AN ODYSSEY FOR OUR FUTURE

WHEN WE CHANGE THE WAY WE SEE THE WORLD, THE
WORLD WILL REFLECT WHAT WE WANT TO SEE

BY
Charles Ehrton Hinkley

©2007 Charles Hinkley All rights reserved

No part of his book may be reproduced, stored to a retrieval system, or transmitted by any means, electronic, mechanical, photocopying, recording, or otherwise written permission from the author.

ISBN 978-0-6151-7585-0

ACKNOWLEDGEMENTS

I did not create this book alone. There were many who helped me over the past years — countless souls many of whose names have lamentably slipped from my memory. My loving mother who, during first nine years of my life, taught me to respect others. My stepmother from Denmark, Christine, expanded my view of the world. My aunt Alice, who was Vice President of the Boston Chapter of the NAACP, taught me to look deep inside every person I met. Miss Dietrich was with my mother when she made her transition and she worked with me closely for next eight years and patiently coached me to see the good in everyone I met. Clayton Ford, my government professor in college taught me to look at every international situation from both sides. As manager of the debate team he trained us to debate both sides of every issue. Dr. Douglas Swett, of Principia College, started me on my journey into fluency of the Spanish language and accompanied six of us to Mexico to study at The University of Mexico the same year Evita Peron died. A fellow student at School of Advanced International Studies of the Johns Hopkins University in Washington, DC encouraged my initial plan to descend the Amazon River and furnished the basic information books to begin the planning process. If there was a fuse that lit the rocket that sent me on my journey it was Helen and Frank Shreider's book, _20,000 Miles South._ I met them at their slide show at the National Geographic auditorium, where they described their odyssey from the Arctic Circle to the tip of South America in an amphibious jeep. This motivated me to plan my 29,000-mile Odyssey and to be the first person to completely circle Latin America. Other students at American Graduate School of International Management shared their stories. Senhora de Naronha, in just four months armed me with the fluency in Portuguese I would need in Brazil. One female AGSIM graduate traveled from Egypt to South Africa, hitchhiking back to the Congo and descending that river. Another student bicycled across South America from Brazil to Peru and helped me in my planning. Professor Lyle Shurz helped me plan the extended journey in both the Amazon and Brazil. He also permitted me to write a book on my 250-day trip for my thesis, which was taken from 500 pages of journal written during the trip.

I am very thankful to Naomi Niles, my wife and partner in life, who has supported me every step of the way. I thank Rita Livingston who was responsible for the title. I am indebted to Betsy Braun for editing the entire book. I am grateful to Amazon John Easterling who partnered with several tribes in the Peruvian Amazon to develop a business, which serves as a model to preserve the rainforest and the Indigenous' way of life into the distant future.

TABLE OF CONTENTS

CHAPTER	PAGE
FORWARD	I
1. A REVOLUTION IN THE MAKING	1
2. A VIEW FROM THE OTHER SIDE	25
3. WATCH OUT FOR ROBBERS	37
4. THE ROAD ENDS HERE	75
5. INTO THE VOID	105
6. DOWN THE RIVER TO THE AMAZON	137
7. DOWN THE AMAZON HEADWATERS	173
8. TO THE AMAZON IN A DUGOUT	187
9. ACROSS THE SERTÂO	237
10. THE EXHILARATION THAT IS BRAZIL	261
11. PARAGUAY TO PATAGONIA	291
12. INTO THE ANDES	311
13. THE PILOT ROAD	339
14. THE EQUATOR AND THE MAGDALENA	359
15. UNFINISHED ROAD	395
16. MAYALAND	409

FORWARD

As the sun burst forth I awakened in my Iowa home. My first view out the window must have been the mile-wide expanse of the Mississippi River, some 500 feet below our bluff. It was love at first sight. My paternal grandparents lived only two houses away and my maternal grandmother overlooked the river, the dam, and the locks. Illinois was across the river and a slight glance to the right was Missouri. Each sharp whistle from the many barges would drive me racing out the door and a mile to the Anshutz' house, which was directly above the dam where I could see the boats being lowered or raised in the locks.

Many times I dreamed of traveling on one of these boats down the entire Mississippi. Sent to a camp in Michigan at the age of fifteen, I unsuccessfully planned canoe trips down the many rivers and streams near the camp.

Water and Peace have always been strong in my heart as I passed through a youth marred by WWII. My Quaker born mother taught me at an early age to talk with God. Added to this was her adopted religion, Christian Science, which emphasized healing and harmony through positive thinking. Many times she asked me what God told me and I would repeat the words I heard to her. I was not allowed to play with war toys and I remember my father getting upset with anyone who bought me toy soldiers for Christmas.

I remember when I was first learning to read I read the headlines of the newspaper because it was easier. On one of the headlines I found a word I did not know and asked my father, "Dad, what's a Hitler?"

"Hitler is a man, he is very evil. He wants to start a war," was his simple answer. Protected from the ravishes of that war, safe in this country, my only participation was obeying the instructions to watch out for balloons traveling overhead while at a camp in Estes Park, Colorado. The war was nearly over and the Japanese were launching balloons with explosives and sending them over the Western United States. That July I passed a newsstand and saw the headlines, UNITED STATES DROPS A BOMB OVER JAPAN. I thought, "Isn't the United States dropping a lot of bombs over Japan? Why the headline?" An hour later I learned we had dropped an Atomic Bomb

FORWARD

on Hiroshima. It ended the war and I was happy for that. However, it was not until five years later while attending prep school in Maine a Japanese victim lectured us and explained in great detail the horrors of that bombing. This made me aware I must see my country from eyes that view it from the outside in.

When I was in high school in Kansas City, a wonderful Latin teacher talked against current segregation policies, which most of the students felt were unfair. It was courageous for her to discuss this in front of the class, and I am still impressed with the number of students she was able to reach to accept her tolerance. The only time she was wrong was when she told me, as compassionately as she could, I would never be able to speak a foreign language.

When I was eighteen I worked on an ore boat for one summer. As we passed through the Sioux St. Marie Locks I heard a dockworker yell out, "We are at war with Russia!" We passed through the locks so quickly I heard no more details until we reached Duluth. "We are at war with North Korea," yelled one of the officials.

"What have we got against North Korea?" I asked.

I finished my last year of prep school and applied for college, hoping destiny would save me from the draft. I was well aware of the forces that finance both sides of every conflict and make their millions off those raising their hands in patriotic acceptance. I knew I was a conscientious objector to war and was all too aware of the consequences of this war. I was caught with even more ambiguous feelings when the Korea Police Action, planned by Truman, was upset by the precipitous action of General Douglas McArthur by marching our troops to the Chinese border. Prior to that action we would probably have soon brought the war to a conclusion. I knew, as our troops traveled North toward the Yalu River, China would enter the war with massive troops. I felt they had every right to protect their hydroelectric power and manufacturing along that river. I wanted no part of our provocative actions. What we are faced with today with North Korea is no more than 45 years of protecting a policy that does not work. Eventually, we will open the borders between North and South Korea, prompted by the threat of nuclear proliferation, but it has become more difficult each day we choose confrontation over diplomacy.

At that time I moved from my conservative, anti-union father to live with my Aunt in Boston, who was vice president of the Boston Chapter of the NAACP. She also helped start many of the garment workers' unions. Her contrasting viewpoints proved to be a mind-expanding experience for me.

I received my draft notice after my first year of college. I had just returned from the University of México and was about to enter my second year of college. While in México a group of us went to see the pyramids at Teotihuacán. I was filled with visions, both good and bad; of past lifetimes intuited I had lived there. Afterwards we went to a nearby restaurant, where the energy was so strong it gave me an excruciating headache.

Simultaneous with my dreaded draft notice came a letter from my church, which had taught me "God is Love and all God's children are created equal" In that letter they informed me I could not use my membership in the church to declare myself a conscientious objector. "Render unto Caesar what is Caesar's" was their quote. I was crushed. How could the religion that taught me to love tell me I had to kill?

The next few years were spent separating my church from my spirituality, one of listening to my Creator rather than Church. Freed from the restrictions of organized religion I experienced tremendous growth and closeness to my Maker. Life is my experience and the only thing that makes it good or bad is my perception of that experience. As I found myself taken out of my safe environment and placed in Korea during the war I held steadfast to my love for humanity. I did not fear being killed in a war, only to be forced to kill others, especially those on the other side who were drafted against their will and taught I was their enemy. When it was inevitable I would be in the war zone I made a last pact with God, in which I told Him/Her, "If you want me this is your perfect opportunity, but I will never kill anyone, so let me take the first bullet if that is what is to be." Shot at a few times but never wounded, I was put on the night crew, in command of ordering all the Signal supplies for Korea. Being in charge of the night crew afforded me the opportunity to teach English to Koreans attending the Chosun Christian School during the day, a connection that led to unauthorized travel in military jeeps to Teagu, Chinhae, monasteries, and orphanages during the day. I was the only person allowed unlimited travel outside the compound. I was able to talk with North Korean refugees and citizens of Korea who gave me an entirely different account of their view of the war. When I asked if they appreciated the fact we were in the country to save them, they answered, "The Japanese ruled

FORWARD

our country for many years and now the United States is ruling it."

To the North Korean refugees I would ask, "Did you flee south for freedom?"

"No, I was starving. We were eating the bark off trees."

I watched in dismay, as most of the students looked in all directions before speaking their truth to make sure their government spies were not hearing them. They would refuse to talk while in a restaurant or teahouse. As military personnel we were not allowed to enter restaurants, teahouses, public transit, movie theaters or private homes. I entered them all. I saw savage treatment on the part of our personnel against the citizens of that country. News from China and India reached me outside normal channels. In 1954 I was one of the first to protest the growing plans for a war in Indochina, which eventually became the Vietnam War. My heart was, and always has been, to seek peace in every way possible.

Most of my passes were available because I learned to sign the captain's name as well as he. Even at Camp Stoneman, California, prior to shipping over, I went AWOL twice, once with a forged pass and another by climbing through a barbed wire fence to go horseback riding. Being in the Army during a time of war freed me to know I could do anything. I not only knew I was protected from death or injury by my Creator but also by the knowledge of, "What are you going to do to me, kill me?" My government had already done all it could do to me by putting me in a uniform, teaching me to kill, and finally sending me to a War Zone. As I look back this training is what enabled me to take a voyage into the void in an eight-and-one-half month spiritual journey through Latin America with $1,750 and little written information on that area. It was a way of seeing my country through the eyes of citizens of other countries.

Following the War, I returned to finish my college education. As a journalist for the school paper I made several futile attempts to write against the de facto segregation at that school. I was pleased to see this practice had ended when I returned a number of years later.

Graduating with a BA in International Relations and Languages, I decided to join the Foreign Service to be an instrument for peace for my government with the Communist Block. With fluency in Spanish and Russian (Middlebury Russian School), I was accepted at the School of Advanced International studies (SAIS) of the Johns Hopkins University in Washington, DC. It was a very disheartening experience witnessing the manipulations on the part of our government, in its move from peaceful neutrality to aggressively protecting corporate interests in other countries. I was little aware my Divine mission was to be placed in situations and locations and to be a part of a major group that would help move this country into its greater purpose.

I was not aware of this at the time but the results were apparent later when I read articles about the meetings with Allen Welsh Dulles, who was with the OSS (the Office of Strategic Services, predecessor to the CIA), who met several times with Hitler's leaders in Switzerland during the War. Numerous articles explained how the Foreign Service became a stepchild to the CIA by installing Allen as its director and his brother, John Foster, as head of the Foreign Service Department. In the 1950s, at the height of the cold war and under the direction of Allan Dulles, its activities expanded to include many undercover operations. It subsidized political leaders in other countries, secretly recruited the services of trade union, church, and youth leaders, along with businesspeople, journalists, academics, and even colluded with underworld leaders. It set up radio stations and news services, and financed cultural organizations and journals.

While at SAIS I saw numerous personnel in the Foreign Service being questioned or ousted for suspicion of being Communists or friends of Communists, also homosexuals or friends of homosexuals. SAIS was known as being the top school for those promoted in the Foreign Service. All who attended the graduate school were there to train for the Foreign Service. Yet, only two of us passed the exam and there were rumors even they probably would not make it past the oral exam. The questions on the exam were impossible. They asked for remote dates in history and other material usually forgotten by most people. Yet, a number of applicants to the Foreign Service were disproportionably accepted from another well-known university. It did not dawn on me until much later that that university was reputed to teach the answers to the questions on the Foreign Service exam rather than the general international courses taught at SAIS.

I felt an unrelenting pull to see the Amazon, which I shared with another student. All my life I wanted to buy a small motorboat and travel down the Mississippi all the way from Lake Minitaqua to New Orleans, but could never get anyone to join me. This student told me there was a Booth Liner that traveled the Amazon every two

FORWARD

weeks and would only take a few days from Iquitos, Perú to Manaus, Brazil. He showed me two books; Norman T. Ford's book, <u>How to Travel Latin America on $5 a Day</u> and an annually published book called, <u>South American Handbook</u>, which contained detailed descriptions of each country. I ordered from the OAS (Organization of American States) the <u>Hotel Guide Books</u> for each country. I was inspired even further when I read a book by Helen and Frank Shreider, <u>20,000 Miles South</u>, and an article by them in the National Geographic about how they traveled all the way from the Arctic Circle to the tip of South America, Ushuaia, with an amphibious jeep.

    Nearly everyone I knew working for the government told me, "Don't join the Foreign Service. You will not have any effect on peace." I finally listened and transferred to a graduate school for international business, The American Graduate School of International Studies (AGSIM) in Glendale, AZ. I met many interesting people there who had been enrolled by their companies after having worked overseas. The average student age was 32. A former graduate owned a travel agency. She shared with me how she traveled all the way up the Nile River, hitchhiked alone through Africa to Cape Town, South Africa, up to the Congo and down to the ocean. Another student had traveled across South America on a bicycle. Two other students traveled by canoe up the Orinoco River in Venezuela, crossed to a tributary of the Amazon, and then by river all the way to Argentina. I began planning on how I would make a trip through parts of South America during the three months of that summer, but soon realized I could not make it fit into such a tight schedule. I, therefore, looked at my bank account and decided I could travel the 29,000 miles on $5.00 a day if I would stay within a rigorous budget. I even thought of the possibility of writing an article for the National Geographic and contacted them. In my research I found no one had written about traveling from Florida, through the Caribbean, Venezuela, Colombia, Peru, down the Amazon, reaching Ushuaía from the west and returning the east through Central America, a complete circle. I decided to be the first. National Geographic answered they already had more than they needed on South America but to contact them again on my return.

    I kept feeling a push to properly prepare for this odyssey. I knew I had to visit all the ancient monuments and ruins to connect with their Spirit and my past. My Inner Voice told me this was going to be a Spiritual journey for me. I was enveloped in both my greatest fears and utmost anticipation. At times I felt I would never return alive from that expedition. Then I would surrender to, "Well, so what? What if I lived and never did this journey? Is that the kind of life I would want?"

I did not realize at the time I was being directed by my own Inner Guidance to witness the dynamic change that was happening in the United States Government, which was thrusting us into empire building. Immediately following the War, Hitler's master spy, Reinhardt Gehlen, surrendered to American authorities, claiming to have the files from the Eastern spy operations, which he headed under Hitler. Allen Dulles, who was in the process of morphing the OSS (Office of Strategic Services) into the newly forming CIA (Central Intelligence Agency) was intrigued and hired him to head up the operations in what he saw as a growing Russian Communist threat. Gehlen significantly exaggerated the strength of Stalin's military as he had with Hitler, which prompted the U.S. to focus excessively on building up our military presence and fearing Communism. Even though Gehlen was prohibited from doing so by his agreement with the CIA he hired six of the top SS Nazis to work under him, such as Klaus Barbie, 'the Butcher of Lyon', and he hired many of the other Gestapo Veterans in the field under the blind eye of Dulles. The CIA then became involved in covert operations, planning the assassination of numerous leaders and the actual assassination of several popular Latin American leaders.

Many of the exaggerated reports from Gehlen were passed verbatim to higher authorities so Presidents Truman and Eisenhower innocently patterned a great deal of our foreign policy under the advice of Hitler's master spy. When Allan's brother John Foster Dulles, was named head of the State Department, there was little distinction between our foreign policy and the Gehlen operations. The significance to the Latin countries was a feeling of neglect and the establishment of dictatorships in these countries that would counter any liberal tendency that might be interpreted as Communist. Once we succumbed to the fear of Communism, we became compliant to leaders that carried us into their agenda of intrigue and covert operations. Everything became a war, such as the war on drugs, war on crime and the war on terrorism, dominated by the industrial/military complex Eisenhower warned us about in his farewell speech. When we, as Americans, change the way we see the world the world will evolve into what we say we want to see.

FORWARD

At a 1958 meeting of the OAS in Panama, the United States dictated to them how each member country was to compliantly accept our conservative agenda. This conflicted with the populist goal of land reform, reducing the gap between the rich and the poor, and taking control of major industries from foreign domination. Still fresh in those leaders' minds was the CIA operation in Guatemala, which forced out their popular elected President, Jacobo Arbénz. Representatives from the participating countries in the OAS meeting returned to their countries exasperated. Argentina and Perú rebelled, only to find their pleas to Washington had fallen on deaf ears. Eisenhower planned a goodwill trip to several of the Latin American countries. In preparation he sent his Vice President, Richard Nixon, to tour Latin America on what was considered by Latinos to be a whitewash journey. This erupted in rioting against Nixon in Perú and Venezuela, which reverberated throughout Latin America. Deep feelings stirred within me. Why were these countries so disturbed by Nixon's visit?

I studied photography intensely and planned the details of my trip as well as attended a full schedule of classes at AGSIM. I especially enjoyed my professor of Latin American Studies, Dr. Lyle Shurz, because he lectured on the people, their governments, and general philosophy. I was concerned because I could find little in any of the books on travel detailing transportation available in remote places. I would locate one village but find nothing leading to or from that town to another. I wrote to the Organization of American States for their books on affordable accommodations. Most of their listed prices seemed affordable if combined with cheaper ones to balance the higher charges. Dr. Shurz, from his research-funded travels through Brazil in the 1920's, helped me with some of my planning.

The last day of school was fast arriving and I was about to step into the unknown. I had to walk my talk and leap into the void I had planned. The $5.00 a day allotment from a fixed bank account forced me to not only travel through these countries but to live with the disenfranchised, not as an observer but as one of them. The students, bankers, corporate officers, government officials, the Indigenous people and travelers I would meet would be an important source for how we, as a nation, look to the common public abroad. This is where the terrorist organizations recruit, from those who feel hopeless against the growing multinational corporations, which control their governments that are protected by the U.S. This is difficult to grasp unless one has lived with the students, workers, the Indigenous people, businesspersons, and governmental agencies. When war becomes our central theme, which began under the direction of Allan Dulles and his German connections, we cannot see the consequences of our footprint on the world, nor will we know peace.

Our government is spying on its own citizens, ignoring judicial protections and due process, denying the right of habeas corpus, and refusing to abide by international laws, treaties, and principles. It is my heartfelt desire, dear reader, that we become the generation that breaks this pattern.

1. A REVOLUTION IN THE MAKING

The ride with a fellow student from Phoenix to New Orleans and bus ride to Key West showed me a poverty stricken part of the United States I did not know existed. I had wanted to travel overland the complete distance but the Caribbean and Isthmus of Panama would have consumed too much of my tight schedule. Island hopping by plane became crucial to save time for more intensive terrestrial forays through South America.

It was a short twenty-minute hop from Key West to Havana, Cuba. Cuba was a rude awakening to what would be normal operating procedure in nearly every city for the next eight-and-a-half months. Quoted rates at hotels would be suddenly doubled at the desk, taxis padded rates, and every con was used to grab my American dollar. In the dark of night the airport bus let us off in the worst part of town as taxi drivers pleaded with me from every side to show me hotels and girls. One driver offered to show me some of the best hotels for a "reasonable price." The first hotel he took me to was a ratty looking place and he assured me a girl would be furnished free with the room at no extra cost. When he quoted me the price of the room I understood why. After a great deal of haggling I succeeded in getting him to keep going. We passed the Hotel Inglaterra, which had been recommended to me in my OAS book. In desperation I jumped out of the cab with bags in hand to get him to stop. I ran into the hotel, the driver right behind me. As I asked for a room the driver tried to get the clerk to tell me there were no rooms. He then charged me extra because he had been able to show me only one of the three hotels he recommended.

Avenida del Prado, Havana, Cuba

"Welcome to Cuba," I thought. My years of study of Spanish were lost in Cuba. Nobody appeared to use consonants and everyone gave the impression they were in a race to see who could speak fastest. "Am I losing my Spanish?" I wondered, "or is the Spanish in Cuba just different?"

Batista, a repressive dictator, had been ruling the country since 1933. Fidél Castro was fighting in the Sierra Maestra Mountains near Santiago. He was getting enormous publicity in the United States and Batista was running another puppet candidate in another of his sham elections. For many years Cuba had lived on weekending Americans coming to Havana for gambling, prostitution and just looking around. Fare was only $10 for a short flight from Key West, making it as affordable as any border town. Bad publicity on Castro's raids on the town of Santiago had frightened away the thousands of tourists that were usually there on any given night and, as I looked around, it looked like it was just hoards of purveyors and me, the token American. I felt overwhelmed. I was not a good candidate for their sustenance. I was a student, making an eight-and-a-half month spiritual journey with a fixed capital reserve (which averaged out to a mere $5.00 a day), an allowance for camera equipment (in the first Free Port), and film.

I was in cultural shock. During the past few years I had been in a cloistered academic environment. A twenty-minute airplane ride had dropped me into a bedlam of noisy, confusing atmosphere where tourism was the only source of income for a majority of the people. My own beliefs on civility, prostitution, and clamor clashed with the reality of where I found myself. My room faced the crowded plaza, speakers blaring political messages amid animated conversations. Even the border towns I had seen in México did not compare to the tumult I was experiencing. I felt I was under attack. I slunk down the catacomb-like halls of the hotel onto the old iron-grilled elevator and out the front door. I could feel the tensions mounting among the people concerning the coming elections. Every one of the many seats in the park was occupied with families and friends loudly proclaiming their allegiance. Postings everywhere promoted the various government approved candidates and the glories of Batista. Statues of heroes were abundant with notations displaying their heroic deeds. A

Capitol Building, Havana, Cuba

poster was displayed with a picture of George Washington and a copy of his famous address, with a short Catechism underneath for the religious. I was in the very center of the city and could not spot another American.

Prostitution was wide open. Before I could walk five blocks ten or fifteen of them tried to latch onto me. Every cab driver stopped to ask me if I wanted a taxi or girl and it took about fifteen minutes to finally shake each one. I had no prejudices concerning prostitution, but my personal beliefs could see no benefit in paying for love with someone who doesn't love me.

I was hungry for a Cuban meal but all restaurants I found were American so I finally ducked into a shabby Chinese one on a back street. Between my Spanish and theirs we had an interesting time getting my dinner. I slept little that night because the plaza never quieted down with speakers and loud voices blasting into the wee hours of the morning.

I searched for another hotel and kept getting lost on the winding streets of Havana. When I needed help I learned to keep my eyes glued forward with confidence and to seek shopkeepers or their helpers. Even that did not work well as another purveyor would usually spot me and chase the clerk off so they could collect money for telling me what I needed to know, which usually ended up with them complaining my tip wasn't enough. I learned to not glance at anyone on the street or they would latch onto me to show me a girl or a taxi and it was impossible to shake them. I finally found a tourist agency and they located a pensión for me and showed me how to get there by bus so I wouldn't have to fight another taxi driver.

As I left the hotel with my bags I was surrounded by a swarm of taxis. I was saved by a police officer who, seeing I spoke Spanish, chased the solicitors away and showed me to my bus. I felt like an escapee as I passed to the back of the bus, sitting next to a boy of about nineteen who was delivering a vacuum cleaner. The boy helped me with my bags, and then sat silently, not knowing if I knew Spanish. Finally he wiped the sweat off his forehead and said to me, "Hace mucho color! (It sure is hot)." My ears perked up because I could understand him clearly.

"Si, hace mucho calor," I said in agreement and then he said something else, which I couldn't understand because of his accent. The man next to him said something in English, which I couldn't understand either. I turned to the boy and asked him where 900

A REVOLUTION IN THE MAKING

Linea Street was. He didn't know but asked the man next to him. Soon the entire back end of the bus joined us. I pulled out a map and we moved into a large huddle. One of the women looked at the boy and said, "That's near where you are going. He can get off with you and you can show him where it is." When the bus stopped everyone in the bus wished me well. The boy pointed to a large house and disappeared down the street with his vacuum cleaner. I knew I had seen the worst and the best of Havana.

The hotel was an old Victorian residence (Mansión Victoria) just a few blocks from the ocean. The señora came out to greet me and a valet ran in with my bags. The room was beautiful and I had my own private patio. Generous meals were served on an outside patio. The señora was a gracious hostess and spoke beautiful Spanish, I understood every word. My fear of having lost my Spanish vanished as we chatted.

The next morning I went back to the center of town. There were still no Americans to defray the constant haranguing. I found one person who spent most of the day showing me Chinatown, old Havana, the prison, and a nightclub at a reasonable price. His presence kept the others away.

Castro and his men had raided Santiago from which I was to take a plane to Jamaica, so I flew out of Camagüay. As the bus moved across the flat plains of Central Cuba I smelled the sweet odor of a pipe. "I wonder who's smoking a pipe," I thought. I looked around the bus and saw no pipes. Then I realized everyone was smoking cigars. A cigar is usually enough to make me want to leave the room, but these Cuban cigars had an unmatched exotic fragrance. One woman who talked incessantly entertained us. The valleys were not nearly as intensely developed as I expected. I could see sugar fields everywhere. Bananas, tobacco, some vegetables, and coconuts were grown in small plots. The bus was like a large chat room as conversations sprung up spontaneously. A couple of men in the front of the bus talked loudly about the hazards of marriage. Finally, the loquacious woman had had enough so she stepped in, yelling about its glories and how she had been married at seventeen, etc. Finally, the bus driver told her to be quiet, that he was a bachelor and didn't care to get married. All the passengers, for the rest of the trip, tried to evade bringing the long-winded lady into their conversations.

Camagüay was a focal point for the big sugar ranches. It used to be the major city in Cuba and was the former capitol under the Spanish. It was, in many ways, a voyage into the past, with narrow winding streets filled with cars, oxcarts, and people.

My final impression of Cuba was its animated pace. The people moved and acted quickly. It was a land of contrast between the very rich and the very poor with a small middle class, which was beginning to emerge in Havana and some small towns. Americans, to them, represented a richness of which they could only dream.

Batista was needed at the time he went in. His type of dictatorship was a benevolent one when it began its rule. A dictatorship was needed to save capital to buy the industrial goods for industrialization, to diversify the production, to draw American capital there and to build the schools. Batista did all these things. However, after some economic stability was achieved the need for a dictatorship passed and Batista refused to step down. The man who was to replace him was his puppet. At that time I felt there would be a gradual move toward democracy. In actuality Castro eventually won the revolution and became another benevolent dictator striving for total power. I had been taught in government classes every country had exactly the government it allowed, through complacency, fear, or lack of real goals. What Cuba did, with its revolution, was to change only the name of their dictator. The jailings, disappearances, assassinations, and repression did not change. Worse was the close association with Lansky, who ran the Jewish Mafia and Trafficante, who ran the Italian Mafia, and who, prior to Castro, dictated who would be assassinated.

Downtown, Camagüay, Cuba

The nation was ill at ease, but seemed to be more concerned with the election than with Castro. Castro showed a lack of control over his men. This was shown by his burning of American sugar plantations and centrals (sugar processing plants) the killing of many innocent people and destroying their property. There was disobedience and disagreement between him and other officers stationed in Miami and Havana. This shook the peoples' faith in him and his army. The people were reluctant to discuss politics and never discussed the election with me. Soldiers were stationed all around the country, every few miles, along the highways.

The country was a contrast of new and old. Some sections were as beautiful as cities in the U.S. Yet the main part of town was crowded with old buildings, which had stood since the early days of the Spaniards. The plazas were rich with the abundance of trees. The drive along the beach was beautiful with many monuments and statues. Even in the smaller towns I would suddenly come upon an extremely modern store, rising from the rubble. Soda fountains and hamburger shops were opening like wildfire, even in some of the small towns. All along the highway there were modern gas stations.

As I was leaving for the airport I had a clash with one porter who ended up moving my bags fifteen feet, called a cab and turned to me, "See I got you a cab." He then swept the bags out from under me and put out his hand. I dropped a nickel into it and walked off. He cried out, "But this is only 5¢."

"I know," I said as I got into the cab.

"But you are an American," he whimpered.

"Yes, but a poor American," I answered as the cab sped off.

The cab driver laughed as he obviously got a big kick out of this.

In Kingston we landed on a thin strip of land, less than a block wide and ten miles long, which helps form Kingston Bay. According to the limousine driver the bay is the ninth largest in the world. At the end of the peninsula was a town now in ruins, built around a Spanish fort. This was called sin town and was a stopover place for pirates and other buccaneers.

Jamaica was the complete opposite of the fast paced, money-grubbing I found in Cuba. At the airport we were welcomed with a glass of rum, elderly ladies met each passenger and located lodging to fit each person's budget. Mine arranged accommodations in a small cottage outside the center of town that gave student discounts, owned by a charming mulatto woman, Mrs. Lindsey.

Kingston was a town of many contrasts. A beautiful park with colorful flowers and paths graced the town, with shops lined on either side. All the buildings were painted Army barracks yellow. The many beggars that roamed the streets veiled the graciousness of the people and the charming locality. Their stories touched me deeply.

They did not attach themselves onto me as had been my experience in Cuba but listened intently to my story as they thanked me for spending time with them. One woman really pulled at my heart when she came dashing up to me with some voodoo dolls, "Here, take these dolls for one dollar."

"I have no need for these," I told her.

"You can have them for 80¢," she begged.

"But I can't use them and it would be trouble sending them to a friend," I said, wanting to weaken and just offer her the money. I could tell she was desperate.

"Sir, just give me anything for them. I just want enough money to eat. I haven't eaten in days." I looked into her eyes and could see the hurt. My heart ached with her every word.

I told her, "If I could use them at all I would pay you the dollar for them but I can neither send them to anyone nor take them with me."

"Bless you, Mister," she said as she slowly walked away. This story, with variations, I heard from many vendors. When people offered their goods for just enough to buy some bread to exist, I wanted to try to help

Mrs. Lindsey urged me go to the beauty contest Jamaica was having at the Myrtle Bank Hotel. I followed her directions but found myself in a very shabby section in the darkness of night. I felt conspicuous, partially because I seemed to be the only white person in town and was wearing a suit, very inappropriate for where I had just found myself. Governor Faubus had just stood outside the Central High School in Little Rock, Arkansas, defying the court order to integrate the schools. Pictures were shown on national TV of white women spitting on the black children trying to enter, and yelling demeaning words at them. I was painfully aware of this disgrace, but knew my skin and nationality made me its representative. I stopped when I found myself in almost complete darkness. The only building with lights was a bar across the street. I caught a glimpse of three young men standing on the opposite side. I turned to go when one yelled, "Hey Mon, what you looking' for."

"I'd better respond to them," I thought, so walked over to where they were standing.

"I'm trying to find the Myrtle Bank Hotel," I said.

"Where you from?" asked one of the young men.

"From the United States," I said as casually as possible.

"I he'ah what you do to colored folks there," said one of the men, defiantly.

"I'm as much against that as you are. Anyway, I'm from Kansas City," as though that had anything to do with it.

The first one looked at the other and said, "I can see this man has nothing to do wit' dot."

Immediately we were all at ease with each other and continued a friendly conversation. Their directions got me to the hotel.

As I waited in the long line at the hotel I felt an overwhelming discomfort with the racial profiling I saw before me. Only a block away I felt I was the only white person in Kingston, yet the long line was all white, with a few slightly colored exceptions. "What am I doing here?" I contemplated. "This is against everything I believe in." I left and went back to my cottage.

I had hoped to hear Calypso music in Jamaica. However, the music pouring out of the Myrtle Bank Hotel as well as the 200 radios blaring along the way, were playing Elvis Pressley and Rock n' Roll. Mrs. Lindsey said, "You'll have to go to Trinidad if you want to hear Calypso but I'll play some Calypso for you before you leave."

Waterfront Drive, Port au Prince, Haiti

The explosive issue in the papers at this time was Chaguaramas, the newly organized Federation of the West Indies.

Mrs. Lindsey explained, "They feel the U.S. air base there is the only place to put their capitol. The university is in Jamaica so they want the capitol on another one of the Islands. As Trinidad is the most financially capable and the next largest they feel they should put the capitol there."

Voodoo Market, Port au Prince, Haiti

The headlines read, "We did not ask to be sold for scrap," obviously referring to the deal Roosevelt made with Great Britain in 1939 to sell some scrapped war vessels to Britain in exchange for a 99 year lease for some air bases on her West Indian Islands. This was done verbally by the Administration because Congress, at that time, was very much against making any deals with England or to become involved in the war. Therefore, there was no bonding agreement. She continued, "The Americans and British confirmed this agreement just recently and the West Indians exploded because there was no conference held with them in it. America doesn't want to let go of the base because of the cost and because it is a perfect place to protect the Panama Canal."

The Jamaicans I met in the shops and streets were quiet, seldom smiled, very polite, and content to live their lives at a slow pace. Even the beggars and hawkers were subdued, noticeably desperate in some cases, but always courteous.

As I looked down on Port au Prince, Haiti from the sky, it was the first city I had ever seen that looked like a slum from the air. At the airport I asked for a hotel. I noticed no one called to confirm a reservation and thought that strange. Later I found the phones only worked during certain times. My French (or should I say patois) and their English provided a challenge for all of us.

Downtown, Port au Prince, Haiti

The taxi driver told me he knew of a nicer pensión that was less expensive than the one recommended by the airport. Remembering my experience in Cuba I demanded he take me to the pensión I asked for. They spoke no English so the driver acted as interpreter. The owner wouldn't tell me a price but insisted I see the room. It was nice but the price high. She kept lowering the price as we drove away. The driver said he knew a place that spoke English and where there were other Americans. It was a beautiful home in the hilly suburbs, which had the same view of the Hilton, located right behind it that charged six times as much. When the driver left I couldn't find anyone who spoke English. A mustached guest stood in front of me, staring at me. I was about to ask him if he spoke any Spanish when he asked me in broken English if I spoke Spanish. He, Antonio, was delighted to find I did. We sat down and talked until dinner. It seems his cab driver told him there were other Spanish guests in the house and the management spoke Spanish. We laughed as a number of other cabs brought guests; I'm sure, with the same story, depending on their language.

My baggage was missing and I needed to call the airport and tell them I had chosen another hotel. I tried to reach the Hilton behind us. Each street dead-ended as we went up first one and then another in our search. We finally saw a sign saying "Gran Hotel." A woman greeted us, speaking beautiful English. She tried the phone and it was not working. She said, "Don't worry, you have plenty of time, and there is not another plane expected until morning.

"The airport is probably closed by now."

"Airport closed?" I said in surprise.

She laughed, "This isn't Idyllwild you know."

Waterfront Park, Port au Prince, Haiti

Antonio, who was from Buenos Aires, spoke a Spanish I could understand perfectly.

As we shared our dinner, he said, "I'm a buyer for a textile firm and am combining business and pleasure. I am on a trip to the United States but I find the United States to be the most difficult country to get into. I went to the Embassy in Buenos Aires and they handed me a security sheet two pages long, which I had to fill out. It asked me if I was a Communist or if I had any friends who were Communists. They then told me I would have to wait three months for a security investigation. I finally decided I would have to go ahead and proceed with the rest of my trip and then try to get into the U.S. next year even though this makes it about twice the expense. I'm quite confused as the need for such rigid regulations and the frivolity that goes with it. I have several friends who are Communists because during the Perón regime there were many Communists, but I have no desire to be one and detest it."

I asked about the present political scene in Argentina. We didn't discuss Juan Perón or Frondizzi (the then president of Argentina) as I felt these might be touchy questions, but we did discuss the Nixon riots in Venezuela.

I said, "Latin American students are known for their wild ideas and little revolutions. Almost every revolution in Latin America starts with a student demonstration. The Communists have made their greatest gains in the Universities in México."

Presidential Palace, Port au Prince, Haiti

"Yes," he said, "Student revolts started the revolutions in Argentina, Venezuela and Cuba. Therefore, the Lima officials warned Nixon at this time of economic downturn, it would not be a good time to step into the lion's den by visiting San Marcos University. The recession hit harder in the Latin American countries than the U.S. because of raw material cuts, coupled with Congressional talk of raising tariffs. Nixon apparently saw Communists wherever things weren't just right so thought he would go to the University anyway. Communist uprisings are usually shallow, unsupported, and easy to handle, as the members are usually acting more out of orders than from their hearts. There probably wasn't a Communist in any of the students at San Marcos. Nixon was apparently poorly briefed as to the tendency of University students to disregard officials, especially government officials."

The other demonstrations reminded me of Governor Faubus. They probably consisted of a few hard core Communists and all the rabble of the town. These people couldn't find work, wouldn't want it if they could, so they took it out on some third party with the guidance of a hard core.

A REVOLUTION IN THE MAKING

The spark that lit the fire of revolt against Nixon in Lima and Caracas was the whitewash trip he took to prepare for a Presidential tour, after having ignored the American States at their recent conference. Smoldering behind this was John Foster Dulles flying to Florida to welcome Perez Jimenez as he fled the country having robbed half its treasury. One statement by Dulles rang offensively in Latin American ears when he was asked by a reporter why he was supporting dictators such as Jimenez, "We don't want states", he was quoted as saying, "We want their governments." That, in itself, was enough to cause a riot. That also is what has been wrong in our foreign relations since the Dulles brothers' takeover during and following WWII. It is this arrogant attitude on the part of a strong nation that sows many of the seeds of terrorism.

Antonio mentioned one thing that did surprise me. He showed concern over our harboring former dictators and sponsoring ones already in power. I didn't think the Latin Americans cared about that because of their recognition of asylum and the spirit of non-intervention. We both laughed over Trujillo's son's incident. Trujillo, son of the Dominican Republic's dictator, bought a Mercedes for the actress, Kim Novak, which received some notoriety in the press. He asked me, "Would you buy a car for Kim Novak?"

"I could afford it if I had Trujillo's salary, which I understand is the exact amount of our foreign loan to him. I do understand Kim is giving the car back because she found out he was married."

It was like a scene from the movie "It's a Mad, Mad, Mad World" as Antonio and I plied the streets in a hunt for my lost luggage and his American visa. He was a mastermind when dealing with negotiating pricing. Taxi drivers were at a loss, eventually yielding to his relentlessness. As we wound through the narrow hilly streets of Port au Prince we found the drivers were sometimes as confused as we. They consistently came to a stop at dead-ends, reversed and darted down another street, only to find themselves even further out of the way. Frustrated, they stopped and asked directions several times before finally finding our destination. One driver, following Antonio's many instructions in Spanish, ended up only three blocks from where we started. I finally realized this driver could not understand a word of Spanish but did understand English, so I interpreted for Antonio, and we arrived at the Mexican Embassy.

Haitians seemed very proud of their country but couldn't seem to come to grips with its problems, which were social as well as physical. The country was founded by former escaped slaves and French immigrants. It was located on the Western half of the island of Hispañola, which it shared with the Dominican Republic. The government was a constant shambles and the people were constantly rioting against it. Yet no one seemed to be able to take any lead in solving its problems. The social set-up was a handful of mulattos running a large population of Negroes who had only their non-industrial culture to fall back on. It seemed like there were hoards of solicitors searching for easy money soaking a tourist ten times as much as a Haitian if they could get away with it. The upper class spent most of their time in the U.S. or Paris, living off money quickly earned during the tourist season or some other small enterprise. I could see no other line of business besides the free-port stores, tourist hotels and guest houses and other small businesses such as small shops, doctors, etc.

The new President was François Duvaliér (Pappa Doc), a popular doctor, who had seized power the year before. Because he did not trust the military he consolidated his power by means of private guards, called the Toutons Macoutes, popularly known as the 'Death Squad'. They were paid no salary so had to make their living through criminal activity. Like Castro and so many other leaders, Duvalier, a man known for humanitarian acts as a country doctor came into power, changing only the name of oppression of his predecessor. It was not comfortable in Haiti. It seemed like everyone was on edge.

Parque Colon, Ciudad Trujillo, Dominican Republic

When the management of the pensión said dinner was at a certain time, the first plate went on the table at exactly that time. I became painfully aware of this when I arrived an hour late and found my cold plate awaiting me. At least I got my meal.

I had planned on traveling overland from Haiti to the Dominican Republic, but delays forced me to fly. My bag finally greeted me from its lengthy trip at the airport in Ciudád Trujillo, Santo Domingo. Ruling the Dominican Republic was one of the last of the dictators, heavily supported by the Dulles brothers and who ruled with an iron hand.

    I was impressed with the pride of the taxi driver who showed great satisfaction with his country, pointing out places of interest on our way to the hotel. I ended up in a hotel, located in the oldest section of town along the bay. It was greatly in need of some TLC. Had the driver not pointed to the door I would never have known it was a hotel, with its four dark holes, which gave entry into the unkempt lobby. I looked up and saw rust stains had run down the unpainted walls, dimly illumined by a bare light bulb hung from the ceiling. Inside was an old marble-topped soda bar with a mahogany base that didn't look like it was still in use. On the other side were benches from which the manager had to consistently chase away vagrants. I walked down a large dingy hall where most of the tables were located, with the other half of the hall encircling an old courtyard. Small peelings of paint hung stubbornly to the barren walls. An old mahogany desk located next to the antique stairway served as the manager's desk. I climbed up the winding stairway, turned left, and preceded through a large ominously dark hall, which headed into an open court, around which most of the rooms were located. An eerie feeling enveloped me as I walked through another hall, which led onto another court that overlooked the docks. The building was crumbling and many parts of it had fallen away. I walked through two swinging doors, which opened, into my room. Shards of light entered through the small barred window about fifteen feet up, another on the other wall, about ten feet away. As I entered the room it reminded me of a jail. On the back wall was an old mahogany bed with a blanket to lie on and another blanket to cover myself, but no sheets. "I wonder if Christopher Columbus slept on this bed," I thought. A large mahogany cabinet and an iron porch chair completed the decór. I could see water had seeped in the glassless windows and had completely discolored the walls. Looking out the window and could see the docks where ships were being unloaded. The ruins of an old fort, presently being used as a barracks, lay next to my room. I was at peace with most of this; bothered mostly by the fact the only public toilet had no toilet seat, just a tile base shaped like one. Here I was, staying in the city with the oldest church, the oldest Cathedral, the oldest fortification and the remains of the first white men to set foot in this hemisphere — and this must have been their hotel.

When I left the hotel one person after another harassed me, wanting to show me a good time, a disgusting reminder of Havana. I tried numerous strategies to get rid of each one, dodging in stores, saying "No," in sundry ways, finally settling on, "No, I'm English. I've been here three weeks and I've already had a good time." That proved to be the most effective.

However, I let my guard down with one affable gentleman who said, "Hi, my name is Henry. Do you remember me? I'm a porter at the airport and I meant to speak to you then." After some conversation he said, "I usually stop by my sister's for tea at this time. Would you like to join me?"

I thought for a moment, "What the heck. This could be a chance to meet some nice people in Santo Domingo."

When we got to his sister's house he introduced me to a rather robust woman who seemed unresponsive to our conversation. She proceeded to remove some icons and candles from a table and change dresses in front of us. I had been conned. Henry looked up at the numerous religious pictures on the wall and said, "These Catholics have to have their saints, you know. My sister likes rum in her coke. Give me some money to go buy a bottle of rum."

"I don't have any money," I said, not knowing whether to walk out, excuse myself or any other way I could think of to get out of there. I only hoped I would be able to make my way down the dark streets to my hotel without a problem.

"I saw you had money when you pulled your money out to pay the taxi," he retorted.

"I have to pay for the hotel and food," I continued.

"Well, do you want to go to bed with my sister?" he persisted.

I felt outnumbered with Henry, a large man and his 'sister' who appeared equally as physically powerful, so felt it was better to argue my way out the door, rather than dash onto the deserted street in an unfamiliar end of town in a foreign country. I was taking no chances.

Christopher Columbus' House, Ciudád Trujillo, Dominican Republic

He finally relented, saying, "Give me a quarter to get a taxi." I handed him the quarter and left. A pit in my stomach grabbed me as I headed back to my hotel.

I had a hard time sleeping that night, as the mattress was paper-thin and the boards extra thick. I was very discouraged with the majority of people I had met so far on this trip and I still had another eight months to go. My heart sank as I was now convinced I would never get to meet any of the decent Latin Americans. I was tempted to leave for Curaçâo two days early and spend more time there. I was very glad I did not because my fortune changed completely the next day. I told myself, "If this doesn't get any better I'm going to abort the rest of the trip and return to school this fall."

As I came to know the ropes a little better, I found ways of evading and getting rid of the parasites that attached themselves to tourists, at least this one time. I discovered most of them knew each other, so as I became more known they were warned by their friends not to waste their time on me.

I was impressed with the central part of Santo Domingo. It was a mixture of Colonial and modern. This city seemed clean, which I found sadly lacking in Cuba and Haiti. While building the new, historical buildings were preserved or restored. There were numerous attractive parks, which allowed me to walk from park to park, each uniquely different from the other.

First Cathedral in Latin America, Ciudád Trujillo, Dominican Republic. Christopher Columbus is purported to be buried here, also President Trujillo's father.

I was most impressed with the open friendliness of the people who were imbued with a marvelous sense of humor. Occasionally someone turned to me, a complete stranger to crack a joke. A permanent fair ground graced a part of the city, sporting awe-inspiring views of the ocean. Although activity was missing, there was an open bar and restaurant overlooking a stage with dancing fountains, which enticed me to return that night when they would be working.

As I had noticed in Cuba the girls stared back. These glances, unlike the soliciting I had been experiencing, had warmth accompanied by an embarrassed smile, some even greeting me. Even the men greeted me in a friendly non-intrusive way. As I walked along the main beach boulevard I caught the glance of three young women sitting on the guardrail. We had our eyes glued on each other for about twenty feet as I approached. I greeted them and one turned to the others and said, "O muchachas! (Oh, girls)." I walked by two others and they smiled. Soon I sat down and the two girls came by me. They waited awhile and then came by me again, crossing the street and sitting in the park. I sat on the railing until a police officer came by and told me I wasn't allowed to sit on the railing after 6:00 pm. I went across the street and passed the girls. One of the girls called out and I started over. Then I looked and saw she was not calling me, but a vendor. Somewhat embarrassed I walked up to the top of the park and admired its beauty from there.

I was walking back when a beautiful girl across the street called out and asked me to come over. I went over and she said she wanted to see the camera and light meter. She invited me inside her house. I was unusually confused as to her intentions, especially after my experience the night before. She called her sister in from another room. When she said 'sister' red flags went up. However, I found she was a graduate of nursing school and her sister had a BA degree. She had written to the New York Cancer Society asking for a job and had received an answer from them with an application form. Soon we were in the sitting room watching TV. Another woman came in and it turned out she had a law degree. She brought out a scrapbook showing me a picture of an old boyfriend of hers in the U.S. who used to work for the American Embassy in Ciudád Trujillo. It was surprising to see the friendliness of these people. One person dropped in for a few minutes, watched TV, and then excused himself. Everyone that walked by stuck his or her head in the window to say 'hello'. One middle-aged woman stuck her head in as I was sitting with my back toward her and said, "How are you?" I could feel her curious eyes drilling into the back of my neck.

The girl answered, "Fine."

"How are you?" she said again as I could feel her peering around trying to see who I was.

"Fine," answered the girl again," quite casually.

"Fine? Well that's good, that's good," she said, as I felt her eyes finally looking away from the back of my neck. The girls filled me in on all the sites I needed to see before leaving. They walked me to the door, saying, "And come by tomorrow and say 'goodbye' before leaving."

This was just the uplift I needed. I had finally met some decent people. I was again accosted on my way back by a lad who said in English, "You getting along all right?"

"Yea," I barked, also in English," and you'd better be getting along!" He took the hint and left. As in Cuba this was an island phenomenon, caused by the lack of income opportunities outside of tourism. Heavy reliance on tourism and close proximity to military bases made Americans easy targets. Any thoughts I had of ending my journey were completely eradicated by the events of this day.

That evening I headed back to the fair grounds to see the 9:00 showing of the Dancing Fountains. Unfortunately, I was informed they were broken and would not be working that evening. I sat on the third floor of the outdoor theatre looking out over the ocean below and enjoying a delicious award winning Dominican Republic beer.

The fair grounds at night were a fairyland of lights, each building lighted in a different color. In the center was a magnificent fountain lit in various colors. It reminded me of the childhood story of <u>Babes in Toyland</u> as the characters stepped from the world of reality into a one of make-belief.

One of the girls recommended I take the bus over the suspension bridge that overlooks the entire city. Evidently I caught the wrong bus because it turned off and started in another direction. As the neighborhood degraded I felt apprehensive about exiting the bus so felt it best to remain on the bus until it reached the end of the line and ride it back to better sections as it returned. As the bus wound through the increasingly shabby streets I felt even more apprehensive. After another hour I was aware we were getting farther out of town. Finally we reached the end of the line and the driver pulled up and turned out the lights. When I asked him if there was another bus going back to town he told me the last one was just about to leave. I ran over to it and was just able to catch it as it started back over the bumpy roads. We got into the shabby section of town and the driver pulled over to the side and turned off the motor. Drunks were stumbling in and out of the bars and the helper, which every bus driver has (who takes the fare, loads and unloads passengers and tells the driver when to stop and go) got off and went into a bar. He came back and we went to an even worse section of town where he again got off. As I sat there I became even more worried about the leather satchel of expensive camera equipment I was clutching. Wondering if we would ever get back. I asked to be let off at Parque Colón, which was near the hotel. The driver was evidently confused as he stopped at a park a mile away and told me this was the park I asked for. Rather than argue with him I walked back. The street was deserted and the dark entrance to the hotel was closed. I pounded on the door, worried I would be left on the streets for the night, but fortunately the night guard awoke and let me in.

The next morning, after dodging another of the self-appointed guides I asked a guard at one of the forts for some information. He took me over and introduced me to three female students. They pointed out most of the places of interest and we ended up in an interesting conversation. I told them I felt Dominican women were very beautiful. "We love Americans," they answered in unison. The guard complained because only American men come to the country. "Why don't you send more women," he asked, "I love American women and would sure like to meet some."

Everywhere I went I heard the same phrase from women, "I love Americans. They are so handsome." At the free-port store where I bought my camera I was introduced to nearly everyone who worked in the store. When I left I was ushered to the door by three of the female clerks gathered to wish me luck on my trip. After my struggle with Spanish in Cuba it was wonderful to hear so many compliments on my Spanish.

"So many Dominicans have gone out of their way to be nice to me," I told one sales clerk I met.

He turned to me, smiled, and said, "They feel a certain duty to be good to tourists, especially Americans."

It was wonderful to find so much love for one's country in all the Dominicans I met, especially when it seems to be so vogue to hate Americans outside our country.

Everywhere I looked, turned, walked, or ran I was conscious Trujillo was definitely the one man ruling the country. On almost every building was a poster, sign, or even carved into the building itself, the name of Trujillo. He even had his father buried in the same Cathedral where Christopher Columbus is supposedly buried. On the surface I found a deep love for Trujillo. I was conscious of the crushingly brutal government, which preceded Trujillo and how it bled the people. When in 1934 a disastrous hurricane hit and destroyed the old city of Santo Domingo, Trujillo instilled a massive program to rebuild the city and peace was restored to the country. Progress became the word for the day and buildings were replaced. Trujillo, fortunately, was a wise man. He established good relations with the U.S., paid off the national and international debt, built houses for the workers, established schools, built hospitals, and did many other beneficial deeds. This gained him the support and devotion of the people. The capital, Santo Domingo, was named after him in 1936, monuments were built to honor him, and plaques were placed everywhere to pay tribute to him. This devotion still remained with a great many people. What opposition there was lay hidden outside the capitol or out of the country. However, there wasn't the extreme terror of him there was of Jimenez in Venezuela. No one had anything definite on him as to murder. However, even if all the charges against him in the States were true (and they probably were), he still could not equal or even come near Jimenez (Venezuela), Somoza (Nicaragua), Perón (Argentina), or Stroessner (Paraguáy) in tyranny. It was humorous to read some of the signs put up for him. A sign over the hotel desk had a picture of Trujillo and said, "En esta casa Trujillo es Jefe — Símbola Naciónal — Rectitúd, Liberdad, Trabajo, y Moralidad — 1955, Año del benefactor de la Pátria!! (In this house Trujillo is boss — National Symbol — Righteousness, Liberty, Work, and Morality — 1955, the year of the benefactor of the Country). At the Fair Grounds was a conspicuously large neon sign 300 yards away. It flashed about four phrases, alternately. The first was "Unidos Para la Paz y el Progresso — Felicidades en 1958 — Trujillo Presente el Mundo 27 años de Paz y Trabajo — Todos con Trujillo (United for peace and progress — Greetings in 1958 — Trujillo presents the world 27 years of peace and work. Everyone with Trujillo). Another sign in front of the new Post Office being constructed said, "Otra obra de Trujillo, Palácio de Correos, El Progresso no Detiene, (Another work of Trujillo, Port Office Building, Progress never stops)" There were pictures of Trujillo in many of the homes. Some of the plaques were religious. I saw one sign that said something like, "Thanks be to God, Father and Trujillo." Trujillo's father is buried in the same cathedral as Columbus and Bolivar's grandfather, the oldest Cathedral in the New World. Columbus's bones are on public display each year on his birthday. There was an obelisk to Trujillo on Avenida Washington, a downsized replica of the Washington Monument. So numerous were these plaques I was caught by surprise when I spotted a statue dedicated to someone other than Trujillo.

Curaçao from hill

I very quickly recognized this was a police state. In some places it appeared every other person was a policeman or soldier. However, the mood of the police seemed to follow the mood of the people. The police I saw were friendly and easy-going. I was not aware of any harassing of the people. Even the girls I met at the railing addressed the dictator as "Papa Trujillo," but the other girl chimed in, "You know, the ruler." They spoke only silently of any objection they had of him. The police corrected me on two occasions for minor infractions of a myriad of trivial laws, but always with a smile. I was aware the people I met rarely discussed politics, at least around me. I was not aware of whether this was from fear or just disinterest. Nearly everyone was gracious in helping me but usually was interrupted by one of the leaches that would dash over, cut them off, and try to drag me away.

I arrived the next morning in Bonaire, Aruba, but my recently

Pontoon Bridge over canal, Willemstad, Curaçao

purchased camera I bought at the airport, which was to be given to me on the plane, did not. Although KLM promised me due diligence to locate and get the camera for me, it followed me all around Latin America for the next eight months.

Willemstad was quaint in Dutch architecture and loaded with free-port shops. When I checked in with KLM in the morning and my camera was still enjoying an extended trip somewhere else in the world, I found the camera I wanted and all the attachments for $50.00 under what I had planned to invest.

Willemstad, in Curaçao, was like a little piece of Holland dropped into the Caribbean complete with a bay, canals, drawbridges, and colorful homes. It was reputed one of the Colonial viceroys complained of the sun (plentiful in Curaçao) and commanded that all houses be painted a color other than white. As a result I never saw a white house on the island.

Curaçao, Punda

I found the people of Curaçao aloof. When I was in a Phillips Agency a Spanish girl was waiting on people at the counter while her manager sat next to her reading the paper with a dour look on his face. As she waited on me he growled and went back to his paper. When an American came looking for directions, barely glancing up from his paper he snapped a curt answer to him. After the American left he looked at me and said, "Some people are really impolite." I told him, "I guess that is the Dutch influence."

He agreed with me and said, "All people are not that way. I'm friendly. You just haven't met the right people. You should have come here earlier." In the interest of international relations I smiled and left that comment alone.

My anticipation of Curaçao's beauty was dashed as we drove from the airport. We passed numerous unkempt shacks and there was an absence of vegetation. This changed significantly as the bus turned a corner at the end of a long canal to enter the downtown area of Willemstad. The drive down the canal revealed all types of Dutch ar-

Punda, from across canal, Willemstad, Curaçao

chitecture, from early Colonial to very modern. The center of the city was even beyond expectation as we left the desert and dropped into a little piece of Holland. A large canal flowed through the middle of the city, each side of it lined with early colonial buildings. As I approached the canals, beauty turned to stench. In places it smelled like a cesspool. Curaçào (Which means heart in Portuguese) is an island with no sources for water, either above or below the ground. It was completely dependent on desalination of seawater.

I thought I would never get out of Curaçào. They required us to be at the airport an hour ahead of time as they did all international flights. They repeatedly called me to one counter or another to question me, "What is your passport number?" "Visa number?" "Your Luggage?" "Where did you come from?" "What hotel did you stay at?" "Where are you going?" "Why are you going there?" "Did you pay any money to immigration when you came in?" "What type of baggage do you have?" "You'll have to pay a fine or lose your baggage if it isn't checked in the right way," etc. I had always thought of Curaçào as being the easiest place to visit but found it the most cumbersome of all the islands. It took literally hours to get people through Aruba and then customs ended up holding my passport until the next day because I wasn't sure where I would be staying for the one night I would be there. I even found it a little cumbersome traveling from Aruba to Curaçào (one Dutch Antilles to another). It is sort of an anomalous incongruity that the Dutch Antilles should be such a dynamic progressive place and have such a futile customs system. However I had heard some hair-raising tales about the American customs, so I was not one to judge.

I still would recommend Curaçào and Aruba to be far more worth visiting than any of the other Caribbean islands, with the possible exception of the Dominican Republic. The money saved would make any trip to these islands worth the expense. Although I spent quite a bit of money, the difference between this and the money it would have cost in the U.S. would have paid for my total trip to the Colombian border. Prices were nearly half what they would have been in the United States and many luxury items were 40% what they would be in the States.

A REVOLUTION IN THE MAKING

2. A VIEW FROM THE OTHER SIDE

It was a very short trip to Caracas. I had been warned beforehand the Venezuelan customs was the worst in the world so I was prepared and patient (even more so than most of the Venezuelans) for what followed. I waited in the long line for passport inspection to get past the door. I then went through another long line to get a special permit. After that I stood at a counter to get my visa filled out. That clerk handed me a paper to take to another part of the airport so I could fill out more forms. From there I went through customs inspection. A man in front of me seemed to have done this many times before. I found he was working for a Chicago construction company in Venezuela. "I'm taking a taxi," he told me. "Would you like to share it with me?" He breezed through the lines much faster than I, as he was a resident, so he got one of the porters he knew to help me. He turned to me and said, "I'll wait for you outside." The porter gave the ticket to the man behind the counter and fifteen more minutes passed while I waited to get to my bags. Then came the dilemma of trying to connect the inspector with the bags. The inspector grabbed one bag after another, none of them mine. Finally, he found one of my bags and left, but it was only one of my bags. I did everything but stand on my head in a vain effort to get him to come back again and look for the other. The inspection was the easy part, a quick feel along the side of the bag and a perfunctory stamp of the visa and I was officially in the country.

By the time he was through I looked around and saw the porter was gone, so I carried my own bags out. I was surprised to find my new friend still waiting. He told me, "You're lucky this was a quiet hour. You ought to see the place during the afternoon when one flight after another is arriving at La Guaira."

The ride to Caracas was fabulous. We conversed as we passed through customs and climbed 3,000 feet by bus the ten miles from sea level to Caracas. The highway was built at a cost of $3 million connecting La Guairá with Caracas.

The man introduced himself, "I'm Recalde Ortéz. I work for the Chicago Bridge and Iron Company, Ltd. I think Pérez Jimenez, former dictator of Venezuela was a good President. He did a lot for the country. Venezuela is in a mess now that Jimenez is out. Now there is nothing holding the country together."

The highway went through many tunnels and over many bridges in its climb to Caracas. I hardly realized I was going through mountains.

I asked him, "What do you feel is the main reason for Jimenez being overthrown? I have the feeling it's merely a rebellion on the part of the army because Jimenez sought to control the secret police force and things got out of hand, throwing the military out and bringing civilians into the government."

"I disagree but I do agree in part," he answered. "The people liked the public works, education and other things Jimenez was doing for the country but they were just tired of having the police over them all the time—once an incident started this all public feelings exploded at once."

As we talked I began to detect a little accent in Sr. Ortéz's English. I thought it must be Dutch or German. "What country are you from?" I asked.

"Paraguáy," he said. This led into talk concerning the politics of Paraguáy. "There won't be any progress as long as Stroessner is President. Paraguáy was a paradise spot for everyone before the war with Bolivia. She had never had a dictator and the people were very 'simpatico'. The war produced many military heroes. As few people had formal education most of the generals had even less education. After the war they went to Asunción rather than back to their farms and demanded recognition. Soon little groups of them began taking over the government. This present president is one of those leftover generals. The U.S. has installed and supported these dictatorships so they can't be overthrown. Before Stroessner a bunch of women getting together in the square could overthrow a government. This kept the dictatorships from getting out of hand. Now the U.S. has given the government arms and even jet planes which drains the economy, sending men to the U.S. for training and then keeping them there after they are trained. It also prevents any group from getting strong enough to challenge the dictatorship. You will enjoy the people in Paraguáy but will probably not be inclined to stay because of the government."

I added, "There's much speculation Paraguáy will one day be a great commercial center in Latin America by virtue of its location in the hub."

"Not as long as Stroessner is in power," said Sr. Ortéz.

This seemed to be my observation of the Dominican Republic. I also remembered the submarine our government had just given to Perú, giving it a military stance against Ecuador and Colombia.

We got on the subject of the Nixon riot in Caracas.

"I haven't been back to Venezuela since that affair but all the non-Venezuelans are glad it happened. There isn't any dislike for Nixon but the Latin American countries are tired of being taken for granted. This seemed to be the only way of really showing everything wasn't all right in the relationship between Latin American countries and the U.S. I feel President Eisenhower was perfectly justified in sending troops into the Caribbean because it was very apparent the situation was not being completely handled by the local police. (During the riot Ike sent troop ships into the Caribbean as a threat to Venezuela.)

"You will find the Venezuelans anything but friendly. They are very nationalistic and a trifle bit hostile toward foreigners, especially those from the U.S."

This was exactly the opposite of what I had expected. I had always felt the Venezuelans were very warm toward the U.S. because the U.S. had contributed so much to their wealth and because they had the largest American Colony outside the U.S.

He continued, "You will find them sort of indifferent toward you in the city but will probably even find open hostility in the country. Be especially careful in Colombia as the Indians will rob you blind and the people will be openly hostile. The Bogotaños are a separate bunch. You will probably find them friendly and will be safer. Get through Colombia as fast as you can as it just isn't safe there."

This backed up the warnings I had heard from people in the U.S. and the Islands. For the first time in my trip I found an area where I was a little apprehensive to enter. "Maybe I'd better go over my $4.00 a day (trying to make up for my over-expenditure in the Caribbean Islands and stay at a good hotel in Cúcuta just to escape the robbers)," I thought.

Both Sr. Ortéz and the cab driver were somewhat lost when I told them the name of the hotel I wanted. It was the cheapest in the Pan-American Hotel Guide Book. I gave the address and the cab driver finally found it. I was fortunate it was located only a half-block off the main street.

I asked Sr. Ortéz, "How much do I owe you?"

"Nothing," he answered as he shook my hand, "Just give the cab driver a tip of about a dollar. Here's my card. Give me a call if your other people don't pan out. I'm going to be very busy during the days getting caught up after my trip but I would be glad to meet you at night."

I remembered what one former Venezuelan in Curaçâo told me that Venezuela wasn't so expensive until you hit the nightspots. Then the prices were outrageous. I, therefore, planned on using his card only as a last resort.

I felt a little lost when the cab pulled away and left me alone on this dark street facing the even darker doorway to the hotel. I was still slightly apprehensive after my hassle with the KLM hotel manager in Curaçâo and a little shaken by Sr. Ortéz' description of the Venezuelans.

The hotel clerk was exactly as Mr. Ortéz' had described the Venezuelans. He looked at me as though I had just stepped out of a space ship and was wearing green horns. I asked him if he had a room for the night. He snapped back, "Yes, of course." He then grabbed my bag and took me to the fourth floor up many steps, turned the light on in the room, threw the key at me and left. His accent was impossible to understand. Fortunately, another person at the desk had a clearer accent, so interpreted for him when he asked, "Passport?"

"Tourist Card?"

"Where are you from?"

"What is your reason for being in Venezuela?"

"When are you leaving?"

"By what means?"

"Where were you before you came to Caracas?"

"Why, why, why," he kept asking as he scribbled in the report that goes to the government?

If I was somewhat let down by the drab appearance of the hotel outside, I was equally uplifted by the appearance inside. It had a patio on every floor and almost all the rooms had windows or doors leading outside. The patio had a skylight over it to protect the guests from the weather. The room was neat and clean with two large windows that opened out on the street. There was an unobstructed view of the mountains rising 3,000 feet on either side. Caracas lies in a deep valley squeezing it into the shape of a long string bean in a deep ditch. I had my own private shower and washbowl (something unusual except in the best hotels on the Islands) and the price was very reasonable.

The next day I looked off my balcony and saw a demonstration against the government in the streets below. It was evidently just getting started as the people were just beginning to gather around a park. Workers from various unions were marching toward the park with signs saying, "Down with the Rightists," and many other signs which were in colloquial language I couldn't translate. I walked through the crowd rather quickly as I wasn't sure if the assemblage would suddenly get out of hand. Police quietly stood guard just in case. The park was the Plaza Bolivar, which is situated close to the government buildings.

When I finally found the KLM office I found it had just closed and would not be open until 2:30 p.m. I decided I might as well settle down to a siesta as everything else was closed. I went into a café and had a very light meal. I had finally gotten myself to the point where I could go without eating for quite a while (to begin saving money). In Curaçao I went without eating from the little continental breakfast furnished by the hotel until we got a little something to eat on the plane to Venezuela that evening. The expenses were running so high on the Islands that I had to do this to pay for the hotel bills.

Caracas, Venezuela

I went back to KLM at 2:30. They had not heard of the camera coming and told me to check the next day. I then started my hunt for the Colombian Consulate. I found it was keeping exactly the opposite hours as KLM and was closed. I left empty handed.

The parade was beginning to gather momentum. Swarms of people were drawn to the street below. Shabbily dressed men obviously their organizers, hopped up and down, racing back and forth, provoking the workers to shout louder. As I watched this it reminded me of what a newscaster said about the Nixon riots, the week before, "These are led by Communists and professional men jumping up and down, forming the crowds into groups to fit their purpose." I finally had seen enough of their signs to piece everything together. The Minister of Education had been dismissed, as were many others after the Nixon riot shake-up. The leaders of a couple of the unions (probably Communist dominated) became alarmed and led their workers out in protest. The Venezuelans seem to love a riot so everyone joined in just to enjoy the excitement.

All of a sudden I heard a commotion outside the window. I looked out and saw the rioters running down the main street at a fast gallop. Soon there were motorcyclists racing down the main street at high speed. All automobiles joined in with their horns. Numerous other motorcycles were warming up to do the same. Then everything went quiet in front of the hotel. Suddenly police cars came from every direction, veering right and left on the street, down wrong lanes and everywhere else there was an opening. This evidently put an end to the parade, as everyone cleared out.

The next morning I went to the Colombian Embassy. Many others, I found, had preceded me. I was still a bit timid about my Spanish. I started a conversation with the gentleman next to me to pass the time. I could hardly understand anything he said and felt my Spanish must really be getting bad. I didn't feel so bad when I found he was a Hungarian refugee.

A woman came out and handed us numbers. I was number 11 but it may as well have been 11,000. Every time a person was through and the secretary came out someone ran up to her and pleaded his or her case, usually winning the plea and getting in the door. If no one was there to take their place, there were always people like one important looking American, three or four nuns, and some friends who came to chat with the Consul for a half-hour or so. Soon it was time to close the Consulate. Fortunately, they took care of the waiting customers before they threw us out so it was still worth more waiting. I was so starved by then I was grabbing walls and chairs to keep from fainting.

Finally the clerk got around to me. My big fear had been my photos wouldn't be the right size. However, she agreed to cut them down for me. She then asked for a police clearance. I told her the rules for Colombia didn't mention this. She then disappeared into the office and came back out with a 15-day Transit Visa. I had fought so long to get at least this many days and had been warned by people to get through Colombia as fast as I could, so I didn't fight to have my permit extended.

I found the food in restaurants so expensive in Caracas I began to starve myself to keep within my $5 a day budget. My expenses through the Caribbean were sorely over budget. I was hoping the rest of the countries would be cheaper so my reserve could get back in balance. It was apparent I would not be able to adjust my budget in Venezuela with its American prices. I searched for a restaurant that would be affordable and finally entered a cafeteria that specialized in lunches, which I thought would be cheaper. I ordered a platter of Spaghetti, feeling that would be more affordable. The only seat available was with two American-looking gentlemen. I asked in English if the seat was taken and got some cold stares. A couple of minutes later they began talking in Spanish. I felt somewhat embarrassed, so when one of them left to go to another table to talk to some friends I apologized to the other and said they looked like Americans. He seemed a little flattered and said, "I can speak a little English. I would like to study English in the United States for six months where the climate is nice."

I complained to him, "The prices in this city are outrageous."

He answered, "This restaurant is very inexpensive. For instance, that spaghetti you are eating is probably no more than $10."

My heart sank. That was twice what the hotel was costing me. He was right on with that price, so I knew I would have to starve until I reached Colombia. I noticed how weak I was from hunger while I was standing for an hour at the Colombian Embassy waiting to get my visa and nearly passed out.

This was when I discovered the two-tier pricing of Venezuela. As I went to eat off the taco stands I found the prices dropped to less than a dollar for sufficient food. I just had to stay away from restaurants.

I was surprised a man his age (about 40) could take six months off for the study of a language he didn't know very well. I told him, "The best schools are in the East."

"But the weather isn't very good up there."

"Well, why don't you try the University of Miami?" Before he could answer I asked, "What is your profession?"

"I have some land about 12 miles from Caracas. My main work consists of coming into town for frequent visits, entertaining and eating."

I remembered Professor Shurtz had told us in Venezuela we would meet many men of leisure who owned property in the country and would come to town to eat and enjoy themselves.

He must have had some income from the land because he was staying in a nice hotel in town and felt the best thing about the cafeteria at which we were eating was its prices.

I went to lunch with Jolly Backer, his wife, and another graduate of AGSIM. Backer was now head of Phillips Petroleum in Venezuela.

"I don't think much of Jimenez," said Jolly. "I admit he's done a lot for the country but it was horrible living here before he was thrown out. People were dragged off and shot without a trial or just disappeared and never heard from again."

Sr. Ortéz had mentioned the P. J. regime had gotten to the point where it was rotten all the way through and therefore was bound to bring much resentment. He mentioned that the Trujillo government would probably last a long time, as Trujillo is the only one who is getting rich off the government. Jolly agreed with this and said, "Somoza (U.S. Supported dictator of Nicaragua) once said, 'Only I can steal from the government' — and he was right, too."

"I've noticed one thing in all political troubles," I said. "Americans seem rarely to get hurt in the revolutions. One has the impression they are considered out of the skirmish."

"We were here during the revolution," said Jolly. "That isn't true anymore. I was driving around downtown during the revolution and was stopped by some of the people. They asked if I was European. I told them, 'No, I'm American.' They told me, 'You look European so you'd better not go further because they are hanging some Europeans on the next block.' They explained to me the secret police consist mostly of former Nazi's, Hungarians, Yugoslavs, and Poles and are the root cause of the people's hatred. Years later I read the book, <u>By Way of Deception: The Making and Unmaking of a Mossad Officer</u>, by Victor Ostravski, a former Mossad officer, in which he outlined how the Mossad had sent officers to several Latin American dictatorships to train them in torture tactics and equipment.

"The people here do things out of the moment they would never think of doing in a normal situation. This revolution was an accident. Once it started it soon got out of hand. You couldn't call the people revolutionaries or rioters because nearly all of them knew nothing about why they were fighting. A hard core of dedicated insurgents led them in the right direction and the revolution was won.

"The same thing happened when Nixon came. The riots started and with the help of a few hard core Communists and some trouble makers turned into a big thing that was soon out of control. Most of the people who participated in it couldn't tell you the next day why they did it. Venezuelans are not very friendly in the first place and when you add the terrific nationalism which exists on top of this you have emotional individuals that will do things other people would never think would happen."

Sputnik, These cars take passengers from the 3,000 ft. level of tramway to Humbolt Hotel

Jolly continued, "The next day the papers came out and really chastised the people for what they did. From then on nothing had even been mentioned about the Nixon incident. The papers only mentioned what they considered the imperialistic move on the part of President Eisenhower in sending troops into the Caribbean right after the Nixon riots. You would have thought the troops were in Venezuela the way the front pages covered this for days.

"We need to warn you about Colombia. We suggest you go through there as fast as possible. It's dangerous and they'll rob you blind."

I admired a tall circular hotel on top of the mountain, so we met later that after-

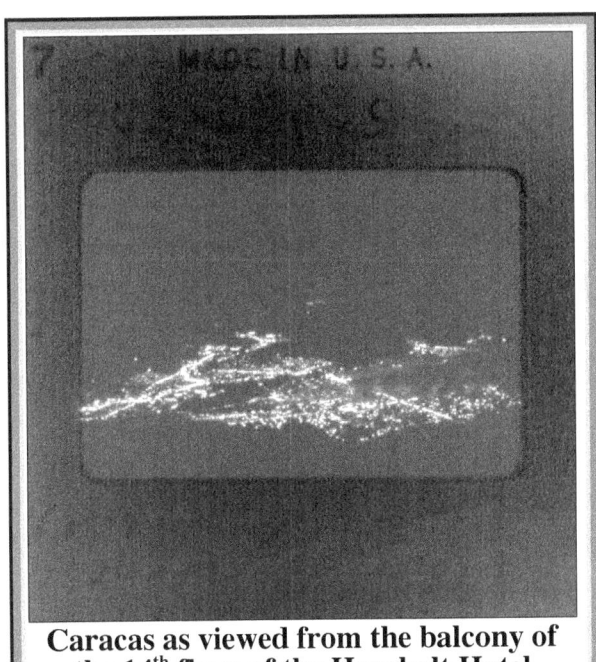
Caracas as viewed from the balcony of the 14th floor of the Humbolt Hotel

noon to go visit it by glass cable cars. The climb was about 4,000 feet, making its altitude 7,000 feet, and we were on top in just ten minutes. The city spread out like a long string of Christmas tree lights, following the valley between two mountain ranges. At the funicular station on top we climbed into little pumpkin-shaped cars, called "Sputnik" (after Russia's first spacecraft), which took us to the very top where the hotel Humboldt was. The interior of the hotel was extraordinarily modern. We stopped long enough for a round of drinks and then went up to one of the rooms on exhibit. The rooms were like luxurious pieces of pie carved out of the circular hotel. Each room had a private balcony, bedroom, salón, and bathroom. Hotel rates were very reasonable, considering the marvelous view and luxury. We went up to see the glassed-in penthouse on the top floor. I felt like I was on top of the world, ocean on one side and the city 4,000 feet below. The hotel was built in the fifties, a dictator's dream. It gradually fell into disrepair but I Google searched and found it had been purchased in auction and would again take its mastering stance, towering over the city.

The workers' apartments that replaced tarpaper shacks, dirt, and rubbish were one of Jimenez' better projects. They were attractive buildings, multi-colored, nicely situated so all residents had a balcony. Rents were heavily subsidized so most of the people living in the slums they replaced could rent on the same land they subsisted on before. This made them unique when comparing them with redevelopment in America, which usually forces the destitute into the streets, replacing them with high-end housing or businesses. Peering into the large glass windows I noticed the former occupants moved in with their previous furniture, which looked a bit incongruous in these ultramodern, tall apartment buildings with those large glass doors that led out to their private balconies. Most rooms were bare, with sparse, crudely made furniture.

When I returned to the hotel the affable clerk greeted me. I still had a problem understanding his Portuguese. Another man was there from Portugal. He started talking to me and I understood every word. I told him it must be the clerk's Spanish accent that prevented me from understanding him. The Portuguese man smiled and said, "It's probably because he's speaking Gaelic, of Portuguese origin which never modernized to become Spanish." Now I was beginning to feel better about my Portuguese.

I bravely walked through the crowds with my duffle bag over my shoulder and satchel full of camera goods at 5:30 in the morning, ignoring the stares that came from every direction. The clerk told me I had better be there before 7:00 a.m. or the bus would leave without me. At 7:30 we were still waiting for someone who had telephoned and said he would be late. As the bus started we all called out in unison, "Adiós Caracas." By then the thirteen-passenger mini-bus was at full capacity. Another passenger telephoned but the passengers convinced the bus driver to go on. We got as far as the older section of the city and stopped again. The driver said he had a customer. They let him on and that was definitely our seating limit. One obese man argued with the bus driver, saying he should by law get on the bus. The passengers refused to even budge to let him in. He started arguing with the bus driver, his helper, and the chief of the depot and was going to take them all on. He ranted and raved for about fifteen minutes while the people in the bus sat quietly and watched. Finally, someone yelled, "He's drunk! Leave him here and get rid of him!" After this everyone joined in—yelling, hooting, hollering and razzing him. This impelled him to take on the entire bus. Finally, the bus left him behind, shaking his fist wildly while all the passengers looked back, still continuing to razz him.

Again we all shouted in unison, "Adiós Caracas!" We were soon traveling on a six-lane autopista, through the mountains lighted all the way to Bariquisimento, followed by an entirely straight two-lane highway. During the night we were stopped about every hour by the police for inspection. The Venezuela police were much harsher than those in the Dominican Republic. They were gruff and took full advantage of their power. The Dominican Republic police had left me with the impression they were civilians in military clothing.

Rest stops were apparently not big on the agenda of our driver. We had traveled several hours before one of the passengers yelled, "When is the next rest stop?"

"Just ahead," answered the driver.

After awhile another passenger called out, "How far is it to the next rest stop?"

"Not too far," muttered the driver.

After another extended time the same passenger pleaded, "When are we going to stop?"

"In a while," sighed the driver, again.

"Well it'd better be now!" yelled the man.

The bus stopped by a field on the side of the highway. Men piled out from every seat in the bus, leaving the women and me, far too shy, to remain seated with them. There was no run for the woods, or effort to hide, men lined up in a long row on the side of the highway relieving themselves. I cursed my inhibited upbringing, which kept me from a much-needed participation. Women just had to wait for the next stop. When we finally reached a rest stop one of the Italian passengers insisted on buying me a beer. I finally talked him into buying me a Pepsi instead of a beer. He then ordered two Pepsis and a beer. To my revulsion he poured the beer into the cup with a Pepsi. I have never tasted anything so awful. I could still taste it the next morning.

I could see what the term, "buses being friendly in Latin America" meant. Within minutes after the bus left everyone broke into animated conversation. A couple of the men on the bus began singing and jokes cascaded from everyone. We passed breathtaking scenery, climbing through the mountains, as high as 15,000 feet. The engine whined as we descended into San Cristóbal at noon the next day. They loaded the three of us who had through tickets into a taxi. We then whizzed up over the mountains and onto a winding mountain road with unsurpassed views of the surrounding scenery, winding down the stunning road to San Antonio at the border with Colombia. Dark clouds capped the distant snowcapped mountains to the South. Eighteen hours of constant clatter in the back of a Volkswagen bus had slowly trans-located us from Caracas, Venezuela to the border of Columbia.

3. WATCH OUT FOR ROBBERS

My nervous system bristled as I faced the bleak picture conveyed to me by numerous Venezuelans of a violent country with unfriendly people who would rob me at every chance.

"Watch your camera and wallet. They will steal it right out of your hands," their voices still echoing in the back of my mind.

"Guards will deny you everything in search of a bribe," The voices continued.

"Neighbors shoot neighbors and even entire families if they disagree with them politically." That one was particularly disquieting to me, being of political predisposition. The Shreiders told of their experiences with this violence in their book.

The day had changed from one of seemingly endless semi-jungle roads, suddenly climbing into cool mountains, followed by a sharp descent from the mountains into cactus desert. A blast of hot air swept through the bus in sharp contrast to the cold of the mountaintops.

This was new country, new people, changing weather and new regulations. Venezuela seemed to be resting on an over dependency on their only income, oil. Her agriculture didn't begin to feed her people. She, therefore, was importing over half her food (formerly as much as 80%). No matter who was in the government the appearance had changed very little. The customs were still as nasty and inefficient as ever. She still had more police officers than she could handle with a disgustingly apparent, large army with its Nazi-appearing uniform and attitudes.

Caracas reminded me of New York. You could make friends with the people if you were willing to go a little out of the way but everyone was pretty well wrapped up in him or herself. There were many foreigners in Caracas and many of them looked like Europeans rather than Latin Americans. The Americans rarely mixed with the natives and the natives did little to meet Americans. The natives were nationalistic and didn't care for the foreign influence in their country. They relied entirely on the petroleum industry and as a result you could go completely through Venezuela and see most land lying fallow. As a result you'd pay $1.00 for a head of lettuce and buy American frozen and canned foods at outrageous prices. There were literally mountains of ore in the country but everyone was interested in petroleum because it was easy money. The government was getting 50% of all the profits of the petroleum industry for doing nothing. It was felt with the New Leftist government there would be a trend toward either nationalizing the industries or demanding 75% of the profits, as was the case with Perú.

Venezuela appeared to me to be very disconnected. The highway was so new it passed through few towns. The few we did pass through, the road went around the outskirts. However, when we traveled the old road I saw women still wore lace shawls and farmers wore the same attire as their 15th Century ancestors.

We sped into the customs at San Antonio quickly and found the Colombian customs courteous and efficient. I turned to leave and a Venezuelan customs official stopped me.

"You will not be able to leave the country for another two hours," he barked.

"Why?" I asked.

"You'll have to wait until the customs opens again," he gruffly answered." Other passengers had warned me of this and told me to pre-pay my taxi. The agent was unconcerned with this and walked off.

As I sat down to wait it out, a shoeshine boy approached me and asked me if I wanted my shoes shined. I felt this was one time I could take advantage of the lower prices in Colombia.

"How much?" I asked.

"One Bolivar," said the young man gazing at his shoebox.

"One-half Bolivar," I interrupted, looking intensely into his expressionless face to sense agreement.

Without so much as a gaze, he sat down and tapped the shoeshine box. I put my shoe on it. After three swift sweeps he half-heartedly tapped the box again, signaling me to change shoes. Three swift swipes and he again tapped the box, indicating he was through. I gave him the half-Bolivar and he picked up his box with absolutely no expression and stumbled off. He started to go up some stairs and fell with the shoeshine equipment scattered all over the place. I got up to see what was the matter and saw he was lying there, still expressionless. I was puzzled and a little embarrassed feeling the people behind me might think I did something to him. I pulled back when I saw people coming over from every direction. I felt it was probably better I let the others handle it in their own way. I was shocked when, instead of helping him, they all just gathered around him and stared. Nobody touched him or tried to help him up. Finally one kind soul kicked the equipment in his direction so he wouldn't have so far to walk to get it. Three or four of the people continued staring at me, their gaze becoming more intense. I was relieved when the boy finally got up and, with the same inexpressive face, put his tools of trade back into the box and stumbled over to me. There were three men left and they were all staring at me. I didn't know what to expect. "What does he want?" I thought. The boy, still impassive, asked me if I wanted a shine. I told him he had just shined my shoes. With that he stumbled off. A blond girl, seeing my concern, said, "Just ignore the incident," and pointing a figure at her head, added, "The boy is a little off."

With that I felt relieved. I walked back to the inspection counter, sat down, and started to read the paper. The three men had all taken up vantage points and were still staring at me. I felt more and more uneasy. I went over to them and asked the blonde-haired person, "Are you, your husband and your friend waiting for the Venezuela customs? If you are, why?"

The husband told me, "We have to wait for the afternoon siesta to end."

We passed our time in endless conversation. He was German but spoke excellent English. "I was in Colombia for five years, working with a foreign company, which was transferring me to Venezuela."

"You will run into a lot of police in between San Antonio and Caracas," I warned.

"Oh, after five years in Colombia I have learned to expect anything and nothing surprises me any more."

I looked up, relieved to find the Venezuelan customs was finally opened. The German exchanged his Colombian money for my Venezuelan money so we could each start out with the proper currency, he for Venezuela and me for Colombia. We went into the customs. The chief was in no hurry to get to us. We waited for a while and finally the German was processed.

As I moved toward the counter behind him, an officer stopped me. "Wait on the bench outside the office," he snarled.

My patience wore thin as I observed people get right out of their cars, run in and swiftly drive across the border and speed into the distance. Friends of the chief came in and visited. Finally, I saw the chief step out for a cup of coffee. I caught him, as he was about to start for the outside door. He looked puzzled, turned to me, and asked, "Do you want anything?"

"I have been waiting on the bench outside your office."

"You shouldn't be waiting out there. I did not know you wanted anything." He stamped a certificate and asked me, "That'll be three bolivars."

"All I have is a dollar bill and some Colombian currency," I explained.

He looked at me and said, "Of course I can't take anything but Venezuelan currency."

I was shocked, frustrated, and now dismayed. I had just traded all my bolivars for pesos so I wouldn't have this problem.

"Where can I get any money exchanged?" I asked, plaintively. After all this was only 90¢.

"Get it at the bank over there," he said, pointing to the Venezuelan side. At this point I was exhausted and obediently ran toward the bank, but I was abruptly stopped by another customs official.

"You can't go through," he bellowed.

"I have to get change to pay the customs," I pleaded.

The guard was unmoved. After I offered to let him hold my camera equipment he let me go to the bank.

I ran to the bank and presented my few pesos and the single dollar bill I had.

"We can't change that. It's too small an amount," the grim-faced teller told me.

Finally, a kindly bank employee took pity on my aggravated appearance and gave me 90¢ for my dollar.

I ran back, retrieved my camera equipment, and dashed into the customs office. The chief stamped my Visa and I turned to leave.

My heart jumped into my throat, as a guard growled, "You haven't cleared Colombian customs yet."

I approached the desk, resigned to another complicated process after recalling how the German spilled out his life history to get out of Colombia. What relief I felt when the customs official dropped everything, knowing he could quickly fill out my short document.

I ran out and grabbed my bags so I could get started, fondly breathing in the Colombian air. My luck changed as I stepped into the taxi. I had not one cent of Colombian money, only travelers' Cheques. The enigma of money followed me like the proverbial can on a cat's tail. The driver was unmoved as he went from kiosk to kiosk of Money Changers only to find them all closed. Tomorrow was Sunday so it would be Monday before I could get my hands on any money for taxi, bus, or hotel.

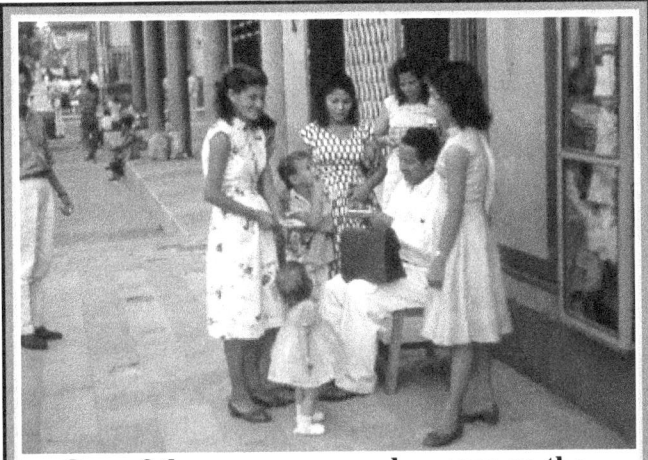
One of the many moneychangers on the streets of Cúcuta, Colombia

The driver was responsive to my dilemma. He took me around to an assortment of bus agencies. We found there were three buses leaving between one and three in the morning but absolutely none before. The numerous warnings of Venezuelan acquaintances echoed in my ear. It would be far too dangerous to run around with $1,000 worth of goods until 2:00 in the morning in a darkened deserted border town, so we drove to a hotel room so I could stay over until Monday if I couldn't get any money changed. When the desk clerk saw me run in with a sport shirt and unshaven face he curtly said there were no rooms available.

I glanced through my Latin American Hotel Guide and told the driver to bring me to the cheapest hotel in it. When we arrived there I gave him some money and asked for change.

"I can't take this. I'm Venezuelan. I don't have Colombian change," he said.

I ran into the hotel and asked for a room.

"All I have is a tiny room," she answered.

"I'll take it," I snapped, without even thinking. "Can you change this bill so I can pay the taxi?"

"Hotel rules don't allow me to change bills," she answered with resignation. I'll send the bellboy out to change it at another place."

When I went outside I could see the bellboy had tried to change it with the taxi driver and they were headed off somewhere to get it changed. They soon returned with the change, with a 10% service fee, which I gladly paid. "Watch out for robbers," cautioned the driver as he sped off.

The sight of my room soon dashed the elation I felt at this accomplishment. It was the worst I had seen since leaving the United

States. A dirty washbasin stood by the door. The bed, with its old wrought iron, must have been brought over by Christopher Columbus when the hotel in Ciudád Trujillo was through with it. It was surrounded by gay-nineties dime-store furniture. My greatest shock was when I sat on the bed and practically cracked my pelvis. The windowless room was hot and muggy; its only source of air came from the hotel through the gap between the wall and the ceiling, a distance of about a foot. I went upstairs to the shower room, waded through two inches of water so I could utilize the facilities. Wisdom told me I was safer remaining inside that night.

Farmers, looking for work, Cúcuta, Colombia

I got up the next morning, had breakfast, and began inquiring about buses for Bogotá. I found that 2:00 a.m. was the only time when the buses left for Bogotá. One of the waiters told me to take the Ferreira, as this was the most dependable. I finally found a place that would change my money.

"What time should I check out?" I asked the clerk at the hotel. "I would like to keep my bags safe and just sit in the lounge until the bus leaves at 2:00 a.m." Actually, I had a deathly fear of walking around the streets at night with my bags.

She smiled and said, "Oh no, Señor. You can keep your bags in your room if you wish. It won't cost you any more."

"Oh, no," I protested. "I'll move my bags so you can rent the room for the night."

"No Señor," she insisted. "You can keep the bags there."

I walked to the bus station and bought my ticket on the Ferreira, a sort of school bus.

I started to leave and was hailed by a young man.

"I'm a student," he said.

I recalled students were the most volatile politically of Latin Americans. He proved to be quite frank when discussing International politics.

After some time in our discussion I said, "The people I have met so far have disproved what I was told by Venezuelans. They told me Colombians were unfriendly and will rob me of everything."

He chuckled and said, "This is not true about the unfriendliness. They are usually very friendly but thievery is very high. They always tell you in one Latin American country the next one is unfriendly. I come from Venezuela, a refugee from the Jiménez regime."

After an hour of friendly conversation, mostly critical of the United States, I said, "You know I'm American, don't you?"

"Yes, I know. Why?"

"Well, you are running down the Americans and I am one."

"Oh, we like Americans. We just don't like what your government is doing. We even like your President. We just don't like Duways."

I didn't understand that word. "What's a Duways?" I queried.

"Duways, Duways, Juan Foster Duwees."

He finally wrote it on a piece of paper, John Foster Dulles.

"Oh, you mean the Secretary of State and his brother, Allen Dulles, the head of the CIA?"

"You are not any more responsible for your government than we are. Latin Americans like Eisenhower and even Nixon, but we detest Dulles. How can a man like Ike keep a man like Dulles in power?"

I asked, "How can Latin Americans like the man who is at the head of our government and dislike the man who is supposed to be his alter ego?"

"Oh no," he said, we actually have a fairly good feeling toward Nixon; many hope he will be the next President. We feel Nixon's foreign policy is good but it's Dulles who runs the Foreign Department. Our respect for Nixon was shown by the fact that although the rioters were right on top of him, both at the airport and in the car, they did him no bodily harm. Had that been Dulles in the car the demonstrators would have ripped him to pieces and spread him from one end of Caracas to the other. As much respect as the demonstrators have for Nixon they couldn't just let the government send him around like a puppet to pat them on the head and say everything is fine. They had to do something drastic to get to Eisenhower, who they feel to be surrounded by officials who give him only soothing news.

"This really helped Nixon in his political aims," he added.

I laughed and added, "The Democrats are now demanding equal time in Venezuela for Jack Kennedy (who was running for President at that time)."

Of equal interest to Colombians was the American engineered creation of Panama from the upper arm of Colombia, which helped us accomplish the Panama Canal passage. Colombia had just successfully revolted against their dictator, Perez Jimenez, a man who took over the country as a humanitarian and ended up consorting with the criminals in a ruthless dictatorship. Due to the extreme violence in the country, mostly between the liberals and conservatives, the revolutionary council voted to come together to rule the country. A liberal would rule for a time and then exchange with a conservative for the remainder of the term. This was unique and especially unpredicted in Latin America, given the volatile nature of that country.

The student had no good words whatsoever for Pérez Jiménez (recently deposed President of Venezuela). "Under his rule students were either put in jail or chased out of the country, learning was prevented whenever possible and very much controlled where it existed.

"I have respect for the government junta. This coming election is a farce and the junta is keeping its citizens from voting, but the government is rounding up other foreigners and giving them the vote in an effort to control the elections, I have little respect for the Dominicans. They are stupid oafs that allow themselves to be dictated to." He continued, "I spent quite a bit of time attending school in Puerto Rico. The Puerto Ricans want independence but the U.S. is hanging onto the island," and thus continued our conversation for another hour.

"I am relatively unimpressed with the new governmental set-up in Colombia," he stated with some finality.

I was amazed at how an internal happening could make such a sensation in another country as the new set-up in Colombia and be regarded so matter-of-factly by the people in that country.

I asked him, "Will the new presidential set-up settle the terrific strife, which has ripped Colombia apart for so long?"

"No," he said. "I don't think it will settle much.

I was surprised to hear this, as the impression left by the papers in the United States was that Colombia had finally settled her problems. One thing I found in Colombia was how little respect the average Colombian had for his or her government. Even Americans, who worked in Colombia and loved it, told me the government was a mess.

I glanced at my watch and saw it was 2:00. I had the promise of the bus office chief he would watch my baggage if I brought it in, so I departed for the hotel to get the bags so as not to inconvenience the hotel. When I was handed the bill I was shocked to see it had doubled. I went back and asked the manager.

"Why is the bill so high?"

"But Señor, I am charging you for no more than if you had stayed the whole night," she said sternly.

"Talk with the girl at the desk," she said as she returned to her work.

At the desk I found the clerk was off for the day.

I explained I had eaten only three meals and stayed one night and the bill was for two nights and six meals. Finally one of the boys at the desk agreed to go back and talk with the manager. He returned in a few minutes with a bill for just the one night.

I had spent half the night before sitting up thinking about shortening the route to the Amazon through a smaller river which might prove more interesting and cut the number of miles I would have to re-cross on my return. I looked at all the rivers in Ecuadór and finally decided the best thing to do would be to wait until I got to Quito, then find out about it through people who knew a little more about it. I, therefore, dropped the matter from my mind.

Divine intervention was with me because I met a Spaniard at the bus station when I returned.

"Tell me more about your trip," he asked politely.

I got out the map and started showing him my plan. "Why are you going all the way to Lima to get to the Amazon?" he asked.

"I had planned on reaching it through Ecuadór but I have yet to find a road there that leads to a navigable river."

"Why don't you go through Colombia?" he asked, somewhat surprised at my answer. "I've done this on a business trip. Let's look again at your maps." When I finally recovered the buried map he searched and began to point. "Take the bus from Bogotá to Neiva. That only takes a day. Then you catch another bus to Florencia and that just takes you another day. There you will find a canoe that can take you to Tres Esquinas in just three days. You can catch a launch to La Tagua in one day, a bus to Puerto Leguízamo on a short trip through the rainforest and a river launch to Leticia from there."

I had never thought of that because the map just showed a river (Hacha and Caquetá) going way down to the middle of the Amazon. By connecting to another river (Putumayo) I would enter the Amazon just east of Leticia, Colombia's isolated outlet to the Amazon.

"How long a boat ride is it from Leticia to Iquítos, Perú?" I asked. "Oh, that's just four hours," he confidently responded.

A wave of relief passed through me. "This is perfect," I thought. "He's made a business trip so he must know what he's talking about."

"Will I be safe there?" I asked, feeling somewhat uneasy inside. "Someone told me I needed to have more fear of robbers in Southern Colombia than in Eastern Colombia."

"No, no need to fear there. The canoes are run by Indians and they are friendly civilized people. Robbers will usually not hurt you. They will just take your money," said the Venezuelan student.

"Is my camera safe?" I asked with still a bit of disbelief.

"They won't take your personal possessions. They're too much trouble, added the student, seeing my skepticism."

I guess I'm safe then. I only have Travelers' Cheques and little money.

He didn't get very far with the explanations of the trip when I realized I was very hungry.

"Don't eat at the hotel. I know a better place that will serve you a la carte," a gentleman said, giving me specific directions.

I arrived at the spot and found no restaurant. I searched the area and finally saw a sign that said "RESTAURANTE." It led me through a dark entrance into an unkempt courtyard, direly in need of TLC. Bare tables with thick layers of dirt adorned the room. I walked around until I finally found a young woman.

"What is it you want?" she asked, somewhat puzzled.

"I want something to eat," I answered.

The girl looked surprised and asked, "What do you want to eat?" she said equally as surprised."

"Do you have a menu?"

"No."

"What do you have?"

"Beefsteak or chicken," she offered.

"Then I'll take the beefsteak." (It was cheaper.)

I looked at the bare tables and then my watch. It was 7:00 p.m., what I thought was the middle of the dinner hour for Latin Americans. I looked around and thought, "I must be their first customer in months."

She finally brought out a beautiful steak dinner, a pleasant surprise for this starving traveler.

I got back to the office and found it closed. It was getting dark and I was worried about being alone on the streets until the station opened, around 2:00 am. Caution made me wary of being alone. I made sure to be surrounded by people I trusted and always made sure I was out in the open on well-lighted streets (few and far between in Cúcuta). There must be a movie house in this town, I thought. When I finally found it I found it did not begin until 9:00 p.m. I went back to the safety of the bus station and found it open again. I read the local paper until 9:00, and then meandered down to the theatre. At least I would be in a safe place until around midnight.

The theatre attendant said I would have to wait until 9:15 to get in.

"That's all right," I said. "It's just about 9:15 right now."

"Oh, that must be Caracas time," she answered. "The time in Cúcuta is a half-hour different."

That was the first time I had ever heard of time changing for the half hour. It must be terribly confusing. The show was awful. All I can say is it kept me off the streets at night.

I got back to the station and found it closed again. I waited in front of it until the theatre across from it closed and the lights went out. This left me in complete darkness. I was really getting wary now. The station could not have been on a darker street. This felt like suicide. I found myself looking down every dark corner for any movement. I felt much safer walking around so I began walking randomly through the main streets. I started to walk down one street and noticed two suspicious looking characters hovering in the dark. I started down the dark street to the bus station and saw them turn and walk down the same street behind me. I walked over to where the bus was standing in front of the office and again started my silent wait in the dark. I could barely see my hands in front of me. "I could be surrounded by robbers and never know it," I thought.

I could see the strangers had changed course and were headed in my direction. I walked slowly to the end of the block, kept on walking around the block until I got to the park, and sat down. There was at least some light cast there by the distant streetlights. I had been there only a short while when the same two men started walking in my direction. I could hear the shuffle of their footsteps and the mumble of their conversation. I felt safer in the park as I was sitting under a bright light and the police headquarters was right across the street. I finally surrendered to their pursuit. They walked up to me and asked, "You waiting around for the Ferreira?"

"Yes," I answered.

They walked past me, smiled and wished me well.

The greeting surprised me, as they used the familiar "Como estas" greeting usually reserved for close friends and family.

As the hour approached 2:00 a.m., I figured the bus station would be opening soon, so again I walked into the dark void. Even though it was still dark my fears were ameliorated by another couple of people who arrived at the same time. Finally, I saw the same two men arriving with several other men. As they approached me I became worried but figured they couldn't do anything drastic with witnesses standing by. They walked up to me, greeted me, and inquired if the office had opened yet. It was then I discovered they were also taking the bus.

Finally, the station opened. It was here I ran into my first trouble with asking for the toilet.

"Hay un 'privado' aquí?" I asked, remembering this was a popular word for bathroom in México.

His blank stare convinced me this was not the word. I remembered 'excusado' above the rest room door on an airplane so asked, "Hay un 'excusado' aquí?" This had worked well for me in Venezuela, but not here!

Another blank stare. I then pulled out my Spanish dictionary, which I used in my moments of distress. I remembered a sign for "Please do not throw toilet paper in the toilet bowl," which was over some of the more rudimentary bathrooms with septic tanks. That also drew a blank stare. He just asked me if I wanted to take a shower. I even used the Portuguese word to no avail. By now I should have been using the word for 'emergency' as I could hold no longer, but he finally caught on and led me to a little room behind the shop.

The uncrowded bus left twenty minutes ahead of time.

I settled back for what I hoped would be a deep sleep. I was barely asleep when everyone was ordered out of the bus. I felt my knees heaving under the weight of continual exhaustion as I waited in endless compliance for the soldiers to thoroughly check each one's set of documents and baggage.

"Get your bags," called the guards. I slowly climbed to the top of the bus to again untie my bag. There was no choice with a duffle bag but to dump all contents on the ground. Everyone obediently submitted to these endless searches. Several of us then climbed to the top of the bus to cinch the gear for the mountainous trip ahead on unpaved roads. This inspection was even more thorough than at the border. By this time I was completely bushed. I had eaten little and rested less over the past 24 hours. It was with welcome relief as I again settled in my seat, ready for another try at sleep. A sudden sharp jolt made me painfully aware we had left paved road sooner then outlined in my book. Sleep was even more evasive with the rumble of the road below. I was soon awakened again as we pulled into another customs inspection. I robotically slipped into my grueling routine, crawling to the top of the bus, unlocking my bag, and unquestioningly letting them go through its contents.

"The only reason for these close inspections is because there is a foreigner on board," I overheard one of the passengers whisper to another.

"Holy Cow!" I thought. "I hope they don't do this every hour for the next seventeen to Bogotá."

We again were on the road. Although there were numerous other police stops, from this point on the police only stopped the bus each time to get a report from the driver of the bus.

I awoke in the morning to lush Alpine panoramic views of wondrous mountains. We climbed around one endless loop after another to reach the uppermost portions of vermilion cliffs, some with unguarded drops into 3,000-foot abysses. I was impressed with the great care taken by the driver negotiating these turns. There was none of the speeding through mountains I experienced in México, where they would even pass on turns. The driver took his time and took great care passing.

I enjoy mountains but soon got my fill of them on that trip. We climbed one range after another over the dirt roads. After about

14 hours of this it became tedious due to the poor shape the roads were in.

As we rounded a turn, after a lengthy climb, the bus straining with every foot, my eyes were drawn into the steep descent ahead. The road wound in an endless twisting string toward the steep drop into the valley far below. The old Bluebird bus slowly ground its way into a descent so steep we dropped from being nearly directly over the tiny village far below where we came to an abrupt stop for breakfast. Every building throughout the village was painted white dominated by a Gothic church at its center. The restaurant was the messiest place I had ever eaten. The food was worse than the decór. The other passengers, more used to traveling in sparse conditions, sat at the dark crude wooden tables in the tacked-together room on a second floor with its unpainted wooden walls. As the food came, the rumble began. The passengers complained an ever-increasing dislike. As I looked over I saw a man fanning himself with his burned pancake-shaped bread. Others threw their food in the middle of the table. I was starving so I was the only one who ate everything. We all paid and left. Everyone was still complaining about the breakfast when we again boarded the bus. In an offering of at least some levity, I mentioned, "At least it was cheap."

They answered sharply, "What do you mean it's cheap?" To change from dollars it is cheap but for us Colombians it isn't." This was the first time I had run into this "changing from dollar" argument and it made me think. From then on I began to think more in terms of pesos, rather than dollars to pesos. I became another traveling peasant, taller and lighter skinned but equally as frugal.

I finally began to meet some people by noon. They saw my interest in their country so they began to point out things along the way. One man came over and sat next to me. We began to converse about the country. This led him into talk about the thievery problem. "These bandits come down out of the hills and kill entire villages and burn their houses. You see there?" he said, pointing to some skeletons of burned-out houses along the road. One of them was large enough to serve as a place for a rest stop, so we stopped there. We went up and looked at the walls. They were two feet thick. He said it had been a store and had stood since colonial times but was nearly totally burned out.

"When was this done?" I asked.

"Probably about 1950. The government sent in additional police and that has cleared up the problem. But the worst part of the country is where you say you're headed. There isn't so much killing going on now. It is mostly robbers taking your money and leaving."

I interrupted, "It is dangerous walking across the street in New York. Every place has its own dangers."

We finally stopped for dinner. I wasn't very hungry but figured I had better eat. We were supposed to arrive in Bogotá at 7:00 p.m. but it didn't look now as though we would arrive until 11:00. I ate a part of the meal but couldn't finish it. We all hopped on the bus. The bus driver again reassured me he would find me a good cheap hotel in Bogotá. I wasn't too excited about the deal, as the price named was so much cheaper than the cheapest hotel I found listed in my book. The student from Bogotá was helping the driver by checking headlights, parking, etc. It appeared as though he had made the run on that bus a hundred times.

About five minutes after I got on the bus my stomach had a conversation with my lower bowel and said it wanted out, the result of the morning meal. The breakfast obviously had not agreed with me. The bumpy road was not helping. Finally, blessed relief was mine when we got on some paved road. There were no sanitary facilities during the roller coaster ride up and down through the mountains. I would just have to grin and bear it until Bogotá. Near Bogotá we suddenly left the main road and were again on a bumpy dirt road. To make matters worse we got lost wandering up and down numerous streets until the driver found the right dirt road, which we remained on until just outside Bogotá. A double lane highway led into the city. We passed by about two miles of elegant English-styled homes. I asked someone "What's with this English styling?"

He told me, "It was a stage the country was going through for a while but it has ended. This happened during the war when a lot of people were suddenly getting enough money to build large homes. Some of these are in a French style, but almost all of them are brick."

My heart jumped into my throat as I got off the bus. The terminal was in the middle of what appeared to be the worst section of town, especially in the dark night skies. Three or four boys who wanted to show me good hotels immediately surrounded me. When I couldn't shake them I ran over to the bus driver.

"You said you could send me to a good inexpensive hotel," I reminded him.

"Sure," he said with conviction. "See the sign across the street that says Hotel Maracaibo?" Although this was apparently a slum section the pressure from my breakfast urged me to go to a hotel immediately.

My fears were allayed when I saw about half the passengers, including the students I had befriended, heading for the same hotel.

"There is another American right next door to you, but he can't speak Spanish as well as you," said a woman, as she led me to my room.

"I don't care to speak English with anyone as it ruins my Spanish," I told her. I didn't want to face two days of straight English ruining my Spanish.

View of the red tiled roofs of Bogotá, Colombia, from the top of the funicular.

The room was very nice, freshly painted, and clean. That spoke well after weeks of staying in shabby hotels. Nevertheless, it was freezing. I hadn't been warm since I left Cúcuta. We had been in the mountains all day and Bogotá is in a valley at 8,000 ft. altitude (1,000 ft. higher than México City). I sat on the bed and once more practically dislocated my pelvis as hip hit board. I had never felt a bed as hard as this so investigated. The springs were replaced with boards and the mattress was only about one-and-one-half inches thick. I found this to be common of the lower class hotels in Colombia that didn't cater to tourists.

I had a very uneasy night with the cold weather, dysentery, and a hard bed. About 5:00 in the morning the American came by. I introduced myself to him. He explained, "I worked for a petroleum company in Venezuela for a while, but finally quit and started traveling through Latin America. When I got as far as Bogotá I decided to rest awhile. I've been staying here for a month. I tried every hotel in the neighborhood and found them all the same price as this and not half as good. I'm going out to mail some letters would you like to come along?"

I stepped into the single shower, which served all the guests and found the water ice cold. When I checked at the desk they told me there was no such thing as hot water in that hotel.

As we stepped out into the bitter cold the American continued, "I find the Bogotaños will steal anything they can get their hands on, but I like Bogotá anyway. You just have to be very careful."

The only way I could stay warm was to keep on my jacket with the fur-lined hood. An attention-grabber, people stopped and stared from blocks away. "Would you like some wild juice that is supposed to be very good?" he said as we approached a small concession stand.

"No, I'm avoiding liquids all liquids and I haven't had anything to eat today, but I guess I can handle some pastry."

In the post office I found the airmail to be run by AVIANCA, the government owned airline. It had a much more efficient look about it in contrast to any other post office I had seen so far. I checked the list and found I had finally collided with a letter. I ran up to claim it.

"I need your passport before releasing the letter," the clerk said with a stern tone in her voice.

"It's locked in my room for safe-keeping," I said plaintively.

"I must have it," was her unyielding reply.

Many minutes passed with little yielding on her part.

"Okay," she finally offered with a sigh. "I'll take your friend's passport number."

Cathedral, Bogotá, Colombia

When we returned I forced myself to eat a meal and suffered no bad effects from it. One of the guests at the hotel asked me, "Did you report to the police when you came into the country?"

"No," I said. "I arrived after 5:00 p.m. on Saturday, too late to report, they were closed on Sunday and I left for Bogotá at 2:00 a.m. on Monday morning," I answered, somewhat uneasy at the possible consequences.

"You were supposed to report to the police the minute you arrived in this country. Colombia has a police network which works separately from the customs, which is something like your FBI. It is called Seguridad Investigationes de Colombia (SIC) which, when translated means about the same thing as Federal Bureau of Investigation. It handles almost all dealings with foreigners. Many of us claim it is a secret police."

"Well, go there with a good story," interrupted another guest.

"Here's how to get to the police station," added another, handing me directions.

Forty-five minutes later I was at the address. I looked around and saw nothing that even looked like their offices. I went into a neighboring store.

"Where's the police station?" I asked the manager.

"I'm not familiar with that," he said, turning to one of the clerks. Soon the two of them had their heads in a phone book, looking for it. He lifted the phone and soon was asking Information. Holding the phone with one hand he copied an address on a piece of paper, and handed it to me.

"That's where I started out this morning," I said, with surprise. As we all laughed, "Oh, oh," I said as I looked at the time. "I'd better take a taxi or I'll be there at their siesta."

Finding nothing at that address, I approached some people.

"It's not here. You'll find it at this address," they said, handing me another address. I went there and found nothing. As I was wandering around in the vicinity, I passed a travel agency. "Surely they would know where the police are."

"Do you know where the Police Station is so I can report into the country?" I asked, trying not to show my inner turmoil.

"It's not near here. Here's another address," said the agent. "It's only about half-mile away. I ran there and climbed to the third floor, as instructed. "I was greeted by a clerk who said, "It's almost noon and we're closing for lunch. Come back after 2:30."

I went back to the hotel for lunch. I was finding Bogotá was not as easy as Caracas to find one's way around. I had memorized the street the hotel was near but had not taken down its address. I walked up streets, down streets and all over the place, but couldn't find the hotel anywhere. I spent about an hour looking for it and finally sat down in a park to rest. Then I took up the search anew and went all over for the hotel. I knew about where it was by the statue of Christ on the mountain and the cold drink sign in the slope below. I finally figured I had been searching on the wrong side of Avenida Caracas. I crossed the avenue and went right to the hotel.

I was back at the SIC office at 2:30 p.m. There was a small line so I took my place, figuring this would not take long. I waited and waited while each person worked out endless knotty problems. I was at the front of the line when one of their officials knocked me out of the way and thrust himself in front of me. I patiently waited for him to finish when a boy came in with an elderly lady that couldn't speak Spanish very well and squeezed in front of me. No sooner were they finished than another guy pushed through from another side. The clerk seemed unaffected by this and began processing his papers. He did finally turn around and notice I had been standing there quite awhile. He mentioned this to the clerk but she just looked at me and went back to her work. Finally, someone pushed one of the other girls toward me. A bit miffed, she asked, "What do you want?"

"I need certification on my visa."

Expressionless, she pulled out a stamp and struck my visa, then, without a word, went back to what she was doing.

"Is this what I was waiting for so long?" I asked with utter dismay.

"Yes," was her unsmiling reply.

We were quite a motley crew, sitting around the dinner table, the other guests with their ruanas on and the other American and me with our jackets on. I wrote in the diary for the rest of the night, still wearing my fur-lined hood on with the jacket buttoned up to keep warm, hands stiff from the cold.

The next morning I awoke with a cold. I started out adjusting my attitude to achieve greater harmony. There seemed to be a lack of harmony through a lot of the trip—baggage not turning up, camera not following, entire days when nothing seemed to go right. If I concentrate on the negative the Universe answers me with more negativity. I knew I needed to change my thinking if I was going to manifest harmony around me. Although the challenges seemed insurmountable they were there to teach me to meet them with joy. This worked well in the days ahead as the people I met responded to me with respect and friendship.

Check cashing and currency exchange continued to plague me. With daily currency fluctuations and the danger of attracting thieves, I cashed only enough checks to get me to each following city. I stored most of the money in my briefcase, some in the duffle bag, just leaving a small amount handy in my back pocket. By keeping checks and money in three or four different places I felt assured if I got into short supply I wouldn't be left high and dry if one of those caches turned up missing.

I found David Hart through the AGSIM alumni directory. The minute he walked in I recognized him. I gave him my card and told him I was traveling around on my own and was calling on alumni.

"I'm heading out to lunch. Do you want to go along?" were his first words.

As we stepped on the elevator he looked closer at the card and said, "I thought I knew you. I'm from Kansas City, too."

"I went to Southwest High."

"I went there, too," he said.

"I went there from 1946-1949." he said.

We went to the Anglo-American Club for lunch. At this place everyone left his or her Spanish behind. Dave was full of enthusiasm for his job and for living in Colombia.

"I love my work," he said enthusiastically. "I think very highly of the bank where I work and I also find Colombia very pleasing."

He gave me some highlights on the banking profession. "Banking is a good background to have. The bank encourages their employees to get in and try banking out. Then, if within five years the employee decides he or she would rather go into business, the bank helps them find a job. The bank feels this will make a customer of the former employee. Their attitude is it's better to have a good customer than a dissatisfied employee. Then, when the employee is looking for a job, he or she finds the broad experience of the banking profession makes her or him more valuable to the companies where they are seeking work.

"The Venezuelans warned me about the dangers in Colombia from robbers," I mentioned.

"The danger exists not so much in Eastern Colombia as it does in Southern Colombia where you are going."

I told him, "I was originally going to go to the Amazon River, via Lima and Pucalpa, down the Ucayali River, but that would mean backtracking through a great deal of the same territory on my return. Some students and traveling salesmen convinced me I could make it by going due south through the Colombian jungle. That way I could come back a completely different route through Perú and Ecuador."

"I'm intensely interested in this route, as I have heard so little about that part of Colombia." Dave said. "Be sure and write me about that area as soon as you get to Belém."

Dave seemed to be keeping current with the old gang from Southwest High. There were a number of our old classmates in South America. I didn't know any of them well enough to look them up. Anyway, it was almost impossible to get in touch with anyone unless I had a telephone number to go by. Most of the people rented their phone with their apartment. This meant the only way to find them was through their apartment or telephone number.

"I'm worried about my visa. It isn't long enough time to get me out of the country through the south. Do you have any ideas on this?" I asked. "The visa says it is non-extendable, once in the country."

"I'm sure it can be extended," he assured me. "Here's an address of a place that can probably do that."

"Good, because I was looking on the map last night and saw there is an archeological park, off on a dirt road, on the outskirts of the jungle. I checked the South American Handbook and found this was a location where there were literally hundreds of carved stones dating from before Christ. I want to visit them but I'm not sure what the transportation is or how I can take this in with the few days I have left on my visa and the distance I have to cover. It would be a shame to go within 80 miles of such an interesting spot and not go in and see it. Few Colombians, let alone Americans, will get to see this within their lifetimes."

As we parted, Dave gave me the address of a travel agency run by an American and his wife. "They can help you out."

When I arrived at the address he gave me I was astounded. It was the same address where I got my visa stamped. I was waited on right away this time. A clerk asked me to follow him to another office. He soon returned and said, "I was told the officer was in conference. Wait here. I waited and waited and finally the officer came out. A woman at the desk explained my problem and got it all mixed up. I again explained it to her and she started all over from the beginning, as garbled as the first explanation. I corrected her and she went into another room and came out with an interpreter. I was sure I had explained it to her correctly. However, just in case I started to explain it to the interpreter in English and found he understood little of what I said. I then switched back to Spanish. I saw a man was standing on the sidelines, listening to every word. He interrupted and quickly clarified it for the official. They sent the interpreter to process me. Then we began the seesaw, so frustratingly prevalent everywhere I went. He spoke to me in broken English I could barely understand. I kept speaking Spanish, hoping he would get the hint. Then he struggled with his English and I patiently waited for him to finish. To his credit he finally took the hint and switched to Spanish.

I followed him into another room where credentials were needed. Fortunately, I had decided not to go to the Brazilian Embassy, so I had all the credentials I needed, as well as three photos. He led me into another office where the first, middle and last name was asked of my mother, father and sisters; father's occupation and residence; and many other non-pertinent questions. He led me out in the hall where my fingerprints were taken several times.

"Would you like my footprint," I jovially asked, hoping to put some levity into an otherwise solemn procession. Noticing no reciprocation, I continued, "Our State Department has been under particularly harsh fire from Latin American countries because they require fingerprinting of Latin American immigrants, who claim this was required only of criminals in their own countries."

He quickly answered, "This is a precaution for identification in case you are killed in an obscure part of the country."

That didn't make me feel any less apprehension about the trip south into the rainforest.

Back in the original room I was handed a very official looking document extending my visa for six days. My only thought was, "All this for six little days, and will that be enough days for this trip?"

I raced to the travel agency because what had seemed like a simple task had consumed the entire afternoon. Slipping in the door just in time I found they could help me very little as they dealt mostly with well-known places and luxury hotels.

The agent stopped a moment and then gleefully said, "I think I have something. I arranged a trip for the Women's Club of Bogotá. Despite the fact they flew to Garcón and chartered a bus the rest of the way, staying overnight at a nice hotel in Pitalito it does give you some more information. There is a hotel and there is a way to get there by bus. Here's the name of a bus company in Neiva."

Now I finally knew there was such a thing as a bus from Neiva to San Agustín.

"There is no hotel in San Agustín," he warned, "so you will have to stay at Pitalito, an hour-and-a-half from San Agustín. I would take the bus in the morning and take another back late that afternoon. I would advise you to take the Auto Ferro to Neiva, as it is safer. There have been quite a few killings in that area. Eleven people were just plain murdered over the weekend. Twenty-one others on two buses were massacred with machetes and pistols in a robbery, staged by robbers dressed as security police."

"That sounds like good advice to me. I've heard this several times. From what I have been reading this is probably the only danger spot I will be going through."

"I agree with you on that," said the agent.

That agent will never know how relieved I was to have that confirmation and advice.

I went by the bank to tell Dave that I had had my visa extended and would be staying over another day in Bogotá. He and the other guy were just going to dinner. Dave had a date that night but insisted on our going to dinner first.

"I just got notice I am to be transferred to the branch in Cali," said Dave, cheerfully, when I saw him. "I like Cali better than Bogotá. Women there are even prettier than the women in Bogotá."

This was a feat I found hard to believe.

"I am dating a Colombian girl," Dave added. "Bogotá is wonderful for dating but it is almost impossible to even think of marriage, as 99% of the women are Catholic. I do not intend to become a bead counter. I need to hurry up and meet someone on one of my leaves the bank gives me to go home."

I didn't feel any healthier after I returned to the hotel. I was still freezing and fighting a cold and only a cold shower to look forward to. I was dealing with not only my physical discomforts, but also the problems of robbery, violence, transportation difficulties and other tribulations. To give in on any of these situations would attract what I feared most. I know I attract what I think or feel into my life. I cannot change what IS, I can only change my perception of what is. I had been taught when I change my perception to joy and well-being I attract that to me. Pollyanna as that sounds, this had always been my experience in life. As I reflect back on this voyage it is the challenges that are remembered and during which my greatest spiritual growth took place.

The writings of others had shown me not only were their physical problems healed but also everything improved in their lives. I looked on this challenge as an opportunity to improve every situation on the travel ahead.

I am grateful I had the experiences related to me by a woman who did quite a bit of traveling in South America. She never let a thing inharmonious enter into her experiences and as a result she had some wonderful manifestations. It showed me, at a time when agnosticism was at its height, by applying the positive thought constantly, every situation could be a positive experience, and i.e. "I am the master of my life." The greatest challenges in my life have been the periods of greatest personal growth. Since my return it is the most demanding incidents of the trip that have been the most memorable.

It was typical weather—cold, drippy, dark, and cloudy. I started walking over to a mountain, rising like a gardened skyscraper from the city, about a mile-and-a-half from the hotel. On top was a chapel and cross, accessed by means of a funicular or path.

The museum was especially interesting because it had works in gold of the Indians (pre-Hispanic) that are processed in the same method we process our gold now, with a wax mold. It also had items from many of the explorers. The museum was housed in the upstairs of the Bank of the Republic (Banco del la Republica). Walking into the vault that houses the jewelry was like walking into a discothèque of gold and silver.

Again at dinner I wore my fur-lined jacket, a necessity to keep from freezing. I began to wail for a nice cool and refreshing drink in spite of the cold. I hadn't had a cold drink since Cúcuta, even at the Anglo-American Club—just warm water and hot coffee.

"Is it possible for you to bring a cold coke from the bar?" I begged the maid.

"Oh no, Señor. You can't find a cold drink in Bogotá," she said. I felt like a fool wearing a fur-lined jacket and asking for such an absurdity. Every drink had been warm, including at the bar, because the climate was so cold.

"I've been searching frantically for my Leica camera, which was stolen from me as I sat in the park," said the American. "I laid it at my side so I could relax while I kept an eye on it. Some one came by and started talking with me. When he left, I reached down to get my camera, but it wasn't there. I have a police official working on the case but I don't think there is much hope. The thieves usually send merchandise they steal to another city to sell. Even if I found the thief I don't know what he could do. The policeman is just sort of sitting back and taking it easy and hasn't done anything so far but ask me for money to work on the case.

"I'm also working to get parts for my car. My car broke down so I took it to a place to be fixed. It turned out it needed some parts the dealer doesn't have. I, therefore, sent to his agency to get some parts, which arrived in good time, as mail service between Bogotá and New York is faster than between most major cities in the U.S.A. a letter can be processed and delivered within 36 hours. However, the Colombian government has yet to work out a decent system for its customs on mail received. I had to go to a place and pick it up. There they told me it was at another place. I went there and they sent me to another place where I found it. I was given a waiting ticket to go through on time. There they sent me through another line to pay the duty, where they told me I could pick it up in three days. After three more days I returned, picked up the parts and took them to the dealer. The next day I got a call. It seems the dealer hadn't taken the motor completely apart the first time and now found it needed some other parts. I sent away for these and am now in the process of clearing them with the government today."

The guests at the hotel reminded me of the characters in the boarding house in a Chekov novel. This was probably the cheapest pensión in Bogotá. The people that stayed there were a conglomeration of lower middle class and higher paid workers. There was an intense desire on the part of everyone to improve his or her lot in life. There were many complaints about the food, exaggerating their jobs and telling about how they were actually staying there for the first time. I did not try to talk up my position. I found it best to play the part of a poor student because the prices went way up the minute an American said anything other than he was barely making it. Some of the people were extremely interesting, many traveling with their own small businesses. One extremely interesting gypsy woman stayed there for three or four days. Occasionally she would excuse herself as her clients came into our salón where we guests congregated, and she would leave to do another psychic reading for them.

The Cúcuta bus driver rushed in and out of the hotel again before I left. I don't know how he endured the 17-24 hour mountain trips with little relief. I found it hard enough just sitting in the seat and sleeping for two or three hours along the way, and that was just one way.

I awoke the next morning and felt a great improvement in my entire attitude. The pessimism and lack of confidence were completely gone. I headed out early to find transportation to the salt mines at Zipaquirá. There was a cathedral built in the lower regions of a salt mine, which had been in operation for at least 2,000 years. I thought I had good instructions on where to catch the bus. When I arrived at the address I went in and got in a long line. When I finally got to the ticket counter the attendant said, "This is the wrong terminal. You have to catch your bus at Avenida Caracas. I went there and waited for about fifteen minutes. When no bus was forthcoming I went down a couple of blocks and waited there. Finally, I asked someone, "Does the Zipaquirá bus come by here?"

"Oh no," he said. "It stops at 18th Avenida Caracas."

I walked down there and waited for a while. It finally dawned on me I was on Avenida Jiménez Quesada, which has the same appearance as Avenida Caracas. I walked down to Avenida Caracas and waited awhile. I asked a man, "Does the Zipaquirá bus stop here?"

He answered, "It does but you can't be too sure of it stopping." This prompted me to walk down the street to catch it. There, in front of the station was a bus marked Zipaquirá, which was just preparing to leave. I looked around for a station attendant but couldn't see any so asked one of the passengers, "Do you pay on the bus?" When I couldn't get a sensible answer I got on the bus. After awhile I began to feel foolish sitting there with the briefcase in my lap. I looked up and saw it was hard to get the briefcase in and out of the basket above where I was sitting. I figured it would be safe in the basket above the seat as it would be hard for anyone to get away with it without attracting my attention. I waited for a while longer and thought I had better recheck on buying my bus ticket. I asked the girl that was taking care of the tickets and getting passengers on the bus.

"You have to buy the ticket at the station, Señor, just around the corner."

I asked, "Do I have time?"

"Oh yes," said the driver.

I ran around the corner and got in line. When I finally got to the window I was told by the clerk I had to buy my ticket on the next block. I literally ran down there and found I had to take another bus that was also located there. I suddenly remembered I had left my camera equipment on the bus as I thought I would be just be grabbing a ticket and get right back on. I ran back in and tried to get ahead of the people in the line to get to the window. They thought I was just trying to push ahead as they do, so they smiled and pushed back. I finally got to a man who looked like he knew something. I told him the story and asked, "Where is my bus?"

"It's down on the other block." I ran back down on the other block. It was filled with buses, none of which was the bus I left my satchel on. I ran back to the station again and this time begged pardon of the people in the line and told them this was an emergency. I got to the window as the clerk slowly looked up. My Spanish suddenly improved and I told him rapidly what had happened and that the briefcase was very valuable.

He turned calmly to his assistant and explained more slowly what had happened. The assistant calmly picked up the phone and waited while the chief went back to selling tickets. After about five minutes on the phone the assistant still wasn't getting anywhere. I asked him for the next station so I could chase the bus in a taxi. He told me his assistant was trying to call the next station to get them to leave the bag there. Finally, the assistant got through. He hung up and said the bus had already left that city and was on the autopista. He gave me the name of the next subsequent stop and the number of the bus. I ran out and got a taxi right away — something unusual in Bogotá.

I nervously explained to the driver, "I am chasing a bus whose next stop is Zipaquirá.

The driver winced and said," it will be hard to catch the bus on the autopista as I can go no faster than it can on that highway."

I was so nervous I was trembling. My anxiety was quite apparent. I could not imagine losing my camera apparatus at this stage of my trip. I blurted out, "I have all my valuable equipment in that briefcase."

The driver looked at me calmly and said, "There's nothing to worry about. We will get to Zipaquirá, drink a small cup of coffee and leisurely return to Bogotá."

Somehow, his calmness put me at ease.

WATCH OUT FOR THE ROBBERS

"My name is Roberto. Come on up in the front seat." I pulled out a map and he showed me where we were going to catch the bus. "I'm afraid it will be a close call to catch the bus because the busses make such good time on the autopista."

I felt like I was racing a sick horse in a derby. I was galloping inside, heart throbbing, as the taxi continued at the same slow speed. It was obvious his taxi had a governor. He reached in the glove compartment and pulled out a list of tariffs. The list said it was 30 pesos to go to Zipaquirá. At that point I would have paid $100 to catch the bus, especially if the briefcase was still there.

I smiled a nervous smile and said, "That price sounds all right." I figured I could pay him 40 pesos with tip, if we catch up with the bus. "I could then take a bus back for two pesos," I thought to myself.

I could never have manifested a better driver. Roberto's calm countenance was reassuring. He placidly pointed out historical landmarks and places of interest as we crawled along at a dawdling pace.

"I have a 23-year-old son who is learning English. Can you write to him?"

I thought of the long list of letters I now owed and tried to change the subject. It was a fascinating drive. We passed through many charming small villages on the way, all of which the driver carefully described to me.

We finally got to Zipaquirá. It suddenly dawned on me with horror that I had not taken down the name of the company that was running the bus. We stopped at the main plaza where there were three bus companies. None of them claimed to have a bus passing through at that time. I described the bus and fortunately there was only one bus that displayed the names of the destination towns over the window. It was located in another part of town. The chief, who was attending us, kindly walked with us to its station.

"It came and left fifteen minutes ago," said the manager. "I suggest you go to the Radio Tower." It was one of the few halfway modern buildings, located on a hill leading out of town. Clean on the outside, it was rather unkempt inside. We checked for an office on the first floor, then on the second floor. Finally, we stopped outside an office on the third floor.

"There is a radiotelephone here that we can use to get the briefcase off at the next place," explained Gustavo, the chief of the station. "Is the case worth much?"

I looked intrepidly around the room, saw several other employees, and whispered to him, "About $800," careful no one else could hear. Gustavo looked up and began calculating what that would be in pesos. His eyes opened wide and he quickly ran to the radio operator. I explained the problem as he made the call. When he finished he turned to me and said, "The office at Ibagué told me the bus has not yet arrived so they will look for a briefcase when it arrives and put it on another bus coming in this direction." It should be here by 4:00 p.m. why don't you come back at 1:00 and they can tell me then if the bag was still on the bus when it arrived.

More suspense. My heart gripped tight as I worked to keep a positive thought on its return. Roberto consistently calmed me, repeating, "Everything is going to be all right. They are going to find your briefcase and return it. Then we can go into the salt mine, see the Cathedral at its base and return to Bogotá. I soon found myself joining his air of tranquility as we walked through town.

I went outside and cornered the man from the bus station.

"Thank you very much for your help. Here's 10 pesos for your trouble," I told him.

"I'm not through with you yet. I want to take you over to make some phone calls just to double check."

I turned to the taxi driver and said, "You can go so I will settle with you now."

"No, Señor. I'm going to take you to the Salt Mines and then back to Bogotá."

"But I can't afford any more than the fare to Zipaquirá." I pleaded.

"I'll drive us over to make the calls and then I'll go," was Roberto's answer.

We went to a small one-story building with a telephone operator behind the desk. This, I discovered, is where the town makes its phone calls. We gave the clerk the name of the place in Bogotá and went in to a booth to wait while she made the call.

That was good advice because the bus company informed me we had the right company but the number was different from that given me by the attendant in Bogotá. We called the bus station in Ibagué and they told me, "If the briefcase is still on the bus we'll transfer it to a bus coming your way, which should get to Zipaquirá around 2:30."

I turned to Roberto and gave him 50 pesos. "Keep the change," I said, hoping that would be enough.

"No, I can't keep this," he protested, handing me back my money. I insisted, but he consistently and firmly refused.

Finally, he said, "I'll take the money on one condition—that you let me stay all afternoon, take you through the salt mines as soon as your camera gets here and then I'll take you back to Bogotá at 5:00."

How could I argue with such a magnanimous offer?

We went to a salt processing plant. Roberto acted as a tour guide, pointing out the architecture of the city with all its balconies, then into a beautiful and well-maintained church.

We then went to a café and ordered a couple of ham sandwiches and a cup of coffee. Roberto continued, "The entire town exists on these salt mines. It is an ancient town. Most of the buildings date from colonial times. It is one of the oldest salt mines in the world. The Indians were working it before the Spanish arrived. No one knows how long they had been working it before then." Deep in its bowels is a Cathedral, which is carved into the mine.

Salt processing at Zipaquirá, Colombia

For a time I escaped from the nervous tension of my missing articles and melded into the calm awakenings of another long-lost world of days gone by. I commented to Roberto, "Everything must be precarious for these people, depending on one salt mine for their entire existence. The salt mines must be close to exhausted by now."

He pointed to a rather high hill and said, "That whole mountain is one big keg of salt."

It was at the restaurant we learned there was a cattle show in town. We got in the car and drove down.

The cattle were impressive compared to those I had seen clinging to the mountainsides on the trip over from Cúcuta. The blend of faces of the owners changed from the usual mixture of Spanish, Indian, and black to Spanish, English, and other European bloods. The main gentleman in the show was about 28 years old and had blond hair. Killing time at the show, it was now time to return to the radio-telephone building.

During the whole incident I clung to the idea that I am protected from any dishonesty. I knew there could be no person with a desire for something that was rightfully mine. I never lost sight of this all through the anxiety and the hours that followed. I knew I had to cling to this idea very strongly because I would be facing this all through my journey—traveling through a part of Colombia as wild as our wooly West and taking canoes down rivers into the rainforest with people I knew little about.

When we reached the Radiotelephone building everyone was still on lunch break. Gustav told us the bag was found on the bus and was being delivered under seal to Zipaquirá reaching here by 2:00 or 2:30 p.m. Roberto suggested we go over to the building and wait, as it was only 1:30. No sooner was this said when I spotted two men coming toward us. One of them was carrying my bag. The one carrying the bag walked expressionless by us, never looking right, or left. The bag was handcuffed to his hand. The other one looked over, smiled, and said, "Is this your bag?"

"It sure is," I shouted as I ran to greet the man carrying it. He pulled back and walked straight through us. He was a man with a mission. We followed him into the Radiotelephone building and up to the third floor. The courier, still handcuffed to the bag, was deadpan, still guarding the bag. We waited for Gustav to return from lunch.

The second courier asked me about my visit to Colombia. "What is your impression of Colombia?" he asked.

"Extremely favorable so far," I said, without even having to ponder my words. "There are dangers here but no more than in crossing a street in New York. The people have been wonderful to me and I have noticed a close affinity between the Colombian people and Americans."

I looked over and saw there were some women in the room so I remarked on the beauty of the Colombian women. They smiled, exceedingly pleased.

While we were sitting there I began to worry about what rewards there would be with so many people involved. This kept gnawing at me as I realized I could be spending all my money, satisfying everyone involved. I wanted to be fair with everyone, yet I could see my remaining finances being depleted. I also was afraid of giving out several rewards and then having others feel hurt or slighted.

I turned and whispered to Roberto, "Who do you think should receive a reward?"

"I feel you definitely should give something to the chief at the bus station, but I don't know about the others," he whispered back. "As the chief at the radiotelephone shop spoke to you in English one time why don't you ask him in English so the others won't understand what you're saying."

The chief came back and greeted all of us. The friendly man accompanying the courier smiled at me and asked, "Is that your bag?"

We said, "Yes!"

Suddenly, the pan-faced courier stood up, walked over to me, handed me the briefcase and smiled. "Congratulations." I thanked them profusely and pulled the station chief off to the side asking him in English, "Who do you think should get tips?"

The chief looked at me, a little surprised, and answered me in English. "This is a service of our organization and therefore there is no need for tips."

Then everyone came up, shook my hand, and wished me well (including the man who carried the case). "I work for a bank and do part-time security work for the organization," he said. "The formal name for the organization is 'Secretaria de Circulación y Tránsito'. There are literally hundreds of individually owned buses that make the short runs. We tie them all together in case something like this comes up. It offers

Right nave, Cathedral in the salt mines, Zipiaquirá, Colombia

passengers of any bus the same service it gave you."

It was a wonderful thing to find at this time. The offices for SIC, the security police, are located in the same building. One of the men involved was located there, so I went by to say goodbye. "How much is that camera equipment worth?" he asked.

"Let me tell it to you like this," I said. "If a robber came up and asked for the briefcase or my life I would give him my life. Without this camera it would be frustrating trying to travel around South America with fifty or more dollars worth of film and no camera."

Roberto and I went straight to the salt mines from the office. I stopped off long enough to give the bus station attendant ten pesos. We stopped off at one of the processing plants. No one was working at the time but the chauffer asked him or her to pretend they were working so they did for the photo opt. The salt is liquefied, and then sent down to a middle of the mountain. It landed in a big vat, and then flowed over the top to the first filter bin, over its top to the second, etc. for four bins. After this it was sent through pipes to the various processing plants. It flowed into a trough where it was poured into buckets. These were boiled for several hours. Then the salt was scooped out in shovels into cloth bags to be shipped all over the country. This whole process was very primitive. That is what made it so interesting.

Inside Cathedral, Salt Mines, Zipaquirá, Colombia

We drove right into the salt mines. Two miles of winding down dark tunnels led us to a cathedral deep inside the middle of the mountain, with illuminated arrows pointing the way. I was surprised to find that salt is black in its original form. I was expecting to find a little white church in the middle of the mountain.

I was thunderstruck by what I saw. The church was carved right into a gigantic room in the middle of the mine. It was like entering heaven itself. The entire cathedral was made out of salt. Silence overwhelmed us when we arrived. As we turned toward the cathedral, monstrous iron gates greeted us. Two lighted gold figures stood on each side of the gate. The quietness and echo gave a reverent ambiance.

A stream of tourists pouring out of busses who joined us in the cathedral soon broke this quiet.

As we wandered in we were swallowed up by the bare immensity of the edifice. Off to the side was a large anteroom, equally as spectacular as the main hall. The walls had niches engraved into the walls with numerous carvings. The lighting effect was spectacular. Each floodlight shown on a different spot for a unique special effect. It amazed me how they were able to give such an impressive effect in just black and white. I climbed some gigantic steps and through a hall, terminating at the dais. I walked across the stage and entered a small, perfectly carved dome room. From here I entered a small niche, for an overall view of the building. I wet my finger and licked it, finding the walls very salty.

I noticed there were quite a few women who didn't have their heads covered. Even in México, which is the most anti-Catholic of any Latin American country, no woman would ever think of entering a church without her head covered. I figured that in Colombia the most Catholic of all the Latin American countries, this would be especially true.

I turned to Roberto and asked, "Why are the women not covering their heads in this church?"

"This," he said, "is more a monument than a church so the church laws don't have to be respected."

Steps to Cathedral, Salt mines, Zipaquirá, Colombia

We climbed for another two miles to drive out the other side of the mountain. In front of us was a sign, which said "Señora." The chauffer asked the attendant, "Is this bathroom for everyone?"

The attendant said, "There's another one on the other side." But the driver did not wait for his answer and barged right in, while I went around the corner to the other bathroom. When I finished I waited for the driver at the café entrance. He said, "Don't you care to use the rest room?"

"I used the one for the men." When it dawned on him what he had done he blushed and darted into the café.

It was after five when we finally started back. The driver kept telling me about his son and how he wanted so much for me to write him. I gave him my card and asked him to write me and I would try to answer his letter. As we drove more slowly on the way back he was able to explain the scenery more fully. We passed numerous interesting houses along the way. They weren't in good shape so I asked if they were large haciendas.

"They are middle-class farmer's small plots of land. The land is rich so they can intensively grow enough on small plots to afford new homes," he explained.

On our way home we passed over a narrow bridge that dated back to Colombian times. On the other side was a castle. "The pieces for this castle were imported from Europe," he noted.

As we entered Bogotá, again I thought it would probably be best if I went by the train station, checked on the train, and bought my ticket. Instead he took me to the section of town where I was staying. We got within two blocks of the place and found he couldn't go all the way. I was about to get out when he said, "I can take you around to the door." Not waiting for an answer he twisted around the streets, came about a block from the hotel and found he still couldn't get to it. I began to feel guilty. I was only paying him fifty pesos for going to and from Zipaquirá, through the salt mines, plus all the other things and all the coffees he insisted on paying for, so I asked him, "Is fifty pesos enough for all you've done?"

He smiled and said, "Well, if you want to give me a little tip?" I asked him, "Is ten pesos enough?"

"Yes, that would be fine.

I got back to the hotel, grateful for getting the camera and equipment back and for all everyone did for me, but very dizzy from the heavy spending.

This convinced me I was what I had always known, an American ambassador. To almost everyone I was as important to him or her as the ambassador they would never meet. I came into a country in which almost everyone complained about thievery, unfriendliness, and bribes and had found camaraderie, hospitality, and honesty. I was master of my world—a microcosm of love in a macrocosm of hate and anger. It was difficult dealing with the inefficiencies of government. However, the openness, helpfulness, and companionship I found around me more than made up for the few frustrations I encountered. What impressed me most was the knowledge of international politics everyone possessed, especially the taxi drivers. Most were as aware of what was happening in the United States as I was.

I asked the hotel manager if he would cash an American Express check for me. He refused. I hadn't expected the banks to be closed for five days so was totally unprepared. I found the American listening to his newscast as he did at 6:00 every night, usually the stock reports, which he marked into a graph he had.

He suggested I go to the Hotel Tequendama and they would almost surely cash checks there.

I went to the Hotel Tequendama. This time I put a suit on in order to blend in. The previous time I had had my fur-lined jacket on and old pants, a little incongruous in this elegant hotel. I asked if I could cash a check. They evidently thought I had a room there because they were only too glad to cash $30.00. (The trip ended up costing me more than $50.00). After I had signed them he asked me for something. He saw I looked puzzled so said in English, "Room number?" I told him I didn't have a room there. He couldn't do anything now as I had already counter-signed the checks so he went ahead and gave me the money.

I met the son of the proprietor of the hotel where I was staying. We started talking about Colombia and the United States. As with all my serious discussions this turned out to be a very interesting one. Almost all my conversations with the Colombians usually started with them telling me they like the people in the U.S. but hate the government, especially Dulles.

We got on the subject of religion when he saw my Bible on the table by the bed. "Are you allowed to work for a man of a different religion in the U.S.?" he asked.

"There's no restriction on who the person works for in the U.S."

"That's wonderful. In Colombia Catholics are not allowed to work for Protestants."

This, of course, was probably disobeyed very much as there were many workers in the banks of the U.S. and Canada and various German and American Companies.

"Religion usually never entered into any dealings except in the Presidency," I told him. At that time there was a great prejudice in the U.S. against a Catholic becoming president. "Many Americans feel a Catholic President's prejudices would lie heavily toward the Vatican, toward giving money to Catholic schools and to many other things, which were against the 75% of the nation, which was non-Catholic."

"Yes, this is a danger," he said. "A Catholic should not be your President."

In only four years from that date Americans were proven wrong on all these judgments with the election of John F. Kennedy.

Governor Faubus had caused the subject of race to pop up in nearly every conversation. I usually found I was best comparing this to the Indian situation of their own country. The reaction to this was, "It's terrible. The Indians don't want to improve themselves. They just want to sell things, beg and rob."

I asked him, "What do you think of the United Action in Colombia?" (Conservatives and Liberals coming together to run the government in concert.)

"I don't think it will solve the deep problem of the Conservatives and the Liberals. My attitude is more one of 'wait and see'. It must be wonderful in the U.S. without the political strife, which tears Colombia apart."

"I'm actually a Liberal and my father a Conservative," I said.

"I'm very impressed something like this can exist without one of you having shot the other," was his swift answer.

The dour Chinese proprietor loosened up and talked for the first time. He had usually stayed almost the entire day pokerfaced with his ruana (a hooded jacket popularly worn by the Indians) on. When people asked him something he would answer in as few words as possible. His Colombian wife made up for it with her liveliness as she ran both hotel and bar.

"This has been a very good hotel and the rates very good," I said.

"At least everything here is safe," he proudly added. "I've been in Colombia 47 years. I moved from Cúcuta just a month ago."

"How do you like Bogotá?" I asked.

"There are a lot of thieves."

"Then how do you like Colombia?" I continued.

He just shrugged his shoulders and said, "My wife is Colombian, and I can't leave."

"I met your son in Cúcuta and someone told me he had to go to Cúcuta because the books were there."

"My son just uses that as an excuse to go back to Cúcuta for a while," he said with a wry smile on his face.

I had to get up at 5:00 in the morning to catch the Auto Ferro at 6:15. I grabbed my duffle bag and briefcase and started toward the station.

4. THE ROAD ENDS HERE

The next morning I ran inside the bus station and was dismayed to see four very long lines. None of the windows said "Neiva," my next destination. I picked one I thought was correct. After a lengthy wait I thought I'd better ask if it was. They directed me to the second line. After a lengthy wait I finally got to the window. The clerk told me I could ride "a piés." Thinking I did not understand her correctly I told her I'd rather have a seat. Overhearing that, everyone laughed.

I ran out and boarded the train, searching for a number that coincided with the number on my ticket. Someone was sitting there who claimed he had the same number on his ticket. When I looked closer at my ticket, I saw it was stamped "standing." So that was what the clerk at the bus station was trying to tell me when she asked me if I wanted to go "a piés" (on foot).

My chaotic experiences, especially from Cúcuta through Bogotá, going from place-to-place for documentation, led by false information and lack of knowledge, even at the local level, gave me an appreciation of travel agents and guided group travel. I would not trade the interaction I had with many wonderful people, but would certainly have shortened much wasted time following a person who had walked the path before me.

I've never been excited about train rides, preferring to travel by bus or car. This is probably one of the more beautiful parts of Colombia, but trains follow the easiest, most level path. The highway looked much more spectacular but I wanted to arrive in one piece. There was great variety through mountains, dropping into arid country and then fields. Some of the country was as arid as the Bad Lands of South Dakota in contrast to the trip from Cúcuta to Bogotá, which was like a roller coaster—up a mountain, down again; from cool mountaintops to arid desolate country.

My head was reeling from the numerous accents, which varied significantly from town to town throughout Colombia. Each town seemed to mirror the accent their original colonists brought from their hometowns in Spain. Several months before I was stymied by the accent of so many Cubans I met, who clip almost all of the consonants; then into Eastern Colombia where the accent and colloquialisms were almost another language. As I became accustomed to one accent I usually encountered another quite different accent and colloquial vocabulary of the next town with its own accent and had to become accustomed to it. Bogotá was the easiest because the Spanish was more formal, easier to understand and I could be understood as well.

We arrived at Neiva at about 2:30 in the afternoon. It lies in a rather flat desolate valley. It was a complete surprise to look down the hill from the railroad tracks and see just a few shacks. I asked myself, "Is this the Neiva everyone was telling me was a good place to find good hotels at cheap rates?"

"Take me to a good but reasonably priced hotel," I told my driver. When he did not respond I presumed he heard me correctly.

As we drove into town the town began to improve in appearance. The taxi stopped in front of a door with a bronze plate on it which said, 'Gran Hotel." This looked beyond my budget but I decided to take it, because I was a weary traveler. The driver honked and honked, trying to attract a porter.

"I can carry my own bags," I said, impatient to get to a room. He finally gave up and got my bags out of the trunk for me.

I dragged my bags in and asked the two who greeted me at the front door with icy stares, "Do you have a room available?"

They looked at me rather strange and said, "Yes, but it doesn't have a bath."

I insisted, "Surely you have a bath somewhere I can use, don't you?"

They answered, "Oh, yes."

The bellhop took me to my room and left my bags. As he started to go, I thought I would try out my new words for bathroom.

I said, "Donde está el baño?" He took me across one of the patios and opened up a door. I looked in and saw only a shower, nothing else. I thought for a moment, then asked

"Where is everything else?

"What else?" was his answer.

"El lava manos (the sink)," I said.

"Oh, it's right over there." He opened another door in the hallway and there was a washbasin—nothing else. He again started to walk off.

I got my dictionary out and repeated all the words I could find, but got no response. He took me to where the hotel clerk and several women were and we all put our heads together. I used the

Portuguese word "toileta" with no response. I opened the dictionary and said, "You probably won't understand this as the guy who wrote this dictionary apparently never had to go to the bathroom."

"We've never heard of any of these words," she said, shrugging her shoulders with a look of resignation. I then asked them where the "poseta" was. They said there was a poseta over there that I could wash my hands in. I then said, "There are three things in a bathroom. You have shown me where the shower is and where the sink is. Now, where is the other thing?" They all laughed in unison. One of them said to the bellboy, "Show the man where the "servicio sanitario" is.

The manager came up to me and said they had a room with bath available. It wasn't half as nice as the room I was moving out of. It had no windows, dingy walls, was only half as large, etc. The one compensation was there was a fan in every room so I could keep cool.

A short bald man with thick glasses stood on the balcony and had not taken his eyes off me since I entered the patio. This gave me an uneasy feeling. I was still not free from some fear of the warnings about bandits in this region. My experience with transportation in this country urged me to get my ticket right away and arrange my transportation forward. I asked the hotel for directions to the bus station. I checked again with the bellboy. He had me going up and down every street in town. The man with thick glasses, who had just left the hotel behind me, then approached me and gave me some better instructions.

When I thanked him he said, "I was thinking of taking a walk anyway so I can take you to the station." I was in a quandary. I did not know this man and did not know if I could trust him, and now I was walking out of the hotel with him on a cloudy rainy day. I decided to go with trust, keeping a wary eye out for any wrong moves.

As we started down the street he introduced himself to me, "My name is Sammy Behár, I immigrated from Greece five or six years ago and own a merchandising company in Northern Colombia." We hadn't walked a block when a friend of his greeted him, looked over at me, and asked, "Como estás?" I became worried as he used the familiar form to greet me. I found this unusual when first greeting someone for the first time.

"Is this a set up?" I thought. I kept an eye out to make sure we were surrounded by a large number of people and there was a get-away, in case I needed to escape. Sami told him, "I'm going to the bus station with this gentleman. Do you want to go along?" We had only gone another half block when another man came up, greeted the other two, looked over at me, and asked, "Como estás?" That was the same familiar greeting as the first man. Now three strangers who knew each other and used the familiar form of address surrounded me. This certainly looked like a set up. My innocence had gotten me in other situations like this numerous times before, not all with good results. I still felt somewhat safe as we were on a busy street with many pedestrians.

The four of us continued walking a few blocks. Sami and his friends continued their conversation but I couldn't hear what they were saying. Finally Sammy said, "Let's get a taxi." He turned to me and asked, "Do you swim?"

That caught me completely off guard. Intrepidly I answered, "Yes, I do. Why?"

"We're going for a swim if you want to go along with us," he continued as we entered the taxi. All I could think of when we were inside was, "I've got to be crazy. I don't know these people. They could be carrying me off and out of the city." My good sense was asking me what I was doing, but my curiosity was urging me to continue and have a good time.

They drove me to the bus station to show me where it was. The guy at the travel bureau had told me the wrong bus, as the one he told me about, Flota Magdalena, only went to Florencia. We then went back to the hotel to get our swimsuits. I told them I hoped they weren't in any hurry as I had a duffle bag and the swimming suit was at the very bottom of it. We then got back in the taxi.

The one who was taking us to the swimming pool was a resident of Neiva. Sami and his friend were vacationing and lived in Bogotá. The one from Neiva owned a small store, which in Neiva put him in the middle class.

We stopped by the store and house of the Neivan. I was still arguing with myself about the wisdom of being in a taxi with several strangers in a dangerous town. I sighed with relief when I saw the Neivan come back out with three women. "Now, it's got to be all right," I thought. As we rode out of town I felt even more relieved by the sense of humor of the two businessmen. We were in stitches all the way out to what they referred to as the Country Club, which turned out to be a mile or so out of town.

I wondered what kind of Country Club this small town in the interior would have. Even though it did not meet the standards of other country clubs I had seen it was unusual to see such amenities in the small town of Neiva. The pool was a large dammed up stream.

The dressing room was rather primitive but I was happy to even see one. Sami asked me if this dressing room was better than those in the U.S. I told him some swimming holes don't have dressing rooms and this, therefore, was better than those. The son of the proprietor was appointed to watch the valuables. I was handing over my wallet for safekeeping when Sami looked at me and pointing a finger at me, barked, "Hand over your jewels,"

We roared and added, "You can't even trust your friends here."

The water was cool and refreshing after the hot day. I had been swimming only a short time when someone approached me and said, "There's a boy who is studying English who wants to talk to you."

I went over to the bank of the pond and the boy came over and said very slowly, "How . . .are . . .you?"

"I'm fine. How are you doing?" I answered.

He gave me a blank stare, saying nothing.

In Spanish I asked him, "How long have you been studying English?"

"I've been studying with an Evangelist woman from the States who was teaching in our school. I've been studying the language for two years but I never get a chance to use it so it's dead to me." Remembering my first two years of Spanish I could empathize with him.

Soon they dragged another man down to the pool to introduce him to me. "He's been in the States for several years and speaks very good English." However, we never could get him past a few greetings. I soon felt myself among very good friends. I was glad I had yielded to trust and gone with the flow.

The son of the Neiva man was still waiting outside the dressing room when we got there with all the valuables wrapped in a handkerchief. "What did you buy with my money?" I said as he handed me the packet. He looked shocked, and then caught on and we all had a laugh.

The day was their state's (Huila) patron saint's birthday, San Pedro. This saint is supposed to have the touch of death. So there was great celebration with masquerade at the Country Club. Sami and I donned two of the festival hats and the whole group of us had our picture taken with a Polaroid camera. We danced into the late afternoon.

We piled back into the taxi and headed back to town. Sami and his friend took me to a bar. Despite my protests they would not let me pay for anything. I worried about getting back to the hotel for dinner. A musician played tunes at the request of Sammy and friend. Finally, after an hour we started out for what I thought was going to be back to the hotel for dinner.

L-R: Emelia, Rebeca, Hinkley, Sami, Esteban. Nieto at Neiva Country Club

Instead, we turned into the next building. It was the Neiva family's house. We stepped into the salón and sat down. The guitarist followed us in and sat down. He had a wonderful, almost operatic voice and was equally as proficient on the guitar. He had an enormous repertory, as he never stopped playing until 11:00 that night.

I began to really get worried about getting back to the hotel. The wife came in and showed us into the back room. There lay a very small dinner. The whole outlay was very simple. The salón was a small room that opened directly onto the street. It was the only room that was complete with walls. Little pictures were evenly hung all around the room at the same height. The room was furnished with simple wooden furniture. The two big French doors opened into a makeshift bedroom. There were three wrought iron double beds squeezed into this room. A path between them led behind a crudely made screen. A table was against the wall for eating. A door led off this to the only toilet. The walls were open at the top and unfinished. Our meal consisted of parts of pork and rice. Sammy apparently remembered my mentioning to him earlier how I dislike pork so he reached over right away and handed me a lemon. That little lemon made it quite palatable.

It was all very simple but the hospitality gave us the feeling of being among royalty. The salón could not have made me happier had it been in a mansion, the pictures would have been no homier had they been painted by Rembrandt and the dinner could not have been better had it been fillet mignon.

The guitarist continued to sing throughout the meal. Afterwards we went in and sat down and talked. As with almost everyone I met they expressed their dislike for Dulles. Their expressions were lukewarm toward Nixon. It always surprised me to find the ambivalence in their love for Ike.

"Do you like Neiva better than New York?" asked Sammy, with his usual wry humor.

"You'll never see this kind of hospitality in New York," I said as a compliment.

"Then we should call this Neiva York." Chimed Sami, roaring with laughter.

We danced while the guitarist played. This was like a dream of paradise in what had been reported to be the most dangerous part of Colombia.

We decided it would be a good idea to supplement the small meal with a little snack when we got back to the hotel so we went back out to bar after bar, asking if they had any food. They were all willing to sell us drinks if we wanted them but none had food. Our final resting spot was a dirty greasy place that said they had food. I ordered tamale because that was something I always liked and hard to ruin. The waitress came out with an entire dinner. The tamale was there and, yes, it was destroyed. "Why did I order this in the first place, I'm not a bit hungry," said the still small voice in my head.

"I think the family had planned on eating the dinner they served us tonight," said Sammy, somewhat concerned. "Did you notice how they served, stood behind us, and didn't eat?"

We felt sad but there was nothing we could do about it after the fact. "What goodness exists in these people. This is the epitome of kindness," I thought to myself.

Back at the hotel I looked at my watch. It was twelve midnight. This meant if I went right to bed I would have less then five hours sleep if I wanted to catch the bus in the morning. The room was hot and muggy. I took a shower and found that gave me some respite from the heat. I pushed the fan in the direction of the bed and turned it on. The blade had apparently been welded on and the weld was bad. The blade flew across the room. Left with no options I finally adapted myself to the heat and went to sleep.

It was a horrible feeling when the knock came on the door for me at 5:00 the next morning. I stumbled out of bed and into the streets walking three blocks before I found a taxi. He took me six blocks, then charged the same high rate as the driver that took me the few blocks from the railroad station to town the day before. I guess the city was so small taxis had a standard rate anywhere in the city.

An old man came hobbling to the car and picked up my bag. I thought I may as well contribute to his daily bread so let him carry it. He lugged and huffed and puffed and finally got the bag inside the station. I told him I was taking the bus to San Agustín so he started processing the bag. There was a mob pushing and shoving their way to the counter. I felt I had better hurry and get my ticket if I was to catch my bus. I tried to get the attention of the porter so he could get my ticket but couldn't get a rise out of him. By the time I got the attention of the clerk all the seats were sold out. I was told I would have to take what I believe was called "La Feirra". I asked him what that was and he pointed to a bus with no driver that was really a wreck. There was an opening on both sides and a bench running from side-to-side, which each person entered and moved toward the center, with absolutely no room for legs. Its only springs were some worn out buggy springs, visible underneath.

I spent five minutes getting the attention of the porter who had my bags. I could not get him to realize I was not taking this bus. When he finally understood me he again struggled with the bag and dragged it out to the bus. Then he couldn't get it over the rail. I reached down, grabbed it, and threw it over the rail. I gave him a peso and he looked despondently at it.

"Is that enough?" I asked

"Yes," he said, and started to walk off. I gleefully found one empty seat next to an opening. I climbed in and started over to it. Suddenly someone jumped over the side, ran across the seat, sat down there and then had the audacity to look at me, still climbing to the seat, and smile. I resigned myself to another spot.

"I am going to have to get more aggressive," I thought. I could not seem to get past my early training to always be courteous, wait my turn and to be fair in all things. Did I really want to trade that all in for the scramble for tickets, seats, lines so I could be an equal combatant in cues?"

After a few minutes I thought I had better double check to see if this was the right bus.

"Does this bus go to San Agustín?" I asked one of the other passengers.

"No, you have to take the "Ferría" to that town," was the answer. I grabbed my bag and went back to the station.

I asked one of the attendants, "Is this the Ferría to San Agustín?"

Before I could say anything more he had my bag and me on the bus. I found everyone had reserved seats as I had expected. One man in uniform motioned to me and said, "Sit down in front of me."

I sat down where he told me.

Just then the attendant boarded the bus and roared, "Anyone here who does not have a reserved seat get off the bus."

I started to move when the military man grabbed my shoulder and said, "Stay in the seat."

At this point I was getting extremely nervous because they were starting to check all the tickets.

I turned and said, "I think the gig is up so I guess I'd better leave."

"Keep your seat," he whispered as he winked at me.

The attendant came closer as he checked each ticket. Finally he came by and I handed him mine. I held my calm expression as a cauldron built up inside my gut. He looked at the price and handed it back. He had not turned it over to see the seat number written in black crayon on the other side. Mine, of course, was blank. That was the first hurdle. I sat nervously hoping they wouldn't sell my seat number. Apparently they marked it as taken when they saw me sitting there. They were turning people away in droves for not having reserved seating. That military man was an angel in uniform. He made my day.

Apparently the reserved seats rule was meant for the originating station because they were stuffing them on as packed as they could at the next town—chicks, pigs, dogs, etc. I was surprised at the length of the paved road. I had no idea any of the roads were paved down there and the recent map I picked up from the Esso station showed them as all weather roads.

We drove into some tropics but mostly traveled through the mountains where it was pleasantly cool. We finally found ourselves on deeply rutted dirt roads. The bus was restricted to a crawl for most of the way. I quizzed several people about San Agustín.

"There is a hotel there that is not frequented by the tourists. It's probably comparable to the hotel in Bogotá where you stayed." We got to Pitalito and I gave a longing glance at the fine new two-story tourist hotel. However, after riding for hours on the rutted road, I was not anxious to add another three hours to the trip just to sleep in a good hotel, so took a chance continuing on this bus to San Agustín.

We arrived at San Agustín at 2:00 p.m. The passengers pointed to a dumpy looking hovel and said, "That's the hotel."

I grabbed my bags and went inside, intrepidly observing its rough exterior. To my surprise the dark entryway led into a large patio with a charming garden, open in back, revealing the mountains in the background. All the rooms were upstairs opening onto a balcony, which surrounded the courtyard. It was not what I would say was hygienic with dogs, chickens, and other animals and fowl running around the courtyard surrounded by time-worn wooden walls. I finally found the proprietor. She didn't seem very anxious to have me as a customer. I followed her upstairs. She opened a door and left without so much as a word. One of the walls was open at the top. A bare bulb hung from the ceiling but there was no electricity. Two army cots, with thin mattresses on them, adorned the room. Boards had replaced the springs and this time there was no covering for the mattresses and no towel.

Whitewashed bldg., San Agustín, Colombia

I asked her where the shower was and the manager showed me a dirty old room with a pipe hanging from the ceiling. There were also two filthy outhouses. I decided not to shower while at that hotel, but to wait until I got to Florencia where I felt the facilities would be better. Although this sounds appalling, the hotel had a rustically pleasing flavor to it.

A tente untying my shoestrings. It is a very playful flightless bird. Natives use it to guard chickens.

As I sat in the patio I noticed a black-feathered flightless bird (a tente, *psophia crepitans*). It was playing with the dog. It chased the dog. Then the dog turned and chased it. This went on for about fifteen minutes until the dog became tired and the bird came over where I was sitting. It reached down and untied my shoestrings, then went back to playing with the dog. Locals use the tente to guard chickens.

I felt I would go up to the park and see how much there was to see.

Lion Sculpture, San Agustín, Colombia

"Do you know how to get directions to the park?" I asked the proprietor. Her directions were confusing so I asked two men who were talking in the street.

"It's 2.5 miles to the park. You should take a car."

I laughed and told him, "I haven't seen a car since I've been here.

"Call the park and they'll come and get you."

"I think I'll walk. It's cheaper that way," I answered.

He continued walking about four blocks with me.

"If you'd like I can walk you to the park," he offered.

"No, you probably have other work to do and I can walk it easily, but thank you," I answered.

He waved at me and said, "Glad to help," as he walked on down the street.

Monument, guide is standing beside it to show their size, San Agustín, Colombia

I was still feeling somewhat uneasy about robbers, although I knew my best protection was conquering my own fear and seeing all beings as my brothers and sisters. I got about a quarter of the way up the mountain and noticed a man who looked like a vagrant stepping into one of the houses. A couple of minutes later I heard his hurried footsteps coming up the hill behind me. I hurried my walk but he was slowly gaining on me. I ducked around a corner and noticed I would be out of sight of any house at just the time he caught up with me. As I turned the corner he caught up. I looked around and he greeted me. "Are you going to the park?" he asked.

"Yes, I am," I replied.

He pointed up ahead and said, "It's just ahead a little ways." He walked with me to the front road, then bid adieu and went off on another road.

A small shack stood by the road, marking the only entrance to the park. A woman appeared at the door and I asked where the museum was. There were two rooms, one for contemporary Native works, and the other for historical findings. I joined three men and three women to follow the path to the monoliths. The guide left us to find our way from there. Huge ancient carved stone monoliths lay helter-skelter along the path. Soon I realized the people accompanying me were drunk. Seeing myself isolated in the wilderness with drunken strangers put me on my guard. It's fine to overcome fear, but discernment was paramount.

"How much is your camera worth?" asked one of the men, taking another swig from the bottle they passed around. That really raised red flags with me.

"I don't know," I said, trying to evade the question.

"Do you carry your money in dollars or pesos?" asked another.

This configuration is called 'Birth'. San Agustín, Colombia

At this point my only thought was how to ditch this group. I did not like the sounds of either their inebriated state or their questions. I was in bandit country and I did not wish to be caught off guard, especially alone in the country.

One of the women offered me some mulberries. This allayed my suspicions a little.

"Can I carry your briefcase?" asked one of the men. I handed him the briefcase but made sure I walked right next to him. I figured it was better to trust one with the briefcase under close surveillance than hold onto it myself. They could easily overpower me at any moment, even if I had the case in my hand.

Downstream was a fountain that had been built by the same Ancient Ones that made the stone carvings. It was amazing how well they were preserved. Some of the stone carvings were higher than a man. Some of them still had their original colors painted on them. There were only two colors used—black and red. No one had any explanation as to the pre-historic people who carved him or her, where he or she came from, or where he or she went. No dwellings have been uncovered. However, this is probably mainly due to the fact so few archeologists have taken an interest in them, and the discovery was so recent. I noticed a great likeness between these carvings and those of Easter Island. It was conjectured their creators could have been the same people.

The sky was nearly pitch-black with heavy cumulous clouds. The director of the museum mentioned I could get a guide for a mere 10-20 pesos, within my budget. I checked with her on the weather, as it had not let up since I had been there. She said it usually let up at least once during the day so I might be able to get some good pictures. She promised a guide would get in touch with me at the hotel.

I was still hoping to ditch the group I was with but soon caught up with them.

I asked one of the women, "Do guests at the hotel usually sleep on bare mattresses, or does the hotel expect guests to carry their own bedding?"

"You have to ask for a mattress," was her answer.

When I got back to the hotel at dusk, all the bulbs hanging from the ceiling were barely flickering. The meal was not bad. On the table was some filtered warm water the color of the Mississippi. I was elated when she served us tea. Everywhere in Colombia I had encountered only overly sweetened coffee, warm beer, or sickening soft drinks, so the tea tasted very good.

"Do they serve tea in other parts of Colombia?" I asked one of the guests.

Several guests chimed in, "This is the only place I've ever heard of it being served."

They stuck to their sugar-laden coffee. The proprietor showed me the package the tea came in. It was from Ceylon and was packed in England.

Monoliths, San Agustín, Colombia

All the men at the table were students. I found them brutally frank and even less disrespectful, even rude; quite the opposite of other students I had met. They were from all over the state, attending a college located in San Agustín. They were helpful in giving me information concerning the trip ahead into the rainforest, a sort of no man's land to most people, a "green hell" to others.

Soon my guide arrived. A quiet but friendly man, he agreed to meet me by 8:00 a.m. to take me to the narrows of the Magdalena River (only three meters wide at that point) and the monuments that were more difficult to reach.

The proprietor offered to make up a lunch for me to take along. It was the first time I had been on a horse in nine years. The guide brought me some leather riding habits. The horse was more mule than horse but the guide said that was so they could climb the mountains easier. He was right, too, as that was the best horse I had ever ridden—smooth riding and unusually responsive.

We rode into the hills and crossed a big pass. It was an extremely interesting ride. There were just horse tracks to follow but they were well traveled. We met more people on the trail than on the highway when I was riding the bus. Everybody was friendly and no one would think of passing us without offering his or her greeting of "Adiós."

We finally arrived at the top of a mountain, which towered over the stream below which was the source of the Magdalena River. I felt this was my compensation for never having seen Lake Itasca, the source of the Mississippi River which I never got to descend. It took about a half-hour to get down to the river, where we crossed a bridge. Three meters may seem like a small stream but the Magdalena eventually becomes as wide as the Mississippi River, and flows nearly the entire length of Colombia on its way to the Gulf of México. The clear weather the director of the museum promised would turn up in the afternoon never arrived. The weather remained almost as dark as night.

We climbed out of the narrows up to the pass again. I felt sorry for the horse, as it struggled up the long, steep hills. We finally encountered a farmhouse. On our return we passed through many small farms, each with large reliefs and stone monoliths scattered about, unattended.

We sat down and I pulled out my lunch. As I started to take a bite out of an egg I spotted the guide sitting next to me with no food and looking hungry. I offered him an egg and some bread. My heart jumped as I saw half the bread being fed to his horse, the guide looking on again with the same hungry look. Fortunately, my travels were accustoming me to get by on very little.

When we finally returned to the hotel at 5:00 p.m., I ran in to see if I could get some change to pay the guide. No one could change a 100-peso note so I came back out. My guide said he would return later in the evening and I could pay him then.

I sat down to dinner and all the college students came in again. Their accent was so thick I could understand very little of what they said. This, with their rudeness, made me feel uneasy.

"Your Spanish is really bad," one of them said. "Do you read Spanish?"

I said, "Of course I can."

I felt even more insulted when they brought in a paper and had me read to them. My Spanish had gone through a daily metamorphosis with each town speaking a different dialect. Fine-tuning my Spanish each time was usually a temporary struggle, and I was able to attain efficiency in the language in short time. Their accent was the most drastic and the most difficult for me to understand. It did not improve during the days in San Agustín and the students made me painfully aware of it.

"There is no bus to Florencia. You'll have to take a bus to Altamira and stay for the day and night, leaving the next morning for Florencia," advised the manager.

"How about the Cuevos de Los Gauchos?" I said. "I would like to see them. The director of the park told me I would have to take a bus to Garcón and wait there for another bus in a day or two for the end of the highway in the direction of the Cuevos. From there he told me it was only two hours by horseback."

They laughed and one of the students said, "There is no such bus. The only way to go there is to go to Pitalito and get a horse and guide from there. It is a six-day round trip by horseback."

The inclement weather supported my not going on that trip. I could get very little out of anyone as to what the Cuevos actually were and whether they would be worth the trip. All I could find out was they were some underground temples with some magnificent carvings in them. No one was sure whether their ancient creators belonged to the same group of people as the monuments. The whole find was very new. I had to get my visa extended anyway to make the trip to Leticia. I, therefore, would do better to make sure I could get my visa extended before I went off on any side trips.

The students took me next door to help me get my ticket. After that we all went next door for coffee (favorite Colombian pastime). The group of students kept getting larger and larger. They kept trying to get their English professors to come over and talk with me. The professors pretended to be too busy, but I can well imagine why they didn't come.

"Do you drink?" asked one.

Although I had no judgments on drinking and enjoyed an occasional glass of wine or cordial with a meal, I felt it was best to just tell everyone who asked that I did not drink when I really just didn't want to drink with a drunk. Looking back I can see this was a wise move on my part.

"No," I said.

This disgusted the group.

"Would you like a cigarette?" asked another student.

"No, thank you, I don't smoke" I said as politely as I could.

This brought on an even ruder rebuff.

"I never noticed a movie theatre in town. Do you have one?" I asked, trying to change the subject.

"Oh No," answered another. "The priest would never allow it."

I got up at 5:00 the next morning to catch the bus. I was getting a little tired of rising at 5:00 a.m. and was looking forward to Florencia when I would be through catching buses. To avert the Bogotá and Neiva ticket problems I was foresighted enough to get to the bus station the night before and reserve a seat. I received seat #1, the very first seat in the bus on the right-hand side next to the window. I ran to the bus to claim my seat and found an army officer sitting in it. He said, "Sit wherever you can find a seat." I, therefore, sat in the back where the bumps push you through the ceiling. So much for averting the bus crunch and crowded lines.

Everyone on the bus had bumped into one another or me at one time during my two-day stay in San Agustín.

"Did you get a guide and take a horse?" asked one.

"How did you like the hotel?" asked another.

"Did you enjoy the trip on horseback?" asked still another.

The man sitting next to me said, "You can catch a 'colectivo' out of Altamira during the day as several of them come through there on their way to Florencia. There's no need to stay overnight to catch the morning bus."

This was a great relief to me. We passed through some interesting little backwoods towns on our way to Altamira, arriving at noon.

"I would sure like to catch some other forward transportation to Florencia today," I asked the driver as I disembarked. "Could you take me to the bus office?" I asked the driver's friend.

I ran inside and asked them for a ticket on the next transportation. They told me there was nothing until the next day.

I turned to the driver's friend and said dolefully, "They say there's no bus until tomorrow."

Someone behind me overheard and said, "There are 'colectivos' coming by at various times during the day. All you have to do is wait at the crossroads and flag one down. Let's go to dinner at the hotel."

We were just starting toward the restaurant when he suddenly looked up said, "There's a 'colectivo' now."

Coming toward us was a truck. He ran to it and asked the driver if he could take me to Florencia. I ran back and grabbed my bags. It took some maneuvering to get them through the canvas opening. I now knew that a commercial truck is called a 'colectivo' in those parts.

The truck just drove into the next town when a passenger in front got out and offered me his seat in the cab. I felt a little guilty leaving all the others in the back but felt I had watched so many officials push in front of me it was about time I got a special privilege. I found the driver had a terrible accent. I had to really focus on his words so I could I could figure out what he was saying.

If I felt San Agustín was at the edge of civilization, I found Florencia to be even farther. I imagined it would be large and have a better road than the one to San Agustín, as it was the capital of this state. The dirt road climbed straight up into the mountains. We didn't stop climbing for more than 2-1/2 hours, and the scenery behind us became more and more spectacular. This deteriorating dirt road was hastily constructed in 1932 during a short war with Perú. On one of the bridges was carved 1934. It had evidently not been upgraded since. The truck hop-scotched around the gaping holes on the one-lane dirt road, hugging the mountains. In places our tires clung to the edges of the road, sometimes as little as seven feet wide, with 3,000 ft. drop-offs and no guardrail. At times the truck had to back up and maneuver around a curve so narrow and so sharp we had to disembark and help the driver maneuver back and forth to find a path, while the truck hugged the sides of the mountains. The road was gutted and parts of it were washed away.

It became colder and colder as we climbed to the top of the pass. When we reached the top it suddenly got rainier and we could feel the warm gusts sweeping up from the rainforest, which spread out like an endless green carpet in the distance below. Also, a mist was rising from the jungle. It was still very dark and cloudy where we were. My misapprehension of the mountains holding the cloudy weather was disappointedly not true. I was rather dejected when I found the other side of the mountains equally as cloudy.

Where I had expected to see a land full of rainforest I saw only expanses of treeless groundcover. The mountains looked rich and fertile, yet there was virtually no cultivation. We traveled miles before even seeing a grass hut.

"I hate this part of the country," said the driver. "I come from Bogotá and I like it there. I can't stand this heat, the roads are in horrible shape, and there are no people."

We stopped in front of a wooden bridge. Even the driver was wondering if he was going to make it across its ten-foot length. He looked at me and said, "That bridge represents the progress in Colombia. All the Colombians know how to do is drink coffee and manufacture boys." After considerable moving, we made it across the ten-foot long bridge.

This was very representative of the type of thinking I was about to run into. Whereas the Northern Colombians had been somewhat pessimistic about the political and economic shape of their country, the people in the South, especially those who originally came from the North, were downright critical of their country, its people and its government.

I was still a bit worried about the people. I didn't know whether I should trust anyone, so desolate was the country. I was a little worried about my bag in the back with the other passengers. I again remembered I must never lose sight of the fact man can be nothing but honest. Almost all fear was quelled through this thought. If I see only honesty that will be reflected in the people I meet. This was certainly true during my travel through the most dangerous territory in Colombia.

As we reached the last peak, I looked down on an endless sea of green, which furnishes 80% of the oxygen we breathe. Scientists estimate 30-35% of all oxygen on earth comes from the rainforests. Just 100 years ago, our air was 32% oxygen; today it's down to 19% because of deforestation and pollution. Approximately 50% of our plant's tropical rainforests have been destroyed in the last Century. At the current rate of deforestation, by the year 2020 80-90% of the Earth's tropical rainforests will have been destroyed. The Amazon is home to more than 200,000 species of plants. Only 2-3% of these plants have been studied for their therapeutic value. Yet, from that tiny percent come one-third of our pharmaceuticals. As I looked down upon the boundless green it barely dawned on me I was looking down on probably the largest pharmacy in the world.

The road came to an abrupt end at the river just a few feet ahead. All the information I had found on its passageways was from the few merchants I had met along the way. I found nothing in written material. This filled me with both the excitement of adventure and fear of the unknown of the mission I was about to embark on, plunging headlong into this impenetrable jungle, accessible only by boat, canoe, or machete. For the next few weeks civilization would be but a distant memory.

We finally got to Florencia at 3:00 p.m. I was quite disappointed at first. I had looked forward to a larger, much more cosmopolitan city. We had followed the Río Hacha all the way down from the top of the mountains. It was very interesting to watch the river all the way from its inception to Florencia, because this was the river where I planned to begin my jungle trek. I had thought I should get a picture of it at its narrows for interest sake, but was a little afraid to take my camera out of the briefcase because the price of the ride might change or people might get ideas. This had been the case all the way from Bogotá. As a result I had no pictures of the extremely interesting terrain in between Bogotá and Neiva, of Neiva itself or of the terrain in between Neiva and San Agustín. The constant stories of robbery and killing had made me camera shy.

We stopped at a rather desolate shack on the road for lunch. One of the "colectivos" was parked there, so this hut must have served the passing trucks. It looked dirty and unhygienic so I stuck to pastries and pop.

When we got to Florencia the driver parked in front of a hotel that didn't look too bad. He let me out and only charged me the equivalent of 65¢ for the five-hour ride. I was dying of hunger. It had been too early to eat when I left San Agustín that morning. I had left Altamira too quickly to catch lunch and had just had some pastry along the way at about one o'clock.

I went inside the hotel and was mildly impressed. It had a beautiful courtyard with a balcony circling it, which all the rooms faced. There was a beautifully flowered dining room, which faced the courtyard.

"Do you have a room?" I asked. My question was received with a blank stare. Their welcome was aloof.

"Is there a place for me?" I asked, hoping to induce an answer.

A boy grabbed my bags and led the way without uttering a word. I got the idea there was a place for me so I followed him to the room. The room was small with two beds. A door led into a larger room with three beds. That room had two big shutters that opened up for a grand view of the street below.

I looked in the next room and noticed two people were evidently occupying it. I was somewhat relieved when I noticed a camera sitting out on the bed stand and a fishing pole. I figured they must be vacationing from Bogotá and they had sufficient money that my things wouldn't tempt them. I looked around and noticed a basin on a stand. A pitcher of water was standing below it. This reminded me I needed a bath. I ran to the shower and found there was no water. I hadn't showered since Neiva so I felt frustrated.

I thought I had better get my visa extended so I could leave the next day. I had found the trip would take closer to 15 days and I only had five days left on my visa so I was desperate. I finally found the secret police office and went in and reported my problem.

Then began the game of musical authorities.

"I'll report to my sergeant," said the CQ.

"We'll have to report to another sergeant," said that sergeant. "Take him to Sergeant Gonzalez.

"This isn't my job," reported Sgt. Gonzalez. "You need to go to an officer in the army. Take the gentleman to the army post."

I plowed through the meal and ran to the army post.

"The officer is not in," said the guard at the post. "I can't let you in."

The policeman argued with him and got him to let us in to check, but we found the officer really was not in his office.

"There's another officer there that might be able to help," said the soldier. He's in the mess hall. Let me take you to him. We finally found him in the mess hall sneaking a snack. They went through all the formalities of reporting as though it were his office.

"What are you doing bringing him to me?" barked the officer. "The army can't do anything about his visa."

We returned to the police headquarters and reported to the sergeant. He told us to report to his captain. I suddenly thought, "This is no way to go about this. Nothing can disturb the harmony, which is rightfully mine." I held strongly, "If this trip is not right I would not have even gotten started on it so nothing can disturb it." This turned out to be another demonstration in holding a positive thought. I hadn't come all the way to Florencia to fly over the most interesting part of the jungle as everyone suggested I do. The minute I took a firm stand in positive thought the situation began to change and was very harmoniously worked out.

We went downstairs and finally found the captain. I was overjoyed when I saw it was an officer I had seen riding down the street on a motorcycle. At that time he had smiled at me and greeted me. I figured a man that was that courteous would do what he could for me. I explained my problem to him in detail. He took me up to his office, ordered some pop for us and wrote out permission for ten more days, then wished me luck.

My search for supplies ran into conflict with the normal process of doing business in Florencia. My American logic told me a store would offer lines of clothes, camera goods or even toiletry items. I was met with a new reality shopping in Florencia. I was favorably struck by the numerous storeowners as well as the friendliness of the people. One person would tell me one place. If I couldn't find it there they would direct me to another place, etc. As there were only four square blocks of shops this was frustrating.

I spotted several women washing clothes on the side of the Río Hacha, the river I thought the canoes were going to be starting their trip down. It seemed strange to me the river was no bigger than a small creek. I could not imagine canoes traveling that stream with passengers and baggage.

It was almost 6:00 p.m. so I thought I'd better hurry before the stores closed. I bought flash bulbs and casually asked, "Where can I buy a hammock?"

"I'll show you where they have them," said a man in the store.

"Good, which store has them?" I said.

"No, I'll take you there," he insisted.

He took me to a big shop, looked some over, and told me, "These are too small. Let's go to another place that specializes in bigger hammocks." He then began bartering the price down for me.

"What else do you need?" he asked me.

He proceeded to offer the same friendly service for the remainder of my shopping. I thanked him and he cheerfully said, "A sus órdenes (At your service)," and walked off. This was a good introduction to the impressive warmth toward fellow beings, which existed in Florencia. By this time I felt I could leave my camera out in the middle of the street and there would be a rush of people attempting to return it to me.

I tried to find out more information about the canoes but wasn't getting any substantial information. My business was slowed by the many invitations I had to sit for a cup of coffee with nearly everyone I met. Each time I would hear, "Vamos por un tinto," I would recoil. The "tinto" was a demitasse half-filled with sugar, almost as repugnant as the "agua de panela." I was not a coffee drinker, and the "tinto" was doing a great job of keeping me that way. My polite rejections were met with, "There isn't any good coffee in Colombia. We ship it all to the United States. If you want a good cup of Colombian coffee you have to go to America." I decided to stay another day so I could make sure I got good connections, but deep down my real reasons probably had more to do with wanting to get to know the town better, I liked it so.

Back at the hotel there was still no electricity. "When will there be electricity?" I asked the house cleaner.

"There hasn't been any electricity here for days," she said with a smile.

A Coleman lantern dangling from the wall was what lighted the dining room. A young woman at the next table greeted me.

I asked her, "Do you know anything about the canoes going down the river?"

She told me, "The canoes don't leave from the Río Hacha in the city. They leave from another river, the Caquetá. You have to take a makeshift bus to get to the river. See NAVEGAL, the government agency for all river transportation, tomorrow."

After about five minutes of conversation she got up, came over to my table and sat down. From then until we finished eating there was not one word spoken. After the meal she excused herself and left.

I went back to my room and started to write by candlelight. At about 9:00 p.m. my two roommates came in. I quietly greeted them as they walked through to their adjoining room. After a couple of minutes they came back in and asked, "Are you a newspaper writer?"

I told them "No, I'm a student. Are you on vacation?"

"No, we work for the government of Colombia. We're looking into the development of this area."

I chuckled and asked them, "Would you mind looking into the development of a little electricity around here?"

They laughed and I asked them, "What are your plans?"

They seemed a little lost for words so I quickly added, "The roads, water, electricity, trade, etc.?"

They looked at me shyly, and then one of the men added, I guess you could say that's what we are doing here. I remembered the camera and fishing pole and silently chuckled within as I remembered the statements concerning the progress of Colombia made by the truck driver who brought me to Florencia. With a look of disgust he pointed to one of the many washed out bridges, "That bridge represents the progress in Colombia. All the Colombians know how to do is drink coffee and manufacture boys."

"I'm Italian. I've only been in this country for six months," said one of my roommates.

I asked him, "How much Spanish did you speak when you came to this country? You speak it grammatically perfect."

"I didn't know a word when I came but the languages are so similar it wasn't hard to pick it up."

I continued writing until the candle was about on its last leg. One of the roommates came to the rescue with their candle as they were retiring but I had endured enough of the flickering light by then, so retired.

The next morning I took my time, as I knew the banks wouldn't be open until afternoon. I thought I'd better pick up a blanket, as it was a little cooler than I thought it would be and didn't want to sleep in my clothes. I thought I would also buy a ruana to wear. I asked to look at blankets. When the clerk showed me a raincoat I discovered the word the woman in San Agustín gave me for blanket was actually the word for raincoat, at least it was in Florencia. Nevertheless, I finally got the idea of blanket across. I told her where I was going and what I would need in weight for a blanket. She pulled a blanket down with black and yellow stripes.

When she saw my reaction to the bright colors, she said, "This will give you protection in the jungle, as all tigers will think you are just another tiger."

Seeing her smile, I told her, "I'm not interested in attracting tigers in the jungle. Don't you have something a little more conservative?"

Each blanket she pulled down was brighter than the other. This was so unlike Colombia, because all the ruanas and clothes of the Colombians I had seen were extremely conservative, usually gray, or black. However, they really seemed to go wild on blankets, hammocks (bright red, green, and yellow) and I couldn't see any conservative colors in them. I observed nuances in the Florencia stores. When I asked the sales clerk the price of the blanket she quoted me was nineteen pesos. I noticed 17 pesos marked on it and told her. She said, "Oh no, that's the price we bought it for." I found this to be true in all the shops. You could always tell how much the dealer was marking up the price on each item. I felt the blanket and it was as soft as soapsuds. I asked if it was wool and she told me it was cotton. They seemed to spin the cotton in a different way there, as it was extraordinarily soft, even softer than a sheet.

I wandered all over looking for the NAVEGAL office but couldn't find their sign. It was very hard to find anything in Florencia as shops were just holes in the wall. If I was looking for camera goods and passed a cosmetics shop, I could find the camera goods hidden on a shelf in a corner. I finally stopped in a store and asked where the NAVEGAL office was. The clerk dropped his work and insisted on accompanying me there. Finding it closed he asked someone standing near, "Where is the boy who runs this place?"

"He's gone for a cup of coffee," interrupted a bystander from next door. The man who was directing me said, "Vamos por un tinto." He filled me in on the town. I told him, "I really like this town. The people are very friendly." After the coffee he insisted on paying. I still hadn't gotten over my Caribbean Island complex where the people I met would invite me to have a coke and then automatically ask me to pay for it, which surprised me someone would pay for something we shared, even at his or her invitation. When we finished he excused himself and went back to his store.

I got to thinking after he left I should have given him my business card. I, therefore, ran over to the store. He turned from his customer and said, "How are you, my friend. What else can I do for you?" I gave him the card and he seemed highly pleased.

I was surprised by everything I found in Florencia. It turned out that absolutely nothing was true what people had told me about Florencia. They told me there would be lots of mosquitoes there. I found none. They said it was in the middle of the jungle. It was in almost barren green hills. They told me I could take a canoe from the city. This was not true as the canoes left from another river. They told me there were thieves all over the place. In actuality this was safer than any place I knew in the U.S. The hotel had locks on the doors but the maids consistently left them open. Valuables, such as the cameras and fishing rods of my roommates, were left right out in the open in the rooms. The main topic of conversation was the thieves in Bogotá. They told me the people would be unfriendly. I was still looking for the first unfriendly person.

I kept finding the NAVEGAL office closed. Frustrated, I finally went to AVIANCA (airline) office and sent some letters.

While there I asked, "Do you know anything about any canoes leaving to go into the jungle?"

With a shocked look, he said, "It's only 80 pesos to go by plane to Leticia. You don't want to go into that green hell. You should fly."

"But that would defeat my purpose." I argued, "I came here to see the jungle, not fly over it."

I returned to the hotel and took advantage of the water working, then lunch and attempted my first shower in three days. I got all undressed and turned on the water—nothing happened. We were out of water again.

Discouraged, I got dressed and sauntered over to the bank. That's when I found they were closed in the afternoon rather than the morning in this town in contrast to other cities. This would give me a late start the next day. My expenses came to more than I had been told and I was afraid of being stuck in the forest without any money.

I went over to the NAVEGAL office and finally found it open. I went in and no one was there. Soon a young man showed up and told me the chief would be there in a few minutes.

When he showed up I asked him, "When is the next bus to where the boats leave?"

He was equally as adamant, "Don't do that. You'd better fly. That is a horrible existence in there."

"I'm trying to get to know this part of Colombia and the only way to do it is to travel overland," I insisted.

"A launch is not due until next week," he said, watching my expression. My depressed look only encouraged him.

I was not anxious to wait around for a week for transportation but figured it would be worth it as this was the most interesting part of the trip. Our conversation continued for some time, but the clerk was no less insistent I fly.

I really had to squeeze to get any information out of him.

Finally, after a bit of coaxing, he offered, "There are canoes, but they do not leave from Florencia. The Río Hacha is too shallow, even for these canoes. They leave from the Río Ortoguaza, about two miles from here at Puerto Lara. It will cost 15 pesos to take a "correo" to Puerto Lara. You will find canoes there that will take you to Tres Esquinas for around 80 pesos. There you can probably catch a launch for La Tagua. Your best bet is to ride down to Puerto Lara with no baggage tomorrow morning and barter for the best price with a canoe to pick you up there, then return for your luggage."

I knew this would cost more money but figured it would be worth it for all the photo opportunities and the adventure. I returned to the hotel for another evening of writing by candlelight. One thing that surprised me about Florencia was the weather. Not only was it pleasantly cool during the day but also was cold during the night. There were no windows in many rooms. Yet I needed the blanket I just purchased.

An Indian man said I would need a hat for the tropical sun. As I hadn't seen the sun in a long time I felt this to be advisable. So I bought a country straw hat. I picked up a can of sardines and some bread for the trip.

I got an early start the next morning. I was at the bus station fifteen minutes early to catch the bus to Puerto Lara. I waited awhile and then got to thinking possibly the chief at the bus station might know a little more about the canoes. I went over and asked him if he knew of any canoes going to Tres Esquinas. He dropped everything and ran around the station asking if anyone knew of a canoe going. He finally led me to someone who said he knew of someone. He soon returned with another man who he said had a canoe and was going to Tres Esquinas with five other people.

The man with the canoe agreed to take me for 30 pesos. He asked me where my baggage was. I had left it back at the hotel because I wasn't planning on making the deal in Florencia. When I informed him my bags were at the hotel, he said, "Go back and get them. I'm leaving from Vitoria but I will meet you at Puerto Lara." I knew making it to Puerto Lara in time meant I had better take this bus, rather than wait for another.

I raced to the hotel. I knew, with the banks closed, I would not have enough money once I got to La Tagua but didn't know if I could ever run into another ride like this. It was 7:55 in the morning I had left everything strewn all over, wet laundry on the line, etc. as I thought I would have more time to do that after I returned. I grabbed everything and stuffed them into the duffle bag. I ran downstairs with it and asked the proprietor if I could pay now, as I had to catch a bus. She seemed completely unruffled and calmly said she would arrange to have one of the boys take my bags to the station. I hesitated at first, as there are so many bus stations. Finally, I felt I had no other choice but let him, as I didn't have time to pay the bill and carry the bags. I repeated three times so he would not forget, "Caquetá" Bus Station and made him repeat it.

Finally, the proprietor came out with a big ledger. She asked me for my passport number, where I was from, where I had last come from, where I was going, what was the purpose, etc, etc.—things the Colombia police require. She slowly wrote everything down as I shifted from foot-to-foot in nervous anxiety. When she finally finished I was a little floored when she asked for 19 pesos for the two nights. I considered that a bit high considering there was no electricity or water and as I was rooming with two others. However, I was in no mood to haggle over the price so handed her a bill. She slowly searched for the change and gave it to me.

As I ran out the door I bumped into the boy who had carried my bags. I gave him the change the landlady had given me and again asked him, "Are you sure you took the bags to 'Trans Caquetá'?"

"Oh, yes," he said, without any hesitation in his voice. I then ran down to the station and was relieved when I saw the bus still waiting for me.

I ran over to the chief and asked, "Where are my bags?"

He answered, "Yes, you'd better get the bags because the bus is leaving right away."

"Where are my bags?" I said frantically, knowing there was a possibility the boy left them at the wrong station.

"You don't know?" he said, with a puzzled look on his face.

"No. Didn't a boy leave them here?"

We frenetically searched all around the station for them. All I could think of was the satchel with the $800 worth of equipment in it.

Finally, I decided to go to "Trans-Federal" and see if the boy left it there. It was the next station so I ran over to it and asked, "Did a boy just bring a bag and briefcase in?"

"Yes, he brought them in," he said as he calmly prepared to sell me a ticket on one of his busses.

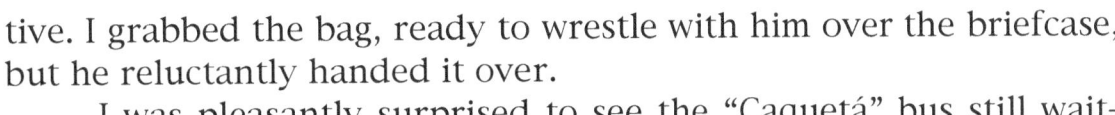
End o the road at Puerto Lara, only jungle ahead. Loading canoes on the Río Ortoguasa.

"No, I'm already going Trans-Caquetá."

Still insistent on selling me a ticket he asked me, "Why?"

Watching my bus get ready to leave I blurted out, "I'm going to Puerto Lara!"

Blank stare.

"Can I please have my bags?"

He impassively answered in the affirmative. I grabbed the bag, ready to wrestle with him over the briefcase, but he reluctantly handed it over.

I was pleasantly surprised to see the "Caquetá" bus still waiting. I ran over to it and threw my bags in. With a typical compassionate attitude the passengers were more anxious to see me catch the bus than to leave on time. The chief at the bus station handed me a note addressed to the guy who had the canoe, telling him I was to get on the canoe at Puerto Lara. He really didn't need to write the note as the owner of the canoe was sitting right in front of me on the bus. It was a bit bumpy and there wasn't any legroom but when they pack those buses full you can't even breathe without having to move everyone in the entire bus.

It was an interesting road to Puerto Lara. Florencia was still in the foothills, almost completely void of trees but which harbored a closely-knit green grass. At times I began to wonder whether the road was going to end right in front of the bus, the environment was so harsh. The road would smooth out for a stretch and I would think the government was doing some work on it, only to discover we had just driven down a landing field which served as an airport for the City of Florencia. As I looked back I could see the mountains I had descended in a truck a couple of days before in the distance. I was looking back at the only civilization I would see for the next few weeks. It was an eerie feeling. The land at Puerto Lara was still almost treeless with closely knit green grass.

5. INTO THE VOID

All six of the boat passengers were in the bus. We soon were joking and felt like old friends.

A very interesting Indian woman, Hilda, was going with us. I was thinking I should get off at Vitoria to make sure I got the canoe at its very inception, but she talked me into going on down to Puerto Lara with her. These people were living in another reality; once we became acquainted they let me in to their world. Some had no idea what a city looked like. Yet they bonded with those they trusted, and expressed an openness, which united us into immediate friendship. The people had almost no ego.

We were out of the hills but this was nothing like the tropics I had read about. The weather was still cool, damp, and dark. It rained all the time I was in Florencia with the exception of a couple of hours one day when the sun shone. I was beginning to miss sunlight.

Loading onto canoes at Puerto Lara for trip down the Río Ortoguasa to Tres Esquinas.

The motorist told us he would leave at about 10:30 in the morning I looked back at the green mountains, looming to the North in the distance. I turned south and saw only a river. This was where the rubber hit the road. There was no turning back from here, no alternate route and no idea what the trip ahead would involve. I was truly traveling into the void. I only knew the canoe would go to Tres Esquinas (Three Corners), where the Río Ortoguaza flowed into the Caquetá. Larger launches plied that river so I could catch one from there to La Tagua. The Caquetá flowed through most of the Brazilian jungle and into the Amazon about halfway to its mouth. Most of the activity in that area was military and merchandisers trading with the Indians. The military was due mainly to the constant conflict with Perú over the rainforest panhandle of Colombia, which reached the Amazon. If I wanted to reach the Upper Amazon Basin I would have to go by truck between two army bases at La Tagua, eighteen miles to another base on the Río Putumayo, a considerably shorter route to the Amazon.

Río Ortoguasa, Puerto. Lara. Upriver trip for the boats was slow because of heavy currents.

Ten-thirty arrived and there was still no sign of the canoe. I went inside and had a cup of coffee. I got into a conversation with the proprietor over accents. I mentioned the fact everyone completely leaves off the "s." I mentioned the NAVIGAL man who had told me he was expecting a boat in the next "Semana" (week). I had thought he was saying "hermana" (sister). The NAVEGAL proprietor felt very pleased to have a foreigner, as foreigners usually fly over this section because it is rough traveling and undependable. I found I still had the key to the hotel so I gave it to a returning woman with my business card to get it back to the hotel. She made so much of a to-do over the card I gave her another one to keep. Cards really made a hit in these parts as nearly everyone had the same elated reaction when I gave them one. While at school Dr. Shurz recommended we take business cards with us because the Latinos appreciate them, so I had some made up for the trip with my father's address. This and other words of advice turned out to be excellent recommendations throughout the trip.

After about 11:30 I began to get a little worried the canoe might have left without us. An Indian woman, Hilda, who I had befriended on the bus said, "They're probably just taking a longer lunch or drinking coffee."

When it did not arrive by 12:30 I was really getting worried.

Hilda said, "The mosquitoes (sancuros) are bad but they bother you mostly at night. The one you have to watch out for is the 'mosco', which will bother you on the way down. Look at the scars on my arms and legs." She showed me huge scars on her arms.

I looked down and wondered how anything could bite like that except an animal. This prompted me to put my 6-12 Mosquito juice where I could easily get at it, ready for the first "mosco."

"The boat is coming," said Hilda. I looked at my watch and it showed 12:45. I looked in the distance and couldn't believe it was finally arriving. It pulled up to the shore and, sure enough, it was our boat. I was enormously relieved.

I snapped a couple of quick pictures of a vulture and a Garza Blanca, sitting on a fence by the wooden port building, which were our only greeters. The vulture was an ominous presence on this journey into the green abyss. It seemed like hours before we finally left. It was obvious we weren't going to get to Tres Esquinas that same day.

We shoved off and started downstream. The river wasn't too wide at that point and was everything I had hoped for. The motorist tried to seat me in the back but I insisted on sitting in front as I wanted to get some good pictures. I finally won out over his insistence, but soon realized I had made a big mistake. I sat with camera in hand, fascinated by everything I saw. It was exciting to know, after all the months of planning, all the miles of travel, with all the discouraging words from almost every corner, I was finally heading into the jungle in a canoe. I don't know whether I expected to encounter a zoo, but was rather disappointed in the lack of visible animals and birds. I saw quite a few Garza (cranes) and one monkey, but very little else. I took a picture of a funny looking bird with no neck that just stood in the shade, eyes fixed on us as we passed. The Garza was a beautiful bird when it spread its wings. I was looking forward to the weather, now that we were South of the Equator. The Northern side of the Equator was going through the worst of its rainy season. It was either raining or cloudy nearly all the time.

Within a couple of hours the rain started again and I began to see why our driver, Eduardo, had wanted me to sit in the back. There was a makeshift canvas tent back there, which he pulled over the rest of the passengers, which unfortunately did not reach me. Worse yet, the motor soon sputtered and died.

It was then I was made aware of how lonely the jungle could be. There we were, on a jungle stream with no motor and absolutely no sound within miles. A boat that had been several miles behind swept past us. The rain clouds began to float a little more our way. I began to think nothing could interfere with the harmony of this voyage. The motor gave no sign of starting but I continued to think positive thoughts about the journey ahead. Finally, the motor started and we were off again. By then the rain was coming down in thick sheets and I could hardly see in front of me. I looked down at my sopping pants, shirt and shoes, and smiled. "This is all in the spirit of the voyage," I thought. I looked back. The only people out from under the tent were the helper and his wife. She had a poncho on and he had a ruana. He smiled and asked me where my pancho or ruana was. I told him I had none as I had felt the price of ruanas was too high.

The rain finally thinned out as it passed over us. The sun came out and my pants and shirt dried in a half-hour. I was grateful for my wash-and-wear clothes.

We wound around the bends in the river and finally stopped on the shore to let Hilda off. She lived in a lonely grass hut. After this we went through another half-hour ritual getting the motor to start again.

The topography of this one-day trip was extremely interesting. We were quite a way downstream before we started seeing trees. They became thicker and thicker until finally we were in the jungle. We saw no villages along the way, just solitary grass huts, built in small cleared areas.

It was also interesting to see the various river launches that came up the river. They were so slow moving against the fast current I began to wonder if they were moving at all. I looked around for the three hotels the man in Cúcuta said existed between Florencia and Tres Esquinas, but saw barely any huts, let alone any other signs of civilization.

The rain again swept over the canoe, harder than the first and it didn't subside as quickly. It finally stopped but the sun didn't come out so I was left with wet clothes.

At five o'clock we pulled up to the shore in front of a grass hut. Eduardo told me to take my luggage out. I couldn't figure out whether this was another customs inspection. I asked but got no response. Finally, I saw everyone going toward the hut, which was built on stilts and knew we were probably going to camp out for the night there.

I climbed up the slippery embankment to the rickety old stairs that led up to the top of the stilts. A railing ran around the house. The chickens, etc. were kept underneath the house. An Indian was at the door to greet us. He spoke a very slow clear Spanish so I could understand every word. His wife and mother also spoke very clear Spanish. Eduardo, on the other hand, had a terrible accent and spoke very fast so I had a hard time getting even half of what he said.

I was getting ready to pull out my sardines and bread and start eating when Eduardo invited me to partake of his food. I tried to refuse but he already had a plate made up for me, so I could not politely continue to decline his offer. All the other passengers sat around and looked on. This made me feel even more ill at ease.

Eduardo then began a political discussion with me. He started the conversation with the usual, "We don't like Dulles," and branched off into Colombian situations. "No one is safe in this country. If anyone expresses differing opinions a fanatic on the rightist side usually shoots him, his wife and children. The leftists are equally as zealous. You aren't safe with your money as this place is full of robbers, especially in Bogotá. The government is incapable of attracting foreign capital or keeping it once it comes in. The government employees are against any progress whatsoever and will usually demand money under the table for every little thing they do. The education problem is tragic and the country is full of ignoramuses that care little about the future of our country."

I had not heard such daring criticism in all my time in Colombia. He went on and on for hours and I was only getting about half of what he said as his accent was so strong. I found by answering, "Sí, sí," every now and then I could save myself a lot of time in explanations.

I strung up my hammock at 8:00 p.m. and tried to go to sleep. However, Eduardo kept on talking until about 10:00. Some little monkeys outside kept making funny noises all through the night that sounded like about ten of them gnawing their teeth at the same time. I finally went to sleep. It rained hard all during the night and was still drizzling the next morning when we arose.

It was impossible to sleep past 5:00 that morning or probably any other morning. If the roosters didn't wake me, the mothers yelling at their children and the chickens were sure to do it. Joining this chorus were the children yelling at each other.

Eduardo again insisted I eat breakfast with him. I felt a growing uneasiness as the others watched us eat, even hungrier than the night before. I couldn't figure out whether this was Eduardo's food or the hosts. I later discovered his wife had cooked it from supplies the motor canoe people brought along. Eduardo continued the conversation about the political situation. I cringed every time he did this, as I had no idea what other passengers were thinking about his opinions. I cut down on his repeating things by agreeing with him as he changed from subject-to-subject thinking I understood him. He offered me a drink again called "agua de panela." It tasted like petroleum with sugar and smelled about the same. It was heated, which accentuated both the repugnancy of the taste and the smell. I gulped it down just to be polite.

Río Ortoguasa widens

It was 9:30 in the morning before we loaded the canoe and began again our journey down the Río Caquetá. I was anxious to get to Tres Esquinas so I could get a launch out of there. By noon I was driven by hunger to dive into the bread and sardines I had brought. I pulled them out and was about to take a bite when I noticed Eduardo's dog's wanton eyes transfixed on my food, noticeably famished. Guilt and compassion gripped me. My hand moved automatically from bread to him, which he promptly gulped down maintaining his tormented gaze. I pulled out the sardines and offered him one. I finally ended up with half a can of sardine and a piece of bread. Fortunately I wasn't very hungry so the half can of sardines and piece of bread did not leave me wanting. The large dog mascot was becoming an undesirable passenger on a crowded canoe, so I stopped feeding him. Every time I would dry off after each rain the dog would shake water all over me. That dog did everything to ingratiate his presence, jumping off the canoe onto the mud, then jumping back on, leaving half his retained mud on me. Some dogs beg for food, this one wrestled me for it. We went tooth to tooth every bite I dared take in front of him. At last, ten claw marks later, he showed me who was "boss" (P.S. The "boss" enjoyed his food very much, wagging his tail and all).

Eduardo was just not taking "No" for an answer on continuing my trip past Tres Esquinas.

"I'm just going to Tres Esquinas with you, Eduardo," I insisted.

"When we get to Tres Esquinas it shouldn't take us long to go on down to La Tagua," he said, unrelenting, ignoring my pleas.

"I can't afford to pay you to take me to La Tagua. I'll catch the next launch that comes by."

Still unmoved by my refusal he continued, "Why don't you buy a chicken and some crackers for our trip to La Tagua."

"I definitely will be taking a launch out of Tres Esquinas," our rounds of conversation continued, to no avail.

We finally arrived at Tres Esquinas in the early afternoon. The back of the town appeared first. Then we rounded a corner and could see ahead where the Río Ortoguaza (The one we were on) flowed into the Río Caquetá. The village appeared larger from the front, indicating it was larger than first impression. There were also streetlights, indicating it was somewhat civilized. All the buildings were painted yellow; it was solely a military camp.

As I started to get out of the canoe Eduardo called after me, "There's nothing to see here. Stay on board and I'll take you to La Tagua for another 200 pesos."

I called back, "I'll take my chances. Where's the hotel here?"

"There aren't any hotels here, just army barracks," he persevered.

"Can I get a check cashed here? I only have 47 pesos left."

"There are no banks here, but if you let me take you to La Tagua I'll wait for you to go to Puerto Leguízamo, get a check cashed and return." I thought long and deep about this offer. There was no assurance I could get either room or board here and after I paid Eduardo for the trip up to this point I would not have enough to even take a launch to La Tagua. I finally decided to take that chance. When I learned the weekly plane was going to Leguízamo and only cost 40 pesos I was confident I should not continue to La Tagua in the canoe. I could cash my check at Puerto Leguízamo.

I picked up my bags and climbed the hill to the camp. I paid Eduardo and watched him fade off into the distance upstream.

The C.Q. assigned a man to take me to the officers' quarters to see if I could get a room. We put my baggage in the guardhouse and hiked the 100 yards to the other side of the camp. The guard asked me if I wanted him to call me as late as 10:00 p.m. if a boat came by.

Knowing launches only come by once a week or so I told him, "Call me at any time." At the camp, officers were all sitting around in short-sleeved shirts drinking their beers. Off to one side was a swimming pool, which no one was using.

"When does the plane leave for Puerto Leguízamo?" I asked the seated officers. None of them could give me any definite information on the flight.

"Wait until the AVIANCA man comes back and you can talk with him." A crowd of GIs followed me wherever I went.

"How are you planning on traveling when you leave here?"

"How did you get here from Bogotá?"

"Many Americans pass through here." (I think it was probably closer to three in two years).

"This place is known as 'Infierno Verde' (Green Hell)," several of them repeated many times.

"How long do you have to serve in this area?" I asked.

"Eighteen months," was their reply.

"I find it unbelievable men can exist in a womanless green hell for a year-and-a-half," I queried.

They gave me the same calm answer to which I had become accustomed in Colombia, "We have the three things we enjoy most—conversation, coffee and beer," and they seemed satisfied with that. Most of the conversation centered around several things: the rain, the lack of change in weather and the hot sun, but it didn't seem as though the roughness of these things governed their lives. They were a jovial bunch with a great sense of humor.

"How often do launches come through?" I asked them.

"About once a week or so. There will probably be one Monday or Tuesday. I pulled out my map and everyone crowded around me to study it. I noticed I would cross the Equator on my way to La Tagua, probably the first night out. As my rapport grew with the military men and I began to change my mind about flying out. It would be a shame to fly across this fascinating area of the rainforest. I decided the company in this army camp wasn't bad. My newfound friends talked the chief into letting me eat in the technicians' mess hall and promised me I would have a room for the night, despite the original rebuff I received initially. This way I would be able to wait three or four days before leaving. I decided I would definitely wait it out. I could cash my check in the AVIANCA office on the base the next Monday.

Someone told me a guy who was from the States wanted to speak to me. I went over with them and ended up at the AVIANCA office. He spoke to me in beautiful Spanish and I asked him where he was from. He said he was from Spain. Then he asked where I was from. I told him Kansas City and he looked somewhat surprised. He said, "You aren't from Spain? They told me you were from Spain."

I said, "They told me you were from the States."

"Sit down while I work." He explained the base to me.

Everyone always seemed more than willing to talk about the war between Colombia and Perú. They explained to me Colombia had to be consistently on the lookout for any aggression on the part of Perú. I never could get straight exactly how the war started. It was always made clear to me Perú made repeated attempts to wrest the panhandle from Colombia.

After awhile the airline clerk took me to the hanger where there were some typewriters. As I looked around the base I could see the Colombian Air Force in ready, a few raggedy old planes and one big plane in no shape to fly, let alone fight.

"Are these Colombia's fighters?" I asked in surprise.

"Yes," was their confident reply.

"One of the officer's wife is an American. She's from Phoenix, Arizona," said the Spaniard."

"I go to school in Phoenix," I said.

"I'll take you over and introduce you to her." They laughed and said she doesn't speak any more Spanish than a few greetings. Everyone has to speak to her in English or someone has to write a note for her when she wants anything. "She's been here for about six months."

"How can she have a husband who speaks Spanish and live here for this long and still not speak any Spanish whatsoever?"

Three of them pointed to their head and said in unison, "She isn't quite there."

"Does she ever find people to talk with?" I asked. I had only noticed one officer who spoke English and his English was in bad shape.

"Many of the people here speak English," they proudly stated. I had not run into any, so far, who were able to go past a few greetings.

One of the soldiers came in and notified me they had gotten me a room. This was more than I expected. I was expecting only a bed at the most. I went over with them and found it was rather nice. It had screens on the windows and led into a private shower and toilet shared by two other suites.

I went back and continued talking with the men.

Finally, one of them looked at my watch and noticing it was 5:30, asked, "Have you eaten yet?"

I felt that was early so told them, ""I'll eat later." I thought Latin American dinner hour was from 7:00 to 8:00 p.m.

"The dining hall closes at 6:00," added one of the men. It was then I found the typical Colombian dinner was from 5:00-6:00. This clarified why the restaurants were empty in Cúcuta and the many times I was just sitting down as the others were getting up in Bogotá. At Florencia I had noticed the people started gathering for dinner between 6:15 and 6:30. It was hard to keep up with the meal times of every place I went. I had gotten into the habit since Tres Esquinas of asking the meal times at every hotel where I stayed.

I went over to the mess hall and found everyone had already eaten. I felt a little uneasy sitting by myself at the table. Soon, two other couples came in but sat at another table. The meal was mediocre. The other couple had a punch drink that was atrocious.

I went in my room and found there was no light bulb. I was offered the bulb out of the AVIANCA office for the night but found the agent gone and the office locked tight. As soon as some of the boys found out I needed a light they searched the base for one not being used. They finally swiped one out of some place and brought it to me. I had planned on doing a lot of writing but two of the boys stuck around to talk. They helped me set up my mosquito net and get the room in shape. I even had clean sheets.

"I'm the bugler for the camp," said one of the soldiers.

I asked him, "What time do you blow your bugle?"

"At 4:00 in the morning," he said.

"Is that when everyone gets up in the morning?" I asked, hoping he would say, "No."

The 4:00 a.m. warning was enough to encourage me to retire at the same time as the others, 9:00. I turned out the light right after they left and went to bed.

At 4:00 a.m. I heard the bugle. He must have learned to play the day before because I thought he would never make it through the call, let alone have the call recognized by the men. It took a little while before the noise of the arising camp began. I managed to halfway sleep through it until 7:00 a.m.

Breakfast wasn't served on Sunday morning until 10:00 so I waited around for it. I felt this would be late enough to skip lunch and just take dinner, thus saving money, as the meals were so expensive. The guard was, as agreed, looking out for any launch floating down the river. There was no need for me to wait at the pier because I knew they had to stop at every military checkpoint throughout the country.

A padre with a long beard and white garb came in. I greeted him and the agent mentioned to him I was from the States. The padre then addressed me in English. I started to speak English and he quickly changed back to Spanish. Just from those few words I was aware he knew more English than anyone I had met so far in Colombia.

He asked me, "Do you know a couple of Protestant missionaries who are friends of mine in the States and one Catholic missionary?"

I don't know a single missionary. Many people, when they found I was from the States, would say, "Oh, you must know so-and-so." The strange thing is they would usually look surprised that I was from the United States and didn't know their American friend. The padre bought his air ticket, then left.

One of the fellows offered, "We'll take you and show you the jungle. The jungle around here is rich with birds and animals so you can get some good pictures. When the morning is cloudy there is sun in the afternoon and when the sun is out the afternoon is cloudy." I was still waiting for the sun to come out. I hadn't seen the sun for more than five minutes since Cúcuta. Even in Neiva, which is a semiarid plain, the weather was cloudy.

I was just getting ready to go to 10:00 breakfast when the C.Q. came in and told me, "A launch just arrived."

A pall of gloom fell over me as I thought of the adventure I would be missing. I was really looking forward to getting into other jungles and spending a day or two more at Tres Esquinas. Reality told me it might possibly be another week before another launch came and I didn't have that kind of time to spare. "Oh well," I thought. "I can probably get out in the jungle just as easily at Leguízamo and Leticia, Iquítos or Manaus."

I looked at the guard, somewhat sad, and reluctantly told him, "Hold it. I'll be right back. I just have to get money and my bags." I was nervous as I dealt with the slowness of the postal service. I kept looking over my shoulder to make sure the launch was still docked. The C.Q. finally agreed to cash my check, after much protest. Then he had to register the letters, get the stamps, after which he informed me, "I can't accept the film. There's no place to put the stamps."

"They can be put in the sack and the stamps placed there," I said trying to resolve the situation and still make it back to the launch before it left.

"I can't accept that," he insisted.

"Bogotá accepted the film in this way and that seemed okay to them," I added.

"Then I guess it's okay with me," he finally acquiesced. He then had to find places for the many stamps. Then he had to register the film. Then I had to pay for it, after which he proceeded to look for change. I was anxiously thinking of the launch at the pier waiting for me as my feet clawed the grounds. It was with great relief he finally finished and I ran to my room. Everything was strewn all over the place. The last thing I expected was a launch to arrive so soon. Living out of a barracks bag makes it difficult to get at things so I was usually reluctant to put things back every time I use them because I would only have to dig through everything to find them again. I threw everything in and compressed it to fit, then dragged the mosquito net down and the blanket off the bed.

I ran down to the pier and was pleasantly surprised to find the launch still there. The soldiers insisted on carrying everything down for me and about seven of the ones who had been closest to me came right on board with me. I gave them a notebook to write their names in and between the pen not working and misspellings it took them about ten minutes to get all their names written. I expected the captain of the launch to be chomping at the bit to leave, but when I looked around I saw no sign of impatience on the part of any of the people on board.

The soldiers got off after a hearty handshake from each and the boat started chugging out toward the middle of the river. As I looked back I saw about 20-30 men on the shore watching me off. They waved and waited there until the boat was well on its way. I have never run into a friendlier, more hospitable group of people.

The launch was a sort of covered river barge, about fifteen feet wide and fifty feet long, with a diesel motor. It chugged along very slowly in the downstream current and I'm sure had the river been without any current it wouldn't have moved.

We were just around the bend when we stopped at a town (I think Solerno was the name). We docked alongside a small raft where a woman was washing tripe. It was extremely interesting so I wanted a picture of it. Every time I got ready to take the picture her daughter would look at me and tell her mother I was taking the picture. The mother would move around in a position to hide what she was doing. I finally managed to catch them both by surprise.

I walked into town to see what I could pick up to eat. I found the town small and its people somewhat shy, but it met my expectations of what a small jungle town should look like. I stopped some people and asked them where I could buy something solid to eat. The first people I stopped just looked at me and walked off. The second group of people just gruffly replied, "Over there." I wondered if these people had a language of their own or were surprised to hear an accent in Spanish different from their own. I finally found a little shop that sold various kinds of bread. I couldn't find any other type of food in the rest of the village.

As I returned to the launch, one of the men who worked on the boat pointed to a large fish that had been caught. It was one of the largest I have seen so far. It didn't take much coaxing on their part to get me to take a picture of the fisherman holding it up posing for it.

I looked up and saw the captain of the launch beckoning me from the shack above the river.

"Hey, Carlos, come on up and join me for a beer."

I ran up and saw he had a hot foaming beer ready for me. I tried to pass on it every polite way I could but finally gave in and forced as much down as I could. I finally left with the bad taste of hot beer in my mouth. The boat was still being loaded so the captain remained in the shack for quite a while longer.

I heard him calling, "Carlos, come up here."

I ran up only to find another hot beer waiting for me.

"I'm sorry," I said. "I can't stand beer, especially warm beer."

I felt that would end it once and for all, but he still went ahead and put it in front of me, telling me, "Beer is the same thing bread is made out of. Come on, comrade, drink your bread," he said with a broad smile.

By taking little sips I only had to drink the equivalent of a gulp before the boat was ready to go. I ran to my bag of bread and tried to kill the taste of the warm beer, but to no avail. Same stuff? Oof, not the same taste!

A young man wandered on board and asked me about passage. I told him to see the captain about it. He did and came back with passage taken care of. The captain had quoted the same price for him as he did for me—ten pesos. He said he was a worker looking for a job in Leguízamo.

I was approached by the captain of the boat with the same question I had gotten from everyone from San Agustín on down. How much is the camera worth? The price sounded phenomenal to them and I usually tried to hedge the question, especially when someone who was going to be charging me an unquoted fare asked about it.

We passed no villages on the way down, only small thatched huts. We stopped at several to do some trading. Some served as points of commerce for the rest of the huts deeper in the jungle. At one point we unloaded about a hundred bags of bad wheat for the cattle and pigs, mostly pigs, of the area. There aren't many cattle in the rainforest. Meat is difficult to preserve without refrigeration. They would find it difficult to eat an entire cow before it spoiled. Every part of the pig is used. Even the skin is dried and used in every way possible. The intestines of the pigs are emptied and refilled with rice, yucca, and other things to make a sort of bologna.

All loading and unloading was done by manpower so it took hours to load and unload the boats. Each man had to walk up to the unloading point, dump a bag, and come back for another. Also, the men weren't expected to work when it rained. As there was intermittent rain during most of the day there wasn't much work done. If the meal was cooked at the same time as we docked, unloading waited until after the meal had not only been eaten but digested as well.

The captain told me, "We are preparing a meal for you."

This surprised me so I said, "I already brought some food." I felt this answer was satisfactory but the captain called me over and had a meal set out for me. All through the trip I had been eating more or less average meals. They had been somewhat monotonous at times, only varying in quantity from morning meal to evening meal. However, I had never been handed anything as inedible as this. If there were such a thing as a menu it would have been called, "Un gran bloque de sal y un vaso de gasolina para tomar" which in English would be "One great big block of salt and a glass of gasoline to drink." The plate consisted of fried rice, dried yucca, and plántin (a dry sort of banana with no flavor). I swore the drink was warm petroleum with sugar in it. It was that same "agua de panela" Eduardo had given me. I tried not to drink it but the dinner was so dry I was forced to for self-preservation. Fortunately, there was some meat with the meal so it was moderately palatable.

I went back and found the other passenger quite hungry (name of Diego Atahortyus). They had neglected to serve him anything so he was starving. I offered him some of my bread. As there was nothing to do after dark we all looked around for places to sling our hammocks. Diego and I were the only passengers. The rest of those on board were laborers. I found the laborers reluctant to talk with me. This had been my experience since arriving in Colombia. The bosses of the laborers always seemed friendly everywhere, but the common laborers were shy and would greet me but say no more. The Colombians always seemed to proudly point out there was no race problem in their country, but there was a glaring problem, it was social. The laborer of Colombia had little chance to improve his or her lot. I saw many frustrated laborers as well as others who were workers on the same level of society, damning their country and complaining about the very nature of its people.

We had to wait until the workers finished unloading the bags before we could sling our hammocks. We were finally ready for bed by 9:00 p.m. I found the hammock much more comfortable this time. I had had to adjust my body to its shape. The first night in the thatched hut had been a little rough and I was sore all the next day.

I was prepared to meet a hot and humid Colombia, with the exception of the millions of mosquitoes in the rainforest. I prepared for heat and bugs from Neiva to Florencia. I kept expecting to see extreme weather in San Agustín because I was told it was in the jungle. It was a mountainous tropic but was cool and cloudy all the time I was there. I had been told Florencia was a green hell. I found it pleasantly cool but rainy and cloudy. I even had to use my blanket at Tres Esquinas, which is in the selva (jungle). I looked at the map and saw we would be crossing the Equator at about 4:00 a.m. "Can it get hot that quickly?" I thought.

I asked the captain, "Will it be a hot night?"

"No," he told me. "It will probably be cold even with your blanket." He was right. I about froze that night as we crossed the equator. I kept waking up, wondering if we had crossed it. I wondered if the weather would change now that we were in the middle of winter on this side of the equator.

The captain told me, "There won't be much to see at la Tagua but Leguízamo is a large city and has many beautiful buildings."

Everyone with whom I talked confirmed this description. So I looked forward to getting to Leguízamo.

They assured me there would be transportation in buses at least every hour for the 15 miles between the two cities.

It was still rainy and dreary when we pulled into La Tagua. The saying I heard the day before, "When the morning was bad the afternoon would be sunny," had turned out to be true the day before and I hoped it would be the same that day. There was no way to describe my impression of La Tagua without physically arriving there at 6:00 a.m. on a dreary morning by barge. I sloshed up a muddy street that led from the port (a pile of mud), past dirty wooden or thatched houses, to a church which surely must have been in ruins since colonial times. The two blocks of ankle-high muddy street ended at a military base, only a slight improvement over the rest of the buildings that comprised the town. The dreariness of the weather, buildings, road, and military camp looked like a Charles Addams cartoon.

I got off the boat and saw muddy streets leading past many unpainted wooden shacks which served as homes and stores. The captain took me uptown.

He went into some buildings to inquire about transportation and soon returned.

"There is no transportation out today. They have no public transportation between La Tagua and Puerto Leguízamo, only military trucks and jeeps traveling between two bases. They only travel when there are troops brought in on river launches. They hadn't been able to reach the other base for a couple of weeks because of the rains. It's impossible to travel these slippery roads in heavy rain, even with four-wheel drive."

The captain showed me the town hotel, just across the street. Dreariness was everywhere, in the weather, atmosphere, people, and mood. Even the soldiers were more reserved and walked around with grim faces, obviously dissatisfied with their life there. The townspeople remained shut away in their houses. I saw little movement in the town and even when the people were moving there was little exchange among them. The Colombians are usually a very loquacious people so this was a divergent contrast. I was accustomed to seeing Colombians talk energetically in taverns, streets, rooms, and literally everywhere there were other people. I saw cars dodging around groups of conversing people in Bogotá so as not to interrupt their conversation or get in their way.

The captain took me to the military base to see if I should get permission to leave the base. I wasn't too bothered by this as I had found Southern Colombia much easier to travel in than the Eastern. Coming from Cúcuta to Bogotá we had been stopped a dozen times by police checkpoints (as we entered and left every city or pueblo). At two of these points we had to show our passports or identification. Everyone must register with the government and get what is known as a "cedula" (National Identification Card). One must carry it at all times, just as a foreigner would carry a visa or passport. The base informed me I would have to get permission from the police to leave.

I found Diego and another Indian who had joined us and we all sloshed our way through the mud to the hotel. The owner was reluctant to get us a room but finally agreed to after some persuasion. She went outside and opened up a barn door. Inside was a smelly hole with a bar in it where we evidently were supposed to sling our hammocks. We carried our baggage inside and closed the doors. Diego and I decided to tour the town and, as there was no lock on the door our Indian friend offered to watch our bags. The road turned at the church and headed in another direction for about two more blocks. We waded through the ankle deep mud. The road then turned again and went for two more blocks. The architecture was tediously identical throughout—wooden planks put up to keep out the mud and eyes of other people. The road then merged into the jungle. We looked at it and wondered if we wouldn't make it faster trying to walk it. We returned on another street (the only other one in town).

We saw a place that looked like it served food. Regretfully, all they served was bread, not even any pastry (something very unusual in Latin America). They had nothing to drink but warm beer, as did every other small pueblo we had been through.

I was looking around for the police when I bumped into a friend of the captain.

"I'm going to report to the police," I told him.

"That's just a story. You don't have to do that," he assured me.

"I'm looking for a boat from Puerto Leguízamo to Leticia and several people have told there won't be a boat for another month or so."

He took me back to the NAVEGAL office and checked. There we were told there would be a boat leaving on the tenth. This was the seventh so that meant only three more days to wait.

I asked him, "How long will it take to get between the Puerto Leguízamo and Leticia?"

He told me, "Twenty-five days because the boat doesn't travel at night."

"My visa only lasts another 13 days."

"I have another appointment that will last a half-hour. Wait here for me and we'll see if we can get your visa extended."

The half-hour turned into an hour-and-a-half and I wore out the sidewalk (the only one in town) waiting for him.

He finally showed up and told me, "I'll take you to the captain of the base, and the captain will extend your visa. Have you met the padre yet?"

"No I' haven't."

"Let's go to the church."

The padre was a young bearded Italian, about 35. We went out to his patio and sat down. He was very friendly and a gracious host.

"I have some pictures I'd like to show you," he said, offering me a coffee. We shared a large album he had, with hundreds of pictures of an assortment of Indigenous who lived in the rainforest around there. I was surprised to find ninety percent of the men wearing kakis and a white shirt. The women were usually dressed in flowered (pink) dresses. Most of the natives we met spoke Spanish, slowly and clearly, flavored by their native dialects. One of the helmsmen on the boat to La Tagua spoke several of the dialects and was Indian himself. Many were very Spanish looking and some looked as though they had no Indian blood in them whatsoever.

The padre explained each photo, "Now this is the chief of a tribe in this area," and there would be a person in kakis looking very bored with it all. I was just getting into the meat of his pictures and of the stories he had written about the Indians when someone interrupted, "An army truck just arrived."

The professor I had befriended had dedicated himself to finding me a truck that would have room for us. I turned to thank the padre for his hospitality, and he asked if I had met another Italian padre in my voyage down the Putumayo. He whipped out a photo and, sure enough, it was the Spanish padre I met at Tres Esquinas.

We ran out, only to find it was a false alarm. It was only a jeep bringing some officers in from Puerto Leguízamo and was full on its return trip. My confidence was bolstered, seeing a vehicle had made it through the wet jungle. There was great possibility another vehicle might make it that day. Sure enough, another truck was not long in coming. We chased it down and found it wasn't going to leave until after 2:00 p.m. The captain of the base at La Tagua was on it. He spoke good English so I switched over to English with him to give him some practice. He told me he could do nothing about extending my visa but referred me to Captain Durán, the head of the Leguízamo base, whom he said could give me a carta blanca to travel as long as I wanted in the area.

He invited me to lunch at the officers' mess. The meal set before us looked delicious. I hadn't eaten or drunk anything in quite a while, as both food and drink were so appalling on the launch. For breakfast they served us sugared heated petroleum again (agua de panela), dry yucca, fried plántin, and dry fried rice. I sampled each but could not get the courage to eat anything. I was astonished when he charged me fifteen pesos. I complained to Diego that I didn't feel those two meals were worth five pesos. The usual launch charge is three pesos a day for board. Diego said, "You should feel bad? I had to pay the same for the one meal in the morning." Again, I learned to be more conscious of where others are before I spoke.

I was just taking my second bite out of that delicious lunch when someone came in and said, "The truck has arrived and he doesn't dare wait. It looks like rain and he wants to get through the jungle so he can eat his lunch." The captain said, "You'll have to leave your meal. He can't wait." I looked at the beautiful meal I had to leave behind. I grabbed the lemonade and gulped it down. Thirst was my greatest need. I ran out and grabbed the truck. We picked up Diego and my bags at the gate.

"Have a great journey," said the captain. Be sure to see Capitán Durán at the Leguízamo base. He'll get you lodging and extend your visa. Capitán Durán speaks English so you can use either Casatillan or English with him. About ten feet further we picked up our Indian friend, so drunk by that time he could barely walk.

I stopped to pay the hotel woman for the use of the room for the day. She pushed the money back in my hand, saying, "I can't take anything. Some people get stuck here and I offer them the room. If they are stuck here overnight I charge them for sleeping, but if they only stay during the day I don't charge them anything."

Being first on the truck got me a seat in the cab but I again felt guilty with everyone else riding in back. As soon as we reached the end of the town we were in the thick of the jungle. The jungle was cleared on each side of the road to make room for some scrubby looking cattle to graze. Little grass farmhouses dotted the clearings along the way. It looked much more civilized than I had expected of the jungle. I was still disappointed to see all the Indians wearing khaki pants. The truck fishtailed its way through the jungle. All vehicles using this road had to be equipped with wide tires and four-wheel drive, nothing less could get through. Even with four-wheel drive we slid from side to side, swimming over the deep mud.

We stopped at a hut to pick up some things and to give the truck driver his lunch. The sun came out for five minutes and I took the opportunity to take pictures of the road. The passengers were people from all walks of life in the area.

Road between La Tagua and Puerto Leguísimo. It is impassable during most of the rainy season.

We waited a half-hour for the driver to finish eating. He finally came bouncing out and we were off again, trying to beat the rain. We slipped and slid over the rest of the 15 miles. Everyone I met told me what a beautiful place Leguízamo was, which gave me high expectations. We finally arrived at the outskirts, a few grass huts appeared along the road. It was a short drive to reach the heart of town. I found it to be of the same architecture as la Tagua—a cluster of boards tacked up around frames. Some had replaced the grass roofs with corrugated metal, but they still looked dilapidated. This was just a larger version of La Tagua, the streets ankle deep in mud. The only decent buildings I saw were some pre-fab corrugated metal buildings with 5' x 5' rooms (four of them). This was the newest in jungle dwellings for Colombia and I heard them once referred to as "Casas Inglesas" (English Houses).

"Here's the hotel," said the driver as he stopped in front of a shabby green dwelling. Diego got off and the Indian about fell off. As I inspected the shabby dwelling I thought I'd better check with the captain first to see if I could stay at the base. I could always come back if nothing better was available.

"I'd like to go to the base," I asked the driver. He gave me a surprised glance but proceeded down the mucky road. It was only five blocks to the base, where the road ended at the Río Putumayo.

I walked to the base with my bags and the guard looked at me completely perplexed. When he saw me with a duffle bag on my shoulder, he must have thought I was a new recruit arriving without my group. I told the guard I was here to see Capitán Dorán and he motioned me to a seat. Even more unusual was a recruit walking up to the gate with bags in tow, asking to see the commander of the base. After a ten-minute wait I was sent to the captain, accompanied by another guard.

The assistant at the desk asked me, "What do you want with the Capitán Dorán?"

I told him, "I was sent by Capitán Castillán of La Tagua. I have extended my visa twice and now find it would be advisable to extend it again."

He asked me, "Where are you staying?"

I told him, "Capitán Castillán told me I might be able to stay at the base."

"The captain isn't in but will be in another few minutes. We can't help you on housing, because this is a military base." The guard then took me back to the gate where I waited for about another fifteen minutes for the captain to get back. Finally, a jeep drove through the gate, there was a salute and the guard turned to me and said, "That was the captain."

INTO THE VOID

I gulped twice and said, "He's not coming in? It looks more like he's leaving."

"He's going home and won't be back until tomorrow."

"I was told to wait at this gate until he came in," I said, trying to suppress my anger.

"Here are the directions to his house. Why don't you see him there?"

"Are you sure I can see the commanding officer at his home? If I were to do that in the States I would be court marshaled for trying to see an officer at his home."

"No, that's all right. Go ahead," he calmly said with confidence. I walked all over the city trying to find his house and finally found it just a block-and-a-half from the base.

"Come on in," he said, completely unaffected by my intrusion. He listened intently as I told him my problem with the visa.

"I'm sorry, I can't help you because I lack the power to do anything in those matters. The Central Police handle all matters of immigration so the Army can do nothing."

"I'm sure my visa will run out before I get to Leticia and there is a fine of 500 pesos for overextending my stay."

"Don't worry," he assured me. There is an American Consulate in Leticia and you can check with them when you arrive there. Be sure and check with the police before leaving Leguízamo, though."

I went back to the Base and grabbed my bags where I had left them with the guard. I slipped and slid the four blocks up the road, to the hotel, tricky while carrying 65 pounds. There was no doubt left in my mind as to how the truck I came in on was the first truck that had gotten through the jungle in four days. When I arrived at the block where I thought I had seen the Hotel Diego and the Indian went to, I couldn't see a sign, nor could I see anything that looked like it might be a hotel. I fi-

Beautiful downtown Puerto Leguísimo. Hotel is the building on left.

nally entered a doorway I thought I had seen them go into. Inside was a filthy room with an unfinished table on one side and an ancient hand-operated sewing machine near the door. The walls were uneven white washed boards, open several feet short of the ceiling. A woman met me in the hallway. Her face was perplexed, probably wondering what I was doing in her home.

I asked, "Is this the hotel?"

She said, "Yes, I have some rooms." She took me around to the front and down a couple of doors. She opened two barn-like doors and inside was the biggest mess I ever saw. Paper, dirt, and mud were piled knee high. There were some uneven boards, a little taller than me, that made it a room. These had been whitewashed long before. There was an old hand-made table, an army cot, and a hospital cot. A bare bulb hung by its cord from the wall. I looked around and saw that all her children had come in the room and there was a crowd looking in. There was no type of latch to lock the door on the inside. The maid came in and swept the tons of dirt out while I went out to seek passage on the boat the people in La Tagua thought might be leaving on the tenth.

Army camp at Puerto Leguísimo. The last old boat is the one I took. Last boat is cañanero (military boat); first one is a small launch.

The clerk at the ticket office looked surprised when I told him I wanted 3rd class passage. He seemed to feel it would only take ten days to get to Leticia. I felt that would just barely get me there before the visa expired.

"Mr. Rosa, who is the manager, was in the States for seven years," they said as they went back to call him. He was a nice older man of about 79. His English was getting a little shaky, as he hadn't been in the States for too long.

"I lived in Chicago for a few years and then moved to New York before I came back to Leguízamo. My dream is to die in the

United States. Look here. Here are the names of a couple of Americans who booked passage."

"Are they going first class?" I asked

"They already went on the boat a month-and-a-half ago."

I returned to my room and started to clean up. They had brought a pitcher of water and a pan for me. The room was soon full again with people looking on. I closed the doors but the children just opened them back up again. I got the biggest crowd when I started to use my battery-powered razor. They had never heard of an electric razor in Leguízamo and wondered what I was doing. When I asked one of the people where the toilet was I was told, "Go out, and back through the main door, through that room, through the kitchen, out in the back yard and about another fifty feet."

I went out, went in the same door I did the first time. There were two rooms off this one, which were using curtains for doors. I had to step down into the dirt floor of the kitchen. There was a pile of something in the corner, which was the stove. Dirty pots and pans were all over the place. Chickens scattered throughout the room, picking up whatever dropped, and fighting with the other animals. A woman in a charcoal covered dress, standing next to the stove, turned around and smiled. I went out in the back. Sure enough, through the trees, was an old privy. The only thing it lacked was a half-moon on the door. I did have to marvel, though, as I had really been through some rough parts of Colombia and this was the first privy I had run into. It did differ from comparable ones in the U.S., as there were cockroaches all over it you had to fight

Kitchen in hotel, Puerto Leguísimo. Definitely not recommended by Duncan & Hines.

to sit down. I found, much to my dismay, I had left behind the most important thing one carries in the backcountry of Latin America — toilet paper. A few leaves off one of the trees did the trick.

I went back to the kitchen and asked where I could bathe. I got a blank stare, but was finally told the Putumayo was where everyone bathed. The Putumayo is even dirtier than I later found the Amazonas; so bathing was a new adventure.

Dinner was really quite tasty, even better than the hotel in Bogotá. The other guests were interesting. One of the guests, who was there with his wife, was a mystic, excusing himself from the table as his various clients arrived. Two others were traveling salesmen.

We all got together and felt we would partake of the only entertainment in town—go to a movie. I was surprised to find a building set aside for movies way out in the sticks. Between the Argentine accent and bad speakers I understood nothing. The rest of the group had to explain everything to me on our way back.

It was almost mandatory that every person have a flashlight in Leguízamo as the streets were so muddy and there were no streetlights. I was glad I had brought the ankle boots along because I never had to worry about shining them.

I got up early the next morning expecting to get everything out of the way, as the boat captain had told me we might leave sooner than expected. I ran out to take my laundry down and wash it. I got to the river and found it so muddy nothing would ever come out any cleaner. I noticed upstream some women had some rafts and were washing on them. I ran upstream and couldn't find a vacant raft. I approached a black woman washing and asked her if she minded my coming out to do my washing on the other side of her raft. She, instead, sent her daughter up to get the clothes. She insisted on doing them. After she was through she sent them back to me. I asked her, "How much do I owe you?"

She called back, "I wouldn't ask for anything for just doing a few clothes and not even drying them for you."

I thanked her and went back to the hotel where I hung them wherever there was a clean spot. There wasn't any water there so I couldn't wash up. I could feel the dirt growing thicker on my skin.

I wandered over to see the NAVIGAL office. I met Mr. Rosa on the way there.

INTO THE VOID

After greeting me he said, "The boat will be delayed because we just received a pile of sewer pipes to take to Leticia. I can't give you a date the boat will leave. Have you seen the boat?"

"Only on the outside," I said.

"Would you like to see it?"

We climbed down the muddy banks and onto the boat. On the outside was painted the name, CUIDAD NEIVA. It was an old paddle wheeler, which looked like it had transferred many years ago from the Mississippi. It was a dark gray with an engine at river level, which burned wood for fuel. Mr. Rosa explained to me, "These boats are converted to burn wood as fuel to provide a living for the Indians whose huts dot the shorelines of the rivers."

A hallway led to the third-class eating table. Two freight barges were in front. One was covered with a corrugated steel roof and housed a pig, some wood, cargo, and the third class passengers. A narrow deck wrapped itself around the hull on the second story. Inside the hull were the camarotes (tiny rooms containing a double decked bed). This was what first class passage bought (a bed, not the room). One look at that made me glad I was going third class. In the front of the hull was a screened in room with a table and chairs. This was the dining room. The top deck contained just the shell and the officers' quarters. I was surprised when I saw the captain's quarters, a small dirty room with a hammock. His only luxury was a small gas refrigerator. There was a cage behind the captain's quarters where all the chickens were housed. The officers slept in camarotes, the same as the first-class passengers.

Mr. Rosa told me, "The captain is the same person you were talking with yesterday." Capitán Mendes Ballestas was inside his room. He was still complaining about his sickness but remained friendly and exuberant.

He told me, "I'm going to let you put your hammock in the dining room where the mosquitoes can't get at you. You can hang your hammock right after dinner each night and take it down before the 7:00 breakfast. You can also eat in the dining room. You don't want to eat and sleep in the third class.

"I'm very dissatisfied with this part of Colombia. I had a boat on the Magdalena River for 40 years and they suddenly stuck me on this line. I made them promise I would only have to take this line for six months before they would transfer me back. I have only four more months to go. I have no loving words for this boat, which looks like it's about to fall apart."

He took me down and showed me around. The WC was a room about three feet by two-and-a-half. It had a pile of cement with a hole in it for a toilet. Overhead was a pipe that hung down with a valve on it which served as a shower. A window on the side served as a doorway for mosquitoes. He took me next door to show me his facilities.

Seeing the look of disbelief on my face he said, "It's not much better but at least I have my own."

"How is the food?" I asked. "I experienced such abysmal food on the launch I don't want to be stuck with the same rubbish for the next ten days."

"Let's say the food is average," he said, "I'm hoping that will answer your question." It did. Average had to be better than what the last launch had served me.

At lunch I found a new set of guests. The two schoolteachers only ate at the hotel. They were wise enough not to stay there. The meal was good as usual. They even had filtered water. I didn't want to ask what it was filtered through. One thing that struck me about all the places I had eaten in Colombia, especially this place, was the complete lack of any cleanliness. Even the plates were filthy, the glasses were so dirty I couldn't see through them and the silverware usually still had the food from the day before left on it. The chickens, dogs, etc., ran around under the table, picking up the crumbs. Eating and sleeping spoke well for my strong immune system. Other than a slight dysentery and cold in Bogotá I remained in even better health than before I began the journey.

At the police station I told the chief, "Capitán Dorán sent me."

"I'm sorry. I can't do anything about visas." He dug in and got a letter from his commander in another city. "You can see it says here I can do nothing about visas. There is a consulate at Leticia for the U.S. so go straight there when you arrive." He evidently spoke good English because he read my passport instruction in English with perfect translation. One wonderful thing about the Colombians I met; they did not insist on speaking English once they saw I could speak Spanish. Usually, all the people of the other countries I had been insisted on speaking English even if they only spoke a few words.

INTO THE VOID

After I returned to my room I again had to fight to keep the children out. I was loudly and rudely made aware for the fiftieth time of one child who incessantly screamed at the top of his voice until he predictably got his way. I have heard many children cry but never one that could scream as loud as this one. He would screech every fifteen minutes, lasting for at least five minutes per shriek. As my room had only partial walls he may as well have been in my room.

The afternoon was the clearest I had seen since leaving the Dominican Republic. There wasn't a cloud in the sky.

Diego told me he had decided to go back, pick up his wife, and move on to Bogotá. I told him I felt this was probably the best thing because he could find jobs in other larger cities from there. There was more work to be found in Cali, Medellín, and Barranquilla than in Bogotá. Going to Leticia would have meant it would have been at least another two months before he could see his wife again.

I did have to watch everything but not from stealing. The children grabbed things while I was cleaning lenses and camera and have a fingerprint on the lens before I could grab their arm. I had to check everything before I closed the bag to see that none of the children still had it in his or her hand. There was absolutely no discipline in the family. The children ran the house. Wherever one of them wanted to relieve themselves no attempt was made to stop them. I never heard the word "No" and don't think the children had ever heard it either. I never witnessed a spanking, if ever there was one. The fathers seemed a bit stricter in speech than their American counterparts but the mothers seemed to spoil their children.

That evening my room was again filled with people. I tried to remove some film, which had broken off its sprocket the day before, but every time I tried someone would open the door and come in. I had to open the camera under a blanket at night as all the light of the hotel (all 25 volts) flooded in my room over the short walls. Although the electricity was only about equal to candlelight it was enough to affect color film if exposed to it. Finally, my room was about filled with people, watching me try to wind the film under a blanket. I finally got the film all rolled and found someone had run off with the lens cap, so I had to substitute foil.

Everyone was full of questions. Do you know the two "misters" (I hate that name) who were here last month?"

"No, I never heard of them."

"One was real tall. Both of them work for a zoological company in the United States. One was a Colombian and the other was an American who couldn't speak Castillano."

I asked, "Could he speak Castillano before they left?"

"After the month was over he spoke perfect Castillano."

They were, of course, surprised I didn't know them—their being from the States and all. They did not leave me alone before it was time to go to bed so again I wrote nothing in my diary.

The next morning I got up bright and early. I had become accustomed to the noise, making sleep impossible past 6:00. However, in this hotel there was no sleeping at all. Radios blasted loudly until late at night. The ear-piercing child howled at diverse hours during the night. By four o'clock the other children were all up and yelling. Added to the incessant noise during the night was the most uncomfortable cot I had ever slept on. Not only was the mattress harder than the floor but also I swear there was a block of wood hidden in the pillowcase. I awoke sore all over. Three mosquitoes found their way into my mosquito net. I couldn't get them out so they bit me at intervals all night long. I am sure they retired for life after that night.

The beautiful day I had hoped for was not yet there that morning. It rained all night and was still raining. At breakfast the proprietor came to me with my missing lens cap, which one of her children had brought to her.

I started to go on over to see when the boat was going to leave but the rain got so thick I couldn't see. I waited and waited under a shelter for it to lighten a little and watched the road turn into a mud slough. Mr. Rosa came by and said the boat would probably leave the next day. I ran from shelter to shelter waiting for it to clear up so I could get back to my room. After about another half-hour I gave up and darted through the rain. This constant rain was unusual. When it rained hard it generally cleared up within at least a half-hour. I went back to the room and started writing in the diary again. I now had everybody trained so they only came in when the door was open. The only trouble was there was no window so it was fairly stuffy and hot in the room with the door closed.

I didn't do much in the evening except hope the boat would leave the next day as the child ceaselessly bellowed all day long and his shrill lasted until 11:00 p.m., and periodically during the night. All I could think of was that I was glad it was only costing four pesos a day. I had had to cash a check that day and had taken a big loss on it.

I awoke the next morning to the screams of the spoiled child joined by the yelling of others, etc. at 5:00 a.m. The alarm clock I bought in Curaçâo was a waste of money. I didn't need it.

The Señora came in and asked, "There is one favor I want to ask you before you leave. She led me across the street to a storage place. There was a refrigerator with the door partially open. She said the latch wouldn't work. I started taking it apart to fix it and found the spring to be strong when it smashed the latch against my finger. I worked on it for about a half-hour and finally fixed it.

The children followed me into my room. As I packed I had to swiftly grab something out of one child's hand, turn around and quickly grab something else out of one of the others. I turned around and saw one of them was peeing on my floor. The women laughed outrageously, but I failed to see the humor. My room was a mess. I finally got everything safely out of their reach and in the bag. The mother wanted me to take a picture of them and send her a copy. I didn't want anything to remind me of them, as well as being rationed to three pictures a day, so I tried to dissuade her, telling her I couldn't send her a copy for six months. "Oh, that's all right. I don't mind," she answered. I managed to get out of it by delaying.

Dugout canoes. The main mode of travel on the Putumayo. They are made from burning out the middle of a large log and carving out the interior. They will sink if inundated with water.

I was beginning to feel like W. C. Fields, who always portrayed an older man who hates children. Actually. I loved children; I was just not accustomed to what I perceived to be a complete lack of discipline or respect.

I went out to the kitchen to pay the landlady. I asked her how much and started to get the 12 pesos ready. She said, "Thirty pesos." I was astounded. I mentioned my friend had paid about half this and asked why she was charging me more. I gave it to her and told her that if that was what she wanted to charge me I guess I had to pay it. She told me to wait a minute, got three pesos off a man sitting at a table, and paid that to me. I felt that was a rather feeble compromise and just took it and left without even a thank-you. I got my bags and brought the key and lock to her. She had a somewhat guilty look on her face. On the way out I checked to see what the others were paying. I found they were paying eight pesos. She was charging me only two more pesos than everyone else. I know it is impolite to complain like I had at several hotels, but if I didn't do that I would ruin it for other Americans who followed me. This double-price system for Americans starts from people paying inflated prices without asking questions.

6. DOWN THE RIVER TO THE AMAZON

I grabbed my bags and headed for the boat. The rain had deepened the mud and made the riverbanks even sloppier than before, as I slid down them to the boat and carried them up the plank to the third class passenger department. The pig was noisily eating its dinner. I saw a couple of workers there and asked them if the boat was leaving on time. My heart sank when they called back that it wasn't scheduled to leave for another day. I did not want to spend another night in Leguízamo so I ran to the office to make sure this was correct. The chief assured me it would definitely leave that night. Mendes came in and said it would leave at 5:00 p.m., definitely by 6:00. I was greatly relieved.

I remembered a rather strange looking pet near one hut the owner called Lulle. I learned later it was a Capybara, the largest rodent in the world. I had seen it wandering around town so I knew it must be someone's pet. I inquired around to find its owner so I could take its picture. I finally found the owner and she ran out in back and enticed it out with some food. It was the funniest looking animal I had ever seen. People told me the Capybara play with the children. They used them for house pets although they resemble pigs in some ways, but they seemed to be as clean as dogs. However, their bristles were as brittle as a pig's.

Capybara, largest rodent in the world, about the size of a small pig. Docile and playful.

I got on the boat, sat on a bench, and started writing in my diary. Capitán Gonzales was hopping from one place to another, obviously drunk. It wasn't too long before the boat was preparing to leave. People were beginning to gather on the shore. Other than the Cañon (Colombian naval vessel), which plied up and down the river at uncertain intervals, this was the only boat out of Puerto Leguízamo every six weeks.

The first-mate, whom I had met the day before, got on and told me Mendes was fixing sleeping quarters for me. Mr. Rosa got on and wished me a good trip. I wished him luck in getting back to the States.

There was a large crowd of about fifty people standing on the shore to see us off. The boat tooted its whistle and we slowly inched our way into midstream. We soon passed the Cañoneros, which made up the Colombian fleet (and which Perú could probably have crushed in two seconds with the three submarines and six battleships the U.S. had given her). The third class passengers slung their hammocks on the barge we were pushing. It cost about the same as first class on the paddle wheeler as it did to go third class, but it only took four to six days to go to Leticia where the paddle wheeler made the voyage in ten to fifteen.

Narrow passage on the Putumayo. Tile pipes on barge in front of our boat is destined for sewage system being introduced in Leticia.

The old sternwheeler picked up the first load of wood at about 10:00 a.m. At about 4:00 a.m. we stopped again for wood. I felt these two times would be enough to supply us for a while but we stopped again that afternoon and again that evening. As each load took about two to four hours to be hand carried on board I began to wonder whether we were traveling or loading more. I asked Capitán Ballestas if this wasn't enough wood to hold us for a while. He said, "Naw, this boat eats a lot of wood."

One of the passengers came over and began conversing with me. "I'm a traveling merchant."

I asked, "How do you go about your work?"

"I have my goods on the ship." He took me around to the side, opened the door and there, spread all over the room, was about everything anyone could want: pens, knives, machetes, writing paper, medicines, gum, candy, shoes, etc. He pulled out a bottle of liquor. My first thought was, "Oh, here we go again!" He offered me a drink and I politely refused. He kept insisting and I finally took a sip hoping that would satisfy his perseverance. I had yet to learn the second sip was more difficult to refuse than the first. Once I took the first sip they would practically force me to take a second drink. After his fiftieth time of offering me a second drink I told him it was against the principals of my religion and I had only taken the first sip so I wouldn't offend him. I would have been delighted to share a glass of wine with him, but I was careful with whom I shared drinks; it kept me out of trouble. Gomez rambled on, "There were two Americans on the boat last month. One of them drank a lot but wasn't very smart. The other one drank very little and was very smart. The one who drank a lot ate very little but the other one ate a lot."

Huts along Río Putumayo

He then plunged into the topic of religion. He asked me, "Are you an Evangelist (a dirty word in Colombia)? There are many religions in the world. All have faith in God. One religion cannot claim it has a monopoly on God. The Indians are called atheists because they don't believe in God. Yet they can walk through fire and do many other things through their faith." What differed in my conversation with Gonzales was his willingness to step out of the constraints of religious dogma into philosophy.

I mentioned, "My mother taught me to rely on God for my good health, a healthy mind is a healthy body. I know my thinking is what makes it so. I am responsible for everything in my life and when I perceive it at its highest level, harmony and joy become my way of life."

He said, "No one has a monopoly on the Bible and the Bible is for everyone."

When I was a child we lived in a Catholic neighborhood. My father cautioned me religion and politics were something I never should discuss with anyone. Here I was, in the most Catholic of all countries I had experienced. They had just been freed from the forbidden fruit of discussing either politics or religion other than what had been a state religion, and nearly every conversation turned to politics and religion. I never initiated either topic, but found the Colombians to be like escaped prisoners of conscience enjoying their newborn freedom. This was not true of all the people. Perhaps it was because some felt free with a foreigner to express themselves without restraint, or because being with a non-Catholic aroused their curiosity to investigate new thought they could not find among their own constrained beliefs.

I could see the others were shying away from becoming involved with our conversation. It was against the law to talk against the Catholic Church before Rojas Pinilla was removed from power. This happened so recently I found most Colombians reluctant to take advantage of their new freedom as there was still quite a bit of intolerance left over from the Rojas regime.

Gonzalez continued, "The two Americans who were on the last trip were interesting. One had a jar with poison in it and went around the deck catching insects. They caught animals and were doing other zoological work. One had a paper where he copied all the names, information on pictures, etc. They told me they were going to work in Leticia."

I kept trying to get away from Gonzales as he droned on and on, slurring his words as he sipped from his bottle. The first-mate and Mendes were both drunk as well. "Are you planning on eating in the screened-in dining room or upstairs?"

Peruvian village along Río Putumayo

"No, my passage is for eating downstairs," I said.

"It's only a peso more a day to eat upstairs."

To which I gleefully replied, "If that's the case I'd like to eat upstairs."

However, when I asked the labor chief about this he told me it would be five pesos a day. Gonzalez lit into the chief, "It is only

$4.50 — that $5.00 was for the privileged who eat with me. He continued babbling his argumentative dialogue with the labor chief as the labor chief kept trying to get away. The chief finally managed to get away after about a ten-minute dressing down by the drunken Gonzalez. This accomplished nothing but it put an end to whatever rapport I had with the chief. He was quite gruff with me and never again befriended me after that.

Gonzalez raved endlessly about what great friends we were. He addressed me, as what I thought was "camarote." Camarote is the word they used for a bed in one of the rooms on the ship. I figured I'd better get that settled immediately, so I told him I didn't understand what he was talking about. He went into a long explanation. After the third explanation I could see we were getting no closer to an understanding so I acted as though I understood everything, in order to stave off any further explanations. I was finally saved from a seventh explanation by the call to dinner. I eventually found he was addressing me as "comerade", which is comrade.

The ship's passengers consisted of two young ladies from Leguízamo, a woman with her daughter and me. Gonzalez ate with us rather than with Mendes because it was cheaper. The food wasn't bad and the tablecloth was clean. My only complaint was all we had to drink was "agua de panela." Fortunately it was not heated which made it somewhat palatable.

The second day I noticed the bottom deck was filled to the brim with wood. This gave me a satisfying feeling because I figured they couldn't get any more wood on board. The most uncomfortable time was when we stopped for more wood, with oppressive heat accompanied by thick layers of mosquitoes, I mentioned this to Mendes and he said to my dismay, "Oh, we've still got the two barges we're pushing to fill yet."

That day a 12-year-old boy sat next to me and began a very intelligent discussion about trade in the area, the various values of the currencies of Brazil, Perú, and Colombia and the aspects of the area in which we were traveling. I was amazed to be having such a scholarly conversation with such a young man so I asked him about his background.

"My mother lives in Iquítos; my father left my mother a long time ago and moved to Puerto Leguízamo, where he married another woman. I took a boat from Iquítos to Leticia, a journey of about three days and then caught the Ciudád Neiva to Puerto

Leguízamo, which took about twenty-five days. I had a short visit with my father and now I'm going back to Iquítos to be with my mother. This is the first time I have seen my father I can remember."

I guessed such experiences had made him mature for his age. He had only been over this area once and yet seemed to know more about it than nine-tenths of the crew. I usually found Colombians to be very nice and seemed to have much interest in their surroundings. I noticed the boy had a sort of whining accent. He sounded as though he was whining all the time he talked. However, I have heard that same accent from many of the natives of the villages in the rainforests of Peru where Spanish is their second language.

All the women on board were named María except one, and that was because her sister was named María. One María was a young girl of about eighteen. She reminded me of a butterfly, flitting and flirting with every man in sight. She was traveling with another María, about nineteen or twenty years old and much more levelheaded. She was no less flirtatious, but it was obvious she knew how to handle herself. Both girls spent a majority of their time reading romance comic books. Another María was a woman of about thirty-four who had a daughter accompanying her. She rarely stopped to take a breath in her conversations. What made this most grating was when she didn't talk, she yelled, mostly at her daughter. Even that yelling was only for a short break in her endless conversations with the passengers and crew on the boat. This left only Gonzalez, the only remaining passenger. He ran a concession on board, selling goods to the passengers and the Indigenous living along the river banks. It was obvious he felt himself to be a failure because he was constantly making excuses for it. He anaesthetized this with strong drink. He made a consistent unsuccessful drive to conquer one of the two young girls. They rather enjoyed the attention and made sure their "no" was not emphatic enough to scare him away.

The complete change of weather was blissful since we crossed the equator. There was only one completely cloudy or rainy day and that was one day in Puerto Leguízamo. Intermittent showers, which usually passed over us in the late afternoon, were refreshing. Mornings were clear. At noon billowy clouds began to form in the distance. By late afternoon sun-rimmed clouds thickened in the distance, and I could observe them creeping closer and closer, finally blotting out the horizon with a thick soup of drenching rain. A pleasant cool breeze buffered us from the humid heat of the jungle.

After dinner I settled down in the dining room and got ready to put my hammock up. Mendes's maid, who wanted to iron some clothes, passed by and began eying the dining room. I could see this was the only table on the boat so told her to come on in and do her ironing.

After a couple of minutes we heard a great commotion on the deck. I looked out and saw Gonzalez coming in. We could see Mendes wrestling with one of the women passengers who was dressed in nightclothes. Every fifteen seconds Gonzales peeked out to see what was happening and give us a report on the progress to the maid who just smiled as she kept ironing. Soon the woman started crying. Gonzalez complained he couldn't figure it out as he had offered a price and she had refused him (it seemed to be common to offer a price to any girl you met). It soon became evident the woman was not in the best of health. Several people rushed her into the room and pumped sedatives into her. Gonzales, drunker than ever, continued ranting and raving, even though no one was paying any attention to him. Everyone on the boat was crowded around the little door offering his or her comments. It was not long before we discovered she was three-months pregnant. Gonzales really had a fit when he learned that. He ran all over the boat, ranting and raving, "I don't want any problems on my boat. I'm going to put her off at the first port I get to."

It was obvious to all of us he couldn't accomplish that, as there was no town of more than a few huts for ten days and no transportation to get her out. I was trying to get the whole story but the accent made it so I could only comprehend about half of what was said. This frustrated me to only understood bits and pieces of sentences following an extended conversation.

One of the women ran all over the boat, telling everyone, "When I was pregnant I went everywhere without any trouble."

It took hours before everyone quieted down, especially Mendes. Once they were gone, Gonzalez went in to conquer one of the other girls with no luck whatsoever.

I finally got my hammock up and the last person left the dining room. I found the night very refreshing. I really began to wonder where all the droves of mosquitoes were that everyone talked about. I found a few in Puerto Leguízamo but they were more a bother to me than the onslaught I had been led to expect.

I found it impossible to get any sleep on the boat, as the boat frequently stopped to load more firewood. Each time the boat stopped it took from two to four hours to load the leña (firewood). I woke abruptly when the boat stopped for the second time in the morning. Each time two thousand splits of wood were loaded by hand. The Natives who lived in villages along the river cut the wood for their livelihood. I could see why Colombia converted the boats to burn wood, to offer at least some means of support for the Indigenous peoples. They chopped wood for about two weeks to accumulate about four thousand and sometimes six thousand pieces of wood. This they piled in stacks, waiting for the boats. The sticks that covered the bottom enabled them to count the wood. Ten more sticks were stacked in the other direction on top, etc. until they had a stack of something like a hundred. The stacks were counted and a certain price was paid for each hundred sticks of wood. The Indians then came on deck during the loading to buy things at outrageous prices from Gonzalez and another dealer that was on the boat selling beer, gasseosas (a very gassy soda) and clothes (mostly khakis).

For breakfast we had Quaker Oats (they must have had the rainforest market sewed up), rice and some fish. The conversations at the table filled in the gaps in last night's happenings. I learned that the troubled girl had a husband in Puerto Leguízamo and had snuck on board with her sister to go to Leticia. No one seemed to know why. Mendes finally calmed down enough to let them work their passage to Leticia.

The second day of the trip from Leguízamo I was awakened at 5:00 a.m. by the squeal of the pig, which was housed on the barge. His cries for mercy grew louder and louder until they finally ceased at 6:00 a.m. At 7:00 a.m. it was of little surprise when at breakfast I was greeted by fresh bacon.

The dried fish was the most revolting I had ever eaten. It tasted like a block of salt. The rice was fried and fried and fried until it was so dry it was completely void of flavor. Plátino was a very dry type of banana, which was about as flavorful as biting into a cube of starch. Yucca was a dry, stringy plant, which was used only for flour in the more civilized parts of Latin America.

The third day we coasted down a little further, stopping to pick up more wood at regular intervals, which by this time filled the entire bottom of the boat from deck to overhead, as well as both of the barges. The mosquitoes, which had been surprisingly scarce during the first part of the journey, began to appear, but thicker than anything were the little creatures the natives called "mosquitoes", not to be confused with our mosquitoes. It looks like a flea but infected me with every bite. By this time I had blood spots all over my arms and legs. I'd never seen anything so vicious. There was no escaping him or her because they poked through all protective clothing or cover.

I still couldn't find any two people who agreed where we were. I ran around with map in hand trying to orient myself. Even when we'd pass by a cluster of huts each person would give it a different name, ninety percent of them not even listed on my map. At the end of the day we arrived at a little Indian village that was on the map, Aríca.

The fourth day out we were sure the pig was finished. However, our plates came in piled with erect ears, hair still intact. The pieces I had I easily recognized as the ear lobe, clear down to the eardrum and another piece was the tip of an ear. Others had the nose, cheeks, and other such delectable parts, also with hair still intact. I could not hide the disgust I felt when I spotted the hairs in the ear lobes standing erect in my plate. I started extracting the hair from each piece as I cut it. I finally found this too vast a task. Gonzalez saw my consternation so he quietly mentioned, "You're not supposed to extract the hairs. That's the best part." I went back to my eating and found cooked hair wasn't that bad. About halfway through the meal one of the girls suddenly excused herself before she had even finished eating the nose.

As the water of the Putumayo is dirtier than the Mississippi (more like the Missouri) the water was run through a filter. As they never cleaned the filter the water was as dirty after being filtered as before. To mask the dirty water they made it into what they called "agua de panela." This is done by taking the brackish tasting juice from cinnamon and squeezing it into the water (through an old dirty cloth). This changes the water to yellow and gives it a taste something like petroleum with sugar in it and a smell about the same.

Mendes kept mentioning to me I could buy a monkey small enough to put in my pocket for five pesos. I felt this would be a good thing to have for the trip so I began looking around as we came to each village. The first day we found no such animal.

Soon, everyone was helping me look for a pocket-sized monkey. We ran up to one hut and asked if they had anything to sell. They said they just had "farina." I had never heard of this before so I didn't ask for any. About a half-hour later the girls came out with a saltine can full of the driest powder I had ever tasted. It was tasteless, crunchy and about broke my teeth when I bit into it. It is made of dried yucca and is a favorite of the Indians. They use it for sprinkling over their food and chew on it during the day as an appetizer. It is called "farina."

The coming of the boat is a big event because it is the only contact the indigenous have with the outside world. It was also their only means of support. It took about three weeks to chop the wood. They sold this, along with anything else extra they night have. Some venders plied the river, trading with the villages, but they were few and far between.

Someone came running to the boat and said they had monkeys for sale. I got off and ran up the hill. One of the Indians said he had some that could fit in a pocket. I asked him how much they were and he tried to evade the question. I finally got him to name a price. He said, "Twenty pesos but they are wonderful!!! Sits in your pocket and looks out."

I told him I wouldn't pay that as others were selling them for five pesos. I looked to the ship's mate to help me but he just said that was a good price for that type of monkey. I finally got the villager down to 10 pesos, with no help from the mate. Full grown it was about five inches long. The natives called it "leoncito" (little lion) because it had the face of a lion. Its big eyes poked out through the mange covering its face. I stuffed it into my pocket and it actually did fit, with its paws holding the top edge and face looking out. It made no noise most of the time—just sat in my pocket, watching every movement around me. They are highly valued by the people as pets and very rare. I only saw two on the entire descent down the Río Putumayo. It was accustomed to travel on the back of a person and would crawl up there if I put it on my arm. However, this one was not housebroken. To get around this the natives usually tied a soft piece of cloth around its waist, tight but not too tight. A string was tied to this for a leash and they didn't have to worry about whether they pulled it too hard. The main concern was keeping the animal warm. These little monkeys are very fragile and my little pet nearly froze to death coming up the Amazon, as the wind was quite cool at night. In the U.S. they are called marmosets.

The Indian who sold me the monkey was quite talkative and expressive, much different than any others I had met. When he named his price, he said, "You're the captain of the boat, aren't you?" I told him I wasn't and he went on talking about the wonders he had seen, even though it probably covered no more than to Iquitos and back. He was completely enthralled with the riches of Iquítos, the people there, and the financial remuneration from the work. He worked on a boat for a while.

I looked at his hut on a small hill overlooking the river and said, "You are probably better off in the middle of the jungle than working on a boat, from what I have seen of the life as a worker on one of the boats."

He quickly retorted, "I'm not so sure about that. I'm never sure of my meals from one day to the next here. The only contact I have with the outside world is this boat which plies the river, passing here once every month-and-a-half. The boys of this village work three weeks to cut enough lumber to sell to the boat. This is their only means of livelihood. Occasionally they sell something else like a monkey, a few bananas, some dried yucca or maybe a hen or two. On the voyage upstream we can sell the dried and stretched skins from the hogs we've killed." These, unlike the food products, could eventually find their way to the more industrialized parts of the country or the international market.

The boat was too undependable to carry fruit or meat to the markets, principally because the boat had no refrigeration (aside from a little gas refrigerator Mendes had). There was also the problem of even being able to sell anything on the boat as the boat picked up food and supplies at random as it went along. As each unit was self-sufficient they couldn't sell anything to each other aside from some extra fish they caught, a few bananas, etc.

All the Indians mistook my Spanish for a Bogotá accent. Even though I talked with the monkey salesperson for a half-hour I think he still thought I was from Bogotá after I left. He again asked, "You said you were the captain of the boat?"

"No, I'm not."

"Are you sure you aren't the captain?"

I pointed to the boat and said, "The captain is the little man in pajamas running around on the top deck."

"Where are you from?" he continued.

"I'm from the United States," I answered.

"Is that near Bogotá?" he said in all seriousness.

I began to realize I must see the world through the eyes of people who had no concept of the breadth of the world—what is big, what is modern and even what a city looks like. As the United States moves closer to empire building and a power never invested in any nation before, our news media ignores, for the most part, what we look like from the eyes of the civilians dodging our bombs, watching their houses being destroyed and being deprived of a living. We tend to see people with myopic vision formed by our religious beliefs and fear of the unfamiliar. If we could stand in the shoes of the many civilians whose only crime is being in the wrong place at the wrong time, we would find fewer enemies and experience a more peaceful world. The question we need to constantly ask ourselves is, "What do we look like to other peoples and nations? Have we walked a mile in another's moccasins before we judged them?"

I went up to see the rest of the town and ran into an army camp. One of the soldiers stopped me to ask me questions about the boat just as I was stopping him to ask him about the town.

I asked, "Are you with the police or army of Colombia? Your uniform is different."

He laughed, "This is the Army of Perú." It was then I learned the boat crew had even told me the wrong side for Perú and Colombia.

"Are you from Bogotá?"

"No, I'm from the United States."

He looked a bit surprised to see an American there. The tiny monkey remained standing in my pocket, observing everything around as I again boarded the boat. Everyone assured me I had a rare pet and that other small monkeys die but this type was stronger than the other small species.

The river suddenly opened up, becoming wider, more like what I was expecting. Islands began to form and it began to appear like the description I had of the Amazon. We could not figure out whether we were at Puerto Arturo or Eré. "We passed it last night," said the captain. "No, we won't pass it until tonight," chimed another. I had taken a photograph of a good-sized village but finally left it without a name in case National Geographic would accept it. Mendes said we would arrive at Aríca that night. When I asked if it was of any size, he said, "Naw, just another three huts." He was rather disgusted with his new assignment and was looking forward to the day he would return to the Magdalena.

The girls went into a small store run by a boy called "Lindo" (translation: pretty). His charm sold them every sort of useless thing he had in the store—golf caps and men's shirts. The girls ran ashore at every stop along the way and found new men on shore to flirt with.

Mendes kept himself well up in hot beers, always attired in pajamas. Gonzalez also kept himself inebriated with his tonic, which had a licorice taste. This kept him unusually well humored (except in the mornings) and gave him the extra strength he needed to chase María.

The late afternoon of the fourth day we finally arrived at Arίca. Mendes was right, there were barely more than three huts. I was about to photograph it when I was informed the boat didn't stop there because we didn't need any wood.

We arrived at Puerto Alfonso either during the night or early morning, having had to fight off the mosquitoes again when we stopped for wood. All during the trip we had been safe at night because the only thing that bothered us was the "mosquito", which bites during the day but sleeps at night. At this point we ran into what we would call a mosquito but what the natives called sancuro. It bites only at night and rests during the day. I put the mosquito net over the hammock to keep the mosquitoes out. At about five in the morning I found a couple of mosquitoes inside with me. I fought them off and felt I had gotten rid of them. Outside the net was the deafening buzz of a million mosquitoes. I could feel hundreds of them biting my back but was confident they couldn't do that because I was lying on my back and had the hammock and blanket folded underneath to protect me from their proboscis. I felt my back and it was all welts from one side to the other. I looked inside and couldn't find any mosquitoes. I then lifted the net and looked under the hammock. The bottom was just one black cloud of them covering the bottom of the hammock.

"There were millions of mosquitoes on my back, piercing even through the padding I tucked underneath me for protection," I mentioned to the mate as he passed by me."

"Oh, that type of mosquito has a proboscis that is unusually long and can bite through almost anything," was his answer. I was very happy when I heard the boat whistle and the engine started again.

I went back to take a shower and found the shower was still full of mosquitoes. After about an hour's airing in the wind the dining room was free of them. I went back about an hour later and found the shower was out of water. I decided to wait it out and went back after another hour. By this time we were heading to shore again for wood. This meant another long wait, as the shower didn't run while the boat was stopped. Every time I wanted to take a shower the water was either not running, we were on shore, we were headed for shore, or it was occupied. Having one shower for all the passengers was extremely inadequate, especially since it wasn't operating most of the time. I wasn't sure the shower took water off the body or put dirty water back on. My clothes never looked the least bit clean after I washed them. I was told we would arrive at Tarapacá at the Brazilian border that night.

"Why is the boat just barely creeping along?" I asked one of the officers.

"The motor is broken and we will have to repair it tonight at Tarapacá," was his answer.

"Will it take long to fix it?" I asked.

"It'll probably take all night."

I winced as this meant another delay. We were making such excellent time that it looked as though we would make it to Leticia in ten days.

We hobbled along with the broken engine and I began to wonder if we would make it by that night. That afternoon the boat pulled off to the side and rested against some tall grass. They had to work on the engine to get it to go further. The girls found a boy with a canoe and went off for a ride. I dove into the river but swimming was difficult because of the fast current. It seemed the current was equal to my swimming speed so it took all my strength just to keep even with the beached boat.

As I came up on deck they told me, "The delfines are swimming out there with you.

"What's a delfín?" I asked.

"It is a long fish with a fin and shoots water." This sounded to me like a shark. I described a shark and he said, "That's it."

"What are sharks doing here?"

"They swim up the river every night."

"Do they harm many people?" No, they won't harm anyone unless they see blood." It wasn't until much later I learned I had been swimming with the dolphins.

The crew finally got the boat started. The river here was a series of very wide lakes and very narrow stretches between islands.

That afternoon I was writing in my diary when one of the girls came in and started making conversation. I knew something was up because this girl had never talked to me before. I waited for the hit and she finally said, "I have a problem." I could see this was just the beginning and braced myself for the rest of her story.

"I don't have enough money to get to Leticia, paying for the food and everything. Could you loan me Cr$2,000 until we get there?"

"How are you ever going to pay anyone back?" I asked.

"I have friends in Leticia," She said. "María and I are going there to look for work."

This failed to pull at my heartstring. I had been watching her buy too many silly little things to feel sorry. I told her I was completely broke and didn't know how I was going to pay for everything. That was just about true, too, because I had little cash. My expenses had been more than planned. Gonzalez offered to cash some of my checks at the ridiculously low price of six to the dollar when the Bogotá rate was Cr.$7.65 to the dollar. I was in no mood to have to cash at that rate. María could starve.

María then ran to "Lindo", who was nobody's fool either, and to Mendes, who was also nobody's fool, and finally made the rounds to everyone else with no success. I was sort of glad to see this, as it was obvious she had been very spoiled all her life and needed a challenge to wake her up to the fact that others exist in the world.

That night I was sitting on the bench on deck when the Peruvian boy sat beside me. He started talking about María and I mentioned she had friends at Leticia to give her money. "Oh yes," he said, "Her husband's in the Colombian Navy. They are traveling there to meet him." This was news to me because they were more than free with every man they met.

About ten o'clock we pulled into Tarapacá. This was the border town between Brazil and Colombia. It was historically significant because the Peruvians advanced all the way to that point during the war. This now forms the end of the Colombian Panhandle, which cuts down into Perú and Brazil to give Colombia a port on the Amazon at Leticia. It is only a short distance overland to Leticia but takes at least five days by boat.

The shore looked rather uninteresting in the dark. I was expecting a town but was told there was only an army camp there. There was a small town on the other side of the hill. It looked large after not having seen any town at all for five days.

The boat came close to shore and the girls stood anxiously on the barge getting ready to greet all the soldiers. The soldiers jumped on and within a minute the girls were surrounded. I went on shore but saw nothing worth seeing.

The mechanics started immediately working on the motor. The boat was blanketed with soldiers. You couldn't find a seat anywhere. Gonzalez grabbed me, as I started past. He had his bottle of licorice liquor and was trying to encourage me to drink with him. I told him again my religion forbade me to drink, which was really not true, but it sparked another long dissertation on religion. He ranted and raved about the evils of the Catholic Church and said, "We are all one religion. Everyone has his faith in something. The Communists believe in Communism, the Indians perform miracles with their faith and yet the Church calls them heathens. Everything is possible with faith—healings, physical handicaps overcome."

I cringed when he began these religious conversations, looking around to see others' reactions. I became increasingly concerned about the reaction of others to these loud conversations. I noticed they looked on shyly, listening to every word but trying to act as though they weren't participating in the conversation. I became increasingly embarrassed, as I well knew the terrible dictatorship Colombia had recently been which forbad criticizing the Catholic religion.

"I'm a Catholic," said Gonzalez, "but I am well aware of the terrible powers of my Church. I refuse to give it power or to let it act as a power over me. It wasn't so long ago I would be shot for talking like this. It was against the law to say anything against the Catholic Church. It is somewhat better now, but still people kill others for talking against the Church. The same goes for politics or other beliefs. If a man doesn't like you here he just goes in and ravishes all the women in the family and kills both them and the men. Whole families are getting butchered every day."

The inner turmoil I was feeling prompted me to ask, "Is the new political set-up any better now, and is it making an effort to improve the situation?"

"No, it's not doing much and things are only a little improved," was his non-empathic answer.

As the conversation switched to politics he stated he was a Liberal. I told him what a liberal was in our country and asked if that was the same in his country. He said it was. I then felt it was safe to reach into my belongings and pull out the picture of the Liberal candidate in Colombia (who was now President). On seeing this, Gonzalez ran over and embraced me, saying, "My friend, my friend." I mentioned this was a gift of a boy in Neiva and I never dared wear it since then, as the political situation was still so volatile.

When I told him I was a Liberal in the United States he had to drink to that. I went back and got him a hot beer and got myself and another passenger some hot soda. We had no sooner finished this than Mendes came stumbling by. He asked me to buy him a drink. Unfortunately this meant I would have to buy the entire gang a round of drinks, which would drain me of most of my cash.

Gonzalez mentioned religion again and Mendes chimed in, "Y'know. I'm very religush. Yes, I'm, very religush. I may get drunk, but y'know, every time before I start the boat I cross myself—yea, no matter how drunk I am I cross myself."

Someone butted in with, "Is this to vindicate you or save the ship?" That offended Mendes so he made a quick exit.

By 9:00 p.m. I was looking forward to putting up my hammock and going to bed. However, one of the women was using my traveling iron in the dining room so I waited. The noise got louder and louder and the number of soldiers grew rapidly. The girls had paired off and were busy entertaining their companions, sitting on my hammock, which they had set up in the back.

At midnight nothing had quieted down. Mendes was drunker than ever and so was everyone else. The woman was finally through with my iron so I went back to retrieve my hammock. The solders looked rather disgruntled when I asked them to move. I was so tired I fell asleep in spite of the noise. It was then about 1:00 a.m.

At about 4:00 a.m. I felt a bump on my hammock. Someone excused himself and I settled back again. Then the stranger said, "Would you care to have a beer with me?" I said, "No, thank you."

He then repeated louder, "Will you have a beer with me?" I again answered, "No, thank you."

He then said in broken English, "Will you have...a ... beer?" I again answered, "No, thank you."

He then said in English, "Will . . .you . . .have . . .a . . .beer?" By this time I figured my best bet was to not answer him. He continued, "I hate . . .American. I love to fight American." I said nothing as I figured it would only aggravate the situation. He repeated, "You . . . hear me? I say, I love to FIGHT American! Whatsa' matter, you chicken? Why you no fight me?" Again, I just lay there. It was pitch black out and I couldn't see my hand in front of my face. I was in no mood to fight a drunk, especially one I couldn't see.

After a few moments of silence he went on, "I'm Indian and I hate Americans. Do you hear me? I'm Indian, INDIAN, INDIAN!" I like to kill Americans. Raise your head. Raise it just once so I can smash it with my fist. I'm going to ram this knife right through you. Get up so I can kill you."

At this point I was scared for the first time since I was in Korea. I thought I had lost the power of fear but I was shaking so hard the hammock must have shown it. I lay there expecting a knife to come through the bottom of it any time. At last, whoever it was left the room. I tried to sleep but now found it impossible, adrenalin running high. I turned to prayer and really sought strength. The thought came to overcome fear with love. My first effort then was to fill my thinking with a love for everybody and everything. I must harbor no resentment against this man.

After a few minutes he returned. I stuck my head up and could see Gonzalez sticking his hand in the door. However, I couldn't see the other person. Gonzalez extracted his head in a minute and went on down the deck.

"I hear there is American on this ship. Where is he?" was the first phrase I heard. "I think American in this country is (bleep). American on this boat is (bleep). Do you hear me (bleep), (bleep) (bleep)? Are you a man or are you a mouse?"

I figured it was best not to fight as I thought I recognized the voice as an Indian who had come on boat with a machete and I was in no mood to raise my fists against a machete. He chided me some more and left.

I looked at my watch and it was close to 5:00 a.m. I then felt almost sure this must be some sort of a joke. I couldn't get back to sleep so got up and dressed. I walked to the back of the ship. On the way I passed the girls' room. There was a soldier sleeping in there. He looked very un-Indian to me. I smilingly mentioned there was someone on board who spoke a very good slang English. There was no response so I mentioned someone doesn't like Americans. This also brought no reply.

Finally one of the girls mentioned the soldier in the room had come down to my room a couple of times. I told her what happened.

"This man is the commander of this base. I saw him go down to your room and tried to stop him from going in because it was so early. He insisted on going, saying he wanted to drink with you. He came back in a little while and said, 'He doesn't know how to speak English.' He asked me why you didn't travel first class. You are American so you are supposed to have enough money to travel first class. After the second time he gave up and came back. He chased us girls out of our room and took one of our beds. We had no choice but to go back and shift for ourselves on the back deck."

As soon as the sun came up I went ashore to take pictures. This was the most beautiful land I had seen so far—all green pastureland. Everyone was only too anxious to tell me the history of the battle between Colombia and Perú. I asked them, wasn't it hard fighting in thick jungle?" They answered, "Our army fought hard!"

They never really mentioned how the war started or how they ever got the Peruvians out of there. I saw the great value for Colombia in having this extension, giving them a port on the Amazon but couldn't see why the Peruvians wanted it. When I asked that question once, their answer was, "Because Leticia is such a big town." I gathered from this Leticia must be a city.

When I returned to the boat the mate grabbed me by the hand and said, "I want to introduce you to the commander of the base." I was not anxious to meet him but couldn't break the grasp. The commander looked about as glad to meet me, as he was the night before. Someone proudly introduced me and he grunted an answer. I left, feeling I had done my duty in meeting him but felt more like punching him in the jaw.

I ran into Mendes's office and got my camera out of hock where it had been put for safekeeping. The hills looked so green it almost surprised me to see anything like this in the Amazon.

A few minutes later the commander came out, sat across from me and started to stare. He asked me a couple of questions, which I curtly answered and went on with my conversation. He finally retired to Mendes's quarters.

Mendes came up to me and blurted out, "Estás bravo, Carlos?" I was rather offended, as this seemed like, "Are you brave, Carlos?" When I ignored him he blurted out, "Estás bravo conmigo, Carlos?" I thought he was ridiculing me for not having fought the company commander the evening before. I was even more offended as he was a puny little character. I blurted out, "Of course I am," and left. A couple of minutes later he met me again and said, "Estás bravo, Carlos? Estás bravo conmigo?" By this time I was getting angry, as I was certain he was referring to my not fighting the commander. I kept ignoring him and he finally said he didn't think I understood him. I told him I understood well and asked, "Why do you keep on asking me this?"

He said, "Because I was so drunk last night."

I said, "I don't understand."

"I don't think you understand," he said. "When you say 'Estás bravo' to someone it means 'do you have confidence in them.' I was drunk and felt I was a bit gruff last night and was wondering if you still had confidence in me after all this."

I said, "Of course I do." He looked rather relieved. I told him, "I thought you were referring to my not fighting the commander last night."

"Fighting the commander? What for?" he answered. It was plain he didn't know what I was talking about so I told him the story. He looked amazed and went marching off to his quarters saying he was going to bawl the commander out. He was still rather drunk so I didn't feel there would be much telling off.

In a few minutes he came weaving back to me, shook a finger at me, and said, "I told the lieutenant he was a bad man and that he did the wrong thing. Yes, I told him he had done wrong. I just stood there and told him he aught to be ashamed for what he had done."

It was all I could do to keep from laughing. I thanked Mendes for doing his duty as captain of the boat.

I kept having to dive into Mendes's office to retrieve objects from my bags. Yet I couldn't take them back to where they were because the soldiers were still milling around. The lieutenant was sitting in Mendes's office groaning with pain from his morning after the night before. Mendes was still gulping down one beer after another so he wasn't feeling the after-effects of his drinking.

We finally went in to eat breakfast. Gonzalez hadn't slept at all so he looked the worst of all of us. I thought we were going to have to carry him away. I was so amused I couldn't help but laugh and the girls chimed in. All Gonzalez could manage was to flick the edge of his mouth in a general direction of a smile.

After breakfast things quieted down. I was told the engine was almost fixed and we would leave at 9:00 or 9:30. Sure enough, they tested the motor and we were off at 10:00.

Tarapacá is a good port. The river turns there and leaves a large cove, almost completely free from the current of the river. There was an old river steamer there just in case the one we were on broke down. We had to stop alongside it for a little while so a few of us went on board. I thought it was a much better boat than the Ciudad Neiva. It had a larger upper deck with a few compartments, a large dining room table with two big fans above it and a large buffet with a mirror behind it. I felt it gave more room to spread out, as we had to cling to the side decks on the Ciudád Neiva to get back and forth. Mendes and the mate told me our boat was much faster and when you add the total space on our boat it was more. Lindo had just embarked, and we sat down to a game which resembled our game of "Point Sorry", which we discovered in the buffet. I was just about to win when the whistle blew and we had to jump back to the other Ciudad Neiva.

Tarapacá, an army camp near Colombian border with Brazil. Río Putumayo becomes Río Içá.

We were supposed to arrive at the little Brazilian border town on the other side within an hour. After about two hours we came to one of the most beautiful little villages I had seen on the Río Putumayo. When we crossed the border the river changed names and was now the Içá (pr. Eesáh). The first painted villages I had seen were on this part of the river. I found the Brazilian propensity to paint their buildings white made them the prettiest villages in the Amazon area. The Colombians seemed to have an abhorrence to paint and therefore left the original mud or sticks showing.

Before we left Puerto Leguízamo we stopped at a place for leña (firewood). The hills, which are typical of the area around Tarapacá, were especially steep. We climbed up to the Indian hut that dominated the area. This was the most interesting of all the huts I had seen. It was not only the largest but also very well taken care of and very typical, and the woman was doing some cooking. One of the workers was interested in a parrot they had to sell. It was the meanest parrot I had ever seen. It screamed and scolded as we neared it, then flew as far as its wings would let it. The worker took off after it. By the time he got it back the family was about to sell it for nothing just to get rid of it. He went off with it screaming and biting him every chance it could.

Kitchen in hut. Hut in back is for cooking.

The helmsman, who was Indian, came up and started joking around with the family in their native dialect. The Indians would grin a little but seldom openly laughed.

Indian woman making cassava bread from the yucca plant. The cassava is wound in the far straw thatched item. She is using a stone mallet to crush the powder. It is then flattened on a sort of pizza pan and baked in the enclosed cooking hut in back.

Most of the house was open; a large hammock was the only furniture besides a bench. The family spent the day out here looking over the Putumayo and enjoying the cool breeze that swept over the hill. There were a few banana trees, some yucca, and a couple of other trees. They could easily walk out and pick the fruit from their trees. The woman of the house was making cassava bread. The mate ordered some of it so I got to see the total process of making it. The yucca plant was sort of like a gourd. Its contents were opened out into a wooden trough and some water poured in. Then the dough was meshed into the water band and left to soak. When she wished to make bread she took straw matting down from where it was hanging on the wall, alongside other kitchen utensils. The yucca was poured into this and the straw matting wrapped around it. There was a rope around this, which tightened it when twisted. The matting was rolled so it formed a funnel, narrower at one end than the other. She twisted the rope tightly until just about all the water was squeezed out. She then took this and shaped it into a large pancake. She took this back to a large kitchen straw hut in the back, shaped like a beehive to draw all the smoke out the top, and set it on the fire. The kitchen hut was dirt floor and rather barren. It was roomy so she could move around but had no furniture, just some handmade kitchen utensils and four stones to support whatever she was cooking under which she built the fire. The bread took about twenty minutes to cook; the result was a large, very thin pancake-shaped bread. It was very hard, rather tasteless, and crunchy to chew. However, it could be rather good after one acquired a taste for it.

I went back into the kitchen and asked to take a picture. She looked rather surprised that I would want to take a picture of such a dark disheveled place but granted permission. I was preparing to take the picture when the girls yelled to me, "The boat is leaving."

Unbeknownst to me, this same year a woman named Nicole Maxwell had obtained a small grant from a drug company and made a special expedition to obtain samples of many of the medicinal plants. She spent twelve years there after a visit with friends in Ecuadór. One day, hacking their way through the jungle, she received a deep machete gash on her arm. She worried she might bleed to death or die from infection. Her guide ran into the jungle and hacked some dark-red tree sap, called Sangre de Drago, urging her to drink it. The bleeding stopped within minutes and healed rapidly without any scarring. Her guide told her there were many plants used by the natives to prevent tooth decay, painlessly extract teeth, dissolve kidney stones, heal burns and cure or prevent scores of other maladies. More than half of all plant and animal species on Earth reside in the rainforest, but an estimated 100 species are lost to extinction every day.

She asked the natives about the secrets of healing plants but found most of the curadores (healers) secretive about their information, which was passed from generation-to-generation by word of mouth. It dawned on her that every curador who died without training another was a library of information destroyed. Realizing much of this information was being lost to humanity she began cataloguing many of the plants. Most Indigenous in the Amazon are no longer aware of the healing properties of the plants that surround them. If they ever were aware of the healing power of these plants, a curador had died and taken those secrets with him.

Nicole gained the confidence of the tribes and was able to extract a great deal of this information from them. She lived to be 92 and made a trip to the Amazon with John Easterling when she was 84. Easterling, who is known as Amazon John, has made numerous trips to the Amazon, has partnered with a growing number of Indigenous tribes and built a sizeable business, Amazon Herb Company which has formulated many of these herbs under the direction of a consortium of doctors. John, like Nicole, was introduced to the herbs through weathering his own health crisis. His original intuition had told him he was looking for lost gold in the Amazon, which led him to form a company, Raiders of the Lost Art, which imported crafts from the Amazonian tribes. During those years he developed a close friendship with several of the Tribes. He had been weakened over a number of years with Hepatitis C and before one of his trips he was hospitalized, had compromised his liver and acquired Rocky Mountain Spotted Fever. While on a buying trip at one of the villages he became so weak he could barely move. The people urged him to lie in a hammock while they boiled some tea. Within several weeks he felt free of the debilitating effects of hepatitis. Within six weeks he felt even better than he had before he contracted hepatitis, ten years prior. He told himself, "I think I've found my gold."

As John's herbal business, The Amazon Herb Company, expanded he asked the tribes who were then partners in his business what they would like most. They said they would like solar operated short wave radios so they could communicate with other tribes. He took some of their leaders to Lima so they could register their land. It was the first time they had ever owned any land. Before John's healing the tribe was about to sign an agreement with the lumber companies due to their desperate needs. Fortunately they did not sign that agreement and are now operating computers, and many neighboring tribes have shown an interest in joining them in John's joint venture.

Since the fourth largest cause of death in the U.S. is from properly prescribed pharmaceuticals, the knowledge and availability of these plants is doubly important: first, in providing a natural alternative to prescription drugs, and second, in providing the ability for the many Indigenous people to support themselves in the same sustainable lifestyle they have enjoyed for thousands of years. The leading causes of death for the Indigenous are snakebites and falling trees rather than the degenerative diseases we experience, such as the first three causes of death: heart disease, cancer and stroke. It is an amazing turn of events; our growing need for alternative cures will help preserve the rainforests during this critical time.

According to the New England Journal of Medicine two-million-two-hundred-thousand people suffer side effects from pharmaceutical drugs so severe they are permanently disabled or require a long hospital stay, and more than half of all drugs possess side effects not detected prior to approval.

Fungus, yeast, molds, viruses, parasites and bacteria and environmental toxicity—are at an all time high. Many of these strains are not affected by modern antibiotics due to indiscriminate use during the past fifty years, so over half the world is turning to alternative treatments to improve and maintain their health.

Leslie Taylor, while researching alternative AIDS and cancer therapies in Europe, began researching a medicinal plant from the Peruvian Rainforest called Cat's Claw. She was also dealing with a health issue, cancer, and this research took her to the Peruvian Rainforest for the first time to learn firsthand more about this new medicinal plant. Upon her return, Leslie founded the Raintree companies to make this important new medicinal herb available in the United States. She wrote a book, <u>Herbal Secrets of the Amazon,</u> which catalogues over 100 of these herbs and their health benefits. She, like John, has merged her knowledge of the medicinal plants with phytochemists, botanists, ethno botanists, researchers, and herbal medicine practitioners to document, research, test and validate medicinal plants.

Large commercial farming had killed the small farms of Southern Colombia. The independent farmer could no longer compete in the open market. The only options for them was to continue a sparse living by cutting wood for the wood burning boats, leaving their villages to live in the slums of major cities or plant cocaine and other illegal drugs. Most of the indigenous peoples are caught in the cross fire of our so-called War on Drugs, which is being approached from the wrong end—defoliating their only viable alternative to starvation, while offering pittance for rehabilitation programs for addicts in this country to help reduce the demand for drugs at the consumption end. We are offered by the Universe an opportunity to partner with our indigenous neighbors in the Amazon, but are placing emphasis on hopeless conflict, which is like killing a mosquito with a bazooka. Many indigenous are forced to sell their land to the lumber companies or compete for fish with large commercial organizations, which over-fish the waters, increasingly contaminated from mining and cattle grazing. The reason the plants of the Amazon possess such healing qualities is due to the interdependence the plants, trees and creatures, which have to maintain life in an otherwise hostile environment. These life-sustaining qualities are synergistic with the body's catabolic system.

Colombia is the third largest producer of oil in Latin America, and is the tenth largest supplier of oil to the United States. Even though this is compensated by plans to use the profits from oil in the region to go to social causes it is like the proverbial "feeding a man a fish rather than teaching him how to fish."

When we landed at the Brazilian border station we got off to see the town. This was the first time I had heard Portuguese for over one-and-a-half months. Amazingly, I understood everything. We tried to find a place that sold food as we walked around. We finally found the only store in town, in the back room of a house. The girls started rattling away in Spanish asking the woman if she had ice cream. The woman smilingly acknowledged the question but it was obvious she didn't understand. I asked her the same thing in Portuguese but my Portuguese was so terrible it took three times before I got the sentence over to her. She said she didn't have any ice cream, which I was sure was the case. I asked if she had anything to drink. She didn't have this. I then asked if she had anything to eat. She said she didn't have this either. She had a monkey sitting on the rail. The girls wanted to buy it but she said that wasn't for sale. The other few items she had for sale were of no interest to me so I thanked her and we left empty-handed.

It was an interesting town with about fifty or so whitewashed huts, the government building behind a small park with flowers and a tiny church. The church was so small it would barely hold more than ten people at once. There was a small rosary in front covered with glass, a picture on either side and a cross above in front—all very simple.

It took about two hours to get the boat through customs. The sun was blazingly hot that afternoon so it was good to get going and get some breeze stirred up by the moving boat.

It wasn't long before we passed the town that was shown on the map as the border town. Nobody seemed to know the name of the new border town. It had just come into existence several years before. The other city was Ipuranga, a very good-looking hut village but nothing like the border station. We passed it in a short while and were on our way. I was told it would only be about a four-and-a-half day ride to Leticia. I was somewhat happy the time was ending. I was getting very tired of the dried fish they were giving us morning, noon and night and was getting weary of stopping so many times every day in mosquito infested places to get firewood. I also was finding the journey a bit dull as all the villages usually consisted of a communal house and just a couple of other huts. I was anxious to get on the Amazon where there was more movement. In all days we had spent on this river not a single boat passed us. The biggest water vessel we had run into was a motor canoe. The Tarapacá experience with the commander of the base dampened my enthusiasm and made the trip less enjoyable.

We got only a short way into Brazil when we passed one of the prettiest places I had seen. There were just a couple of huts situated at the branch of a very small tributary. This was what I had pictured a jungle river to be like when I read about it. I would have liked to have had a small motorboat to take up the river. I was rather short of pictures of any animal life. I hadn't even seen a decent boa to photograph.

Bela Vista Village near Río Içá

I, therefore, ran around trying to seek someone to go ashore with me and take a walk through the jungle. It looked as though we would be there for quite a while loading the wood. I ran up to the house to ask about the paths. My Portuguese was so bad this was quite a job. I finally got a young boy, called "Negrito", to go along with me. He carried the briefcase with the camera equipment in it. This was the first chance I had to get inside the jungle. I could see how thick it was. It was like a green wall on both sides.

We headed into the woods on a path at the other side of a clearing. We came to a tree, which had fallen across the path. It was covered with ants. I could see why my professor told us the biggest pest of the jungle was the ant. There were literally millions of them. Leading from this was an army of them marching into a hole. We carefully crawled over the log as I was in no mood to fight ants.

The woods were completely void of animals as far as I could see. It was very noisy with a myriad of birds flying around. I couldn't find any of them, as they seemed to be hiding themselves behind bushes and up in trees. We finally came to a clearing with a couple of houses. I was a little worried about what people might do upon seeing strangers appearing out of the jungle like this, so we approached with caution. It appeared as though school was in session inside the first hut, built on stilts. As we approached, all the students and teacher had moved to the window and were staring out. An elderly man came up to us. I greeted him with "Bom día". He politely responded with, "Bom día" He asked if I wanted to look around. I found that as I talked with him my Portuguese improved a little. All I needed was to get away from Spanish for a while. The two languages are so similar they kept getting intertwined. He took us across a mooring to the other house, which was evidently his house. A tree in front attracted about twenty little parrots. After I had taken a couple of pictures we went back to the other hut. I told him I was going to take a picture of it and he went up and told the teacher to call all the chil-

Bela Vista (Beautiful View) school & its pupils

dren out. She brought them down. "What do I do now?", I thought, overwhelmed at the production I had caused. I felt with all this formality I had better act as though I was attempting to take a professional shot for a magazine. I had the man chop down all the weeds in between the children and myself and arranged them by height. After this they all went back inside to finish their lesson. I thanked them and they thanked me. I then bade farewell to our charming host and headed back to the boat. I finally found some ducks called "patos pescadores" (Fishing Ducks) that got close enough for a picture with the telephoto, my only wildlife photo.

That night we stopped for wood. The usual Indians came on board. I noticed the Indians were now getting whiter and whiter with a few blond Negroes mixed in now that we were in Brazil. There were a lot of mulacos that came on board (mixture of Indian and Negro). This is usually a handsome combination as the Indians soften the African features and the color is usually a deep copper.

One of the older Indians had some monkeys and fish he was trying to sell on board from his canoe. One of the passengers was about to buy one when someone yelled up from the barge the old man's canoe had just broken loose. With it went the monkeys, the fish, and Cr$100. I couldn't help but feel deeply sorry for the man because Cr$100 to him were about the same as $100 US would be to us. When it was seen there was no hope, Mendes hooked the motor onto a little dugout canoe we dragged alongside and a couple of the men took him back to his hut. He took it amazingly well, never uttering one complaint. It was amazing how accepting the Amazon people were. They lived in the NOW and seemed to take each day as it came.

By this time a menagerie was growing on the boat. The mate bought a well-behaved parrot that loved to have its neck stroked and one of the girls bought a parrot, too. Also on board was the parrot someone had bought on the upper river, my little monkey, and Lindo's two monkeys, one a ringtail and the other a mongrel that liked to growl at everyone and wrestle with them. The deck was a mess. Someone else also bought a woolly monkey, which was loving but very lazy. The tiny sink that spilled out dirty river water when the motor was running was busy with everyone giving his or her pet or pets a bath. Also, Gonzalez bought a squirrel monkey, the most vicious I had ever seen. It looked like a little black squirrel. If anyone came near it, it squealed and bit, inflicting a rather nasty bite.

Gonzales tethered him on the busiest corner of the boat, so we all passed this noisy one with extreme care and at a safe distance. One thing I found was the bigger the monkey the smaller the bite. The little ones had little sharp teeth and bit more often. The big ones had flat teeth that did little damage.

"We'll be loading twenty stacks of wood tonight near Santo Antonio do Içá," Mendes told me.

"That's a lot of wood. It'll hold us there for most of the night," I said.

"The price of wood went up when we entered the Amazon so we needed to store up and this was the last town on the Río Içá."

At about 10:00 that night we stopped for wood. There was wood as far as you could see. I decided to get some sleep so went to bed a little after landing. Amazingly I was able to sleep through the noise of the wood being thrown on the metal deck, stack after stack, and the cheer as each piece of wood was thrown. At 5:00 a.m. I awoke to the continuous pounding of wood. I looked under the hammock, which had now changed its name from 'hamaca' to 'carapaná'. Again my back was like a waffle iron. I looked out and saw we hadn't moved, the wood was still not completely loaded. I looked down below and saw they had already filled the bottom deck and one of the barges. I figured this ought to handle us for a while and mentioned this to someone. "Oh no," he said, "We are going to stop again tonight for wood."

María was still walking around half-starved. I don't know how she was getting each meal paid for. She seemed to be facing a challenge for the first time in her life. Her usual jovial approach to life was no longer a joke to her. It was about this time Mendes finally must have given in as she was now eating with confidence — anyway, with as much confidence as you could have with the ghastly meals we were fed. I had forgotten the wonderful tang of hunger, which ordinarily improved any meal, no matter how unpalatable.

That afternoon we reached the village for another load of leña. It was located on a very steep hill, a 200-foot climb. We trudged up the hill to an Indian hut halfway up. It was here we noted the great difference between the Colombian Amazon people and those of the Brazilian Amazon. Whereas the Colombians were friendly, even loquacious, the dwellers of the Brazilian side seemed serious, melancholy, and not so interested in improving their lot. They stood around us and stared but never made any effort to talk to a stranger. This made me feel ill at ease in their presence. We ran around and picked some fruit. The fruit looked like an overgrown lemon but consisted of a soft woody material. It was good when I ate it during the short time it was ripe but it could be quite bitter if it wasn't ripe. This didn't seem to bother the natives, who ate it whether green or ripe. The girls kept bringing me these, telling me they were just right. Perhaps they were just right for them but not quite ripe enough to please my palate.

I kept asking for lemons, as I was constantly thirsty. All they had to drink was hot beer, some kind of hot gaseous soda water that was made in Leguízamo and agua de panela. I was hoping to get some lemons to quench my thirst a little and save one to put in the aqua de panela. This was the only way I found agua de panela drinkable. However, no one seemed anxious to sell anything, even less so in Brazil. I had the feeling if there were ten bananas on their trees and only nine people to feed, they would throw one into the river so they wouldn't have to sell it. Looking back now, it probably had more to do with the subsistence level which produced so little food for the residents.

Río Bocanos from Río Içá at Tambaquí

We were scheduled to arrive at the Amazon by 6:00 p.m. I was hoping we would arrive a little earlier because I wanted to get a picture of the rivers flowing into each other. I had never seen such desolation as I had for the trip down the Río Putumayo/Içá (same river, Putumayo in Colombia, Içá in Brazil). We had traveled for seven days without seeing one other vessel, and only a few huts along the way. The mosquitoes were not as much trouble as expected and only at night. It was the mosco that bit and left welts on my arms.

This was another place where a little advance knowledge would have saved me a lot of time. It was Thursday evening when we arrived at Santo Antonio do Içá. Hindsight tells me I should have

Barasanta trees along Amazon. These are the only color other than green I saw from the rivers. The blossoms turn from green to red to orange as they ripen.

disembarked here, taken a plane to Iquítos, and seen the other places on my way back down the Amazon, mostly to miss the four-day holiday which began the day I arrived in Iquítos. This would have saved nearly a month of travel and put me on a brand new SNAPP liner instead of the bag of bones I ended up with.

I sat on the front of the barge in the hopes of getting a good view of entering the river. After it darkened I put my camera away and went back out again. By 7:30 we still hadn't passed anything that looked like the confluence. I saw a few lights pass but still couldn't feel we were entering a larger river.

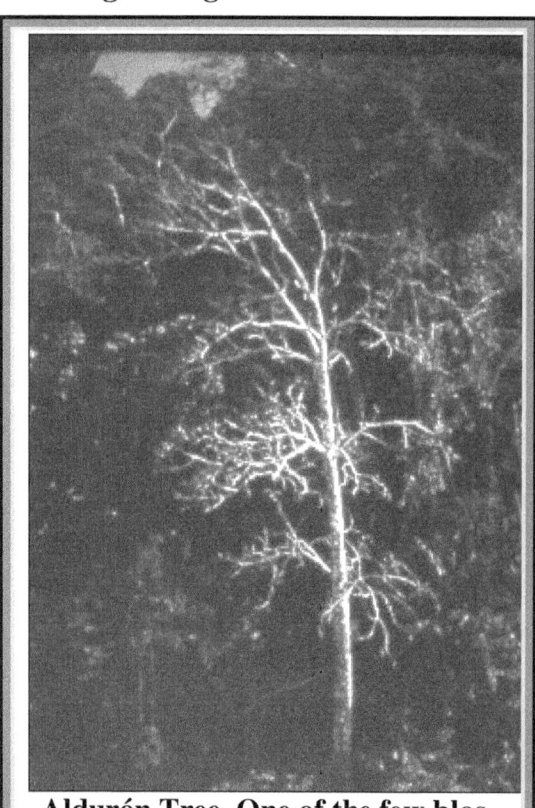

Aldurón Tree. One of the few blossoming trees I had seen. Red colored buds are food for parrots.

Finally someone came by so I asked, "Are we about to enter the river yet?"

He responded, "We already entered the river a half-hour ago. Those lights you saw were Santo Antonio do Içá."

I was confused. I told him, "This River doesn't look any larger than the Içá."

He said, "We are in between a large island and the shore."

I guess it was a long island because I finally got tired of waiting to see how wide the Amazon was without the island and went to bed.

Before long we passed into a clearing that was recently burned out. This gave me a chance to see the process of farming which is characteristic of the jungle. A small clearing was first burned out and a thatch hut thrown up, a few banana trees and yucca were planted and that was it. The larger organizations sustained themselves on collecting their production from small farmers, which they sold for a large profit, rather than attempt to grow crops on large plantations. In the rainforest trees and plants intertwined to give a solid organic base to sustain them. There is very little topsoil in the rainforest. It supports itself literally on the roots of the trees and other organic groundcover. When small areas are burned and then allowed to replenish every few years, as the Indigenous have done for thousands of years, the forest quickly replenishes itself. After a couple of years the cleared land is no longer productive so the tribe moves on to another spot. In the case of rice this is about two years. If trees are planted, rather than crops or cattle the land will produce indefinitely. However, when large plots are burned as there is with the raising of cattle, it will yield about $60 an acre per year, but the forest will become a desert in as little as three years, forcing cattle operations to destroy added land to sustain the same number of cattle. In extensively cleared areas, such as is required for raising cattle, the topsoil that sustains the rainforest erodes. Many Indigenous are attracted to the $400 an acre the timber harvesting will yield, but that leaves an almost equal desert behind so income becomes short-lived. However, if the rainforest is harvested sustainably for medicinal products it can yield $2,400 per year and the Indigenous are able to sustain their way of life indefinitely. While we have identified only 3% of plants of the Amazon, many are disappearing for eternity before we even have a chance to catalogue them. In spite of this understanding the forest is being depleted at the rate of 75 acres a minute or 39 million a year.

Barasanta Tree. Natives claim the fruit cures many infections, even syphilis.

The next morning after entering the Amazonas I awoke and found the river wasn't any wider. I was informed we were going around another island. It was becoming a little warmer earlier than usual and I was afraid this day was going to be a hot one. We had our usual dehydrated, salt-laden fish with dried up rice and dry yucca for breakfast. I could feel I was losing a lot of weight. We had picked up a few passengers at Tarapacá so it was becoming increasingly crowded on the small boat.

The menu for the journey can be written very simply:						
1st Day:	Breakfast	Meat	rice	Plátino (dried banana)		agua de panela
	Lunch	Meat	rice	Plátino	yucca	agua de panela
	Dinner	Meat	rice	Plátino	yucca	agua de panela
2nd Day	Breakfast	Bacon	rice	Plátino,		agua de panela
	Lunch	Pork	rice	Plátino	yucca	agua de panela
	Dinner	Pork	rice	Plátino	yucca	agua de panela
3rd Day	Breakfast	Pig's feet	rice	Plátino	yucca	agua de panela
	Lunch	Pig's liver	rice	Plátino	yucca	agua de panela
	Dinner	Pig's head	rice	Plátino	yucca	agua de panela
4th Day	Breakfast	Dried pigskin	rice	Plátino	yucca	agua de panela
	Lunch	Dried fish	rice	Plátino	yucca	agua de panela
	Dinner	Dried fish	rice	Plátino	yucca	agua de panela
5th Day	Breakfast	Dried fish	rice	platino	yucca	agua de panela
	Lunch	Dried fish	rice	Plátino	yucca	agua de panela
	Dinner	Dried fish	rice	platino	yucca	agua de panela
6th Day	Breakfast	Dried fish	rice	platino	yucca	agua de panela
	Lunch	Dried fish	rice	platino	yucca	agua de panela
	Dinner	Dried fish	rice	platino	yucca	agua de panela
7th Day	Breakfast	Dried fish	rice	platino	yucca	agua de panela
	Lunch	Dried fish	rice	platino	yucca	agua de panela
	Dinner	Dried fish	rice	platino	yucca	agua de panela
8th Day	Breakfast	Not hungry				
	Lunch	Dried Fish	rice	platino	yucca	agua de panela
	Dinner	Dried fish	rice	platino	yucca	agua de panela
9th Day	Breakfast	Dried fish	rice	platino	yucca	agua de panela
	Lunch	Not hungry				
	Dinner	Dried Fish	Rice Plátino		Yucca	agua de panela
10th Day	Breakfast	Not hungry				
	Lunch	Not hungry				
	Dinner	Not hungry				

By noon it was getting oppressively hot. I was looking forward to the afternoon rain. However, at 2:00, when the billowy clouds usually start closing in, the sky was a radiant blue. Even the old pipe-smoking woman was succumbing to the heat. We all sat as close as we could to give room for all the extra passengers.

I was filled with anticipation from all the wonders everyone on board had told me about the town of Leticia. I had yet to readjust my expectation to their reality, based on their limited encounter with the world outside.

"They have skyscrapers just like New York," declared one little girl.

"They have a beautiful hotel, there is a Marconi (radio tower) and the streets are paved," stated another, animatedly.

"They have beautiful homes," another girl said with excitement in her voice.

It was hard to imagine such a beautiful place on the Amazon, so separated from the rest of the country in the middle of the rainforest.

"Leticia is right next to a city in Brazil, Tabatinga, a border town," said one of the girls. "There is a road and an international bridge which you cross to get from Brazil to Colombia," added the boy.

I should have known from the overstated descriptions of Leguízamo to expect the same exaggerations about Leticia, but I never came close to guessing the extent of these embellishments. As we traveled up the Amazon I was pleased to see the moscos had stayed in the dense jungle of the Putumayo/Içá. I felt I would buy another one of the leoncitos (marmosets) to send to my girlfriend in New York. One of the workers on the boat had bought one and offered to sell it to me. I paid dearly for it but figured I would probably not see another one again, they were so rare. We had traveled nearly a thousand miles since I bought the first one and I hadn't spotted even one other.

The shoreline along the Amazon was an endless wall of tall green forest. I saw no flowers on the trees; except for one tree the natives called Barasanta, which I suspect is *Triplaris surinamensis* or Longjohn tree. It formed a pink blossom, which eventually turned a deep red. Parrots loved its blossoms. People also told me there were many medicinal properties to it, and that it even healed syphilis. I have never been able to locate its proper name but later mentioned this to a Colombian friend. He recognized it immediately and said he had a friend in Medellín who had syphilis and the doctors had tried everything to eradicate it with no luck. He told me he picked up some on a trip to the Amazon and fed it to him. His friend was quickly healed. Twenty-five percent of Western pharmaceuticals are derived from rainforest ingredients but, as I said before, scientists have tested only one percent of the tropical trees and plants. It's a sea of untapped healing richness. The rainforest has given us herbs to treat or cure inflammation, rheumatism, diabetes, muscle tension, surgical complications, malaria, heart conditions, skin diseases, arthritis, glaucoma and hundreds of other maladies. The U.S. Cancer Institute has identified 3,000 plants that are active against cancer cells of which 70% come from the rainforest. It is unfortunate, most Indigenous in the Amazon Rainforest are no longer aware of the healing properties of the plants that surround them because the verbal intergenerational linkage has been broken. We have barely touched the potential of the economic potential of the rainforest and reasonable alternatives to a troubled medical system.

Amazon John Easterling, Leslie Taylor and many others have carried Nicole Maxwell's dream to a new paradigm for balancing the growing health needs of the world with both the lifestyle needs of the Indigenous people and environmental sustainability of the rainforest. His company now partners with some fourteen rainforest communities, which have saved over 300,000 acres of rainforest. As the health demands increase in the rest of the world more tribes can enter into this type of partnership, saving even more forest land, which would otherwise be despoiled by the cattle, fishing, mining and lumber industries. As each community is added to the partnership, new medicinal plants are added to the records with plants not available in previously documented communities. As this industry expands, others are pursuing this model, gradually saving a good portion of the Amazon while healing the world.

7. TO THE AMAZON HEADWATERS

On the third day on the Amazon we were told we were approaching Leticia. I looked in the distance and saw only a few wooden buildings. As we approached the shore I saw only dirt streets, a mud embankment, shacks and the least friendly people I had met so far on the Amazon.

Leticia, Colombia. Brazil is across the river with Perú to its right.

I disembarked and slid up the muddy slope leading to the town. One boy pointed out a rather ramshackle building to the left, near the Marconi as the hotel. I set my eyes on the radio tower and headed for that building. I was not sure whether they would permit animals in the room so I put one Marmoset in each pocket and they quickly settled in. There was a long open hallway leading to what looked like the center of the building. As I headed down the hall a dignified middle age lady approached me and asked what I wanted. I asked if they had rooms and, without uttering a word, she proceeded down the long open hallway and led me through one of the many doors that lined it. Like so many of the others I had met on the Amazon she was serious and uncommunicative. We stepped inside the room and she went to the other side of the bed to pull the covers down for me. When she looked up, this quiet and rather matronly woman burst into uncontrollable laughter.

Leticia, Colombia park.

"What's so funny?" I asked in bewilderment. In my embarrassmenI tried in vain to see what she saw in me that was so funny. I asked her again what it was but she couldn't stop laughing, just kept pointing at my shirt.

"Allá," she finally blurted between her laughter. I looked down and there was a monkey looking out from each of my top shirt pockets. The hotel manager and I became best of friends after that.

As I stood on high ground in "beautiful downtown Leticia", I looked in vain for the magnifence and cosmopolitan depiction, which was described so enthusiastically by the boat passengers on the Ciudad Néiva. In sharp contrast to the dilapidated appearance of the town and its lone radio tower, was the spectacular view toward the river below. On the far side of the river was Brazil. If I turned my glance slightly to the right I could see Perú. Leticia was in Colombia; Benjamín Constánt was in Brazil, and Ramón Castillo in Perú, bordering Brazil. Three kilometers to the left of Leticia, on the same side, was Tabatinga, Brazil. As I glanced across the Amazon I was reminded of my birthplace on an embankment of the Mississippi River where I could look out my bedroom window and see Iowa directly in front of me, Illinois across the river and Missouri directly to my right on the same side of the river. My dream to motor down the Mississippi had been supplanted by this adventure on the Amazon. The sight across the small Leticia Park and expanses beyond was no less beautiful than I remembered from my Iowa birthplace. The rainforest was a beautiful place. It was not a 'green hell', as described by the soldiers at Tres Esquinas but Our Creator's gift to humanity. The shantytown behind and the rough exterior of the hotel next to the radio tower were "New York" to my fellow travelers.

Leticia had a small zoo, which was connected with the Tarpon Springs Zoo in Florida. It served as a holding tank for animals from the rainforest before they were shipped to Florida. This was an opportunity for me to see some of the animals, which I could hear but never encountered in the jungle. I tried to get the manager of the zoo to help me send the Marmoset I bought to New York. He said an American originally from Greece, Mike Tsalikis, was now in Iquítos, Perú and he owned the zoo. Wildlife was housed here, many sent to Tarpon Springs Zoo in Hialeah, Florida.

I discovered a vintage Martin seaplane would be leaving from Benjamín Constánt very early in the morning in two days. When I asked how I could get there everyone I asked declared, "Check with the 'Gringo Negro'. He takes a motorized canoe to the plane in the morning." I was surprised at the name, which means "Black Foreigner". I finally located his store. Behind the counter was a black man, name of Mike, who did not look like he was from this part of the country. I could tell from his accent he was not a native, and he finally addressed me in perfect English. I laughed when I found he was an American. He owned the store.

Martin Sea Plane owned by PanAir do Brasil. They were an excellent way to see the Amazon as they stopped at many river villages.

I asked him, "Whatever brought you to Leticia?"

He answered, "You know, the rat race and all that. I feel more comfortable here." We talked at length and I arranged to cross the Amazon with him in his motor canoe early in the morning.

I went to the government office to straighten out my overextended stay. The officer roughly dressed me down for allowing my visa to overextend. The official seemed unimpressed when I told him, I tried to extend it in Cúcuta, but they would only stamp it for two weeks. Then the consulate, police and other government offices were of no help in Bogotá, finally extending it only a few more days. Further complicating this was the difficulty I found in Tres Esquinas, La Tagua, Puerto Leguízamo, and Florencia locating anyone who had any visa authority."

Río Japurá from the air. Now I could see why it took so long to go short distances down the rivers. Storms loom in the distance, wandering around the Rainforest, dropping buckets of water underneath, leaving other areas dry.

He finally stamped it when I told him I was leaving in a couple of days. Whew!

Mike arrived right on time in the early morning and we slipped into his dugout canoe on the Amazon. The Amazon is about eighteen miles wide at that point but flows around a number of islands. The water rises as much as thirty feet during the wet season so many of the buildings were built on stilts, and the piers were wooden platforms built into the low shoreline on pontoons which rose and lowered with the river so boats could load and offload during all seasons.

It was a longer trip to Benjamín Constánt, Brazil than I had figured due to the large islands, which separated both sides. The wharf had lowered to accommodate the reduced shoreline of the river during the dry season. Almost the entire town was built on stilts along this wide wharf. Meat was drying in the open on a railing next to a restaurant, which would eventually be cooked with whatever the flies left behind. A few flowering trees decorated the bland surroundings. I looked out at the expanses of river extending into Colombia and watched Mike head back to Leticia.

Ice cone vendors on every corner. An excellent way to beat the heat during the heat of the day.

I located the plane resting on the mouth of another small river that flowed into the Amazon. It was a Clipper Sea plane, manufactured by Martin in the 1930s, now owned and run by PanAir do Brasil, an offshoot of Pan-American Airlines. We climbed down the banks and onto the plane. The cabin was a long empty cargo-like hull, housing many webbed seats for the

Park fountain, Plaza de Armas, Iquitos, Perú.

passengers. I sat in one and looked out the narrow slits, which served as windows. Once we were airborne, I looked down into an endless sea of green carpet, the center of the Amazon and Peruvian jungle. Winding bands of rivers flowed from all sides. Large cumulous thunderclouds drifted aimlessly around the forest dropping massive amounts of water directly under them, leaving the peripheries dry.

Iquítos was as much a surprise in its unexpected beauty as Leticia was a shock with its unanticipated shabbiness. I fell in love with the town immediately. Picturesque weathered tile buildings lined the streets. Unlike Leticia and the many other towns along the rivers, the streets were paved; many with cobblestone placed years before during the rubber boom days of the early 1900s. I was pleasantly surprised at how beautiful the Amazon River was, viewed from a lofty perch where there stood a statue of Ramón Castillo, a Peruvian hero. The people were friendly and helpful. Air conditioning in this heat was supplied by means of the iced drinks and cones sold at every corner. Little machines shaved ice and a selection of fruit drinks were poured over the ice. I became very aware of my weight loss when I stepped on the scales and found I weighed 166 pounds (a loss of 35 pounds). I struggled to keep holding my pants up as the gravity of the heavy Peruvian coins pulled them down. I bought most of my food at the markets, which lined one of the parks, picking up a little rice tidbit here, something else there, etc.

Fountain at night, Plaza de Armas, Iquitos, Perú.

I had to wait around Iquítos for eight days for transportation as they were celebrating the Peruvian Day of Independence and everything stopped for five days. I enjoyed my stay there very much and hated to leave when the fiesta ended. Iquítos was very pleasing, with its numerous charming tile buildings and two beautiful parks. The people were very pleasant, friendly, and open. It was not long before I had made numerous friends.

I found a hotel and was soon introduced to the American everyone was talking about all the way from Puerto Leguízamo. He got into Iquítos the day after I did. He was a 21-year-old student from California named Jim Conner. He was a snake expert and lived in San Francisco. His travel partner had already returned to the States. He told me about his trip and it made mine look like a pleasure cruise. He spent months in the rivers getting to the Indians and was planning on hiking back through Panama. A tall blonde-haired person with a beard, he turned all heads as we walked through the streets. I told him I was jealous because he was getting all the stares usually directed at me. He told me I should shave off my mustache so everyone wouldn't keep mistaking me for a native. It was true, though. I ran into some men from Sears Roebuck and had a difficult time trying to get them to talk to me in English.

Statue to Ramón Castillo with Amazon in the distance, Iquitos, Perú.

While in Leticia I spoke in English for the first time in a month. It really shocked me. I had a hard time talking fluently. I had to stop every now and then to think of what the words were in English. I talked with a girl later on that afternoon in English and did a little better. I also had endless conversations with Jim. I now spoke English again like a native.

Jim went to find Mike Tsalikis, who owned the zoo. When he returned, he informed me Mike would not be there until late that night. I was disappointed because I had waited four days and was about to catch a boat that was leaving for Benjamín Constánt that night. I finally located another man who shipped animals to the zoos and he said he would make sure the Marmoset went out with the next shipment. He would ship it to the zoo in Florida and they would transship it to the New York address from there. It was still summer so it would be safe for the animal to travel to New York. He had been in Peru for twenty years and spoke Spanish grammatically correct, but like an American reading Spanish for the first time.

I finally found a launch that carried passengers, but it was going only as far as the Brazilian border town of Benjamín Constánt. I had to do some hedging to ditch another American who was staying in the same hotel, keeping the departing launch a secret from him. He had been traveling in Latin America for four months and had learned only one Spanish word for every month he had been there. His vocabulary then totaled, "Good Morning," "How are you," "how much" and "beer." I couldn't see nursing him for the next fifteen days I estimated it would take to get to Manaus.

I bumped into two Spanish immigrants from Sâo Paulo who were also traveling third class. I met them at the Brazilian Consulate's office that afternoon as I was getting my papers in order. They seemed cold and unsociable, despite my overt gestures of friendship. It was hard to break the ice and get them talking, but once I did they never shut up. As a result, writing in my diary suffered badly. Before we left, Conner came to where I was waiting for the boat and told me Mike was back in town. We ran to a restaurant and sat at his table. When Mike found I had shipped a marmoset to New York he was visibly incensed.

Tiled fronts to houses and businesses, dating from the Rubber Boom days. They still give the appearance of elegance.

He looked at me sternly and admonished, "Those marmosets are very fragile. It will never make the trip. Whenever I send marmosets I send a bunch of them, as many don't make it. I doubt if this one is going to make it to New York." (I recently discovered through an Internet search that Mike was caught smuggling cocaine along with a lumber shipment, and imprisoned.)

Unfortunately I had to break away to get back to my boat. I didn't want to miss this one after so many days' waiting.

From the moment I returned and everyone boarded, the Spaniards, Guillermo and Gumercindo were my constant companions. The food was exquisite. We had fish every day but the cook made it taste like filet mignon. My head ended up with constant bruises from having to navigate through a maze of five-foot ceilings and hanging pipes and doorways. The other passengers, with their moderate heights, had little problem. I asked Guillermo about their lengthy stay in Lima. I was interested because Perú was on my return agenda.

Guillermo went on endlessly about his distain for the people of Lima. "We are both disgusted with Brazil. It is very backward and doesn't make any sense in anything it does. We wanted to get out of Brazil into a more progressive country, so we went to Lima, hoping maybe to find employment and move to Perú. Lima was awful. It was hot. The people treated us like dirt. You probably wouldn't have a problem because you are American but they still remember the Conquistadors. We could feel hatred from almost everyone we met. The minute they heard our Spanish accent they either stopped the conversation or treated us rudely. We're glad to be out of there. The weather was miserable, constantly foggy and cold."

Benjamín Constánt. The raised boardwalk leads to the pier and protects the town from the water when it rises thirty feet in the rainy season

I was fascinated with the dolphins that were our constant companions as we plied the river. They would jump, swim along beside us, and follow in our wake. I never expected to see dolphins on the Amazon, especially 2,000 miles up the river.

Forty-three hours later we stopped at a few huts. I was told this was Ramón Castillo, the border of Perú. A quick check of our documents in the ship's hold, and we rounded the corner to Benjamín Constánt, Brazil. The ship's captain offered us room and board on the ship for the three days he would be there. He then charged us only $6.60 for the trip from Iquítos, including those delicious meals.

Having suffered through the three-day bank closure in Bogotá, the festival of the Patron Saint of Neiva, three days of bank closure in Florencia and four days of Independence Day in Iquítos, we were now faced with the Rubber Festival Days of the Amazon, which stopped all river traffic for another week. When the boat left we found ourselves on shore with no existing hotel, no place to eat and a town we were weary of the first time we stepped onto its shore. The boat captain told us we could stay on his boat out at the raft if we wanted, but we felt we had already imposed on him enough.

My Spanish friends, Guillermo, Gumercindo, and I were sitting on the shore and suddenly Guillermo mentioned going down in a canoe would be faster and more interesting than waiting around for a half-month for transportation. By this time there were only two of us. Gumercindo ran out of money and was being furnished his room and board on a river launch by a friend we met. This was exactly what I was thinking of doing, and hadn't known how to broach Guillermo. Actually, the thought of it was kind of exciting, to actually paddle down the river in a dugout canoe. "We're here," I thought. "We'll never have this opportunity again." I quickly agreed with Guillermo and we swiftly found ourselves looking for a dugout canoe to buy.

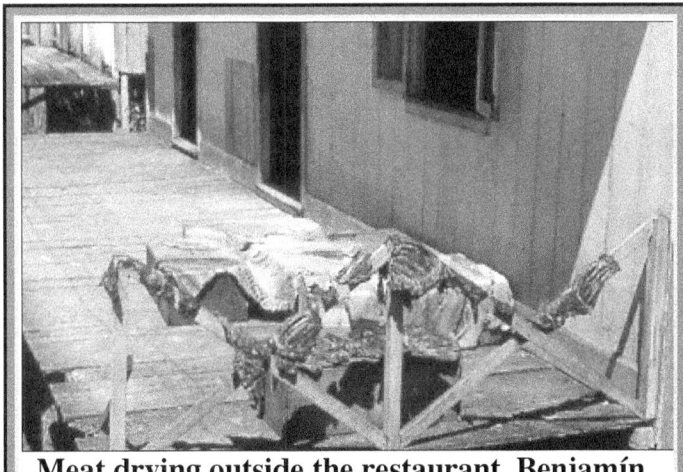

Meat drying outside the restaurant. Benjamín Constant.

We found, to our consternation, the people just didn't sell canoes anywhere in Benjamín Constánt as well as anything else we needed for canoeing down the river. We even went outside the town to individual huts to see if we could buy one, thinking at least they would have one for sale because that is where they were made. The few who offered to sell us a canoe wanted an outrageous price. At the end of the day we found ourselves with no canoe, no place to eat, no room to sleep in and no hope of transportation. I had my hammock and blanket but Guillermo had nothing to use for sleeping.

We met an older man who told me there were two American Baptist missionary families living there. I thought perhaps they could help a fellow American. I went by the house of one of the missionaries and encountered his wife working in the front yard. I greeted her in English. She gave me a dirty look and grudgingly returned my greeting. To make conversation I mentioned, "We are stuck here with no transportation and are looking around for a launch to Manaus.

She sneeringly snapped, "Yea, all the Americans that come here are in the same fix. Would you care to see my husband?" I found him in the yard. He was as cold as she at first but soon warmed up.

"Look out for snakes," he warned. The worst one is the mapanare (Bushmaster or fer-de-lance). If it bites you, you die within ten minutes. Many of the natives fear it when they travel any distance away from their village because they can't get anywhere to treat it in time.

Also, don't jump into the river. It's full of piranha. They travel in schools and they can finish you off in less than a half hour."

"I have seen children swimming in the river. How do they keep themselves from being bitten?" I queried.

"They know where and when to swim," was his answer. "There are certain places the piranha go. They usually will not attack unless there is blood, but a splashing of the arm or wiggling of the toe can attract them. Once one bites you, your blood attracts all the others to finish you off. I once knew a small boy that was just entering the water when a piranha fish bit off his toe. Fortunately, they got him out of the water in a hurry before any other fish bit him. Once I opened up the door to my shed and there was a bushmaster. I managed to get him before he got me. You need to be careful in the jungle and waters."

Business district, Benjamín Constánt, Brazil

He thought for a minute and said, "I know of a man that used to rent rooms. I also know a place that serves meals by the day. Would you like to have dinner with us?"

"Thank you but we'd better seek out the pensâo (room)," I said, knowing we'd better get settled and make sure we at least had a place to sleep. I was sure glad I ran into him. We were about to die of starvation.

The room wasn't much—just four hooks on which to hang two hammocks. An old hand-made table and two hewn chairs were brought in to complete it. It had some boards tacked up which separated it from the outside. However, it looked like a palace to us. It even had a shower—a cistern with a bucket and rope. The guy at the pensâo was a good-humored Peruvian. This was certainly not helping my Portuguese. Guillermo naturally used his Spanish because it was his native tongue and both of us spoke it so much more fluently than Portuguese. He explained this was a room used as a meeting room for political meetings. There was no one running for office so they could rent it out.

Tabatinga, Brazil, connected by a path with Leticia, Colombia. At this time it was solely an Army camp. It has now grown into Leticia as a tourist center.

The meals served at the small eating-place were delicious. I was beginning to gain back some of the weight I had lost. It was at this time I was introduced to a Brazilian drink, called Guaraná. It is made from a climbing vine in the Amazon Rainforest. It was not only delicious, but also stimulating. Guaraná became my drink of choice throughout Brazil, giving me the extra strength I needed for extended travel.

After exhausting every possible resource in the area for the purchase of a dugout canoe, we were told we would find it easier and cheaper purchasing one in Colombia. This meant finding some means of transportation back across the river to Leticia. We found a barge going to Leticia that left at noon but the captain would not allow us to go to Leticia with him because we had no visas. However, he said he was going to Tabatinga, Brazil and would drop us off there. We could then take the "highway" to Leticia. It was 5:00 p.m. when we arrived at Tabatinga, with its small assemblage of army buildings, and chapel—nothing more. Guillermo and I began looking for the highway and international bridge but we saw nothing to the west except a green wall of trees. Seeing not even a path, we approached a group of soldiers playing soccer in an open field. I searched for a path while Guillermo approached the soldiers to point out the highway. I went in every opening in the forest I could find. All were dead ends.

Guillermo yelled back at me, "They say there's a bridge here and that leads to the road. They say it's just past a white building. Look for a bridge, Carlos." All the buildings were white but Guillermo was sure he had found the bridge. We whacked our way through a rough patch to two white buildings. We then spent fifteen minutes trying to find the "highway".

These were the first houses of Leticia we saw at sunset, coming out of the jungle from Tabatinga.

After about ten minutes Guillermo yelled, "I found the international bridge." It was a made of small makeshift wooden planks over a small ravine. On the other side was a narrow path leading into the forest. We stood in the tall grass, which was higher than our heads.

Afraid we would end up in the forest with no way out I exclaimed, "Guillermo, this can't be the highway. This is just a little footpath leading into the forest. It could dead-end at any time. Surely this is not the International Highway, the people on the Ciudad Neiva said was so popular."

The declining sun was fast fading behind the trees and would soon be gone. The grass was over our head so the trees were our only guides. We ran into a big wide wooden bridge about fifty feet long, then back into the jungle. I told Guillermo, "If it gets any darker we won't be able to spot any Bushmaster or Onças (Jaguars). We had not brought the flashlight because we didn't think we would need it with a "highway and international bridge". The more we contemplated the faster we ran, trying to get through the jungle before night fell. If this was a wrong path we were doomed to spend the night in the jungle, without blankets, hammocks or flashlights.

Racing between the trees I looked intently at every step for bushmaster snakes. The missionary's tales of piranha attacks, aggressive Bushmaster snakes, and animals that attack haunted us with every step into the intimidating darkening skies. All of this created pictures that conjure up snakes at every dark corner. I dreaded having to sleep in the jungle at night. I had heard the noises of the animals at night. The trees closed in on us as the sun passed beneath the horizon. Finally, at about 5:50 we spotted several grass huts in the darkness. The huts became more numerous as we hurried along the path. Suddenly I recognized one of the grass huts to be one I had seen before on the outskirts of Leticia. I looked for a border guard or even a sign that said we were now in Colombia—nothing, just huts. The first thing I could think of doing was to go to the general merchandise store owned by Mike, the American, to see if he could find me a motor and canoe at a reasonable price. His shop was closed for the day but someone else told us about another motor, which was available.

The next morning we rushed around like two kids in a toy store, getting all the stuff we needed. After due consideration we decided a motor was too much expense to chance. A motor would cost close to $300 US and the chances were it would work for only ten miles before breaking down, in need of a part we couldn't get. We, therefore,

The fading sun as we paddled from Leticia to Benjamín in our newly purchased canoe.

bought a dugout canoe, paddles, utensils, cooker, and food. Guillermo went out to talk with a man who had offered to sell him a canoe and told me to wait at the wharf for him. I was sitting there when a customs officer came up and greeted me. I was shocked, but tried not to show it, reflecting on the overextended stay when I passed through here before, and our lack of visas. I breathed hard, smiled, looked relaxed, and shook his hand. The officer laughed and said, "Your buddy was shocked too, when he saw me the second time. Guess it must be the uniform."

"Oh," I thought, "He knows Guillermo." Just then Guillermo came up and said, "This is the man who sold me the canoe." When the guard was out of earshot, Guillermo whispered to me, "He wasn't in uniform when I made the arrangement but when I met him to close the deal he had changed into uniform to begin work." He only had one paddle but said he would include another short one his son, obviously very small, used. This was an unusual experience, a customs officer selling us a dugout canoe, helping us carry it to the wharf and seeing us off—two illegal aliens he was helping leave, without ever having inspected our papers. This was hilarious after all the hours I had spent in Cúcuta, Bogotá, Florencia, and Leticia, trying to have a few days added to my original visa.

8. DOWN THE AMAZON IN A DUGOUT

We found two challenges immediately when we pushed off from shore. I can paddle a canoe but a dugout handles entirely different and the Amazon is full of shifting currents and whirlpools. Secondly, Guillermo had never paddled a canoe and, in typical Spanish pride, could never allow himself to admit anything was wrong with what he did. We, therefore, found ourselves going around in circles and switching back and forth in the rough current while Guillermo repeatedly castigated me as the canoe began moving in circles. I was getting increasingly angry at both canoe and Guillermo. To make matters worse there were a number of Indian men living on the island who were bursting with laughter and taunts. That made Guillermo even angrier. This circus continued for close to two hours. We finally managed to maneuver around the curve that took us out of the main channel around an island to Benjamín Constánt. I observed one Indian rowing and saw how the back man was guiding their canoe. I followed suit and everything went along fine until Guillermo traded with me for the back again. Then it all started once more, Guillermo bawling me out every time he pushed the canoe around. I finally found if I let him harangue me, we would eventually find what he was doing wrong and correct it without hurting his pride. It was when I tried to show him a correct way the tirade would begin anew. We both learned from this. I learned many Spanish curse words from Guillermo as he kept trying to change my rowing, and he was able to hear many disreputable words in English as I exasperatingly told him it was he who needed to change his rowing. When he explained something to me there was occasionally a key word I didn't know or the phraseology didn't make sense. I usually

The author and Guillermo in the dugout, cooking tea over the sterno, a constant occupation with the heat.

answered, "Si," to avoid a re-explanation. This was like pouring gasoline on his fire and he would catch on and say, "You aren't understanding me, Char-leis! You aren't understanding a thing I'm saying!"

With all flare-ups aside, I could not have picked a better partner for the canoe trip. The Spanish pride, which made him unwilling to admit his mistakes, also made him one of the trustworthiest people I had ever met. I would have trusted everything I owned with him. He also had a keen interest in everything around him. He was a great help to me in my picture taking. Also, the times of laughter far outnumbered those few moments of anger.

As we rounded the island and began paddling toward Benjamín Constánt the last rays of sun lowered through the trees in the distance. We had not expected to stay all night in Leticia and had to pay our 12¢ apiece for the room at Benjamín Constánt. It was actually good to be back at Benjamin. The hotel in Leticia was expensive, the beds hard, the noise loud, the room hot and the food abysmal during our short stay there. As we had left a bill at the pensâo in Benjamin Constánt the Peruvian owner was glad to see us, as he was sure we had skipped without paying our bill.

We got off the next morning with our focus set on Manaus. Seeing us off were a large number of acquaintances we had befriended during our short stay. We were given estimates ranging from eight days to five months to reach our goal. I was sure we could make it in 8-16 days. The first day we tried to reach São Paulo de Olivença. I had marked up the AAA map, which was all I had brought with me from Phoenix. I didn't think I would need anything more because all this traveling into the void was momentarily planned. So in our descent to Santo Antonio do Içá we just followed our noses. To maneuver through the numerous islands we had to be sure we picked the main channel because a wrong turn on an island could mean two or

One of the Indian traders who approach each launch for bartering.

three hours wasted.

By nightfall we still hadn't reached Sâo Paulo de Olivença so we kept on paddling. We still hadn't seen anything by ten o'clock. I knew electricity would be shut down by then so we wouldn't be able to see it if we passed it. We then decided to stay at any hut or village we could find. At last, seeing a light we paddled and paddled toward it. When we got to the edge we found we had misjudged the current and shot past the flashlights on the shore. We finally paddled over to the side where the current wasn't so swift and tried to push against the current. Guillermo guided us out into the stream and said the current was not so swift there. The closer we got to shore the thicker became the mosquitoes. The flashlight on shore shone on us and soon a couple of more flashlights joined. We rowed and rowed for about twenty minutes and moved only about ten feet. Finally, I could hold my angst no longer so I insisted we go to the side where the current was less swift, thick with mosquitoes but faster getting to the flashlights. When we got to quieter waters we quickly made it to the point where we had seen the flashlights. The natives had climbed up the banks about twenty-five feet overhead and were looking down on us. I was shocked when I saw Guillermo unloading everything ready for the night. We weren't even sure of being invited to stay with them so I urged, "Hadn't we better ask them if they have room for us first?" I looked up the steep incline and could see a small group of natives shining their lights down on us. Behind them were a few grass huts.

I let Guillermo be our spokesperson because my accent was so thick and my facility was tarnished in Portuguese. Also, they spoke with such an accent only someone who had been speaking the language for some time could understand all they said. Guillermo, ignoring me, kept getting things ready while all the Indians stood on the banks flashing their Eveready's down on us.

We went up the embankment slipping and sliding while the Indians laughed among themselves. When we got to the top Guillermo asked them in Portuguese if they had any room for us. They said, "Nâo" and seemed reluctant to talk. I saw they had room but were probably afraid of us. Two bearded foreigners, I in bare feet, paddling a canoe didn't generate much confidence. Guillermo, with his flamboyant Portunhol (Portuguese with Spanish thrown in), was almost demanding in his tone of voice, which I am sure added to their mistrust. In answer to Guillermo's pleas they offered to let us stay with the cattle below. This was not an option, as the mosquitoes would have eaten us alive (or dead) by morning. Even the cattle were showing their dissatisfaction with this arrangement.

We begrudgingly headed back into the dark night. We had been told the dugout canoes do not float because they were made out of hard wood and hard wood does not float. The canoe is made by cutting a large hardwood log in half, forming the outer shape for smooth paddling, then burning the inner core, leaving about two inches of hull for support. We decided we would paddle through the night, with one of us sleeping at the other end of the boat.

Guillermo warned me, "Remember they told us to be careful of any squalls because waves can come over the canoe, sinking us."

"I'll watch out for that so you can get some sleep," I assured him.

"Stay close to the shore so we can get to shore in a hurry in case of wind," he warned.

"I will, just go to sleep," I reassured him. "Don't worry."

We were alone in the world with the chatter and howl of every living thing in the jungle. Especially menacing was the roar of a lion. "I didn't know there were lions in the rainforest," was my thought. "How would we ever get ashore without a machete, with the lush green growth blocking our every move?"

We were a captive of the water, its sheer size dwarfing both the canoe and us in its vastness. Swarms of mosquitoes were sucking us dry with their invasion techniques penetrating every pore of our skin. Guillermo wrapped himself to the top of his head to evade our aggressors. He was soon sound asleep and I was left alone to fend off the beasts and fight the heat. The vast expanse of water was serene and I was hit with an irresistible urge to move out of the calm shorelines into the center of the river away from the mosquitoes. A crimson half-moon reflected brightly off the murky waters, which enveloped us in its remote vastness. I felt at peace with the world, stranded in an ocean of forest and water. I looked back to make sure Guillermo was asleep and then paddled out toward the middle, free of the mosquitoes. I soon grew tired from the tranquil setting and dropped off to sleep. Suddenly I was rudely awakened by the wind agitating the waters, slapping the sides of the canoe. I was both aware of the warnings we had received concerning squalls and a fear Guillermo might wake up before I could get us again close to the safety of the shore. I wasn't sure which I feared most: his "I told you so" or drowning. The waves soon began to splash light sprays over the bulkhead. I paddled with full force to reach shore before Guillermo was awakened by the thumping of the waves, or the bits of water that sprayed over the sides.

Suddenly Guillermo awoke, "What's going on here Carlos?"

"Oh, I just noticed some waves so I'm heading for shore," was my feeble answer.

Closer to shore we were again eaten alive by the mosquitoes. I recalled at every downstream end of almost every island was a small sandy beach. It was winter on the Amazon and the river was at its lowest, some thirty feet below its summer levels. This left long stretches of beach at points within the islands in half-curving stretches and at the end of islands. Maybe if we could make it to one of the islands we could find a place to sleep on shore the rest of the night. We proceeded downstream, paddling toward the island as the small tempest abated.

We rowed endlessly until we passed another island. I looked in at one spot and the full moon shone on a small indent in the middle of the island with what looked like a small elliptical beach. We rowed toward it, making sure we approached it from the upstream side so we would not overshoot it as we had at the small Indian village. Our rowing had improved. We landed at the exact spot of the beach we were aiming for. We rowed to shore and Guillermo stayed in the canoe to hold it safely. I stepped on the beach and shone my light at the trees to see how thick the forest was. Twenty green eyes stared back at me, from a distance of about twenty feet. I was immediately aware we were in the middle of a den of alligators. I'm sure they were as curious at our presence as we were of theirs. It was a no-brainer; we would not be camping there for the night. We were exhausted and were sure

The author and Guillermo at one of their landings

we would have to stay offshore that night. We pushed away from our party of alligators and anchored the canoe as best we could. "Two men sleeping in a dugout canoe for the night? This is going to be interesting," I said to Guillermo.

"I guess we can sleep end-to-end and might have room," was his suggestion. We rustled for about fifteen minutes trying to fit both of us at opposite ends of the canoe, Guillermo's feet in my face and mine in his. Neither of us had bathed in several days so it was an odiferous venture. The mosquitoes, due to our close proximity to the shore, were having a feast. We covered ourselves as well as we could but the sweltering heat forced each of us to remove some cover every now and then so we could breathe.

The next morning was hot and muggy. We cooked our cornmeal and tea and were on our way. We did our cooking on the little Sterno Swedish cooker in the canoe while we drifted with the current so we wouldn't lose any time. As we passed a small sandy beach on one of the islands Guillermo said, "Stop here. I have to go to the bathroom."

"Hang it over the side," I said, not wanting to lose any time.

"No, Carlos, it's the other thing," he pleaded.

Dust storm on the Amazon. This is winter so water level has dropped thirty feet, exposing sandy shores. This demonstrates the fragility of the Amazon floor with its lack of topsoil. This is how the Rainforest becomes desert when it loses its trees to cattle and timber operations.

"Oh, you mean you have to have a bowel movement?"

"Carlos, it's been three days." I was surprised. It really had been three days since either of us had had a bowel movement. I guess this food was stopping us up.

The islands were an interesting discovery of environmental laws and civil disobedience. The

Brazilian government was trying to protect the turtle population because it was being decimated by over hunting of both eggs and young turtles. The government allowed hunting to continue on most islands but marked others with white flags, meaning 'off-limits to poachers'. We noticed that every island with a white flag had at least several canoes tied up; the ones without flags were barren of people. It was obvious the white flags meant, "Come and get my eggs, they're protected."

We were just leaving the island at 8:00 a.m. when we ran into a motor canoe that came out to intercept us with another canoe at its side with several men. One of the men had an old long-nosed pistol across his lap. We didn't know whether we were going to end up minus our baggage or our baggage would end up minus us. The first thing the man with the pistol asked was, "Are you foreigners?

"I am," I said.

"I'm a naturalized citizen, originally from Spain," said Guillermo.

"Can I have your passports?" asked the man with the gun.

He inspected each of them, and I was sure he did not understand a word of mine. However, we were both feeling more at ease, knowing this was an official of the government.

"Do you speak German?" he asked.

I told him, "No. I am an American."

"I'm assigning a deputy to go with you to the town where my municipality is, Santa Rita."

This all sounded very legal so we said nothing. The deputy got in and took over the paddling on the front of our canoe while the motorized canoe left with the official. The searing noonday sun was too much for me so I put my dying breath into every stroke. After about an hour we stopped and another canoe pulled up to our side. Guillermo saw how tired I was so he took over the paddling. The burning sun was about to drive me nuts. I had never experienced such a scorching sun. Every so often either Guillermo or I pleaded, "Where is the town?" They would always respond with, "Around the next corner."

We waited out in the middle of the river for about an hour-and-a-half. Guillermo asked, "Does the deputy have an office?" only to get the same reply, "Nâo." We began to suspect a hold-up but couldn't make any sense out of what was going on. Finally, we were held captive for another hour, experiencing the pleasant relief of several light rains, which granted us short-lived respite from the intensive heat. We pulled over to the side of a peninsula and the deputy tied the boat up. The others went ashore and the deputy stayed with us for about an hour. None of them had said more than three words to us since our arrival. Finally, they went ashore and kept watch on us from there, holding their guns on us and conversing with each other. I was burning up from my exposed back, arms, and legs that were becoming intensely burned.

I looked at my watch and saw it was 3:00 p.m. I asked Guillermo, "Can you make any sense of this?"

"I'm as much in the dark about this as you are," he said, shaking his head. "I've dropped all suspicions of robbery. It's all too complicated for that. Then, looking overhead to the three men Guillermo called the deputy over and said, "Maestro, we've got a long road ahead of us. Hasn't this man got an office where we could process and get on our way?"

"He said to wait here for him," was the answer. We could get no more out of him besides, "That's right." At 4:30 it started to get dark. I figured my watch was between one-and-one-half hours slow so it must have been about 5:00 or 6:00 p.m.

I then began questioning Guillermo in a loud stage whisper, "Where are we were going to sleep for the night?" We could see no response from any of the men.

"This has got to be the Brazilian government. Nobody else pulls a dumb stunt like this, especially robbers," Guillermo said repeatedly.

At times Guillermo or I would say, "Why don't they go ahead and shoot us, if that is what they are going to do?" There were times when we wished they would shoot us and get it over with, if that was to be our inevitable conclusion, so we could end this suffering.

Finally, at 5:00 a motorboat came roaring our way. It was the man with the pistol. He handed some eggs to the other men, gave them some directions we couldn't hear, and was off. They then started to eat in front of us. As we had only eaten some mush for breakfast the day before, a can of meat for lunch, nothing for dinner and mush for breakfast that morning with no lunch, we were starving. They didn't offer to share anything.

We finally pulled into a small inlet on an island. I recognized the island from my ascent. The deputy finally broke the long silence and turned around and told me that Santa Rita was on the other side of the island but we were going on this side. I judged that the customs was on this side. We pulled into a spot where there were three shacks on a hill. He explained, "You can go to Santa Rita tomorrow as there are two American missionary families living there." We finally pulled over to the dock of one of the buildings. There was a man bathing on the end of the dock. He looked very European so I asked the deputy if he was American. The deputy said, "Yes." I figured this must be one of the missionaries. We approached and the man greeted us in Portuguese. I was astounded at how good his Portuguese was as the other missionaries at Benjamin had spoken it so poorly.

I said, "Hello." He answered, "Bôa tarde."

"The deputy said you were American," I offered.

Enrique Geissler in front of his home.

He said, "Oh, I speak a little English. What other languages do you speak besides Portuguese?"

I said, "Castillano, Portuguese, Russian and English."

"Oh, you're Russian," he said.

"No, I'm American," I answered.

"But you were born in Russia?"

"No, I was born in the States."

"Well, where did you learn Russian?"

"In the U.S."

"Do they teach Russian there?"

He motioned us forward and said, "Take your bags inside as the Indians steal everything they can get their hands on."

I asked, "How many languages do you speak?"

"Eight, more or less," he said.

I told him, "Add my Russian to the more or less."

I took it for granted we were going to stay there for the night and started looking right away for a place to hang my hammock. I felt it was cruel of the police to impose on this kind old man like this. The hut was a shambles. It was just a cluster of boards carelessly tacked up with a grass-thatched roof. The only furniture was an old hand-made wooden table in the middle of the floor covered with paper and two wooden benches on either side of the room. There were three hand-made stools around the table. The decoration on the only windowless wall consisted of political posters.

As good as the old man's Portuguese was I detected a slight German accent. I asked him if he was German and found he was a German Jewish refugee who had come over in the rubber boom days about fifty years before. He asked me for my name and teasingly said, "That sounds like 'Hitler.' What are you doing here?"

I said, "Oh no, you're the German."

"Oho," he chided, "But I was here all during the war."

He asked Guillermo what part of the States he came from. Guillermo said, "No, I'm from Spain."

"Oh, Franco," said the old man, again laughing in jest.

I could see Guillermo's natural embarrassment, as he could neither deny he was Spanish nor denounce Franco. The Spanish government and Franco repulsed him but felt it was the only type of government that could keep Spain from virtual anarchy.

The man then introduced himself, "I'm Enrique Geissler. We can speak German, Hebrew Yiddish, English, Spanish, or Portuguese. Which do you want?"

"I prefer Portuguese, if you don't mind. I need to brush up on my Portuguese and Spanish just makes it worse."

The whole evening was spent in a most fascinating conversation. Enrique was as much abreast of the world events as I. He could discuss the political situation of the United States with much greater knowledge than most Americans. He was also very aware of the political situation in his own country. He gave me personal experiences of the rubber gathering, the U.S. interest during the war, prices paid, type of life of the people, etc. The rubber boom, which began in the late 1800s, petered out in the early 1900s, due to unrealistic prices on the part of the Brazilian government and the blight, which wiped out most plantations.

I finally got to bed. Most huts we saw were built at the top of high embankments. While mosquitoes gathered in hordes within the first few feet of the river, they would usually thin out as people ascended the embankments to the higher levels, especially the level of the living areas, making them non-existent at the living areas. This hut was no exception, except there was a wind blowing across the water. This blew in the mosquitoes up to our level and they aggressively carried off every drop of my blood they could. The mosquito net I was carrying wasn't made for a hammock and mosquitoes kept sneaking in. Every part of my body was sunburned, exacerbated by the aggressive mosquitoes and the weight of the blanket covering my skin. As tired as I was from two sleepless nights I never was able to drop off to sleep.

Our host came in bright and early the next morning to wake us up and began chatting. All of a sudden the horrible thought dawned on us this was Sunday and the customs would be closed. We would have to wait another day. As much as we enjoyed our host we were anxious to reach Manaus.

We asked our host when we could leave but every time we did he would say, "Make yourselves at home. You can leave tomorrow." He took us out to show us some of the native vegetation. He showed us a rubber tree and bled it a little so we could see how they extracted the latex. He showed us some of the fruits, etc. "There are over 3,000 fruits in the rainforest. The Indians use over 2,000 of these. Of these we are only aware of 200."

When we got back we began dropping hints. Every time he asked us how we were doing we said we were thinking about how much time we were losing.

At some point in our extended conversations, it was revealed the man with the pistol was Enrique's son. I took Enrique off to the side and asked, "I would like to know, for any future people coming through here, why we were incarcerated on an island for seven hours, hauled around the river from place to place and then kept for a day or so in a home against our will?" He looked surprised and said, "Is this true?"

"Yes, this is true and I really feel it goes beyond reason."

"This is the fault of my son. He is the official and he told me you all wanted to see me because I am a foreigner."

"You mean we were here as guests? We thought we were prisoners."

I truly felt sorry for the man at that point. We were now able to piece everything together. We were all innocent victims of his son's ignorance. The son had evidently felt I would like to see his father as his father was a foreigner, so he assigned one of his men to guide us below and wait until he could get some of his vending out of the way. In typical upper Amazon absence of detail, he failed to explain things to the deputy. Therefore, the deputy felt he was doing his duty to hold us there at gunpoint and as someone given authority, he was going to obey it to the last word if it meant waiting all night. The son completely ignored time or the fact people were waiting on him while he continued buying and vending food at the various houses along the way, even though it took all day. The father was delighted someone wanted to see him and threw open his doors to us. "I wish you would stay here five months," he said to me, "so I could improve my English and you could perfect your Portuguese."

His vocabulary in English was excellent. However he couldn't speak it. His vocabulary helped me when I got stuck as he could translate the English word I wanted. He had proverbs in English on his door and several books on the English language in German and Hebrew.

For breakfast he gave us a delicious meal. We had some turtle egg cake, which I really enjoyed, turtle liver (delicious) and turtle stew. I love turtle when it's cooked right and this was beautifully cooked by a woman who never was introduced to us as his wife or maid. We gave him a half-pound of sugar, a bunch of crackers and furnished the tea (which he refused to drink). He claimed he was a true German and drank only beer—when it was available.

We even discussed religion with Guillermo, who was a Catholic but in true Brazilian manner refused to show any intolerance of any other religion. We discussed the Baptist and Catholic missionaries in the Amazon. I got the feeling he had more respect for the Baptists than the Catholics. Guillermo was Catholic but felt very strongly the Catholic Church had too much power and the missionaries were bleeding the natives.

As much as we enjoyed our host we felt we had to move on and loaded up the canoe. Enrique apologized for his son. We told him his hospitality had more than made up for his son's error.

We left with a feeling we had never been

Amaturá

entertained so royally. I don't think I have ever met a more charming host. Before we left Enrique said, "Promise me one thing—that you will write me a letter when you get to the United States and let me know how the trip came out." I did, when I returned, but never received an answer. We left a good friend and I have thought about him many times.

The next day we planned to make it to Amaturá. I needed medicine for an infection, which had persisted since leaving Iquítos. Shortly after beginning our descent we looked to the north shore and saw several western-type, freshly painted buildings. This was Santa Rita, which I recognized from our ascent. It was the missionary village for which we were first held captive, but which we never reached. We became increasingly concerned when nothing seemed to agree with any part of the map. The endless green wall on each shore and the islands swept us along a tedious path of questionable achievement. Guillermo kept a steady supply of tea from the boiled water from the Amazon. The sweltering heat from the noon sun accelerated our consumption past the ability to boil enough tea to supply two thirsty men at work in endless paddling to nowhere.

Over two-thirds of the Earth's fresh water is found in the Amazon Rivers, streams, and tributaries. I could see, as explained in David Childress' book, <u>Lost Cities and Ancient Mysteries of South America</u>, in previous civilizations this had been an inland sea. In many ways, it still is. Our greatest fear was becoming trapped in an endless loop of side streams and eddies that wind in ribbons throughout the vast forest. Caught in one of these we could find ourselves delayed for days. Already we were delayed for a good part of the afternoon due to a wrong turn trying to find another town and were again forced to continue rowing into the night.

Mouth of the Río Putumayo (Içá) at San Antonio do Içá.

We were both exhausted from lack of sleep but felt we

should make it to a town that night so we could get a good rest. We pushed and pushed and finally at about 9:45 p.m. we spotted a couple of lights ahead. They were located about where we were told the town should be so we pushed on. I fell asleep three times while paddling. Finally Guillermo said, "I can't go it any more." I had reached the end of my strength so I grabbed my hammock and put it up in what little room was left in the canoe. The bottom of the hammock fell into the water soaking bottom of the canoe, but I was so bushed I could have slept standing up. Suddenly I heard a crash as we brushed the bank. Guillermo pushed us back out into the stream and called for my help but I was too sleepy to even lift my head. The mosquitoes grew into thicker and thicker swarms. There were so many of them they sounded like airplanes soaring over our heads. I pulled the blanket over my head and that gave me at least some protection. I could hear Guillermo repeatedly calling to me at various times during the night to row out to midstream away from the mosquitoes but I was too exhausted to move. At sunrise the next morning we looked out and there was Amaturá right across the river from us. We couldn't have moved more than a mile or two all night. We looked at the town, then at our reserve energy and decided even though it was directly across the river from us; it was not worth paddling to it. My sulpher drug could wait until we arrived at Fonte Bôa.

Last view of San Antonio do Içá as we shoved off in our canoe. The priest is sitting in the center doorway of the closest house. His church is on the hill.

Exhausted as we were, we paddled hard that day. I was in better shape than Guillermo as I had slept for five hours, whereas he had had virtually no sleep. We made it to Santo Antonio do Içá that afternoon. We both searched everywhere for a room but no one in town was eager to rent us one. Guillermo came back; pride hurt and said, "I'm tired. I'm not going to try any more."

I finally convinced him to go to the launch we had seen in Santo Antonio. Finally, through a friend of a friend we found a man who would let us put our hammocks in a room.

The room turned out to be a sort of barn with a machine in one corner and a table in the other. Rudimentary, but to us it was home.

The people of the town were extremely friendly once we were settled in someone else's facility. We drank the only two cold drinks (Guaraná) in town, and then went up on the hill. The church was gathering for a meeting. The padre, dressed in a brown robe, was seated in front of the doorway, a light shining on him through the darkness, blessing each parishioner in a long line of people. He sported a long beard, which bounced up and down off his chest as he talked and laughed with each parishioner that entered. When he spotted us he called us over broadly smiled and asked, "Where are you from?"

"I'm from São Paulo," volunteered Guillermo.

"And you?" asked the padre.

"I'm from the United States."

"Oh, you are at war with Russia."

"What?" I said, in shock. My heart jumped a mile to my chest. I was still in the Army Reserves. I did not want to go back to war.

Seeing my consternation, he smiled and said, "Your country just went into a confrontation in Lebanon and Russia is saying it will go to war."

I felt a little more at ease with that and continued our conversation. With the world situation the way it was I felt it best to inform the draft board I was moving about and using my father's address as a permanent address. I really sweated it out when I heard the U.S. sent troops into Lebanon and the USSR delivered an ultimatum. The news was a week old when I got it and I couldn't get hold of any more recent news. I finally got BBC and found the news reassuring. The Russians had backed down.

"Where have you come from and where are you going?" asked the padre.

"We are paddling down the Amazon. We started in Benjamín Constánt and are hoping to reach Fonte Bôa by tomorrow and eventually Manaus."

"How are you traveling at night?" he asked.

"We've had to drift during the night because we can't find a place on shore to hang our hammocks, the forest is too thick to enter and I'm not interested in fighting snakes."

The padre looked at us in disbelief. "You've been drifting at night? You've got to be crazy. Even the Indians don't travel down that river. There are the dolphins that can overturn your boat and snakes that will pull you to the bottom. The Amazon is not like any other river. It has eddies and whirlpools. If you paddle into one of those they can sink your canoe and carry you to the bottom. You know, that dugout won't float if it gets water in it. If the snakes don't get you the piranha will. Wait here for a boat. Stay here and wait for a Brazilian boat, due in five or six days."

The priest had to leave to conduct mass, but his stern advice did not go unnoticed. Both of us left in deep silent contemplation. What intimidated me the most was when, not only the padre but also others we met told us, "Even the Indians don't travel any distance on the Amazon."

As we ambled down the dark streets in the moonless night on our way back to our abode, Guillermo looked at me in deep thought and said, "You know, he's right. We really ought to consider selling the canoe and catching a boat." Everyone we met echoed the padre, telling us it was dangerous to travel the Amazon in a canoe and spoke in opposition to us continuing this insane journey. It was when they repeatedly told us, "Even the natives don't take long trips on the Amazon in non-motorized canoes," that finally convinced us not to continue.

Lagos above Foz do Jutaí — We slept on the large island in the middle

I became conscious of my dreams during the night. I had always wondered during my years struggling with Spanish, whether I would dream in Spanish. Several people had told me I would really know I was proficient in a language when I dreamed or thought in that language. I concentrated on the process of my dreams and discovered, to my amazement, I didn't dream in a language. Because of my close relationship with my father I held imaginary conversations with him, during which we talked endlessly. Occasionally I would switch to conversations with others I had met during my trip. When I talked with my father it was in English, but when I talked with others I would hear and speak the conversation in their language, much simpler than I ever thought it would be. I had somehow passed through the invisible barrier to speaking fluently. I had long ago ceased to translate, which had given me speed and facility.

We awoke to a cloudless morning and I boarded the launch and did some shopping. Our friend, the skipper of the launch, was not as negative as others concerning our descent of the river. He told me, "There isn't much danger except during tempests. You can just pull over to shore during those turbulences."

That was all I needed. I bought a flashlight and went back to get Guillermo. He had also recovered from the demanding rigors of the trip. We were soon all packed in the canoe. As we shoved off we looked back at a good portion of the town, which had come down to see us off. We had not had a chance to see the padre to tell him of our change in plans. As I looked back toward the houses on the hill my eye caught the door of one of the homes. There sat the padre in his brown robe, waving to us from his chair, his beard bouncing up and down with laughter. We had been blessed, both by the town and its padre.

Lakes above Foz de Jutaí on the Amazon

We gave up our dream of making it to Foz do Jutaí in one day. However, we were able to read the map now, as I hadn't marked that part. We passed Tonantíns and felt we were right on track with the map. Finally, we both ended up with a different count on islands. Soon nothing looked like the map. We kept rowing and finally felt we were near Foz de Jutaí. We pushed on and on, passing beach after beach. I finally figured we had passed Jutaí and were at a point way on the other side of it. It was night so I felt we might as well bed down, but Guillermo was intent on making it to Fonte Bôa before ten o'clock that night. By 10:00 nothing looked like anything on the map. It was dark and we could see we were heading into a huge open body of water. We then began looking for a beach. There were none. We kept rowing and rowing but it was just one big wall of trees on either side. Finally, at 1:30 a.m. we began nearing the end of an island. I remembered that at the end of every island is a beach. We reached the end of this one at two o'clock. I went ashore and dug the paddle in to anchor the boat. Guillermo told me to go out further so the boat could drift and insects couldn't get at us. I stepped out on the sandy shore and soon found myself in quicksand. I should have recognized it as quicksand because I had run into enough of it before. I sank immediately to my knees. I remembered I had been instructed long ago not to try to wade or climb out, as I would only bury myself deeper. I stood and contemplated so I would not make a false move. I called out to Guillermo, but he was busy unloading the canoe. After the third sharp call he turned and calmly asked me what I wanted. I yelled out, "Throw me an oar! Throw me an oar!"

I didn't know the Spanish word for quicksand and Guillermo could not see I was sinking in the darkness. I looked about for a flat instrument and saw I had the oar in my hand. I laid it flat on the ground and put my weight against it. Gradually I managed to work myself out.

We anchored the boat and this time moved all the baggage from the middle. We lay side-by-side. There was exactly room enough for the two of us squeezed in and no room left over. I woke up the next morning stiff as a board, having slept little. Guillermo said he slept like a log. It was, therefore, he who carried the brunt of the work the next day as he had gotten the most rest.

Masses of butterflies, sometimes many colors, found on beaches along Amazon.

We got an early start and at about 10:00 a.m. ran into some natives. We called out to them, "Where's Fonte Bôa?"

They said, "E Longe d' Aquí. (It's a long way off.)"

"How far back is Foz do Jutaí?" we asked.

They answered, "Oh, that's about a half-day ahead of you."

We were very much distressed by this news. My AAA map wasn't helping us at all.

One of the most beautiful sights on most sandy shores was a large mat of butterflies of every color imaginable grouping on the sand, forming a carpet sometimes as much as three feet in area. We saw many of these assemblages on nearly every sandy shoreline. A number of these beaches were bordered with some of the tallest grasses in the world, a few as high as twenty feet.

We must have taken many wrong turns because after a day of canoeing around nearly 180° canals all day long we still hadn't reached Foz do Jutaí. My fear was accentuated by the many eddies and side streams which traversed the forest. If we were side tracked into one of these it could be days before we found ourselves getting through the maze back into the Amazon. What added to this deception were the islands, which made the river look narrow at points so we couldn't tell if we were on the Amazon or one of these side eddies or streams. The map, at this point, was worthless. In the afternoon we found ourselves in a narrow estuary. It was miles before we saw a hut. Standing beside the hut was a woman. I called to her, "Are we on our way to Fonte Bôa?" The woman ran into the house and looked out, not answering our question. I could tell she was acutely afraid of us. We finally gave up and continued paddling.

Tall grasses of the Amazon, behind Guillermo.

I had a great deal of time to reflect on my life during the five days and nights in the canoe. Many times, the only sounds we heard were the crashing of the oar propelling us at snail's pace down the river. There was a green sameness to the surrounding forest, interrupted at night by the numerous calls from the animals and birds that shared the forest with us. I found later the lion's roars we heard were from the howler monkeys. I contemplated on the preceding part of my trip and life in general. This was one of the first times in my life I had stopped to do nothing but think. Foremost in my thought were the many years of education—grade school, high school, college, and graduate school. I compared those years with the two months' journey I was on. I had learned more in that short time than all my years of study. I had not only met people from all walks of life and heard their stories. I witnessed, first hand, the desperation of the forest people who, for thousands of years, had lived, laughed, fed themselves, and raised children in peace. I saw their struggle just to get enough to eat, chopping wood endlessly and trading trinkets to buy sufficient food. I saw their plunge into the jungle and to the city in search of a job that could sustain them and eventually allow them the luxury of returning to their families.

I not only saw these people, I lived in ambient circumstances, which enhanced my understanding of them. I had bonded with people I might never have known, so disengaged were our lives. We were on the same earth, but only under the conditions in which we met, bonded, and lived for a short time, could I say I truly knew them. I knew I was treated as a novelty, but we knew each other as friends. I found great compassion and attachment, even in short acquaintances, such as the store manager with whom I shared a cup of coffee and who helped me with my shopping in Florencia. The bus that waited for me going to Puerto Lara impressed me. No one on that bus had complained about my delaying them, because their primary concern was to help me get to the canoes. I thought of the family I met in Neiva, a town famous for its robbers, who shared their home, food, and music with me. I remembered the truck driver who gave me a ride from Pimineta to Florencia. We all joined as a team to guide the bus around corners where the wheel was nearly off the edge on a 3,000 ft. cliff. I was reminded of the Indian who owned the hut on the Putumayo, who kept insisting I must be the captain of the boat. I wondered what happened to Diego, the only other passenger on the boat to La Tagua, who left a wife and children at home to search for work in the rainforest. Discouraged by his fruitless pursuits he returned to his wife and was going to look for work in Bogotá. I wondered if the Marmoset had made it alive to New York. I later found it did, but died on a night Louise forgot to shut her window during a cold spell. When she said to me, "I never could tame it. It kept biting me," I knew it was the same Marmoset because I never could tame it and it even made my tame one wild.

"Everyone should travel for two years and return home, a changed person," I speculated. All those years in school were nothing more than repeating dates, phrases, problems and events, most of which were forgotten moments after each exam. All my time, money, and effort had gone into completing tests, grades, and degrees and I was nothing more than an educated parrot with a short-term memory. What would rest with me for my entire life would be the travel I had done and the travel I was about to do. This was the best investment I had ever made in my life. Now, I had met a Spanish immigrant and was now paddling a canoe down the Amazon. I was learning what it was like to feel starvation as we ran out of food and found none.

A thousand thoughts raced through my head during my hours of silence. "Why can't we make travel an alternative to the draft?" I had never wanted to kill anyone, nor had I felt any ill against anyone because of his or her race, religion, or lifestyle. Yet I was forced into the Army, taught to kill, and sent to a battle zone to kill people of another race or face imprisonment. Wouldn't it be better to draft men and send them to other countries to live and work with the people?" I'm sure there would be fewer wars.

I had attended Middlebury Russian School and was doing graduate work to join the Foreign Service to make peace in the world. What I had witnessed of the American Consulates, and the numerous discussions I had had with people from all walks of life, convinced me the United States lacked understanding of other countries. What stuck in my mind were John Foster Dulles' comments to the press when he was criticized for flying to Florida to welcome the former dictator of Venezuela when he arrived in Florida with half the treasury of that country, "We don't want people,

Guillermo cooking on the dugout canoe.

we want their governments." Supporting dictatorships and overthrowing democracies has been the action under the veiled results of our constant assertions we are supporting democracy in the world.

What has happened in the southern part of Colombia is an abomination, partially due to our demand for drugs, also the war that has been foisted upon these people by the United States in our failed drug policy. It wrenches my heart to see the Indians and small farmers, forced to work in turbulence controlled by both the government and the drug lords. We have fed the violence and robbery that existed sporadically throughout the area by concentrating on the wrong end of the drug problem. We pour billions into furnishing and training armies to attack and decimate the growing of cocaine, and more into warehousing low-end offenders in prisons, while offering pittance for drug rehabilitation. The innocent suffer for it on both ends of the spectrum. I would not advise traveling to Southern Colombia today. It is just too dangerous.

Guillermo was usually in charge of the little Sterno burner we used to boil our tea. Our food was down to a few saltine crackers and some bananas. The bananas available to us in the rainforest were quite different from the bananas sold in our supermarkets. They had tough cores and were tasteless. Eating these staples, combined with the endless rowing, drove us past the ability to boil enough water to make tea for our bodily demands. We were constantly thirsty and hungry for eggs or meat. Many times we would see a small grouping of huts and hear the crowing of a rooster. However, when we approached the natives to buy some eggs, the rooster had stopped crowing and they claimed they had no eggs to sell. Until now we would dip our pan into the Amazon and fill the boiling pot. However, we were beyond that capability and still thirsty, so we decided we were going to have to drink the water from the Amazon

Village of Foz do Jutaí at the mouth of the Jutaí River.

without waiting to boil it. We carefully filled our cups, taking care it did not contain any piranha. The picture of a piranha biting my lip as I took a drink was not appealing. We had to trust we would not be drinking either toxins or parasites. Quenching thirst was our primary concern.

By 9:00 that night we gave up rowing and started looking for a beach to bed down. It seemed like miles to the end of each island where we expected to find sand and a small barren spot. We found a semi-beach and pulled up. The mosquitoes, which had been unusually bad in the middle of the stream, were not so thick on the beach. I started looking around for two stakes I could drive into the sand to hang my hammock. I found absolutely nothing, the mosquitoes got thicker and thicker until I could hardly walk through them.

Porto Benjamín Afonso, Brazil where we sold the canoe and waited for a boat.

Stairway leading from commercial area to the living area, about 200 ft. above. Mosquitoes slept during the day and would rise only about 20-30 ft. at night, except when the wind was blowing.

We tried to use the mosquito net but it just wouldn't maneuver the way we wanted it to and the mosquitoes found their way inside. The night was hot and muggy. This was unusual for the Amazon as it usually cooled off at night. The only way we could escape from the mosquitoes was to dive under the blanket, but only briefly, because the night was hot and muggy, making it miserable to remain under the blanket. The sound of the millions of mosquitoes nearly drove me nuts. I thought I would go crazy before morning when the sun came up. Guillermo kept ranting and raving all night so neither of us slept at all—we just wished morning would hurry up and arrive.

Finally, the first rays of sunlight appeared against the azure sky. As Guillermo and I sat on the narrow shore and looked out at the expansive river, Guillermo turned to me and said, "I can't take any more. I've had all I can take. It's silly to keep traveling this way. We just aren't equipped for it." I was sad at first and hoped Guillermo would change his mind.

However, deep in my heart I knew he was right. We were poorly prepared and inadequately outfitted. I was suffering from severe sunburn and my legs and feet were just one big scab. The heat from the searing sun had sapped all my strength. The mosquitoes were getting objectionably thicker as we went along. The natives refused to either sell us food or let us put up our hammocks in their huts. We hadn't been able to bathe because the Amazon River had so many man-eating fish, including the Piranha, which could devour a man in 30 seconds.

We decided to await the Brazilian liner at Foz do Jutaí. The fierce sun was searing my bare legs and hands. I thought we would never make it to Jutaí, located at the confluence of the Río Jutaí and the Amazon. It turned out to be no more than a few grass huts, about 50 feet above the river. As we approached I heard roosters crowing. "Good," I thought. "We can buy some eggs here, spend the night, and take the Brazilian liner."

Upper area where residences were located to escape mosquitoes at night.

One of the natives approached and I asked him, "Do you have any food you can sell us?"

"Nâo," was his answer.

"Is there any place here we can stay until the Brazilian liner passes?" I continued.

"No, there is no place to stay and the Brazilian Liner does not stop here," the man continued.

"There's a town ahead a little ways, called Pôrto Affonso. The boat stops there." This we considered strange because that town was not on the map. Since then I have never seen it on any map.

We decided we would have to go another day and suffer through another night if we wanted to reach Fonte Bôa. We grudgingly hauled ourselves into the canoe and headed east again. By then we were really feeling hunger. We kept pushing on and on and finally found some buildings, which the native had mentioned. We were surprised by the size of its commercial building near the shore. Pôrto Affonso was in lights on the front of the closest building and a PANAIR sign in front with an aluminum model airplane over it. Some had told us it was the headquarters for the Lebanese Mafia, which controlled the smuggling into Brazil through the Amazon. Guillermo went on shore. Somebody came up to me while I was guarding the boat and assured me, "It's all right to go ahead as all your goods are safe here during the day."

I didn't know whether to trust this so I stayed with the boat. Guillermo returned in about twenty minutes with a dozen eggs.

"I don't want eggs," I barked. "I want to know if they have a place to put us up for the night and whether the boat stops here."

Guillermo disappeared again and came back with the reply, "The boat is going to come by tonight and we're looking at about a half-day to get to Fonte Bôa by canoe so we had better hurry. That was too chancy for me with all the other delays and false estimation of times we had experienced.

I said, "We'd better stay here then. With all the other delays and false estimated times we have experienced, we'd better not take a chance on missing that boat."

We befriended several of the men at the warehouse. They offered to find us a place to stay until the boat arrived and buy our canoe and other equipment we had

Chicle, used to make chewing gum, wrapped for shipment in banana leaf.

bought for the trip. The canoe sold for half the price we paid for it but the person who bought it put us up for two nights and gave us meals for those two days. His wife was an excellent cook

The far side of the building led to a small storage area for chicle (the source for chewing gum), castanha (Brazil Nuts), balls of rubber, etc. The chicle looked like white chalk, wrapped in a large bulk with banana leaves. The rubber was in hard latex balls with a hole through the middle, like a large pregnant donut, hardened after hours over a spit of smoky fire. Almonds grew on the trees outside. To evade the mosquitoes the business was located below, about thirty feet above the river. Wooden notched planks led up to the houses, about another fifty feet up the hill. Cross-planks were nailed into the planks every two feet to give good footing in the rain. The mosquitoes were non-existent below until dusk, when they swarmed into the business area in menacing waves. The climb to the homes was above their feeding area, a height seldom reached by mosquitoes, except in winds such as were present at Enrique's, so we were relatively free of mosquitoes both day and night. The boat didn't arrive that night as predicted, so we spent the night in an open-backed shack they offered us as a part of the payment for the boat. We hung our hammocks on the built-in hooks.

Crude rubber balls, ready for shipment.

They showed us the toilet facilities, another door down from us with boards over an empty hole we could stand or squat on. In the middle of the night I was awakened with the urge and walked in bare feet to the facilities. It was dark outside and completely black inside. I stood for a second over the hole and suddenly felt a thousand ants attacking my feet, ankles, and legs. I jumped and brushed until I could feel them no more. I was reminded again about what my Latin America professor had told us, "Ants are probably the most destructive creatures in the rainforest."

The boat never arrived during the night so we found ourselves again seated for a delicious meal cooked by our host's wife. I never knew turtle could be cooked in so many wonderful ways: soufflé, omelets, steak, liver, and several others. We could not have dined at a better restaurant. By this time we had bonded with the people of the small port and soon found ourselves welcoming a small launch, which had just arrived. Hearing our names called we looked around. There was Gumercindo standing in front of the store with the same people who were putting him up in Benjamín Constánt.

We waited all day for the Brazilian boat but it never arrived. That night we again slung our hammocks in the open-backed shack for the night. Our host was losing the advantage he weaseled out of us, buying our boat for half-price. The dinner they served that night was as delicious as the others.

Tavares Bastos. It carried cattle and people — together, observe bottom deck.

At 4:00 a.m. we were awakened and told the boat was arriving. We stepped out into drizzling skies. This was one of the few times I heard thunder on the Amazon. Our host was standing there to see us off. He handed me a can labeled "Peixe" (fish) to take with us. I put it in my bag for emergency, in case we found ourselves without food.

In the distance was a tramp steamer, the Tavares Bastos. Its appearance ran a close race with the paddle wheeler on the Putumayo for ugliest boat of the year. I was shocked. I had planned on going third class. I had slept in jungle shanties, barns, canoes, and other third class vessels but had never seen anything that could equal this. It was even worse then the hurriedly built WWII troopship I was shipped from Japan to Korea on. I made up my mind I would definitely buy first class on this boat.

"I'd like First Class passage," I said to the dour faced purser as we stood in the rain.

"There's no First Class left," he barked back at me. I had no choice. My Spanish friends were even more indignant than I. Gumercindo told us the captain of the launch had offered to take him on down the river so he was going to do that. Guillermo boarded the boat with me.

The shallow waters required the boat to anchor in the middle of the river, so we paddled out to it. Third Class was an open bilge on the bottom. On each side were cattle bins, which reeked with a foul odor. There were about four to six head of cattle, several hogs, and about 25 chickens in these bins. Between these bins were about 200 hammocks passengers had strung between the steel girders in the middle. They were slung so close together there wasn't even room to pass sideways between them, let alone find the space to sling another hammock in between. I picked one spot and was quickly chased away. I then picked another and found some workers tearing it down to load some freight. They stridently chastised me for putting my hammock there. I then moved to the other side to get out of the way. A worker yelled, "Get your hammock out of there."

Parrot on board the Tavares Bastos.

I finally started to put my hammock up over some others and was told to move three different places before I was able to sling it with no reprimands from either workers or passengers. I then got up in the hammock, now at the top of two others. A passenger was lying in the bottom hammock. The rope on mine gave way, tumbling me on top of him, taking his hammock and another down

Taper on board the Tavares Bastos.

with me. I heard, "Quí bôm que é fraco." (It's a good thing he's skinny.) I turned and saw an older woman on the top hammock next to mine, smiling down at the two of us lying on top of each other with our surprised expressions. Then I realized she was commenting on how good it was I was skinny. Now I was aware of my vast weight loss.

I was repairing my hammock when I noticed the workers washing the decks and dispassionately spraying water on my bags. I quickly moved them to a dry spot only to find someone had moved them to the other side and workers were spraying them there. I put them on top of some barrels and turned around only to hear a worker behind me shout, "Who put their bags on these barrels?" I finally found a safe place in the middle of the deck on top of some other bags.

Monkey in his hammock on board the Tavares Bastos.

The call to breakfast came and everyone got in line. The man in front of me asked, "Where are your utensils?"

I couldn't believe my ears so asked him, "Don't they furnish them here?"

"No," he answered.

One of the passengers politely offered to let me use his cup after he had gone through line and was through with it. The line had dwindled to just a few by then. I ran down to the pot they were serving from and

River widens at Tefé

was given a little piece of bread and a half-cup of lousy coffee. That was all there was for breakfast. I didn't know what we would do as neither Guillermo nor I had any utensils. We had given them away at Pôrto Affonso.

Lunch was as bad and sparse as breakfast. The cook managed to scrounge up three plates from First Class and gave me a spoon, which broke the first day. We were given a half-bowl of slop for lunch and that was all. Dinner was the same. Guillermo and I were both starving by then. I was beginning to wonder how I was going to last the three days to Manaus when I found it was going to take four. I was only glad I had gone as far as I did by canoe, as we saw absolutely nothing out the open sides, which were blocked by the cattle. If I was able to get in a position to see out without getting knocked over by the hoards of people, I could see some jungle as we floated by through the open cracks.

Tefé as seen from the Tavares Bastos

An elderly American was traveling First Class and I could tell he was lonely. Because he could speak neither Spanish nor Portuguese he lacked anyone with whom to talk. This was the perfect excuse to climb up on deck occasionally to breathe and talk. I became his friend and translator. My fluency was making me more relaxed with my Spanish, but when I had to inter-

Looking into a storm on the Amazon. It could drench areas twenty feet from us and leave us dry.

pret a conversation between a Dutch missionary who spoke Portuguese the elderly man and myself, I felt challenged. The American had recently retired from the Post Office in Chicago and was taking a lengthy tour through South America arranged through a travel agency. His complaint was the fact they had limousines to meet him at every airport, prepaid porters at every juncture and luxury accommodations. This was as much a cultural shock to him, after years of pounding the pavement, as the third class accommodations were to me.

The officers looked down their noses at my bare feet, pants rolled up to my knees and beard. With the burns on both legs I could not stand any covering on them—not a pretty sight in First Class. However, I didn't feel a bit embarrassed as I felt the way they treated passengers below was worse than they did the pigs and cattle. At Tefé we stopped and another 100 people got on board. Third Class was nothing but a mass of cloth and rope as hammock over hammock was strung. There was absolutely no place to sit down. Our only refuge was our hammock.

First view of Manaus from the Río Negro

On the third day the workers' showed even more disregard for the passengers. At five a.m. I was awakened by a sudden swoosh as tons of dirty water poured down from the deck above on some of the hammocks. We all raced to the center for shelter. All of a sudden we heard another swoosh from the other side as tons of water came gushing down on people, hammocks and baggage and livestock. Suddenly the breakfast

View toward central part of Manaus, Brazil

bell rang and we all hurried through the water to get our piece of bread. I stood in one corner with Guillermo trying to avoid the traffic but was shoved out of the way by some of the workers. I saw a torrent of water coming my way as the workers boorishly sprayed their fire hose in all directions to clean out the cattle bins and our "living" quarters. I rushed to the other side but soon they began spraying on that side. Finally, things settled down and I sat on the side to catch my breath.

Opera House, Manaus. Performers came from all parts of the world, traveling by boat 1,000 miles up the Amazon River to perform here during the Rubber Boom days in the early 1900s.

Inside Opera House, Manaus, Brazil. Beautiful painted fresco on the ceiling and golden columns.

Suddenly, swoosh! A torrent of silt-laden water fell on me from the deck above. I was completely drenched from head to toe. I got up, started forward, and banged my head on a low-hanging beam, almost knocking me cold.

I finally decided Guillermo and I had better get some substantive food into us so I pulled out the can of Peixe. My mouth watered for the fish inside. When I opened it I found only sugar-sweetened guava. The thought of sugar in any mode, at this time repulsed me so I looked around for someone to give it to. One of the passengers looked hungrily at my can. He offered me a morsel of food for the guava. I looked closely at the label and found the manufacturer was Peixe. It was not Peixe, the Portuguese word for fish.

I was never so glad as when the boat finally pulled into shore at Manaus. It was past five o'clock and customs was closed so we had to wait until 8:00 the next morning on the ship. I finally got through customs by 9:00 and got off the boat, free at last.

Guillermo and I walked through the streets. I was very disappointed to find the people even more disagreeable than they were on the Upper Brazilian Amazon. They were rude, teenagers chided us with insulting remarks about our beards, and nearly everyone refused to talk to me when they heard my accent. In direct contrast to this were the numerous women who stopped us on the street to talk to us. A man explained this to me, saying, "The women have interest in you—but men don't chase men, they chase women. That's why the women are nice to you and the men rude." A rather simple explanation. Of course I did have about five of the women I met compliment me on my good looks; must have been my new slim figure (now 40 pounds less).

Igreja do Pobre Diablo (Church of the Poor Devil). Manaus, Brazil. The wife of a businessman built this in 1897 following his death. Notice the size comparison with woman in front.

Guillermo had bought passage on a boat going to Belém so we parted, he to his boat and me to find a hotel.

The Hotel Amazonas was $12.00 a night so I did some checking and found an older hotel, the Hotel Grande, that must have been a fashionable hotel in the rubber boom days. It reminded me of some of the old movies I had seen about the Amazon. The only furniture in my room was two hooks for the hammock. Wide-open windows let in the breeze from the Río Negro River down the hill. I immediately showered and began the painful process of shaving off months of facial growth with my battery-operated electric razor. It felt refreshing to again feel my bare face. The meals at the hotel were terrific. For lunch they served fish and rice, filet and macaroni, another meat and more rice, banana and Guaraná. This was more than I wanted but I forced myself to eat it because I had become so thin.

I went back to the boat Guillermo had transferred to and began searching for him to say farewell. At last I saw him leaning up against the side at the back of the boat, looking despondent. I greeted him and threw my arms around him. He drew back and glared at me with a shocked look.

I was surprised at his reaction and said, "Guillermo, how are you?"

He looked several times, deeply into my face, then smiled and said, "Carlos, I didn't recognize you without your beard." I had forgotten he had never seen me without my beard.

I found Manaus a beautiful city. It had supported at least a half-million during the heydays of the rubber boom and fallen as low as 50,000, nearly becoming a ghost town, but was gradually reviving and had now mushroomed to more than 130,000 inhabitants. Trees beautifully shaded many streets. There were many classical buildings left over from the rubber boom days, palaces and many beautiful parks. This amazed me when I became aware this city was way out in the middle of the jungle with no transportation except by air and boat.

Hidden in the jungle, Manaus was one of the most exciting cities of the entire trip so far. Ocean liners made it up the 2,300 miles of the Amazon to load and unload passengers and goods to and from the upper tributaries of the Amazon. One of the outstanding achievements of the Rubber boom days in Manaus was the opera house. It was still in pristine condition, with an azure painted ceiling and gold accent. The people of Manaus managed to attract opera tours from all over the world, which would traverse the 930 miles up the Amazon River to Manaus to give performances. Another testimony to the cultural aspects of the city was a theatre in the beer factory which my professor, Dr. Shurtz, told me about. He was invited into

One of many canals for harboring small craft. Manaus, Brazil

the factory by the owner in the late 1920s and was told to sit in a small amphitheatre. He said, "In a few minutes the owner came out on the stage and sat at a large Steinway and played Beethoven for me." The beer factory is the originator of the drink, Guaraná, which gave me such great energy in Brazil. The owner went to New York in the late 1920s to introduce this drink to the U.S., but his son contracted infantile paralysis while they were there so he returned to Brazil and never again tried to export Guaraná.

A constant line of small boats drifted in from both rivers with small loads of goods. The goods were loaded onto the larger vessels for shipment to the rest of Brazil, Europe, and the United States. Two large English vessels were able to travel up another 1,000 miles to Iquítos, Perú every month. There was quite a bit of manufacturing and the town was modernizing, as if coming out of a deep sleep.

The reaction among strangers to my accent was the same even without my beard. If I asked where something was, like "Onde e qui está a Igreja do pobre?" (Where is the Church of the Poor), a tiny church built by a poor man to honor God, I would get a, "Sim" or "Yankee", as they shrugged their shoulder and walked off without another word. This was extremely frustrating to me!

'O bonde'. Floating bonds financed the early streetcars; hence they are called 'the bond.' Manaus, Brazil

I searched for the navigation office of SNAPP but found the directions confusing. I stepped into a store and asked a young woman where the office for SNAPP (Pronounced snoppy) was. She answered me, "E pêrto do coheiu." (It's near the coheiu.)

I asked her, "O coheiu. Que é qui é un coheiu?" (The Coheiu, What's a coheiu?)

"O coheiu, onde mandan as cartas," she said, surprised I did not understand her.

My eyes lit up. "O correo." (Post Office) I now had the key to why no one understood me. My Portuguese teacher was from Lisbon, Portugal, so I had learned Portuguese with a Portuguese accent. These people talked with an accent, akin to a Texas accent in English. I needed to speak with their Carioca accent so they would understand me. It was also an excellent way to have a more definitive separation between my Spanish and Portuguese words, as the two languages get mixed together because they are so similar. The Carioca accent sounded more like Spanish with a French accent. Guillermo spoke what he referred to as "Portunhol", a mixture of Portuguese and Spanish.

Former Governor's Mansion, Manaus, Brazil

I went to the brand new airport at Manaus. I must have looked like a bum in these pristine surroundings because I wasn't able to find a laundry in Manaus and just couldn't get the dirt out of my clothes. I had on my sports shirt, baggy pants (which were even baggy when I was 40 pounds heavier) my big straw sombrero and muddy ankle boots.

All I could see at the airport was a long line of suits. The only English I had run into since leaving Iquítos was an older gentleman I met on the boat. However, that was all I heard at the airport. I noticed everyone was together so figured it was a convention. One of the men approached me and introduced himself. He was the headman for that area for the Baptists. He traveled extensively as a liaison. His name was A. D. Moffet and he was Dean of Boys at Shelton College in Ringwood, N. Y. They were Baptists from all over the world. They had just attended an international convention in São Paulo and were visiting Manaus

Aerial view of the black Río Negro flowing into the brown Amazon

on their return to the States. Many Baptists emigrated to the Amazon after the South lost the Civil War and this piqued their interest.

Río Tapajós upstream where it widens

We got up in the air and I managed to maneuver around to get near a good window to take some pictures. Suddenly the sign for "Fasten your Seatbelts" lit up. The plane turned around and started back toward Manaus. I began to pray when I noticed a couple of passengers running to the front and a couple of the crew running back to the rear of the plane. I noticed one of them was smiling, which put me more at ease. Finally, someone said, "The pilot is just running back to let someone get a look at the Río Negro flowing into the Río Amazonas. Sure enough, we got to the point and he flipped around so a couple that missed it could see it. Below was a wide expanse of black ink, called the Río Negro, flowing into an even greater expanse of coffee brown water.

The small launch the author took to get to the town of Itaituba. Its mayor owns it.

No one paid any attention to the seat belt sign. Everyone was running all over the plane. The double doors to the pilot's cockpit were open and there was a steady stream of people going up to visit. The crew were running back and forth with detailed maps to show people where we were and serve us food and drinks.

Moffet looked over at me and said, "When the pilot flew us into Manaus he buzzed the city before he landed."

I said, "I wish I could have been on it to get an air view of Manaus."

Schoolhouse in Fordlândia

To which Moffet added, "You could have gotten a good picture when he almost brushed the top of the buildings. It seems he had a friend on one of the river launches in the port."

When we got to Santarém we buzzed another boat friend before landing. It is really something to see a DC-3 buzz a city. I got off and bid all the Baptists bon voyage. A porter grabbed my bag and put it in an old beat-up station wagon. Several others got into the car so I figured that should run the price down. It was a nice bumpy ride into town over a dirt road. He proved he had more horn than brakes. I suddenly began to wonder how much the fare would be. If you know the fare you can always catch the drivers if they try to overcharge. As Santarém only had a population of 14,604 it wasn't much of a trip to the center of town. I noticed the others didn't pay so thought I would wait until the last minute before offering to pay. The driver turned to me and said, "That will be Cr$100." I couldn't have been more surprised or felt more robbed if he had stuck a gun in my face and asked me for it. He smiled, whistled, and said, "That's a lot of money isn't it?" Caught again, I paid and left.

First view of Fordlândia, built by Henry Ford in the 1920s, complete with a Country Club.

The hotel was so terrible I at least felt it would be cheap. The walls of the rooms were stacks of boards tacked up to separate the rooms in a big barn, similar to Puerto Leguízamo. The senhora of the hotel was extremely nasty making me feel quite ill at ease. I was putting up my hammock when I heard the plane with the Baptists go overhead. I got everything in order, ate, and returned to my room, when I heard some

English-speaking people checking in. "You sure meet Americans in the oddest places," I thought.

I went out to greet them and found it was a couple of the Baptists. "I didn't know you two were staying," I said. "We were grounded," one answered, very disgruntled.

"I thought I heard you go overhead," I said.

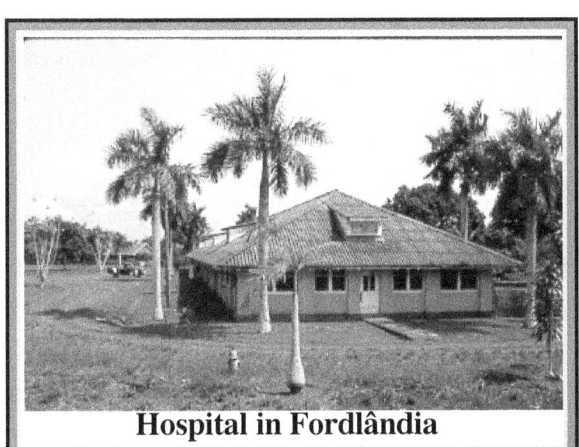
Hospital in Fordlândia

"Oh, we got a half hour out and had to return because the radio went out," they replied. They were none too happy with their unexpected stay. I couldn't help but laugh it was so funny. They did admit that as horrible as this place was they would probably remember this part of their trip the most and get the most laughs out of it. This meant they would miss their flight home from Belém. They were disappointed at this.

Falls and narrows at Sâo Luís where the Río Tapajós narrows from five miles wide.

I went out the next day and found a man who had a small twenty-foot wooden boat with a 26-HP motor going to Itaitúba, which belonged to its mayor. I could catch another boat out of there going the rest of the way to Sâo Luís on the Río Tapajós. I wanted to see the interior rubber tree and its processing area. Sâo Luís's location made it the closest riverboats traveling up the Tapajós to reach the rubber growing and processing. The river at that point narrows from as much as twelve miles in width to a series of waterfalls, making passage further upstream impossible. All river traffic south of Sâo Luís must be transported by land around the series of water falls (Cachoeira Maranhâo Grande). There was a village built by Henry Ford in the 1920s by the same river, called Fôrdandia, complete with a country club and swimming pool. I wanted to see if it was still there.

We got to Fôrdlandia at noon the next day. I ran around and tried to get a look at the place in the few minutes the boatman said he would be there. This model city, with its huge processing plant, was abandoned by Henry Ford in 1946 when it transferred its purchasing of rubber to Malaysia, due to the blight and high prices in Brazil. The place was extremely neglected and in shambles, but still intact due to the hard woods used in their construction. I was about to get on the boat when someone told me there was an American priest there. When they informed me the boat would be another fifteen minutes I ran up to the church to meet the Franciscan Father. I finally found him in front of a line of people giving blessings. I stood in line with the others and when I approached him he greeted me in Portuguese and started to bless me. I addressed him in English and he looked up at me, stunned. He finished his blessings for the others, introduced himself as Frey Miguél, and invited me into his house to have something to drink. The parish house Ford had built was quite nice, neglected on the exterior but beautifully paneled inside with hardwoods. He offered to take me around in his truck but the roar of the boat's motor prompted us to run down to get me back on it.

Galley on the Ze Antonio. Out of this small space came some exquisitely delicious meals.

The Ze Antonio, which took me from Itaituba to São Luís with a falls that prevents further travel.

Executive housing at Fordlândia, still in amazingly good shape after years of neglect

"Stop by here on your way back, day or night, and I'll show you around," Frey Miguél said as I boarded the boat.

The diesel engine chugged up the river at a snail's pace to Itaitúba. Itaitúba had a glorious past, since it was a very rich town in the rubber-boom days. They told me they used to send their laundry to Portugal. Now, the price of soap was almost too elusive for the remaining residents. The river is quite wide at that point, more like a big lake—very little current and as much as 12 miles wide at points. We got to Itaitúba at 12:01 a.m. I was about to sling my hammock to spend the night on the boat when the captain came in and told me he had me on a boat for Sâo Luís, the Ze Antonio, leaving at 3:00 a.m. This boat would remain in Sâo Luís for two days, giving me plenty of time to look around. The charge for the trip from Santarém to Itaitúba with three meals was only about $1.80.

The Ze Antonio to Sâo Luís was a bit larger. Everyone was surprisingly friendly on the boat, making it an enjoyable trip. At Sâo Luís one of the crew took me by the arm to show me the town (a God-forsaken place, just a bunch of grass shacks and some warehouses to store latex balls for shipment). Another crewmember tried to get me on a truck to Pimenta where they process rubber. I was hunting around, looking for transportation there when the captain told me we would be leaving in two hours; not the two days I was expecting. This gave me no time to see the rubber processing—two days lost and nothing seen. The captain told me he was just going to stay in

Brazilian government worker's houses, Fordlândia

Itaitúba for a half-hour and in Fôrdlandia for a day. This seemed just what I wanted after all.

The Ze Antonio was a small launch, possibly thirty feet in length. On the stern was a small area with a charcoal stove and some storage for food. A thin black man was our chef. Out of that kitchen came some unbelievable delicacies. All of us bonded as family for the short duration of the trip.

Catholic Church and parish house, Fordlândia

We were about to pull into Itaitúba at about 2:00 p.m., when the motor broke down. One of the parts was beyond repair. There was no small motorboat to run and get help and no current to take us on down. We just drifted while a couple of the men took a rowboat down river. Two young Indian men took a swim in the river and asked if I wanted to join them. I declined, preferring to rest in my hammock. Following their swim they walked into the forest. One thing was common on every boat. When it was siesta time everyone headed for his or her hammock. After resting I decided the water looked inviting. I stripped off my clothes, stepped up on the edge of the boat, and prepared to dive into the water.

Fordlândia, rubber factory, which Henry Ford built on the Río Tapajós to process rubber. Abandoned in 1946

I was stopped when I heard, "No, no! Don't go in there! There are piranhas!" The captain and two others raced toward me in shock.

"But the two young men went swimming," I said.

"There weren't any piranha where we were then. Piranhas look for still water. We are experienced to look for those things."

I was thankful for my watchful friends. That could have been tragic.

The crewmembers returned in about six hours with a mechanic. The mechanic said he was out of the part so we would have to take it to a missionary school up the river the next day to weld it. The next day they spent all day fixing the motor and we were finally able to proceed that night.

Woman and child stripping leaves to make an addition on their hut. Belterra, Brazil

The next morning I started out bright and early to see Itaitúba, mostly grass huts. I then stopped in to see the American Franciscan, Frei Martín, whom Frei Miguél had suggested I look up. A dour nun met me at the door, announced me to the priest, and started to leave. He yelled something at her as she headed to the door. He was extremely happy to see another American. I wasn't too impressed with either his Portuguese or his treatment of the people. I figured after eight years in the sticks he should speak better Portuguese. He invited me over for lunch and dinner. We had quite a talk about the area. He was very nice to me but extremely grumpy with the parishioners who often dropped by the window to greet him and the nun. I was embarrassed at the way he treated everybody. He talked so pessimistically about everything in that area, I found I had to reverse his negative misconceptions as I continued my travels.

Housing in Itaituba

When I mentioned the huge Baptist church in Santarém he laughed and said, "They're always in competition with us. They built that church so it would be larger than the

Catholic Church."

The next day the boat still wasn't ready to leave. The Mayor's boat had come in during the night so I changed over to it. By this time I had gnawed all my insides out with anxiety. My original plans

Río Tapajós at its widest point.

had called for July 27 to be out of the Amazon. I had reset August 27 as the very last day in order to keep my schedule. Here it was already August 29 and I was drifting out in the middle of the river and on shore for three days. I had seen nothing of Sâo Luís and nothing at Fôrdlandia. I laughed right along with the others at the motor and delays so they wouldn't get a bad impression of an impatient American, but I think they could see through my facade. The captain refused to charge me anything for the meals or ride from Sâo Luís to Itaitúba.

We got to Fôrdlandia that night. I ran to the parish house. Both Frey Miguél and the priest at Itaitúba were cut off from the world, without access to either radio or newspaper. All their news came by way of rumor from traveling natives, who have a pattern of exaggerating. Frei Miguél and I hopped right in his truck and he took me around. The small boat would be at Fôrdlándia for such a short time I knew we would not get to see much. I could see there was quite a bit to explore so it did not take much coaxing on Frei

Main avenue, Belterra, surrounded by hundreds of rubber trees.

Miguel's part to coax me into staying overnight and leaving on Humberto's boat the next day. He put me up in a nice pine-paneled room on the second floor of his parish house. That was the first time I had had my own private room for a long time. It was also the first time I had seen a bathroom with shower for months.

We went around the next morning after Mass. He showed me the clinic, which he supported for the workers. The government was two months behind in paying the workers so he was personally supporting them in food and some expenses because they were starving. The government allocated the money each month, but officials along the way pilfered it before it could reach the projects. The large factory Ford built was still standing but in shambles. A large water tower dominated the little village. Although the exterior of the houses was shabby, the hardwood floors remained in perfect shape.

These are some of the original rubber trees growing at Belterra before the town was built. The blight killed most of them

I mentioned the problems I had converting traveler's checks and that I was going to be flying to Belém upon my return. He gave me the name of the head of the Franciscan missionaries who he said could help me if I had trouble cashing the checks. He told me to be sure and stop at Belterra, another town Ford built. Since the blight had wiped out most of the rubber plantations, including Fôrdlandia, manufacturing and cultivation were now concentrated in Belterra and the villages lining the upper Tapajós River. The Brazilians had let Fôrdlandia fall to pieces.

Tapping a rubber tree at Belterra. Townsend said the cut was made too deep, which will probably harm the tree, preventing its future production.

231

The buildings were crumbling; the machinery was shot. The people were starving.

"Stop off at Belterra on your way down. There's a road from there to Santarém so you can easily catch a ride that short distance."

Belterra, Brazil. Ford built workers' housing

Humberto came in that afternoon. Miguél warned me he would steal me blind and others had given me similar warnings. He also had a habit of stopping to see friends at various huts along the way so you never knew when you'd get to your destination.

Humberto reminded me of an overgrown pig. He was always growling, shouting, and ordering everyone, including me, around. I wanted to eat with the rest of the passengers but he insisted I eat with him. I felt very uneasy sitting in the middle of the cargo eating with the captain, with all the passengers looking on. There was an urge to decline, which I often tried to do, but officials who offered these privileges always insisted until I would finally acquiesce.

Guesthouse at Belterra. Beautiful hardwood interior

The passengers were very friendly. I found the Tapajós River to be a complete change from the rest of the Amazon. The people of Manaus and Santarém (especially Santarém) were very rude and would yell things at me or laugh at me on the street, but on the Tapajós they were proud to have an American among them and treated me as one of the gang. We slung our hammocks wherever we could find space between the cargos.

We stopped at Boím, famous for its hardwoods, for about five hours the next day. They loaded it by floating it, piece-by-piece, to the boat, handing each piece onto the boat. The Tapajós had many beautiful beaches. This was good for swimming but the shallow shoreline made it difficult to load cargo onto the boats. So many places had Piranha, Boa Constrictors and were a danger to a swimmer.

Worker housing, built by Ford.

We didn't get into Belterra until next morning at 4:00 a.m. This town had nearly the same architecture as Fôrdlandia, except the buildings were well maintained. Henry Ford built Belterra and this is where most of the rubber was grown. The officials of the company led me to an American, Charles Townsend, who was with the ICA, an international organization for agriculture. He was there to introduce a blight-resistant tree that would produce a better rubber plant for the Brazilians.

Baptist Church in Santarém, Brazil

He took me around, got me settled in the guesthouse (quite elegant with beautiful hardwood paneling and floors inside) and took me through the factory and experimental station where he was developing the blight-resistant strain of rubber tree.

The failure of the rubber production was due to poor planning and unrealistic marketing. Dr. Lyle Shurz, my Latin America Professor at AGSIM went to Brazil in the late 1920s to research the market for rubber. His advisors warned the governments there was blight on some of the rubber trees, which was not threatening when sparsely grown in the wild, but would spread quickly if they tried to plant large plots. Both Ford and the Brazilian government were anxious to modernize production so, despite the warning, proceeded planting large plots, dotting the area of the Tapajós and Amazon Rivers. In a short time, the blight just about wiped out the entire rubber forest. When the blight attacks the rubber tree it does not kill it, it stifles the sap flow so it no longer produces latex serum. It takes new plantings seven years to grow to production, so each experiment to produce blight-resistant trees took seven years for each test. Townsend was hastening the process by grafting young trees rather than seeding and experiencing some success. He pointed to the gashes on the trees, beneath which hung small cups, some with good production and others gashed too deep, harming the trees. Production and manufacturing of rubber was now confined to small villages, individual plots, and this plantation at Belterra. Also, Brazil, in its desire to generate more capital during its days as sole supplier, kept raising the price of rubber until it became feasible for someone to create a new source of income for Indonesia and other countries with ambient climates. Brazil lost its plantations and monopolistic position within a short time.

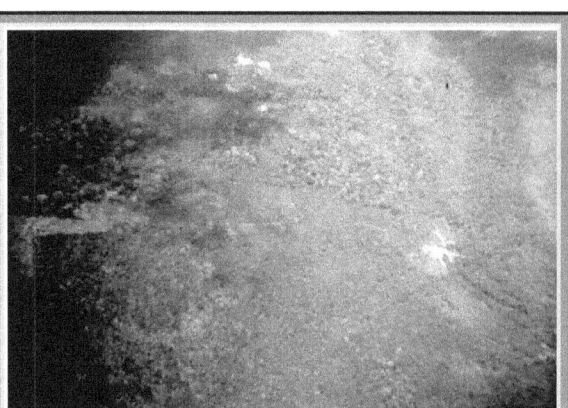

Indigenous clearings in the jungle from the air. These will be abandoned after 3-5 years as they move to another spot. Large clearings for the cattle and timber cutting will revert to desert, lost to the world and future generations.

That evening Charles invited me over for dinner. I had a million questions that had been building up inside of me and there was little time left to get them all answered. He invited me to stay another day and take a boat trip with him to an interesting village, but I felt I was far enough behind on my schedule as it was.

The truck to Santarém had already left and there was no transportation until the next day. I began to worry as I only had Cr$80 (about 50¢) to my name and couldn't cash a check, as money was scarce in that area.

The next morning I got a ride on the back of a truck for the 2-1/2 hour ride to Santarém. I ran over to the air ticket agency and found the plane for Belém was leaving in ten minutes, but no one, not even a bank, would touch a traveler's check. Money was tight there, too. PanAir offered me 100 to the dollar. This would be a loss of about $4.00 on the $10 check. The agent ran me over to the local Parish House. The American head of the Franciscan Order for the entire area, who Miguél had recommended I see, was there. This was a job usually cherished by the Italians. He ran to his desk and pulled out Cr$2,400 and said, "Here, take this and you can cash your check at a good rate in Belém and leave the money for me with the Vice-Council there." I was amazed at such a trusting attitude toward a virtual stranger.

I bought my ticket and got out to the airport fifteen minutes after they told me the plane was scheduled to leave. Fortunately, the plane was a half-hour late.

This airline had lost a plane in the drink just a while before but I felt it was safe to fly it. We had a rough trip into Belém and I felt the pilot had better brush up a little before his next flight with passengers.

9. ACROSS THE SERTÃO

One of the passengers on the Tapajós recommended a cheap pensâo. Even though the airlines furnished the taxi and stated the rates, I was charged extra as an American. I never seemed to be able to win at this game. I grabbed my bags and ran upstairs when I arrived at the pensâo. The bottom floor was just a dirty hall with a couple of boys repairing shoes. When I asked the senhora if she had a single room, she grimaced and said, "Yes, I have a single room." That was just what she had—one room for everyone, together. There were three of us in the room; a fat man who slept most of the time and snorted rather than talked, and an older black man who carried a small pistol, which he obviously removed from his bag. I was not comfortable with this, especially with my satchel of camera equipment.

Belém, mouth of the Amazon River. River is around 100 miles wide as it reaches the ocean.

I found the people of Belém very friendly. As I was about a foot taller than the average Latin American and had a foreign face, everyone usually stared at me. I considered this impolite so would stare back until they looked away. However, I soon decided not to do this any more as one of "the boys" mistook my stare back as a look of amour. I couldn't get rid of him. As he followed me down the street I saw a padre who looked American. I stopped him and asked him in English if he was American. He stammered a bit and then blurted out, "Vd. habla Español?" He turned out to be from Spain. It worked because when I turned around the boy had disappeared.

Market. Belém, Brazil

I went down to the port to see if the ships I had missed had come in. I was standing there when I heard, "Carlos Hinkley." Startled, I turned around and there was Gumercindo.

"I'm waiting for a boat but couldn't find one until the 15th. Guillermo found a cheap boat right away but I didn't have enough money to go with him. Meet me in the morning and we'll see the town together. You've got to see this," said Guillermo, sporting a wry grin.

Loading rubber balls and castaña (Brazil Nuts), Port of Belém, Brazil

"What?" I asked, not knowing whether this was a joke or an interesting find.

"There is a beautiful park in front of the opera house that is named after—you're not going to believe this—Benjamin Constánt."

"You mean, the same person as that awful town on the Amazon?"

"Yes, and it is beautiful contrasting with that miserable town."

First thing the next day he made a point to show me the park. "I'll bet Benjamín is happy he got something other than that decrepit village named after him."

That night was one hell of a night. The fat one snored so loud I could hardly sleep. There was only one bed so two of us slung hammocks. The other guy relieved himself on the floor in the middle of the night, which didn't go too well in this stuffy room.

Statue to Benjamín Constánt and Teatro de Paz, Belém, Brazil

I reasoned I'd better take another airline after my experience with Lloyd. Several had told me they had lost three airplanes in the last few months. However, when

I checked out the other two airlines I found Lloyd was the only one that had room for me, so I finally had to buy a ticket on it leaving in two days.

One of numerous Victorian Mansions in Belém

I found the pensâo that Gumercindo was staying in had another room so I decided to change. The people in Gumercindo's pensâo were absolutely the lowest class in Brazil. They cussed, swore, fought, etc. The senhora smoked a cigar, the ten-year-old girl also smoked, along with the 11-year-old boy. They spoke terrible Portuguese, running at the mouth all the time, babbling away. His main saying to me was, "You don't know Portuguese very well, do you?" I said, "I speak a little." He replied, "Well, you don't speak it very well!" This came at a point when I was really patting myself on the back for

Crazy bus in Belém, Brazil. They came in many different styles, each individualized by the driver-owner.

finally getting some fluency. I did find I was conjugating almost all my irregulars in Spanish and was mixing Spanish words in with the Portuguese.

The next day I spent sightseeing. It took me two days to get used to the shock of the dirt in Belém, with narrow streets and old broken-down palaces. I'm not sure whether it was more unkempt than Manaus, Santarém, or Iquitos or just that I had a high anticipation of

Victorian house and garden, Belém, Brazil

what it would be like. However, the next day I appreciated more the quaint streets, old cathedrals and palaces and parks. "Gumercindo, let's go to the museum to see the animals Guillermo and I kept hearing in the jungle and never saw," I suggested. Of course we couldn't miss the statue of Benjamin Constánt, facing the opera house from its beautiful setting in the park.

I got a cheap plane next day for São Luís. I swore I would walk before I ever flew on Lloyd again, for this was the first time I can ever remember being frightened on a flight. The plane gunned down the runway without even warming up or testing its engines, and then stopped halfway to the end. Several mechanics came, the crew got out to meet them. Everyone looked the engine over and adjusted a couple of things like you would on an old Ford fliver. They started the engines again. The plane again raced down the runway, faster and faster but with little lift. As I watched us race past the tall forest on the side I wondered if the field was long enough to rise above the tall trees at the end of the runway. Finally, we lifted a little just as the tar went out from under us. I watched the trees whiz by on the side and noticed we were only about halfway to the top of them. I wondered how far they had cleared the trees ahead. We lifted a little more, just barely clearing the tops of the trees as they swayed below our draft. We then slowly lifted until we were safely above them. It took about a half hour to climb to cruising height. Once at altitude, the plane did a series of dives and pulls for the entire journey as we fought the updrafts from the jungle below.

Modern architecture, Brazil. Rowing Club in Belém.

Road through Sertão, Northern Brazil, between Fortaleza & Natál. Dusty & hot.

As I looked down at the massive carpet of green below us, a matrix of small brown circles were visible. These were the burn areas in which were built temporary villages. Every two years these dots would change to another spot, allowing their former clearing to return to forest. This is ecologically sound for the indigenous that live in harmony with the forest. However, it is an ecological disaster when done on a massive or more permanent scale. Juselino Kubichek, the President of Brazil at that time, was draining the treasury, focusing on completing the construction of the new capital, Brasilia, in the high plains of the rainforest and the Trans-Amazon Highway before the end of his term. This is why an area as large as the state of Vermont is lost to erosion in the rainforest every year. Plants, trees, and birds are intricately interconnected in the rainforest. When larger tracts are burned, that collective existence is forever lost, leaving only eroded desert in its place.

I looked down and could see what looked like a city below. Rather than descending for a landing the plane continued until it was directly over the it. Suddenly we dove down and, in an instant, landed on a large hill in the center of São Luís. My heart was still in my throat when we finally hit ground. I was never so glad to arrive at a place in my life. It was later I learned that Lloyd had lost three planes within a little over a month and had the worst maintenance in Brazil. I was fortunate to be on one of the planes that made it.

The ride into town was about as bad as the airplane ride. The car was barely in one piece. The door wouldn't work so the driver took it off to let the passengers board and then tied it shut. He started the engine and you could hear the clatter for miles. He fought with the gearshift, trying each gear unsuccessfully when finally second gear took hold and the car began to move. The clutch churned and groaned and then finally held. We immediately swerved to the side and he fought with the steering wheel, which was so loose it took two turns before it moved the wheels. We then swung from side-to-side as he fought to get speed. The trip to town was down a

São Luís, Maranhâo, Brazil

narrow, winding cobblestone road with a continuous row of buildings lining each side and many sharp corners. We just barely missed truck after ox cart as the steering mechanism gave little sign of reacting. The driver pounded the horn constantly as people ran for shelter and slower vehicles left the road. As we got into the narrowly winding, hilly streets he slammed his foot on the brake and nothing happened. It was a game of "dare" and fortunately no one took our dare. Amazingly, when we were through the narrow streets we headed for a park. The cab glided to a stop right in front of the hotel, which faced the park. I wasn't sure whether this was a well-engineered preplanned expedition, perfected by the driver's repeated trips or just plain luck.

My first impression of São Luís was, "When does the train leave?" A blast of hot air hit me in the face; the streets were all small, no new buildings in town, etc. However, after being there awhile I found it one of the most enjoyable places in Brazil. Very little had changed from Colonial times. Burros and oxcarts still plied the streets; the people were still very formal. The language was the closest to the Portuguese of Portugal I had been taught, and the people seemed little changed from their farming ancestors.

Church and Park, São Luís, Maranhão, Brazil

This time I went to the best hotel in town. They told me they had no rooms but would see what they could do for me. They finally showed me to a room with salon and bath. It was the most spacious room I had seen in months.

I was suddenly gripped by an extreme case of oppressive loneliness. During the past two months I had never been alone, even at night. The walls of the room closed in around me and compressed my chest. I thought at least eating in a public dining room would help me overcome this lonely feeling. The restaurant refused to serve me without a jacket, which was wadded up in the bottom of my duffle bag. I tried to get it ironed but there was no service. I was left with no choice but to eat in my room. I felt like a caged animal being fed by my captors. I nibbled on a couple of things and left. I couldn't eat. I went out and walked around, hoping I would meet anyone that would stop and talk to me. I finally returned to get some sleep. I was informed on my return I would have to move, as they needed the room I was in. They wouldn't move me right away so I went up and lay down. In the middle of the night they woke me up to move. The room they gave me was small, had another man in it, and had no bathroom. There was just room enough for the two beds. This was too much. I went out and walked and walked until I was so sleepy I could walk no more.

I was so engrossed in enjoying the crowds at night I didn't notice the streets were clearing off about 9:00 p.m. I rounded a corner and headed down a narrow street surrounded on both sides by shops. I suddenly woke from my drifting mind and looked around. I found myself walking down a dark street with no one in sight. I thought, "I'd better get back to a broader, well-lit street. This is not safe." As I started to turn around I noticed three men apparently breaking into one of the stores. The moment I noticed them, they noticed me and let go of the door. I thought, "If I run back they will know I spotted them and will probably chase me down." They had already begun to walk toward me. I continued walking in their direction, although I knew I would have to pass them as they moved toward the center of the dark narrow street where I could not avoid meeting them. A still small voice in my head told me to keep walking. I did not look sideways, but stared straight ahead as they moved nearer to the center of the street. I could see one had a rock in his hand, the other another instrument like a bat and I couldn't see what the third one was doing. As I approached them I could feel their eyes on me, waiting in the dark. I walked straight into them, careful to not even glance in their direction. Out of the corner of my eyes I could see the look of shock on their faces that I would walk

Mode of transport, São Luís, Maranhâo, Brazil

right through them. When I passed they were no more than two feet away from me. I did not look back but walked to the end of the street and back to town. I did not feel any fear as I passed them. I knew I had the hand of a very welcome angel on my shoulder guiding me through the maze.

When I went to pay my bill I found they charged me for the room with Salón and bath rather than the little room with "companion" that I finally ended up with. Later, when I had lunch with an American associate my father referred me to, he said to me, "Now you can see why all of us with PETROBRAS (The Brazilian oil company he worked for) hate that hotel."

I took the bus to Terezina (21 hours, stopping for two flat tires) to get to Fortaleza (another 14 hours with three flat tires) on the advice of a number of people who warned me the train never makes it. The road was dusty with a deep bed of soft red dirt, and the heat was oppressive. After each flat tire the driver could not find the right tools and passengers would search for a lone tree to give us some shade during the long waits. After the trip I was beginning to wonder how the bus ever made it. As we pulled into Forteleza the usual crowd of porters surrounded the bus. One of them grabbed my bag, tripped, and fell over it. I reached down with my right hand, threw it over my shoulder and picked up the briefcase. The porter, still on the ground, looked up at me in surprise and shook his head in disbelief. That night I couldn't sit in my room but had to go sit in the park just to be around people. Fortunately someone came by and chatted with me for a couple of hours.

Water truck, Sobrál, Brazil

I was crossing by bus through what Brazil refers to as the Sertâo (which in Portuguese means Inland, "Terra Adentro"). The entire upper portion of Brazil alternates between rainforest and drought. It was presently in about the third year of drought. The sparse vegetation looked the same as the rainforest would look if it stopped raining for several years.

Much of the vegetation reminded me of many of the trees in the jungle, but they were dry and looked like they were dying. You could see canals threading their way through the dry desert-like climate. Some carried water, if they were close to a reservoir or natural lake or river, but most were dry ditches threading their way through the arid region. I was told Brazil was making a concerted effort to bring irrigated water to the North. However, corruption skimmed most of the money so most of the projects could not be completed. Where there was water there were small farms, using hand scythes, machetes, oxen, and wooden plows to eke out subsistent farming. Even harvested crops were carried out on their backs. Farmers were migrating in droves to the South to seek work in the factories.

Beggars stood next to every arriving and departing bus and on street corners. Employment was sparse. I was standing on a street corner next to a gasoline station when I heard a band playing in the distance. I looked to see where it was and saw nothing, but the music kept getting closer. Finally I looked at a passing Model A, filled to the brim with people. Inside was the orchestra, playing beautiful music. We laughed together as they drove into the station and waved at me.

Harvesting wheat near Natál.

Every street corner was a musical band and dance hall. In many places several people stood and played hand-made instruments, even if they were just two sticks or a can. Their music was rhythmic and beautiful. Little girls walking down the sidewalks would suddenly break into a dance, twisting to the music.

My Portuguese improved with every hotel as I argued vociferously over the constant overcharges.

I took the bus to Natal the next morning. We had a flat tire a little ways out but I was surprised to see how well equipped this bus was. It actually carried tools to fix the flats.

We stopped off for a couple of hours while the driver fixed the flat and were soon on our way. We got a little ways further and had another flat. The driver stopped and was looking at it when we heard another BANG and a leakage of air. It was hot out in the middle of the desert. (Sertâo area of Northern Brazil). He managed to bandage up one and change the other tire so we were soon on our way. I was amazed when the bus arrived at Fortaleza on time.

I was tired of getting gypped by the big hotels, so I asked around for a cheaper one. Two other men who were looking for about the same price hotel as I talked me into using a portreiro again. The portreiros tried to fleece me as usual. I got together with the other two men who helped me barter my price down. They were still working on bartering theirs when I left. It turned out to be one of the nicest hotels I stayed at. They were pleased to have an American stay there as Americans don't usually patronize lower-price hotels and there were virtually no traveling American students in Northern Brazil. It seemed like I was the first American who had traveled by bus in Northern Brazil. Americans who came down the Amazon usually flew back to the States or sailed on. Even the man who first talked me into taking the Amazon trip told me not to go overland in Northern Brazil. It was a rough, dirty trip through hot dry country, with grinding poverty worse than any I had ever seen, but it gave me an insight into Brazil I would never otherwise have had.

My first night in Forteleza I decided to eat out, rather than eat at the hotel, which had a fine dining room. I walked the streets looking for a restaurant and was surprised to find none, anywhere. As I turned one corner I saw a number of cargo trucks, parked for the night. It was a wide street but deserted, which concerned me so I was about to turn around and return when I noticed a small open café at the end of the street with some tables inside. A man was standing in front of the empty doorway. He did not even greet me. After I sat down he came over and stared down at me. I was hungry so ordered the best meal on the menu, desert, and drink. He continued

Children's City in Fortaleza, Brazil

serving me in silence until it was time to pay the bill. He approached my table, nervously laid the bill in front of me and stepped back and stared. I calculated the bill in dollars and found the entire meal was only equivalent to 60¢. I paid and tipped him, thanked him and left. The next evening I felt that was such a great meal I returned to the same restaurant. As I walked down the lonely street the proprietor saw me, ran over to me and greeted me with a radiant smile. He was a most solicitous waiter, treating me as a long-lost friend and sent me off with solicitous goodbyes.

Beaches at Natál, Brazil

When I returned to the hotel I realized this was a restaurant that served mostly truck drivers. He was overwhelmed when he saw a foreigner coming to his restaurant, surprised when I ordered one of his most expensive meals and timid when he handed me the bill, which to a truck driver must have seemed like a great deal of money. When he saw me return the next night he was thrilled to see I came back after what he probably thought was a huge bill.

Each city had its own unique red light district, limited to a few blocks. This was legal and government run or licensed, carefully placed out of sight. I remember thinking what a sensible way to treat an act, which harms no one, compared to the United States where the Johns are free to roam while their objects of relief are hauled off to court or owned and controlled by pimps.

Band in car on way to Joâo Pessoa

A 16-hour bus ride

landed me in Natál, the end of the Sertâo. I had great expectations but found it to be just another small town with a few modern buildings. Its major attractions were the beautiful beaches north of the city. I left the next morning for Recife. I ran to a bank, quickly before they closed, to cash enough money for the trip ahead. When I arrived at the bank a guard blocked me and said, "The bank just closed, come back tomorrow when we open."

"But I've got to cash a check so I can take the bus early tomorrow," I said in anguish.

The guard and I bantered back and forth for several minutes and he finally said, "Wait here. I'll go talk with the manager."

He soon came back down and said, "Follow me."

At the top of the stairs was a small office. A very courteous gentleman behind a desk greeted me, "Come on in. My name is Manuel Peres." He then proceeded to ask me where I was coming from, where I was going, how long I had been on the trip and numerous details on the Amazon. He finally asked me, "How long have you been studying Portuguese?"

"Five months," I replied.

"How many years before that?" he said, with a surprised look.

"No, I just studied it for three months."

"Well, you speak better Portuguese than a priest I know who's been here for twenty years."

Recife, a city built on three reefs, connected by a series of bridges.

Considerable time passed as we conversed so I thought I'd better get back to the reason why I came, so I asked, "I really have to cash this check. Can you do that?"

"Don't worry about that. I'm going to cash it for you. Let's talk first."

We chatted for another half-hour.

The ride to Recífe passed miles of sugar cane fields, which extended up like a green carpet covering verdant rolling hills as far as the eye could see. In the middle of the ride someone yelled, "Pneu."

I thought, "Oh, no, not again." However, It wasn't a flat, just something wrong with the steering mechanism.

If I was surprised at the smallness of Natál, I was even more surprised at the bigness and beauty of Recífe. It was full of beautiful modern buildings in a picturesque setting. It showed great promise of becoming a major city in the future for Brazil. Recífe means reef, and that is what it was built on, a series of reefs extending out into the bay, with numerous bridges connecting each peninsula.

There were three places I wished to visit in Northern Brazil; mostly motivated by my readings in the language books I studied.

Colonial buildings in Recife

One book named several places of interest in the North: Natal as a major city, Joâo Pessoa as having beautiful beaches and the falls (Cachuera de Paulo Alfonso) on the Río Sâo Francisco.

What had sounded like a romantic journey past beautiful beaches, short trips through breathtaking vistas and magnificent waterfalls explained so delightfully in our language book was nothing like the flowery descriptions in the book. It was a two-day trip to the falls with an overnight stay in Arco Verde. Lined up at the bus were the usual beggars. Most of the passengers were farmers from the Sertâo who spoke a dialect closer to Portuguese from Portugal rather than the more familiar Brazilian.

Woman beggar between Natál & Joâo Pessoa

The difference was probably like a person from New York communicating with someone from the hills of Tennessee. I noticed even many of the Brazilians from other parts of Brazil found it difficult to understand them. Most of them had been forced to leave their subsistence farming during the drought and were looking for work in the cities until the rains again returned. We were soon on a dirt road with desert surroundings.

As a foreigner, it was disturbing to me, not so much because of their accent but what they were saying about me. itself. As I strained to listen to their conversations I would hear things like:

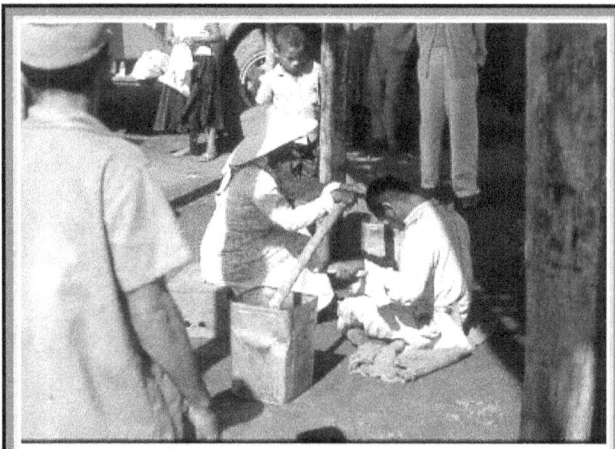
Man playing wire strung on pole held by his assistant between two large cans.

"Foreigners are really strange people."

"He's taking pictures indiscriminately out the window. They really are strange."

"He stops and looks at the musicians playing and doesn't pay them anything," referring to a man who was playing a wire between two cans at one of the bus stops.

"He really is strange. He doesn't enter our conversations."

"Foreigners don't pay the beggars."

This was the unending conversation I heard coming from the passengers in the rear during the trip to Arco Verde. I was embarrassed and somewhat incensed by their rude conversation within earshot of me, but did not know how to enter their conversation.

Terrain between Arco Verde and Petrolândia

At Arco Verde we ended the bus ride at a small café. As we filed in I purposely picked a table alone so I didn't have to listen to them. Instead of discouraging them, the table acted as a magnet to a large portion of the group who sat around me. As soon as I heard negative comments about me, I thought I'd better end this right away. I picked a conversation I knew I could speak my most rapid Portuguese, and asked them questions about who they were, where they were going and about the trip I would have to Paulo Alfonso the next day. They immediately and respectfully answered my questions. After about fifteen minutes of conversation there was a moment of silence, during which I heard one of them say to another in a whisper, "I'll bet he understood every word we were saying on the bus."

I was sure this had settled the negative conversations, but was unpleasantly surprised after we transferred to the bus to hear, "These foreigners sure are funny. Look at the way they dress, [etc., etc.]" My friendly conversation with them in the restaurant had not had any effect on them.

When the bus arrived in the town of Paulo Alfonso I was sent to the only hotel in town. The town was divided between the collection of shanties and the newer town completed by the government for the hydroelectric plant. The manager opened a door to a small room containing four cots. To get to the last one I would have had to crawl over the rest. A man sleeping in his underwear slowly sat up. The manager told him to get up because he had to put someone in the last bed. I was reminded of the disgust of the first room I rented in Belém. Something inside me said, "Don't do it." I just couldn't spend a night in that stuffy room with three strangers, especially with a satchel full of expensive camera equipment. I asked the manager if they had "um cuarto solo" (a single room). He looked surprised and said, "But senhor this is 'um cuarto solo'. One room for everyone."

"Is there a hotel in town that has a private room where I could stay?" I asked.

"No, no hotel in town has such a thing."

"Is there a sort of guest house at the power plant where I could stay?" I continued.

"Yes, why don't you go to the power plant and beg your way into their guest house."

"But isn't this restricted to officials of the

Coacheira do Paulo Alfonso

project and their visitors?" I questioned.

"Tell them you are a foreigner wanting to inspect the hydroelectric plant. They'll feel you are an official and let you stay there."

I followed his directions, caught a cab to the plant, and was stopped at the gate. I told the guard I was from the United States and was not used to sleeping three to a room in the only hotel in town. He made a call to the plant and let me in. The small hotel for the hydroelectric plant was beautiful, with a private shower and air conditioned room. We had been traveling through red dust for the past two days so I was thrilled as the water washed the thick crust of red dirt off my body.

At the visitors' shack I was informed that to visit the falls I would have to hire a taxi, which they called for me. I waited endlessly; finally seeing the same taxi that had overcharged me back in town arrived to pick me up. But fortune was with me. A family from Joâo Pessoa, who had driven down for a visit, was also touring the falls and the plant invited me to join them in their car. The company furnished a guide. This was the greatest blessing that could have happened to me. The trip, since Belém, had been a lonely one. My encounters with the Brazilians had been from perfunctory to hostile. I was traveling with desperate people, out of work and neglected by their government, fraught with a hostile natural world. They were

Carrier bucket strung across canyon to reach the Coacheira do Paulo Alfonso

sad, frustrated with their lot in life, and completely unfamiliar with foreigners. Traveling through hot territory, dusty and bumpy roads made our shared experience uncomfortable. Hotels would fudge on exchange rates, pad bills; the myriad of porters, who were usually out-of-work laborers living on subsistence income would invariably charge me 300% of their going rate for minimal service. There was practically no opportunity to converse on the buses. Seeing people in such poverty distressed me. Even in the hotels there was little dialogue with other hotel guests or employees. I felt isolated from the constant interaction to which I had become accustomed during my expedition through Colombia and the Amazon. I found myself in loud arguments with hotel clerks and stores where I was persistently overcharged. Colombia had caught my heart and the Amazon, even with the chaos on board the paddle wheeler on the Putumayo and the mistreatment on the Tavares Bastos on the Amazon, was full of life and connection with people from all walks of life. Even standing in lines I found myself disregarded as others in front of me were taken care of while I, a foreigner was forced to wait. I could never, as a white person, claim to feel the pain of discrimination experienced by a person of color, but my treatment throughout the Sertâo gave me a glimpse of what their life must be like in the U.S.

The Brazilians built a large dam on the Río Sâo Francisco, which would soon be producing 348,000 Kws. for Northeastern Brazil. The falls was higher than Niagara, but was squeezed into a narrow canyon with an enormous volume of water roaring through the narrow opening. We crossed the deep canyon by means of a two-person bucket suspended from a cable with a handle, which one of us pumped back and forth to move the bucket forward. The couple's father was still recuperating from a heart attack, so being suspended in a bucket over nearly a thousand feet of roaring water was done very slowly, but the view was worth it. The power plant is deep within the walls of the canyon, some 267 feet below the surface.

I turned to my host and confessed, "I keep getting overcharged for everything. They do this because I am a foreigner and they think I have a great deal of money."

"Don't feel bad. You pay in dollars, which are worth more than the cruzeiro. It's not because you're an American. They charge us the same thing they charge you because we are tourists and they sense right away we are from another city so must have a lot of money."

"Do they really charge you as much as they do me?"

"Yes, we get charged triple just like you do and we have to earn back the money in cruzeiros."

This made me more tolerant of the shake down I seemed to be experiencing with every service. "It would take a large part of Brazilians' earnings to travel, even short distances as a tourist," I thought. The power company furnished the guide and these people shared their car with me.

In Natal I was told there was a bus every day from Paulo Alfonso to Salvador. Reality proved there was only one bus a week going to that city. A plane left the next morning but I had only sufficient money to go by bus or hitch a ride on a truck.

The next morning I walked out to the police roadblock on the outgoing highway. Everyone was shocked as they watched me carrying my heavy bags through town. I remembered what Dr. Shurz told us in class, "Brazilians never carry their bags. If they can scrape up two cents they will find a boy to carry even their briefcase." Watching a foreigner carrying two heavy bags must have been an event. It was small wonder there were so many boys at each station vying to carry my bags. No one carried his or her own bags.

The guard at the border station was friendly and told me he would help me find a ride. He looked at me as I walked up to his shack and said, "No wonder you Americans are so strong."

As we waited for a truck to pass we talked for what seemed like hours. Politics was, of course, at the top of the agenda. His conversation turned to race. I glanced at the open window. A tall, thin black man was leaning in the window, smiling and listening to our conversation. The guard continued," Here we have the mixing of the races. You Americans have the right idea. You separate the races and send them to separate schools."

"There are only six states where the races are separated," I retorted.

"I don't believe that," he said.

"The mixing of the races, where it has occurred, has been good in most cases," I retorted.

"But we have the mixing of the Portuguese with the blacks. The Portuguese just want to get rich in a hurry so they won't have to work and the Negro doesn't want to get rich and doesn't want to work. The sensuality of the two is like rubbing two sticks together—it only makes fire. And what do you have when you mix the Portuguese with the Negro—nothing. The result is you have a Northern Brazilian who is frustrated, resents work, overly sensual and not very good-looking. Such a thing would not happen if the U.S. had a mixing

Shopping in Recife

of the races as great as Brazil because we have so much more to mix the Negro with. If the father of the family has made something of himself the resulting mulatto will try to rise to an equal level with his father. I think with heavy immigration places like Salvador, Recífe, Belém and Natal can pull out of this cultural lag and progress with the rest of Brazil. There is strong evidence this is happening." I looked at the window and saw the black man, still listening and still smiling, so was sure he was either stifling any resentment to the guard's bigoted ranting or was not fully comprehending what he was saying. Nevertheless, I was embarrassed at this conversation, especially since it must have been very insulting to this very nice gentleman standing at the open window.

I was surprised at the guard's conversation. I expected to find complete racial tolerance in Brazil. The tolerance I had been taught to expect in Brazil was not widespread. Every conversation shifted to race, and not all the Brazilians I met were open-minded. Some Brazilians told me they have a culture, whereas the United States has none because of Brazil's miscegenation. I found even more territorial divergence in Brazil than in the U.S., as each state was as complicated to cross from one to the other as our Canadian border. Each state collected duties on goods crossing its borders. I found great resentment of one state for another, and the people as divergent as their views of each other. The fourth and fifth generation Portuguese farmers of the Sertâo had a language probably better understood by farmers in Portugal than Brazilians of the big cities. Each state had its own songs and people seemed to see themselves as citizens of Pará, Pernambuco, Maranhâo, etc., rather than the nation.

View of Alta (upper city) from Baixa (lower)

A number of trucks stopped with an assortment of surly drivers. I was relieved when a friendly driver pulled up on his way to Feíra de Santana, a city that had considerable transportation to Salvador. The officer started asking him in low tones if I could ride on his truck to Feíra. I sat by helplessly while he demanded I pay nothing and ride in the cab. There was nothing I could do, as the officer persisted on putting me in nothing but the best accommodations. My heart sank as I watched each driver drive away.

Finally, at 2:00 p.m., I found a truck. I thought we would never get to Feíra. He started by wanting 500 cruzeiros. As we rode along I began to add up what I had and concluded I might not even have enough even if I went without dinner and breakfast. I knew I was being far overcharged, as the bus would have been less than he was charging. I asked if I could sit on the back of the truck to pay less. He said it was the same price. I told him I didn't have enough money to make it to Salvador. He finally said, "For you I'll make it 450 crucieros. Is that low enough?"

I told him if I went without dinner that would almost definitely be enough. He then said, "I'll make it 300 cruceiros. I won't have you running around hungry."

Elevator, which carries people up from Baixa to Alta, Salvador, Brazil.

We would go for a half-hour, then stop for a half-hour, etc., etc. We weren't making any time at all. Finally, that night we pulled up to a gas station and slept until about 4:00 a.m. The truck only went about four mph whenever it hit any type of grade at all, so I felt I could walk faster than it was going. We finally pulled into Feíra at 2:15 p.m., just in time to miss the last bus that day. I ran around town inquiring about other transportation but couldn't find anything. When I told one man I had no money and had to get that bus he ran around helping me. Finally, he gave up. I peeked around a corner and saw two different Mercedes buses standing there. I ran down and found one marked for Salvador. I guess the men I had asked about buses gave me a bum steer because they wanted to let them carry my bags for a price. I got on and was on my way by 3:30. I then found the two hours everyone told me the journey would take was closer to five hours. When I had given the truck driver his 300 cruceros he gave me another fifty back because I was so short on money that I had had nothing for lunch. My experience with Brazilians was they would gyp me for all I was worth, but once they found I was low on funds they'd go out of their way to help me.

The man I sat next to on the bus directed me to a low price hotel. It was not one I would have chosen in the middle of the worst section of town. However, it had good rates, served good meals, and was right across from the train depot where I would be taking the train to Belo Horizonte. There was a gracious ambiance to Salvador. My hotel was in a predominately black section of the city. Here, the people were joyous, cheerful, and friendly. It was called the Baixa (meaning lower), because it was on a shelf, which extended out to the ocean. The rest of the city was located on the Alta (Upper), which extended to a precipice, which looked down on the Baixa, about a hundred feet below. Although roads wound their way to the top at the far south end, pedestrians moved between the levels on a series of elevators. The Alta appeared to be primarily Portuguese. There the mood was somber, with people seldom smiling or responding.

Recífe was purported to be the starting place for most revolutions in Brazil. Many shared their class resentment with me. I was eating in a restaurant at one of the nice hotels where I was staying in Salvador, when the waiter began talking with me every time he approached my table. At first it was conversational, but as he got to know me better he began pointing to people in the restaurant, chatting about the coming revolution. He pointed at one stocky man sitting at another table and said, "These pigs think they own us." He then turned and walked back to the kitchen. The next time he passed the table he quipped "We're going to kill these people when we revolt," glancing at four men seated at another table while slicing his finger across his throat." Then he zoomed to another table. I cringed every time he came to my table.

Alta (Upper City), Salvador, Brazil

When he returned he repeated, "We're going to slit their throats." Then he flipped to another table. I looked around very quickly to see if any at the other tables were looking my way. They weren't. I almost felt like eluding him every time he came to my table. He returned several times, slid his finger across his throat, and again repeated to me, "We're going to slit their throats." Wonderful restaurant, great food, but was I ever glad to be out of there.

President Jucelino Kubitschek was making every effort to unify the country, industrialize it, and push the population, which was concentrated on the coast, into the interior. To facilitate his goals he was able to make a deal with the Americans to place a satellite relay station on the Island of Fernando de Naronha in exchange for financial support toward building a new capitol at the edge of the rainforest. He felt moving the Congress from Río to the interior would change the thinking of the governing body. The great development happening in the Southern States of Río Grande do Sul and São Paulo was making people look to the central part of the country. Kubitschek was ousted in 1961 by a military coup. According to historia.net, in 1964-1985, Operaçâo Condor, a political/military alliance was set up to place military dictators in Brazil, Argentina, Uruguay, Paraguáy, Chile (September, 1973), Bolivia (August, 1971) and Argentina (March, 1976). In 1976 Kubitschek and another past president of Brazil were both killed under mysterious circumstances. The military government initiated major ventures into the rainforest, seeking great revenue from its many resources. They brought in major capital investment from the Japanese, using their vast Nisei population for guides and interpreters. Thus began the destruction of the vast Amazon area. I was there in 1973 at the invitation of the Brazilian government, when planeloads of Japanese business people were arriving with no knowledge of Portuguese. At that time the international community was talking about Brazil eventually becoming third largest GNP in the world. However, I felt a tremendous dearth of emotion from the part of government officials I met, and a coldness emanating from the buildings. They left me with the impression of robots in empty boxes — the complete opposite of the jovial Brazilians I had encountered on both trips.

I planned to take the train from Salvador to Belo Horizonte, the city in which the visionary Kubitschek was mayor before he became President. I could not understand why the voyage took fifty hours to travel just 540 miles. When I asked the hotel clerk where to get tickets for the train, he looked at me with wide eyes and said, "You're not taking the train, are you? The train is awful. Take a bus or fly, but nobody takes the train."

I figured it couldn't be so bad. I had traveled on many rough roads and rivers, so I was undeterred. However, everyone I asked told me the same thing, including the shoeshine boy. "Don't take the train. It's awful. I would never take the train. I would fly if I had to."

"But," I asked him, "What if you didn't have the money to fly?"

"Then I wouldn't go."

That got my attention. When a shoeshine boy tells me he wouldn't take the train I thought maybe I should listen. However, I talked myself back into the train and bought my ticket.

Wood burning train from Salvador to Monte Azúl & Belo Horizonte

I thought, "The train has a restaurant car and is probably at least a little comfortable. I am tired of riding the buses with two inches between the seats to stick my feet and then bang my knees against the seat in front on the bumpy roads. The train is cheaper and travels at night." I bought first class to be sure.

ACROSS THE SERTAO

10. THE EXHILARATION THAT IS BRAZIL

I made sure I got a reserved seat because I knew the train would be crowded. I sat next to a very pleasant matronly woman and we exchanged hilarious jokes as the train waited to leave. Seating was a scramble due to the many third class passengers who had boarded the car and were grabbing all unoccupied seats. I managed to befriend several passengers and they helped me seize a seat in the mishmash. Soon every inch of the car was filled with third class passengers, many with confiscated seats. The conductor was a little man with a Caesar complex. He barked, commanded, and cajoled in his effort to clear the car of all but first class passengers. Some he managed to drive to other cars, but most escaped his grasp and were soon joined by the relentlessly returning evicted. I became increasingly aware of the marvelous Brazilian humor. It is difficult ordering a car full of laughing, jovial people out of where they were collectively resolute to be. One of the many times he entered the car with a determined look on his face, threatening the crowds with dire circumstances, one of the passengers in the rear bellowed, "Too bad he isn't an Onça (panther). Then he could eat us all and be rid of his problem." The crowd roared and the little man left, mission unaccomplished.

Wood burner train from Salvador to Monte Azul

I was fortunate to be seated next to a man who made an agreement with me to guard the seat if I had to leave and I would do the same for him. The train, like the boat on the Putumayo, was a woodburner. Soot passed the window, puffs of smoke entering with each change of direction, which also gave us a view of the many passengers hanging onto the outside of the train.

"Why does the trip take 50 hours to Monte Azúl and why do we spend the night in that town?" I asked my neighbor.

"The train has no lights so we don't travel at night. We will be spending the night as soon as it starts to get dark. Then we continue traveling to Monte Azúl tomorrow morning."

"Where do we sleep?" I asked.

"In our seats," he answered. "When we get to Monte Azúl the rail line ends and another train company picks us up to take us to Belo Horizonte. They are never on time so they leave a night in between and let us stay in the town."

"Why don't they connect the lines so we can make it in one trip?" I asked.

"Because we are in different states. You are traveling in the state of Salvador. You will be met by a train company from the state of Minas Gerais."

I was hungry and several times we stopped by numerous vendors who lined up to sell tin plates of delicious chicken gumbo. I was tempted to buy one but the filth raised a red flag within me.

Belo Horizonte. The city streets radiate out from the circular central park, forcing flatiron shapes to the buildings closest to the park.

"I think I'll go to the dining car. Save my seat," I told my friend.

"Don't go there. This is only 30¢ U.S. The dining car will serve you the same thing and charge you a dollar," he insisted.

"I think I'll take my chances," I said as I headed to the diner. When I opened the door to the diner I found it as crowded as my car, mostly third class passengers with no seats. Not one person was eating but the car was full. An employee wearing a dirty white apron saw me standing, came over to me, and asked, "What do you want?"

"I want something to eat."

"Oh," he said. He went over to a crowded table and told the people to get up. They glared at me and reluctantly complied. I sat alone at the table and waited. After a lengthy period I called the waiter and asked, "When can I get something to eat?"

"Just a moment," he said. I could see no one cooking in the little room he came out of. After a lengthy time the train stopped at another large collection of vendors. The waiter went into the room and soon emerged with the exact aluminum plate I had seen the vendors selling while I was seated in my car. I ate the meal and found it tasted good. I knew he had bought one through the open window in the little room. When I finished he charged me a dollar.

The sky was beginning to darken so the sun waned for the day. The train stopped at a small village, lined with vendors cooking and conversing. Suddenly, I realized the noon meal did not want to stay with me. It was showing no mercy so I headed for the bathroom. The doors were locked. "The bathrooms are locked while the train is not running," someone said as I shook the secured door.

I was without any alternative so I ran up a dirt road in the pitch-black night to the town. All I saw was a deserted pitch-black dirt plaza surrounded by a few huts. No one was in sight and there obviously were no public rest rooms. The only presences were some

Belo Horizonte, Brazil

pigs in front of one of the buildings. I could wait no longer so squatted right there in the middle of the plaza. All of a sudden I heard the pigs squeal and race toward me. I pulled my pants up and ran to get out of their way. By the sounds I heard I knew I had just furnished them their dinner.

I found it impossible to sleep on the train. The vendors were noisily visiting and selling to the passengers well into the night. I was overjoyed when the train again started its run with the rising sun.

When the train slowly climbed into the mountains the next afternoon the train inched its way up the sinuous path to the top. At the top I looked down deep into the valley that was Monte Azúl, which was one long line of attached buildings. It was an equally dawdling trip, winding down the mountain to the town, three-and-a-half days after leaving Salvador, a distance of only 270 miles. Scores of young boys were there to meet the train, all with business cards for this long line of hotels, which made up the town.

Central Park in Belo Horizonte, Brazil

The next morning I again boarded a train for Belo Horizonte, another one-and-a-half days to go just 300 miles. I was a physical wreck by the time I arrived in Belo Horizonte, so rested two days. I was especially interested in that city, which was supported by the mining industry. It was a totally planned city, inspired by the plans for Washington, D.C., begun in 1910. It was designed like a wheel with spokes leading out from the hub, a beautifully landscaped circular park, a mile in diameter, with lakes, trees and numerous pathways surrounded by skyscrapers. All major streets radiated outward from the park, making many of the buildings triangular, like the Flatiron Building in New York. Cross streets were concentric circles connecting with the radiating main streets.

Central Park, Belo Horizonte

I realized I needed an attitude adjustment after traveling from Belém to Belo Horizonte. The roughness of the travel, day-after-day, on dirt roads, guarding my finite reserves over constant overcharging and the loneliness of being alone in a crowd made me feel resentful of the people of northern Brazil. "I am what I think." I thought to myself. I determined to begin thinking positively to attract positive results in my life.

This was the first time I had reached a city with an American Consulate since Belém, so I immediately went there to see if any mail had arrived for me. I was waiting at the front desk when the assistant returned from the counselor's office and told me to wait. I thought, "What does the Consul want with me? Have I done anything wrong?" The Consul came in and looked very serious. "Have I received any mail?" I asked.

No, first I need to complete business with you, he said sternly. Your father is frantically trying to locate you. He hasn't heard from you in months.

"I will write him right away," I offered.

"No you won't. You will send a telegram right away before you leave this room."

I then realized I hadn't been able to send a letter to him since Iquitos. "The last letter he had from you was months ago when you said, 'I'm going to be going down the Amazon.' He has been sending inquiries to all the consulates in the cities you mentioned on the map you gave him before you left."

Even the school was trying to find me through all their resources. Needless to say, I sent the telegram.

I hopped a bus going to Ouro Prêto (Black Gold), a gold mining town from Colonial days. Like Taxco, in México, no new architecture was allowed. It was a trip back in time, beautifully maintained, and nestled in the hills.

I wanted to see the new Federal District, Brasilia, even though I understood it was still under construction. I had wanted to go there ever since I saw a map of Brazil in high school with an area marked, "Future Federal District of Brazil". There was no road to Brasilia, which was at the edge of the rainforest. Jucelino was so anxious to complete the project during his term he began immediately, hauling in machinery and steel girders by helicopters.

Horse drawn buggy in Goiania, a town designed at the edge of the Rainforest in 1933

I took a plane to Goiania, stopping in Uberaba, Uberlandia and Ipamera. I was standing in the terminal at Goiania when a young man approached me and said in broken English, "Where you from?"

I said, "Eu so dos Estados Unidos."

"No, where you come from?" he continued.

"Eu vin do Belo Horizonte e vou viagar até a Río de Janeiro."

He still looked perplexed and asked, "You speak English?"

The only road in Brasilia at this stage

This caught me by complete surprise. I reached into my memory bank to think of what to say to him in English and finally blurted out, "We-el, Frahnkely Ai Havent spoken Eengleesh in such a long time…" I was absolutely floored to hear my accent. The young man just shook his head and walked off.

Goiania is another city, totally planned in 1933, as was Belo Horizonte. I took a bus just six hours to Anápolis and then to Brasilia, between Formosa and Planaltina. The forest had been slashed and burned almost as far as the eye could see. The government was

Main avenue in Brasilia. This is now the center of the city.

still burning in the distance to expand the city, when basics were completed. Oscar Neimeyer, who was also on the design team that built the UN Headquarters in New York, designed the city. New concepts were sewn into the design, such as living quarters above shops, districts for commercial, others for apartment living, government headquarters, etc. Neimeyer was a follower of Le Corbusier, with sweeping designs, having collaborated with him in 1936 on the Education and Health Building

Presidential Palace, Only one of two buildings completed at the time.

in Río in 1936. Presently, only a few steel girders divided red dirt roads and large artists renderings gave me a concept of the future capitol to be. Traveling across the sparsely built planned city took 30 minutes over red dust road by jeep, which gave me a good idea of its size. Divided highways were being built to it from Belo Horizonte, with another highway to Belém and Manaus. Senators were complaining they did not want to leave the comforts of Río for the interior. Many threatened they would never leave the comforts of Río de Janeiro.

The only two completed buildings were a modern hotel, which sat alone outside the city, pasted in the red dirt. I glanced around at the surrounding scenery, mostly rolling green hills, devoid of trees, which had been burned out of the forest. Fires, still burning, were visible in the distant expanses. Behind the hotel was the Presidential Palace, another modern building on a hill. I found the hotel to be far beyond my budget so caught a bus to the worker's town, which looked like it was out of the Wild West. It was again night as I paced the busy streets to find lodging. The owner of a hotel told me he had no rooms, everything in town was filled. He offered me to room with him. That was not my choice, but it was the only available choice so I took it.

Fording a river on dirt road back to Belo Horizonte

On a return trip to Brasilia fourteen years later, I encountered a sprawling city of over a million, beside a large lake with overpasses and wide avenues around skyscrapers and other rectangular designs. The Presidential Palace and Cathedral were the only buildings that showed the sweeping lines of Le Corbusier. Corridors, hallways, and entryways displayed every color of marble imaginable, but seemed cold and stark. Apartments were built in "O bloke" (The block), identical to endless expanses of square Soviet style numbered buildings.

Prado in Patos de Minas

The next day I hopped on an old brown school bus marked for Patos de Minas, a town about halfway to Belo Horizonte. The roads were a series of old cow paths, all the way to Patos. We crossed farms, forded rivers, opened gates and bounced over dirt roads, zigzagging our way back to civilization. The bus was loaded to the gills with workers with no seats available. I climbed up on the roof to join twelve of the workers I was traveling with. This was fine until we hit our first rain, forcing us to climb back into the crowded bus. The workers, with their wonderful sense of humor and playful ambiance lightened the discomfort of the bus as it swung from one side to the other along the paths before us. As we reached each farm the

Ouro Prêto

driver's assistant had to jump out and open gates and shut them behind us. In some places the entire road was washed out and we had to go around to keep from getting stuck. We had to build a bridge that was washed out to cross the ravine, two of the rivers we crossed on rafts. The workers had a number of political songs, mostly critical of their President. My favorite was "Jucelino me chama, a Brasilia eu vou" (Jucelino is calling me, to Brasilia I go). There must have been twenty verses, all as hilarious as the first. We stopped at each village and I anticipated someone would leave so I could get a seat. I stood for the entire 22-hour trip to Patos de Minas, with the brief exceptions when some of us were able to travel on the roof when it was not raining.

The next day we traveled from Patos de Minas on a paved road to Belo Horizonte. Again, all seats were sold so I had to stand. Several stops later I realized the driver's assistant was offering all available seats to those just loading into the bus so I went up to complain.

"I want a seat," I pleaded. "I've been standing since Brasilia and you're giving available seats to new passengers. I don't think I can stand for another nine hours."

There was no answer. I did the same thing at the next stop with no recognition. That was all I could take. I screamed at him with every swear word I heard Guillermo use on the Amazon, instantly translated into Portuguese. I had been careful, up to now, never to use any swear words in Portuguese so this would never happen in the heat of a disagreement. He took this as a joke and began to laugh telling me I would have to remain standing for the rest of the trip. The Northern Brazil trip had been so rough I was pretty ill by the time I arrived in Belo Horizonte. I didn't have a chance to recuperate, as there wasn't time. Sixteen hours standing on buses had pretty well wiped me out the day before and I couldn't quite face another nine hours, as the roads were so rough. Then I realized what I had done and felt embarrassed noticing all the passengers' eyes glued on me. I was feeling faint, hanging onto the railing for support. At the next stop the door attendant offered me a seat, as it was quite apparent I was about to pass out.

Like Taxco is to Mexico Ouro Prêto is to Brazil. No new buildings are allowed in this former mining town.

Getting back to Belo Horizonte was like coming home. Everyone was wonderful. My hotel had taken care of everything while I was gone and everything was ready for my trip to Río.

I bought my ticket to Río and when I went to use it the next morning found the ticket agent had stamped it wrong. This invalidated it. I explained it to the clerk but they said there was nothing they could do, the ticket was no good. I really blew my top and they

THE EXHILARATION THAT IS BRAZIL

Cable car climbing to the top of Corcovado, Río de Janeiro, Brazil

nearly died laughing. I finally got my bags and had to get another ticket at another place. The ride in an air-conditioned bus over paved highway from Belo Horizonte to Río felt like heaven. We traveled through emerald forests as we passed through the mountains west of Río, dropping down into the city. Numerous retreats, hotels, and country homes were tucked away all through the forested areas.

Río, with its expensive hotels, tourism, and commerce was where I decided to economize. I found a hotel on the Praça Mahuá, near the embarcadero. Its decór was the same as most of the other cheap hotels I had seen, with rooms separated by partial walls, which allowed air to pass, giving welcome relief from the heat through the open space. I quickly made friends with another guest who worked with radio communications in the North.

Dr. Shurz had talked extensively about the racial mixtures and tolerance in Brazil. He told us no child could physiologically be darker than the darkest parent. This he referred to as Brancamento (whitening), and said this phenomenon eventually produced an in-

Christ the Redemptor statue on top of Corcovado

creasingly whiter race. I noticed, especially in Río, the predominance of white skinned people with African features. The Portuguese, contrary to their Spanish neighbors, venerated the Moors, who established universities and culture. Even when slavery was the norm there was a great deal of mixing of the races. Ending the slavery in Brazil was not violent as was our Civil War. Intermarriage followed the end of their slavery, assimilating not only the African people but the Indigenous as well. The three cultures mixed the mysticism of

Africa, spiritual connection of the Indigenous and the structure of the Spanish and Portuguese for a unique blend of deeply spiritual people, in many cases more similar to us Americans than their Latin neighbors.

The many dilapidated hotels I had stayed in during the past three months had anesthetized me to their deficiencies. I realized this when I was asked where I was staying by some bankers with whom I was having lunch. I sat there dressed in a suit and tie and told them the name of my hotel. One of them asked where it was.

"Right off the Praça Mahuá," I answered without trepidation. Their mouths dropped and one of them exclaimed, "The Praça Mahuá? That's the most dangerous part of town!"

The next Sunday I went to church and met a man who introduced himself as Mr. Bertram Johansson, Latin American Editor of the Christian Science Monitor. We had an extensive conversation, during which he asked me many questions about my journey. He finally turned to me and said, "I have to go. I met an American woman married to a Brazilian and she invited me to lunch at their condominium in Copacabanha. Maybe I can get her to include you."

Río de Janeiro from top of Corcovado

Soon he came back and told me to follow him. We stepped into a Cadillac with an elderly woman, Mrs. Chavez. She uttered one of her three Portuguese words to her chauffer she had learned during her twenty years in Brazil with her insurance agent husband. We sped off to her high-rise condo overlooking the beautiful beaches of Copacabanha. She asked me where I had gone to college and I told her Principia. Her eyes lit up, "My daughter, Ruth, went to Principia. She's married and her name is now Petrinovich. She lives in Santiago." I knew Ruth in school. Small world. That afternoon, as we were swimming at the luxurious Río Yachting Club, I thought of what I would never let them know, that I was staying at the Praça Mahuá.

THE EXHILARATION THAT IS BRAZIL

My eight days in Río were spent being a tourist and meeting with business people who I found in my alumni directory for AGSIM. The Christ Statue atop Corcovado (Hunchback), reached by a cog railway, gave a radiant view of the cities below: Río de Janeiro, Ipanema, and Copacabanha. The cable car to Pâo de Açucar (Sugarloaf) was beautiful in the evening as I glanced back at the angelic lights of the city, circling the bay, which is now my screen saver.

One of the most favorable practices I found in Río was the queue, which formed at every elevator, shop, bank, or public transit. This was a welcome contrast to the mayhem of squalling pandemonium behind every counter throughout Colombia, and intense favoritism in Northern Brazil. Nearly always a quiet single line would automatically form, which was especially noticeable in Río.

I mentioned to Malcolm Gleason, an official of one of the overseas banks, how fascinated I was with the modern architecture I found in most cities. He said, "Yes, it is beautiful and original but so many times the essentials are left out of the design. One evening a female friend was visiting me and asked to use my bathroom. Soon she came out laughing hysterically, giggling, 'Has anyone used the bidet in your apartment? If they have they must be an acrobat.' She led me in and showed me how impossible it would be to mount it."

Praça do París, Río de Janeiro. They were in the process of building a beautiful bayside park.

Nearly all the beach side of Río was under construction. Wind carried dirt and sand from the construction sites to the city, at times blocking the view. Río was now utilizing the tidelands along the main avenues as parks and beaches. When I returned thirteen years later, the city was transformed into a Jewel of the Atlantic. The harbor side of the city was changed from a busy traffic-congested thoroughfare, squeezed in front of a long row of glass skyscrapers to a ribbon of beautiful vistas of the harbor and Pâo de Açucar — a place of splendor.

Sâo Paulo was a sharp contrast to fun-loving and genial Río. Brazilians referred to it as the Chicago of Brazil. It carried a dynamic energy of growth, reaching for the clouds of prosperity. It may have been the Chicago of Brazil but the streets appeared to have been laid out by the same cows that created the paths of downtown Boston. I didn't dare leave the hotel without a map in hand. I could get lost in a sea of skyscrapers just by going around the block from the hotel.

Few streets ran parallel and few were more than three blocks long. Building construction was in a frenzy. I concentrated on memorizing enough landmarks so I could get around the center of the city. People who had lived here for years couldn't tell me the name of the street they were standing on. The streets also had names like, "Presidente Joâo Luís Lubechebsky" and other such lengthy designations, many corners without even a street sign or just a small sign tacked onto the side of a building. When I stopped a person to ask them what street I was on they would answer with embarrassment, "I don't know." In some cases I found the general or politician the street was named after had fallen out of favor and the name was changed so even a map or sign was not necessarily correct. There was no coordinated bus system in the city. All buses and trolleys converged on the center of town with no transfer system. If I wanted to go to a place two miles from where I was I had to go six miles to the center and ten back out to where I wanted to go. All this contributed to the massive increase in the

Dom Pedro II's house in front of Museum, Sâo Paulo. He was Emperor of Brazil from 1825-1891

number of cars in the city.

São Paulo had become the fastest growing city in the world. A major building was going up every three minutes. In 1825 there were 25,000 inhabitants, in 1950, 2,500,000 and in 1958, 3,500,000. In 1948 you couldn't buy a handkerchief made in Brazil. Now they had about every type of item you could think: trucks, refrigerators, cars, motor scooters, furniture, etc. — all made in Brazil. Over 95% of the parts for the Fiat trucks and cars were now made in Brazil and all the other companies — Ford, General Motors, Wyllis, Mercedes Benz had been given orders by the government to manufacture over 90% of their parts in Brazil by the next year or leave the country.

There were mountains in Brazil that were said to be 90% ore, creating an expansive raw materials market for the country. Even though as little as eight years previously Brazil was an importer of meat, they were developing into an exporter of beef. It was amazing to watch the growth. São Paulo was the largest manufacturing city in South America. Brazil was the most populous country in Latin America and was the fifth largest country in the world in land mass. Immigrants were pouring in from all over the world. Brazilians (those born in Brazil) were a minority in São Paulo with Japanese, Germans, Italians, Spanish, Portuguese, Syrians, and Lebanese making up the majority. The president of the Sears operation, Howard Davies, told me it was impossible to go out of business in Brazil. There was a propensity in Brazil to raise prices to equal the availability of products. For instance, Sears ordered some wastebaskets. The baskets were packed so poorly it raised the total cost about five times. However, Sears was still able to sell them at half the cost of one made in Brazil.

São Paulo from top of bank

I contacted Guillermo, who paddled down the Amazon with me, and he agreed to meet me the next morning. He came by Sunday morning and I met him sleepily at the door in my shorts. The first thing he said was, "Carlos, what happened to your tan?" It was the first time I had realized how quickly I had lost my Amazon tan. I hardly recognized Guillermo standing there in his blue suit because I had only seen him in ragged clothes, both of us with beards.

He was anxious to take me to the Butantán snake gardens, where the government extracts snake venom. Unfortunately, it was closed. It would have been a perfect opportunity to meet the snakes that were hiding behind the bushes and in the trees where we traversed. Guillermo was so disgusted with the disorganization in Brazil, especially after his trip through Northern Brazil, he was thinking of moving to Buenos Aires. He was disgusted with the lack of culture in Brazil. "If you talk about anything but women and drink you're over most people's heads," he raved.

It was fortunate I had loaned him the 450 cruceros, because when he got a boat out of Belém he was told at Forteleza he would have to pay two passages to continue because a Brazilian wanted a place and he was a foreigner. He then had to get off and take a bus. This took him across most of the territory I covered so he saw the worst of Brazil.

Sixteen years later we again met in São Paulo. I was Vice President of HMR International, Guillermo was manager of a factory and Gumercindo was vending from a fruit cart. As we conversed in Guillermo's condo that night, he turned to me and said, "You know, Carlos, that trip paddling down the Amazon was completely crazy. I mean that was a crazy thing we did."

Sightseeing presented some formidable challenges, similar to tracking down the police in Bogotá. After a late start I checked on a train for Santos. The bus I caught to go to the station took me six blocks out of my way. I made it to the station just as the train was pulling in to load passengers. I ran in to buy a ticket, waited in line for a while, and felt I'd better ask if this was the right window. I asked and a fellow gave me a dirty look, shoved me out of the way, bought a ticket, and ran after the train. I was informed that I needed to go to the window across the way. I went there and was told it was the window I was just at. After waiting in line there the agent told me it was in the other room. I started to go there, looked down, and saw my train pull out. I suddenly decided I didn't need to go to Santos after all. I then made plans to go to the Parque do Estado where they have an orchid farm with 25,000 different varieties, a zoo, and an observatory. I got out the map and learned I could take a tram out there. I walked a mile to catch the tram and found they were poorly marked. I made the mistake of asking a Brazilian which trolley to take. I had been warned against this in Latin American Studies Class. I remembered Dr. Shurz saying in one of his lectures. "When Brazilians are asked a question from a stranger they do not know the answer to, they, usually do not like to admit it and will tell you anything to satisfy your question, sometimes with grave consequences." The gentleman told me to hop aboard #66 and it would take me there. This was an open sided trolley, which was built to hold 35 passengers, but had about 50. In the crowd I could not pull out my map to check the streets we passed. We traveled for a half-hour before I could sit and look at the map. I then found it had none of the streets listed we were passing. Apparently the City must have felt the street we were on was big enough not to put signs up, as there were none. After ten blocks we passed a street sign but it was stuck behind a lamp. I finally found the name but it wasn't on the map. The trolley ended up on a dirt road and *that* road was on the map. I found I was at least two miles from the park. I thought, "I won't go down in defeat." I started walking. I found the road I was following suddenly ended way out in a field. I wandered around for an hour and none of the roads I was on were on the map. After an hour I ran into a bus stop. I gave up at that point and figured I would return as the park closed at 5:00. I finally located where I was going and found I had been walking in circles. Ah for a travel agent.

I met Howard Davies, the manager of Sears Roebuck operations in Brazil who was also a graduate of Thunderbird. He was a fountain of information on both the history and soul of Brazil. It was the right time for our encounter because I had just traveled over 3,000 miles in Brazil. Brazil is a great tale of homogenization of a mixture of races, lifestyles, backgrounds, and spiritual connections. The dominant Portuguese did not have the feelings of superiority and separation predominant in the European cultures, which populated the Spanish and English Americas. They did not have the aftereffects of our bitter Civil War or the stigma against mixed race children. The Portuguese farmers not only mixed freely with their slaves but also merged the esoteric way of African ancestry with their own Catholic background. There was a respect of the Native cultures not readily found in other countries. Although the Portuguese farmers who settled the Sertâo were more serious and somewhat reclusive than their Southern cousins and still spoke with a dialect akin to the farming areas of Portugal, they respected people of color. They could not understand foreigners. Davies told me there were still African ceremonies that were practiced at the beaches at certain times of the year.

He continued, "There is no divorce allowed in Brazil because of the Church. The adaptive Brazilians do not let this bother them. They separate and, if they find another partner, they have a marriage party at their house or apartment and everyone recognizes the new couple as married and the others as no longer bonded. Everyone has a mistress. That is considered copasetic, even getting wife approval in most instances, but the rules are very strict. The mistress must be kept in a location well out of sight of the wife and she cannot mix at all with any social or business functions. In other words she is to remain completely out of the mainstream life of another's husband, with no rights whatsoever to the man.

"Many of the Indigenous change partners regularly with no problem. One village had been doing this peacefully for many years when a Baptist minister came to their village. He told them this was heresy and ordered them to return to their original partners. This caused great dissention in the tribe for the first time in their memory as partners, happy with their present brides and then forced back together with their original partners. It was a mess."

Davies' history with Sears was quite interesting. He was only 33 years old when I met him. However, he had been with Sears since their entry into the country. The population growth and growing middle class prompted the company to open branches in Brazil. Preparations were made and ships were loaded with the original merchandise destined for that country. This coincided with Brazil's industrial awakening. Mercedes, General Motors, and many other giant corporations were initiating manufacturing in Brazil. The problem was nearly all raw products were imported for the manufacturing, put together by cheap Brazilian labor. This caused an insular economic growth, which did not expand into the general labor and supplier market. Laws were passed about the time the Sears shipments were ready to leave the U.S. that a large number of retail items and manufactured parts must be locally supplied.

"We were caught in a bind," said Howard. "The Sears shipments were returned and his crew was given the responsibility of finding items locally. We found nearly all items were manufactured in small family cottage industries. Brazil had been importing nearly everything. Like Venezuela they were even importing most of their food from Europe and the United States. In the short time since then Brazil is now growing, not only most of its food items but exporting fruits not grown in any other country.

"We went to every manufacturing operation we could find, which was almost entirely a family cottage industry. When we found the items they were not made in large enough quantities for a large retail operation. Most were sold through small shops. When we told them our monthly requirements they resisted. Businesses were a family operation. They did not want the hassle of hiring outside employees with all its problems. That was what the family was there for. But we finally were able to obtain enough goods to open the first Sears store. The remainder of items permitted by law, were shipped in to complete the merchandise.

"Then there was the problem of Brazilian taste. For instance, we received a large shipment of the latest styles in women's slacks. We couldn't sell one. They just sat there on the racks. A Brazilian woman would not be caught dead wearing pants. Finally someone suggested appealing to the Brazilian fascination with the latest styles and new things. We advertised them as the latest fashion. It was not long before we had women in Brazil wearing slacks. Look around now and see how many Brazilian women are wearing slacks, and it hasn't been that long.

"The Portuguese and Spanish who populated Brazil favored either the farmlands of the North or preferred living along the coast. There were many efforts to populate the interior but that was heavily forested. They opened their doors to immigration in a way that more equaled the United States than any other Latin American country. A mutual agreement was made with overpopulated Japan to offer $500 to every Japanese willing to move to Brazil. They were, however, prohibited from working for the government. They were given small plots of land for growing food. This attracted the Italian immigrants who bought trucks to bring their vegetables and fruits to the markets on the growing number of roads. The German immigrants were attracted to cattle operations and populated the grasslands further into the interior so Brazil is now exporting meat. Many Germans moved to the Southern states of Río Grande do Sul and Santa Catarina. Seventy percent of the people of Santa Catarina speak German and half in Río Grande do Sul. Over half of the populations of São Paul are immigrants. Brazil has the largest population of Japanese of any other country in the world, except Japan."

This large reserve of bilingual Nisei (Japanese Brazilians) was later very important when Japanese (few speaking Portuguese) became attracted to investment in Brazil, years later. It also built a growing middle class, for awhile making Brazil one of the fastest growing GNPs in the world.

The auto industry had an even more difficult time adjusting to the new importation laws. Mercedes Benz and Volkswagen were two companies that successfully made the changes, opening up and sponsoring suppliers to make their quotas. The American companies did not, and left. Mercedes was making most of the buses and Volkswagen the cars. Although there were imported cars, the tariff on them was very high, making them only available to the very rich. São Paulo had now become the largest industrial center in South America.

Dock at Presidente Epitacio on Río Paraná

I mentioned to Davies the danger I had found crossing the wide streets of São Paulo. He laughed and said, "They must hand out licenses to all the mental patients in this city. They drive like crazy and refuse to give way to pedestrians. You take your life in your hands when you walk in this city." Upon return to São Paulo fifteen years later I experienced the same craziness when walking in traffic. I felt like I was at the Gran Prix while driving Guillermo's Carmen Ghía through the city, seeing three serious accidents on one trip.

Capitán Haitór, boat on Paraná

The Mato Grosso was calling me with the same

siren call, as had the Amazon. I wanted to see the interior river, which divided Brazil from Paraguay, the Alto Paraná. Of special interest were the Sete Quedas, or Seven Falls, and the Falls at Iguassú. I could find no tickets anywhere for purchase so I chose an all-inclusive tour, which included the two falls, lodging and meals to the border of Argentina.

We started from São Paulo Friday morning. I went down to the station to meet the "tour". I found the tour was not a tour but merely a pile of tickets any travel agency could get for you, only doubling all charges. The train my ticket was on was the second best in Brazil. It was a streamliner. As they collected the tickets I gradually began to spot those out who were on the tour from those that weren't by the packets they were carrying. They were a fascinating compilation of people. I was soon very well acquainted with three single women, an Englishman, the girl he was traveling with and two other girls accompanying them.

The country was beautiful. The Japanese had colonized much of the interior of the States of São Paul and Paraná and had homesteaded some beautiful farms. The compartments were nice consisting of two beds and washing facilities. The beds were foam rubber and placed alongside the direction the train was going rather than on the sides. This, with the heavy rocking of the train, suspended me in the air and rocked me back and forth to sleep a deep sleep.

We arrived at Presidente Epitácio the next morning. A number of canvas-covered carriages were there to meet the passengers not on tour. An old broken-down school bus was there for those on tour.

Lumber boat on Paraná

Thank heavens it was only a short way to the port, as I didn't feel the bus would have made it any further. The launch was a bit old but well kept and I must say it was the best I had seen on any Brazilian waters. It was good to be floating through the jungle on boat and the 61 days I had already spent descending the Caquetá.

Ortoguaza, Putumayo, Içá, Amazonas, Negro, and Tapajós Rivers were not enough to satisfy me. I met some wonderful people. I talked extensively with the wife of a judge. There were three German immigrants, two of whom were in business in São Paulo. An Englishman had an agency in São Paulo importing cameras. He was traveling with his partner and two other girls, his partner being a German immigrant. One couple just about adopted me and many others will be friends for life. It was about five minutes before everyone was well introduced and began bonding. I had a couple of nice roommates. One was an older man from Germany, Hans Reik, who had been in Brazil for 35 years but still couldn't speak Portuguese. He spoke enough to understand our simple greetings and questions. He was with a middle-aged German couple that spoke excellent Portuguese. I did not find the criticism of our government I experienced in Colombia, but was able to talk in depth about Brazil. Probably because we were all traveling as tourists, I felt a kinship with everyone, as close as I would have experienced in my own country.

Rainforest on sides of Río Paraná above Guairá, Sete Quedas

The voyage down the river was beautiful and colorful. The boat carried cargo and people between small port villages. We, therefore, stopped at almost every house. This made the voyage not only comfortable but extremely interesting. I really felt I was on my vacation traveling in luxury. Several of the men and one woman were on a three-week fishing trip. They were

Sete Quedas (Seven Falls) at Guairá, author in foreground

well prepared. It took an hour to unload everything they were taking for camping. They were starting to build a hut when we arrived and had it nearly finished by the time we left. I laughingly pointed out the items they were taking for this little trip to the Captain. "Oh," he said, "This is nothing to what most people take on their fishing trips."

We arrived in Guairá in about two-and-a-half days. Every minute of it was enjoyable because the people were so fascinating. It was good to see a little culture for a change, where the conversation went beyond liquor and women. We talked over politics, economics, and people. I finally felt I was learning a little about Brazil. No one spoke any English to me except the Englishman. However, they must have all had good backgrounds in English because occasionally I would have difficulty with a word. They would ask me what it was in English and when I answered they would say the word in Portuguese. Half the time the Englishman and I spoke Portuguese to each other.

Big Falls, Sete Quedas, Guairá, Brazil

Guairá wasn't much of a town. The hotel was worse and the bus was worse yet. However, the management was excellent. I was expecting we would have numerous tours but found the touring agency had included only one 30¢ bus trip to the falls and back during the two days we were to be there. We decided to take the trip in the afternoon and then hire a motorboat the following day for a trip to a resort island a few miles upstream.

Sete Quedas, 3rd Falls, Guairá, Brazil

The beauty of

the first waterfalls awed us. Niagara looks almost the same from either side. However, Sete Quedas (Seven Falls) is literally what it says it is — seven falls. The Paraná River carries massive quantities of water with a width of less than one-kilometer, so the current is swift. It suddenly comes against an abutment two miles wide, creating not only large falls over 100 feet in height, but a series of other water falls, all different, some more spectacular than others. As we entered the park we encountered some beautiful smaller falls and rapids.

Sete Quedas, Middle Falls. Guairá Brazil

Proceeding down the path we came upon another series of falls, even more beautiful. The path led to endless surprises as we walked through the forest below. At the end of the path was an incredible falls, the beauty of which held us spellbound. It looked like photos I had seen of Victoria Falls in Tanganyika. We sat and drank in its beauty for the remainder of the afternoon. I was told the river travels at 75 mph at the confluence where the numerous falls come together again. The river and falls separate Brazil from Paraguáy.

That evening a group of us hired a jeep and went to see the falls in the moonlight. The falls were even more stunning under a full moon. We made it back just in time to get up the next morning.

The next day we took a DC3 airplane to Iquassú Falls. I asked the hostess to have the pilot dip over Sete Quedas to get a picture. She told him the wrong side so he dipped on the other side and I

Diving into Iguassú Falls with a DC3

found it impossible to take a picture. I explained this to her when we had passed and asked if he would dip over Iquassú. She said there was not a chance because the falls was some 15 miles past the town. I, therefore, settled down to reading. I suddenly noticed the plane was passing the town of Iquassú. I figured this could only mean he was going to go to the falls so got my camera ready. Suddenly the Falls came into view. Only half the quantity of water goes over Iguassú as Sete Quedas but the falls are wider. It is over two miles from the first falls to the last. The pilot suddenly flipped on his side and dove. I remembered dipping on the wrong side before so ran to the other side. I found myself glued to the side as he pulled out of his dive. He then dove down on the other side. I ran from side to side, snapping seven pictures in all. He kept diving in at different angles for about fifteen minutes before going back to Foz de Iquassú. I got off very happy but noticed the girls were a little bit green.

Iguassú Falls as DC3 dives into them

Iguassú Falls from the DC3

In jest I mentioned this hotel was known for telling people with reservations they had no rooms. I was, therefore, not surprised when they told me at the airport they had no room for me. Everyone told me to come in with the bus anyway as I had already paid for the room. We got there and the management wouldn't even talk to me. The women pleaded with them to do something but this only made them more obstinate. Even when the women refused to go to their rooms until the hotel served me they ignored me. I finally managed to flash my America-Tour ticket in front of their eyes. As America-Tour runs the hotel this caught their attention. About a half-hour later they came out and told me to go into the management office. They curtly threw a card in front of me and told me to fill it out. I figured I now had a room but they wouldn't answer my questions. They asked for my passport and I gave it to them. They then started giving the Englishman a hard time. I felt with such irresponsibility I'd better get a receipt for the passport so asked for one. This infuriated the manager. He blew up and said, "Don't you have any confidence in us?"

Diving into Iguassú Falls in a DC3

I barked back, "I wouldn't trust you as far as I could throw you." This infuriated him. He scribbled "Passport" on a piece of paper and threw it at me. I reveled in my obstinate settling of scores.

The next day I tried to find out when there was a tour for the falls. No one knew anything. It wasn't until 9:00 a.m. when I found out the trip wasn't until afternoon. I then ran around trying to get a bus to Argentina to buy a ticket for boat passage to Posadas. I met another gentleman and his wife who were going to Asunción the same way as I and we got to the border. There we were told we had to buy the ticket on the boat. We at least found the time the boat was ready to leave.

Iguassú Falls from bottom of falls

Our tour was suddenly underway, so we quickly returned to the hotel and gulped down our lunch. We went first to the point where Brazil, Paraguáy, and Argentina meet at the junction of the Río Iquassú and Paraná. It was a long ride to the falls. The falls were much more spectacular than either Yellowstone or Niagara Falls. However, they missed the element of surprise of Sete Quedas. We went through the new hotel the Brazilian government had just completed. It was a uninspirational. It looked like a combination of the New York Museum of Art in Central Park and the high school I attended. The Brazilians were very much impressed and I made the faux pas of offering my opinion.

Iguassú Falls from Brazilian side

That night the Englishman ran into a local man with a jeep who took us out to see the falls in the moonlight. During the trip the jeep driver turned to me and asked, "Where are you from?"

"I'm from the United States," I answered.

"No, where are you exactly from?"

"I'm from Kansas City," I said.

"No, what part of Brazil were you from before you went to the United States? You don't act like an American and certainly don't have an American accent."

"I was born in the United States," I reiterated.

"He's a United States citizen and he speaks perfect English. I've seen his passport and spoken to him in English," interrupted the Englishman.

"Then why do you speak with a Carioca accent?" he asked with some disgust.

Great, all the work I had done to perfect the Carioca accent had worked. My Spanish was now completely out of my speech. As I entered Argentina and Paraguáy I now

Iguassú Falls, Horseshoe

found I was mistaken for a Brazilian as I began speaking Spanish again.

I had tried to get the attention of the manager twice to get a ride to the Argentine port, as I had paid for this, and both times he told me he was too busy to talk to me. The girls I had befriended on the trip offered to help me. I took them in and the manager, seeing the girls but not me, came to attention and asked if he could help them. They told him what I wanted and he realized he was stuck with me and had to do something. He finally told me to get on the touring bus and it would drop me off when it passed there. I finally figured this was all I would ever get out of him so I took that bus. The bus got such a late start I thought we'd miss the boat. When we got there they tried to charge me a little extra. I was fed up with fighting so I took back the tip I was about to hand him and paid him off. This came to less than the tip so I was better off.

Iguassú Falls on Argentine side

I had quite a bit of time before the boat left so got through customs, went to the Argentine side of the Falls (much more impressive than the Brazilian) and returned in plenty of time. It was a nice little launch and a comfortable interesting journey. The river was narrow here, crammed into a deep gorge.

I had spoken no English all the way to Brazil so was thinking and speaking it almost as freely as English. When I entered Brazil I switched to Portuguese and worked very hard to weed out all my Spanish. I worked up a reaction against all Spanish words so they wouldn't slip into my conversation. This reaction was so strong after three months of Portuguese I found it difficult to switch back to Spanish. I was shocked to find I had completely lost my Spanish. The Argentines were very patient and helped me along. One older Brazilian insisted on speaking English to me and I had to work hard to break away from him, as this wasn't helping the switchover.

The boat ride to Posadas, Argentina was pleasant. I had met some of the passengers at Sete Quedas so we talked for hours as the boat made its way down the Paraná River — Argentina on one side and Paraguáy on the other. A thick growth of rainforest walled in both sides.

Brazil. Iguassú Falls

At one point in my conversation I was explaining something that happened four years before, saying "hace cuatro anos" (four years ago). Finally, one of the women told me, "You are going to have to change from a Brazilian accent, because 'anus' is something else in Spanish, and I don't think you wanted to say that."

I got to Posadas the next morning. I found out everything the Brazilians told me about transportation and fares was bogus as usual so I had to do some fumbling around. I had to wait all day to get a boat across the river to Paraguáy. Everyone thought I was a Brazilian because of my accent and I felt it was best to keep it that way as I had been told the Argentines love Brazilians and hate Americans, are gruff and not very helpful to them. I was finding this very much the opposite with their friendliness and willingness to be of help. As I became more open about my national origin I found that was the way they were to everyone, not just because they thought I was Brazilian or didn't know I was American.

Río Paraguáy just below Iguassú Falls, Paraguay is on the left, Argentina right.

I ran into town and bumped into a Brazilian couple I had met on the tour. I loved them, but didn't especially want to stick with them as they kept speaking to me in Portuguese. This was ruining my Spanish. They insisted we all go to Asunción together. I could find no information on transportation to Asunción so I caught a ferry that crosses the river into Paraguáy once a day. My Brazilian friends got stuck in Argentina on a technicality and couldn't get out of the country. It took me three hours to get through the exit customs of Argentina and five minutes to enter Paraguáy.

I noticed my energy level had dropped. I thought back about why this happened and finally it dawned on me, "I miss my Guaraná sodas." Every time I drank Guaraná I felt exhilaration and increased energy. I missed my drink now that I had left Brazil.

The dirt road from Encarnación to Asunción had just been completed. It was the first road to unlock Asunción from total dependence on water travel. I found a truck that would be leaving the next morning at 3:00 a.m. Once I crossed the river it was like a new, refreshing and friendly world opened up in front of me. I had to discard nearly every piece of travel information concerning Paraguay I had been told in Brazil. I don't know whether they didn't know or were just embarrassed to admit they didn't know so told me anything to be polite.

11. PARAGUAY TO PATAGONIA

Crossing the border in Encarnación, the guard jokingly said something in English when he saw my passport. Customs didn't even open my bags, simply asked if I was going to sell my camera. When I stopped someone to ask about hotel recommendations he asked what I was planning to do so he could find me a hotel to suit my needs. I asked a couple of men in the hotel where I could get some Yerba Maté and was promptly seated in their circle as they passed their Maté among us. The shoeshine boy who finally got me to weaken and let him give me a shine treated me like a friend. You just can't explain the Paraguayan people, with their extreme friendliness. I had never found such friendliness in any other country. The Guaraní Indians had a great influence here, were peaceful and therefore their culture and language were adopted as a second language. The country was also not conquered by valiant warriors as every other country but by enlightened Jesuits who taught the Indians trades. As a result you had a very friendly Mestizo who spoke Guaraní. Guaraní was the official language of the country and was spoken by preference in almost all places except Asunción. However, everyone could speak Spanish as well. The Spanish the Guaraní spoke was guttural and the grammar sometimes bad.

It was raining when I left but the scenery was fascinating. It was a good thing I made the trip when I did as the roads were closing behind us due to heavy rain as we inched our way on the dirt road through the Chaco. The people on the bus soon became like family. The women were precious. They reminded me of little dolls. Their personalities were the finest I had seen anywhere. A judge sat next to me. Open and friendly, we shared conversation enthusiastically. I kept hearing American English spoken behind me but could not comprehend the words due to the noise of the bus on the dirt road. I looked around and saw no Americans. This persisted and finally I took another look, studying the faces as much as I dared without seeming obvious. I still did not see any Americans. I asked the judge and he said, "Everyone on the bus is speaking Guaraní. I was shocked. It sounded exactly like American English. The judge saw my interest in Guaraní so began teaching me some basic words, all of which I soon forgot. We stopped at a restaurant and he stood next to me at the side of the bus. He told some women I spoke Guaraní. I repeated the few sentences he had taught me, using the American accent and the girls remarked, "He hasn't got any accent."

I waited outside the bus at one station for the driver to return. A soldier stood at attention next to me wearing a colorful uniform, watching the crowd. One shabbily dressed man came up to me and said softly, "That's the military. They are the dirt of the earth. But someday we are going to get them."

I tried to inch away from this man. I was certain we were standing within earshot of the militiaman. I looked up and did not surmise he heard anything the man said. I wanted nothing to do with this. Then the man added, "When we get them we're going to slit their throats. We'll kill the dogs." With that I cringed, looking for an opening to escape before I was associated with any of these words. I knew the military was very cruel and the laws draconian in Paraguáy. People were even shot, I had heard, for not saluting the flag. I looked at the bus and saw there was still no entry allowed; yet the waiting passengers on all sides surrounded us. I inched my way away from the man and the soldier. This was not my fight. I was relieved when the bus began to load and I escaped into it. Fortunately, the man who approached me was not a passenger.

As we approached civilization the Posadas food and wine began to work on my stomach and was anxious to move on. There were no seats on that bus so I was standing, holding onto a steel post. At first my stomach rumbled and then the pressure began to build up. I needed a bathroom but could not see any available. The bus rumbled on past fields and endless houses and my condition worsened. I realized I could not wait another fifteen minutes before we reached Asunción so asked the driver for an "excusado", "privado", "toilette", etc., (none of which he recognized) until I finally repeated the word, "servicio sanitario". He asked if I wanted a "sanatario". I quickly blurted, "Yes, I do."

"Oh, there's one up ahead," he answered affirmatively. He kept driving for another five minutes as I grimaced and struggled. Everyone must have thought I was in terrific pain. Every filling station we passed I asked if there was one there. He would always answer me, "No, a little further." He made a five-minute stop to let some passengers out and unload baggage. We reached a small town and stopped at an ESSO station and I felt surely they would have a bathroom there. I asked the driver if there was a "servicio sanitario" at the station and he said, "No." We waited for another few minutes at that stop and I was in absolute misery. When the bus again started I was hanging onto the pole for life, my eyes watering and face in misery. I didn't think I could make it. He finally stopped in front of a yellow building that said, "Sanatorio". It was apparent it was a health center, not a bathroom (Servicio Sanitario) but I figured once inside I could quickly explain my problem.

"It's a health center, but a health center has bathrooms," I thought. Without hesitation I grabbed my 62 pounds of luggage, threw the duffle bag on my shoulder, and ran across the street to the entryway. Inside was a large room leading to a long hall. I saw there was a woman down the hallway in the back so called out. She ran down the hall toward me and asked, "What can I do for you, Señor?" I asked her where the servicio sanitario was and she gave me a blank stare, so I quickly blurted out, "I have diarrhea."

She said, "Do you have to vomit?"

I figured at least that would get me to where I wanted to go, so I quickly blurted, "Yes."

She then rushed me to a bathroom.

I have since learned the simple word "baño" would have served in Paraguay.

When I came out she was again in the back so I snuck out and crossed the street. The bus had already left but the judge who sat next to me stood where it had been, watching me cross the street.

"What happened to the bus?" I asked.

"It left, but I was worried about you and wanted to make sure you got to town all right," he answered.

I was astonished at this concern. This was beyond anything I had experienced. We soon caught another bus. Once in Asunción he insisted on staying with me until he could lead me to a good hotel I could afford. He then gave me his card and left.

Asunción Paraguáy, Parque Independencia

Asunción was smaller than I thought it would be. It was just in the process of installing a central sewage system. Its charm and well cared for older buildings surrounding a large park was what one dreams about when imagining a tropical paradise. The Paraguáy River, which until recently had been its only connection with the outside world, was about a mile in width and bordered the city from north to south. Vegetation was lush. A Park lined its shore within the city. Across the river was an endless lowland semi-jungle forest, called the Chaco. It covered most of the land, which was Paraguáy to the borders of Bolivia and Argentina. During the rainy season everyone living in the Chaco was forced to move to the Eastern part of the country. When the waters receded they moved back to their homes and planted. The only way in and out of the country during the rainy season was by way of the Alto Paraná and Paraguáy rivers, but was now opening itself to Argentina and Brazil by the recently constructed road from Encarnación and another road, still not completed, to Iguassú. The Chaco was impenetrable, especially during the rainy season.

Asunción, Paraguáy. Downtown and port

I met a group of students in the park who showed me a more intimate view of the government. Of course, theirs was the usual complaint about the United States Government and its support of the dictatorship. They expressed their hatred of Dulles and the gunboats and jet planes purchased by the U.S. This had not only made it impossible to overthrow an unpopular dictatorship (of which this one most definitely was) but also forced the government to squander its budget training pilots to operate and fly them, as well as fuel and maintenance of the jets and gunboats. "We were not a democracy before but we were able to oust any dictator who became unpopular with a coup. The presidents all knew they could be ousted at any time simply by a palace coup. There was a close connection between the people of the country and its leaders, which was successfully blocked by the new military clout backed by American aid and the prominence placed on economic growth."

Asunción Paraguáy. Parque Caballero

I was surprised at how openly and freely people talked about their government. I found this was not a dictatorship of men but of a party. The president changed every six years. This party was very much anti-Communist and aligned its foreign policy subservient to U.S. foreign policy. The U.S. was giving a lot of money to help the country develop. This president was the first president Paraguáy had had who had been interested in economically developing the country. Brazil was also helping them. Argentina had consistently tried to strangle the country and only a few weeks before had tried to start a revolution there, so Brazil had made a Freeport at Corumbá for Paraguáy and also built roads to meet the ones President Stroessner was building.

Asunción lost nearly 80% of its men in the Chaco War with Bolivia and was just beginning to again reach the 50/50 balance of men and women. The Chaco was always in dispute with Bolivia. It became of imminent importance when Bolivia, which had lost its coastal territory to Chile in the War of the Pacific (1879-83), sought a new outlet to the sea through the Paraguáy River and Río de la Plata in Argentina. Small fights began in 1928, turning into full-scale war in 1932. Eventually Paraguayan forces defeated the Bolivians in 1934.

The peace treaty of July 21, 1938, gave Paraguáy title to the majority of the disputed land, but Bolivia received a corridor of access to the Paraguáy River and a port (Puerto Casado). The friendliness of the people was overt and genuine. Almost everyone I met became a friend. People walked up to me in the streets and began to converse. They frankly discussed politics. Everyone I met felt the established government was what he or she needed now. They all shared a common love for their country. During my short stay I made close to forty friends. I was invited to about six or seven homes, all of which I had to turn down due to my short stay. A professor insisted I come and stay with him for a few days and look over his school and meet the students. The Society of Brothers invited me to stay longer and see some of their Mennonite colonies at

El Rosario. Some of my closer friends told me to stay over and leave at another time, but I had to leave because there wasn't another boat to Buenos Aires until the next week and I had used up most of my spare time in the Amazon and Brazil.

Still suffering from the results of my meal in Posadas, I bought a ticket on a small launch going to Brazil on the Río Alto Paraná. It would complete a spiritual loop I felt drawn to make. My original plan had been to pass over the mountains to Pucalpa on the Río Ucayali, take a launch for a short trip to Iquítos and then a Booth Liner down the Amazon for a total of 2-3 weeks on the Amazon. This had turned into a six-week journey down small jungle rivers through Colombia, paddling part way down the Amazon and up the Río Tapajós into rubber country. In southern Brazil I was drawn to the rainforest connecting Brazil to Paraguáy through two rivers. The trip up the Paraguáy River would complete the rainforest portion of that journey. Some of the most compelling locations were those surrounding the rainforest. These places evoked something within me reminiscent of a distant past, many lifetimes ago.

It was not until many years later, when I read David Childress's book on Lost Cities in South America I saw the reasons for the fascination I felt for the rainforest. When David explained how the rainforest was originally a large inland sea, I resonated to that account. I had seen this in visions and did not know how to explain what I saw. Numerous temples and cities, with construction very similar to what I was to find in Cuzco and Tiahuanaco in Bolivia and Perú, surrounded this sea. None of the books I sought satisfied my curiosity or answered my visions in a way that made sense to me. A voice spoke to me as I was planning this trip the spring before and told me, "You are going on a spiritual journey." I did not know what that meant but deep within my soul I knew it would be revealed as I wandered through little known places in search of lost ruins from my past. A few have led exploratory expeditions in search of lost cities in the outer rainforest, some never to return. I only needed to touch these locations and return for later revelations. Whereas I felt constantly drawn to the Amazon, its tributaries, the Mato Grosso and the Chaco, I never knew why; I just knew there was a tie to that land and the Alto Paraná. I later found Colonel Percy Harrison Fawcett had been searching for lost cities in that area. In 1925 he left on a mission with his eldest son, never to be seen again. David Childress writes in his books about how the Amazon Rainforest was a huge inland lake, during an ancient time before the destruction of Atlantis. The locations were revealed to me each day as I traveled. There were no records anywhere I could find of the buses or boats that traveled between cities or even whether any existed. Most conveyances were proprietary, meaning one person owned each bus, canoe, or launch. I could never have guessed the places I would be drawn to or shown by the unofficial guides who would spontaneously appear and lead me to a previously unknown sacred spot.

Rosario on Río Paraguáy

I caught a small motor launch that plied the river, despite my dysentery. I lay down all morning but was well enough to get around by afternoon. I got invitations to spend a couple of days in several homes. I talked over the problems of the country with many of the people I met. My main regret was I was not staying there months instead of a few days. I got to Concepción and got a little worried as I wasn't able to walk around very much, so just spent from 5:15 to 6:00 a.m. there, seeing the city. Then I returned with the same launch. It was a wonderful trip. We passed El Rosario, where the Brotherhood had a center. For the first time I was now forced to return short of my destination in Brazil and Bolivia. Back in Asunción I bought some medicine recommended to me by a friend. Within twenty minutes all dysentery symptoms were gone.

Río Paraguay, Rosario.

I was now noticing the inner awakening within me. I was becoming more Latin in both expression and feeling. I was no longer the quiet person I grew up with. I had learned to express rage rather than bottling it up inside. I expressed myself more freely. I was more in touch with what I wanted and needed. I was feeling more comfortable speaking Spanish and Portuguese than

English. It was almost like having an added vocabulary as I found it easier to express what I wanted more clearly than I had in English.

Main Park, Corrientes, Argentina, on conjunction of Paraná & Paraguay Rivers

I traveled 36 hours by riverboat to Corrientes, Argentina, at the conflux of the Rivers Paraná and Paraguáy. The first night out I met a judge of the Superior Court in Río de Janeiro (Gallería dos Presidentes da Associaçāo dos Magistrados do Fluminences, Río de Janeiro), Durval Passos de Melo. We rapidly became good friends, soon joined by a Russian immigrant businessperson and several Argentineans; we became a five-some for the rest of the trip. Durval spoke perfect Spanish so we switched to that so I could complete extracting my Spanish from my Portuguese. Durval played the piano and two girls sang. Another man had a copious collection of Brazilian and Argentine songs so we gathered and sang. We went down to third class and found a guitarist to complete the repertoire. It was really something, streaming down the river with a full moon up above, and folk music in the background. The passengers were affable and fun loving. It was as though we had been friends all our lives.

At Corrientes I transferred to a larger boat, headed for Buenos Aires. We had two wonderful days of river travel before we entered a widening section of the river and turned toward Buenos Aires. Suddenly we found ourselves in the middle of a vicious storm. The boat was old and the captain was afraid to continue into the deeper

Corrientes, Argentina.

waters of the Río de la Plata so we dropped anchor as the wind whipped around us and the waves lashed at our sides. That night the captain decided we had to proceed, so we bobbed around in the Río de la Plata. The river was so wide we couldn't see the shore on either side and so shallow the water swished the boat around like a toy in a Jacuzzi. Members of the crew, as well as the passengers, were all gripped with fear, especially my roommate who kept his life jacket ready on the top of his bed and ran around like a crazy man, ready to jump overboard at each creaking sound of the boat. I seemed to be the only one who felt we would make it, although I kept listening for any signs of the boat cracking apart. I had not seen such fear and panic since I watched Pusan burn in Korea. I did what I could to calm the others. I was surprised when the distress call was sent out the next morning. I began to look for a life jacket as the rest of the crew and passengers scrambled for the lifeboats. When I reached the exterior of the boat I found one of the workers had fallen overboard. The waves were so rough at that time we couldn't even get a lifeboat lowered into the water. We fought the waves for forty-five minutes trying to find him with no luck. I felt sad when I looked into the blackness of the night at the waves crashing against the boat and knew somewhere in those waters was a young man who had just breathed his last breath in those churning waters. I'm sure others felt equally as depressed but no one discussed it any further. We just stood there with our life jackets, clinging to the side of the boat. We could not safely abandon ship, neither could we abandon her in any safety. We finally had to give up and head for Buenos Aires, arriving there a day late.

Palermo Park, Buenos Aires, Argentina

When I arrived at Buenos Aires, I thought we had landed in Italy. The Spanish sounded like Italians speaking Spanish. They talked with their hands and arms, as do many Italians. Every evening they closed off all motor traffic near Avenida Florida and the streets were flooded with people, meandering back and forth in animated conversation. One young man I met walked with me for a number of blocks in friendly conversation, arms flailing. The streets were crowded and he had to interrupt his conversation with an occasional "Perdóname," "Excúsame" or other apology as his arms connected with others.

Durval and I went to our hotel, took off immediately for our individual chores, agreeing to meet back at the hotel at 5:00 for dinner. Again, I found a contradictory impression of both Argentina and the Argentines. I was told the Argentines hated Americans, were rude, gave poor service, and were arrogant. As with my experience with the Colombians following disparaging descriptions from Venezuelans, I found the Argentines the opposite of their detractors' tales. Everyone I met was extremely polite, helpful, courteous, and friendly. In contrast to the Paraguayans who were warm, friendly, and open, I found the Argentines whom I stopped to ask directions almost too friendly and wanting to do everything they could to make sure I was fulfilled. For instance, I asked one man where the post office was. He insisted on not only pointing in that direction but taking me there, standing in line with me and making sure everything went well. I told him I could find it on my own, could handle the mailing and every other form of protest I could think of but could not free myself from him until everything went as planned. This happened, not just once, but numerous times when I asked directions.

Government Buildings & Park, Buenos Aires, Argentina

I was delayed and did not get back to the hotel until 7:15 p.m. When Durval wasn't there I figured he had probably given up on me and gone on to dinner so I waited until 7:30 and then thought I'd better have dinner before the restaurants closed. The restaurants were nearly empty so I figured Argentines must eat at 6:00. I returned to the hotel at midnight and found Durval had not returned yet. He finally returned at 2:15 a.m. Speaking irately about the Argentines he growled, "I was looking for a place and asked directions from a group of young men. I followed their directions and found myself way out of town in the opposite direction. How can these Argentines lie like that? No one would ever do that

Photographers in Palermo Park, Buenos Aires, Argentina

to me in Brazil."

I tried to suppress my delight at seeing a Brazilian having the same experience with the Argentines that I had had in Brazil, I laughed and Durval looked at me visibly upset. He still didn't believe me when I told him, "That's the same thing that kept happening to me in Brazil. They did lie and they did it many times."

The next night I had an appointment for 6:45 so Durval and I decided not to plan on dinner together. My appointment didn't show up so I went to dinner alone, again in a nearly empty restaurant, and returned to the hotel at 9:00 p.m. and found Durval there. We talked until 10:00 and I started getting ready for bed because I had to be up by 6:00 a.m. Durval looked at me surprised and said, "Aren't you going to eat?"

Buenos Aires from Palermo Park

"I ate long ago," I said.

He pled, "I've been waiting for you to go eat all this time." I felt terrible. The poor guy must be half-starved. I accompanied him to the nearest restaurant. It was packed. There was hardly a table available. It took nearly an hour to get served and eat, and the restaurant was still full when we left at midnight. Durval explained to me no one in Argentina goes out to have dinner until at least 10:00 p.m.

Montevideo, Uruguay shares a border on the Río de la Plata with Argentina. The river, at that point, is more a bay or inlet on the Atlantic, rather than a river. It took us three hours to cross the river to Colonia. The Uruguayan countryside reminded me of Ohio, not only the endless green plains, but the sameness of scenery. The same Italian accent dominated the Uruguayans as in Argentina.

Plaza de Mayo, Buenos Aires

The next day I went to the port to say goodbye to Durval, whose ship had crossed the river and was loading in Montevideo.

He came to the door in pajamas, looking at me out of one eye. He

Plaza de Independencia, Montevideo, Uruguay

suddenly came to and ran to the porthole. "Are we in Montevideo?" he inquired in shock. We had planned on seeing Montevideo together but it was quite rainy so we stayed on board and talked until his ship left at 5:00. I never tired of talking with Durval. He was always interesting. From him I learned more about the Latin mind than any other person I had met. He was even more interesting because he had traveled through France, Belgium, Italy, Norway, Sweden, Denmark, Germany, and Brazil. Like me he was not interested in just seeing buildings and countryside. He was deeply interested in people and the way they think. He was writing a book on his travels. This was the first person in all my travels I had trusted enough to share a room with. All others I had traveled with I had excused myself because I didn't feel comfortable with them, because I felt they would be an imposition or because I didn't trust the intentions of their friendship. The parting words of Durval when I told him it would be a little hard traveling alone again were, "Find a friend in your journeys. Don't travel alone. There is always someone who would enjoy your company." Good advice but I still felt I preferred traveling alone. I could read when I felt like it, come and go at will and did not find myself tied to another's schedule.

Montevideo, Uruguay

Durval was fascinated with the Indigenous side of his bloodline. He traveled extensively to many of their villages and studied their lifestyles. He was active in trying to get the Brazilian government to show more respect for the Indians of the rainforest and those who still lived in remote villages in the edges of the forest. I found on a Google search Durval has a street named after him in Rio de Janeiro.

Montevideo had a European feel about it, with colonnades and monumental construction. That evening I flew back to Buenos Aires.

My original plans had always been to travel by bus to the southernmost part of Argentina and Chile, landing at the southernmost town of the world, Ushuaía. Unfortunately, the extra time I had devoted to the Amazon did not allow the two weeks it would take to travel to Ushuaía and back. The second choice was to cross into Chile through their lowest pass in the Andes, the Chilean Lake District. Crossing was done by a series of launches that traveled across lakes that wound themselves through the Andes, connected by roads which carried people from lake to lake, nestled between snow-capped mountains, ending at Puerto Montt, the southernmost town in Chile. This would not only save two precious weeks of travel but channeled me through some of the most spectacular mountain scenes in the Andes. The train across the endless flat plains of the Pampas was tedious, but comfortable. The service, contrary to that I had experienced in Brazil, was courteous. It did not take long to make friends with other passengers. My cabin mate was a German who wanted to become friends with me but, for some reason or other, I spent most of the journey evading him by spending most of my time in the dining car. The land was as flat as a pancake without a rise for miles. I remembered learning the topsoil was sometimes as deep as twenty feet, making it excellent

San Carlos de Bariloche and Lake Nahuil Huapi

Lago Nahuil Huapi, view of shoreline

for grazing cattle, one of Argentina's chief exports.

A few hours out of Bahía Blanca the train left behind the green, flat and fertile Pampas to travel through a hot desert. The dust was profuse and sometimes made me wonder whether it wasn't cleaner outside. Everything was covered with dust. We followed the Río Colorado, crossed it, headed south to the Río Negro and then followed it on its journey west. Near the end of the State of Río Negro and the beginning of the State of Neuquén we came to the place in Argentina referred to as the California of Argentina. The area was extensively irrigated. Mostly grapes were grown here as far as I could see. We arrived at the end of the line at Zapala at 1:00 a.m.

Lake & mountains from top of boat

I caught a bus from Zapala to San Martín de los Andes. It was November 12th and the scenic road to Chile would not open until the 15th, the beginning of their spring. It was freezing outside and still snowing in the mountains. We climbed into the mountains until we reached a small village built on the end of a long lake. Steep snow-capped mountains enclosed the long, narrow lake on both sides into a distant curve. The town looked like a bit of Bavaria dropped into a winter wonderland. I ate in a small German restaurant. I felt uncomfortable in Northwestern Argentina because I was aware many Nazis had found refuge there. I was told San Martín de Los Andes was one of their places of safe haven. Much later I read a book by a former Mossad (Israel's intelligence agency) agent, Victor Ostrovsky (a former agent), who

Lago Aguas Frías, Argentina

revealed how the Mossad met with many of these former Nazi's to teach the planned cabals torture tactics for new planned dictatorships in South America. This stuck in my mind as I watched the Pinoché and other despicable governments that came into power by force in Latin America, using unmentionable torture to consolidate their power. I was impressed by the unmatchable beauty of this town and surrounding mountains but will always remember the negative energy I felt during my short time in the village prior to catching another bus to San Carlos de Bariloche that same day. Visible at various times traveling either from San Martín de los Andes to San Carlos de Bariloche or as far as Osorno, Chile was the Mountain Osorno, a near copy of Mt. Fujimoto in Japan.

Lake & mountains from boat

The Argentines were all up in arms over the inflation in Argentina. Prices had gone up from 300-500% in just a few months. Even I, traveling with dollars that had increased in value from 200-300%, was feeling the pinch.

The Argentines were very friendly and the view through the mountains was beautiful. I told one Argentine, "The opinion in the U.S. is the average Argentine is the most anti-American of any Latin American, but my experience has shown them to be the nicest of any toward me as an American. Do I just happen to be meeting the nicer people or is this average experience? I lost my temper nearly every day traveling through Northern Brazil the people were so rude. I was even beginning to worry about whether I was just getting short tempered. I never lost my temper once in Argentina, nor did I have any reason to."

Lake & mountains from top of boat

He smiled and said,

"Here every Argentine is your friend."

San Carlos de la Bariloche was a town founded by the Germans and Swiss. All the buildings were in the style of Bavaria and the Swiss Alps. It was a little gem, completely surrounded by snow-capped mountains, and located right on a large lake, Nahuel Huapi. I located a reasonable hotel where every window looked out on the lake.

Lago Todo Los Santos, Argentina

The next morning a bus took me to a small port on the lake where I boarded a small launch with tourists from all over the world. It was November 13th, which, weather-wise, would be equivalent to Estes Park, Colorado on May 13th. It was a three-hour boat ride to Puerto Blest. This lake was dark blue. We had lunch there, and then caught a bus to Lago Aguas Frías, where that lake was light green. It followed a gorge with snow-capped mountains on both sides and in front. At the other end we caught a bus, which took us to Puella, Chile. We reached the border of Chile at the top of the divide and began our descent to Puella. The same man owned the road, the buses, the lakes, the boats we took (in Chile), a monopoly, which made the hotel, and all the land prices high. The scenery was magnificent with cascades, lakes, mountains, and green hills.

Traveling with us were four American women who owned a travel agency, an elderly American man, a Brazilian couple, a Chilean and some Argentines. I found myself interpreting into English, Portuguese, Spanish, and even some interpretation for the Argentines and Chileans who found it difficult to understand each other's accents.

Country Club, Santiago, Chile

In the morning we boarded another boat. It took

us two-and-one-half hours to cross Lago Todos los Santos. Nearing Osorno I was told this was another town heavily populated by Germans. A bus took us to Puerto Varas. This used to be done by boat on Lago Llanquihue (pronounced Yawnkee way) before the road was built. This lake was 26 miles wide. Puerto Varas reminded me of pictures of Alaska in the Gold Rush days, with wooden buildings in 1900 style. All banks were closed in Puerto Varas and none could cash a traveler's check in Puerto Montt. I had so little money I could not eat, sleep, or leave town. I hailed a police officer, which took me to a captain who suggested he take me to an American Air Force Attaché. He was out of town but his houseboy invited me in and said he would work something out. He fixed me something to eat and called another Air Force Attaché. The attaché returned at 9:00 p.m. with his wife. They had just been on a short vacation. The exchange was wild in Chile so he loaned me 2,000 pesos and told me to leave it with a friend of his in Santiago and he would pick it up on his way through there. I found the attaché to be very gracious, but his wife ordered him around like a dog, complaining about everything connected with the trip they had just taken. I was definitely reconsidering any thoughts of marriage after I left their house. I noticed many travelers were carrying dollars, changing those as needed without the exchange problems the traveler's checks were giving me. However, I could never find a bank or exchange place that would give me dollars for my travelers' checks.

Puerto Montt was an interesting town, somewhat reminiscent of some of the fishing villages in Massachusetts. I made a surprising number of friends during my short stay there. Prices were very high and wages were a fraction of the inflated amounts, so most of the people were living in squalor. Every industry here was a monopoly and the owners made as few items as possible and charged high prices to cover their living expenses. If they couldn't sell their goods they just went to the government for a subsidy.

Central Hill Park on a hill in center of Santiago

The weather was miserably cold and wet and the train was not heated so I about froze to the seat. Several little girl beggars came into the car. I looked down and their feet were bare. Brrr! I will complain no more. I was now at the bottom of my circular trip and headed north.

Santiago was a beautiful city with snow-capped mountains (about 20,000 ft.) towering in the background. This was the town all Americans seemed to be crazy about, but I didn't see many Americans.

Again I played tourist, visiting Viña del Mar, and Valparaíso. Several students I befriended gave me a walking tour of Viña del Mar, with its beautiful Victorian homes looking down on the ocean below. Valparaiso was a major port. Houses were built on the sides of steep inclines, reachable by cable car. It reminded me of Salvador in Brazil with the Baixa and Alta (lower and upper parts)

Viña del Mar, beach and homes

I called Ruth Petrinovich, the daughter of the Chaves' with whom I had lunch with Johansson in Río. She and her husband met me at the Country Club for lunch. Her husband was fascinated with my trip down the Amazon and mentioned he would love to do that. But Ruth put the skids on that one in a hurry with a sharply delivered command, "You're not going down the Amazon." Her husband gave me a tour of Santiago in the afternoon.

In Chile I found a different timetable. It was difficult to meet anyone outside the home because time was not by the watch but an approximation that cen-

Palácio Yarur, Viña del Mar, Chile

tered on morning, afternoon or evening. One American banker told me when he first arrived at the bank in Chile he was invited to the boss' party. He wanted to make a good first impression so hurried to arrive on time. A servant came to the door and he found the host and hostess still in their robes beginning to get dressed. He began to think he had the wrong night after waiting for an hour. Finally, the first guests arrived an hour later, with the majority arriving two hours after he arrived.

I did get to go out that night on a double date to a night club famous for its native Chilean dancing, especially La Cueca, a dance originating in Chile.

I looked at the map and read about the interior desert of Chile. It did not sound like anything better than my trip down the Amazon in the Tavares Bastos, but the desert fascinated me. I could not see how I could make that seven-day journey and still maintain my scheduled return to Phoenix in January, so I opted to fly to La Paz, Bolivia.

12. INTO THE ANDES

The cheap flight was made in two laps, Aríca in the North and La Paz the next day. Aríca was once a port for Bolivia. A war in the 1890s carved out a northern port for Chile, leaving Bolivia landlocked. The first lap was a six-hour flight to Aríca. This gave me a good chance to see the mountains of Chile, also the bleak desert that lay in the North. We passed by Mt. Aconcagua (22,834 ft.), the

Mt. Aconcagua, 22,834 ft. Highest in Andes

Dunes from air at Arica, Chile

highest mountain of the Western Hemisphere. It was the most barren land I had ever seen, completely devoid of any vegetation, including cactus.

As we began our descent into Aríca, what I saw below was an inhospitably barren desert stretching to the mountains and sea on all sides surrounding a desolate-looking town on a small peninsula. I could not see how this desolate place could be worth fighting for, although for Bolivia it was their only outlet to the sea. A majority of the population centered in Chile was in the central coastal area.

Upper La Paz

La Paz was the first airport where the plane had to climb to land. The airport was located on a 12,000-foot knoll above La Paz. From the

311

airport we wound down a ravine lined with mud brick houses, to the central part of the city at the 11,000-foot level. Woolen clad women sat behind their fruits and vegetables, each sporting a large bolero hat, introduced to them a long time ago by the British. Every man sported an uninspiring replication of black pants and white shirts. A solemn energy seemed to pervade. Fifty percent of the population was pure Indian and the other half mostly Mestizo. They seemed serious, somewhat brutish, and not openly friendly. Very seldom did I see a smile. In contrast to all other Latin American countries where the park benches were always filled with people in animated conversation, the benches of La Paz were packed with sad-looking families and groups of men or women walking around the park, expressionless.

Looking into older La Paz with mountains

I was amazed at the large denominations on the Bolivian paper currency. I soon discovered they merely moved the decimal point over to accommodate for runaway inflation. After I completed a small lunch at one of the restaurants I went to pay. The meal was $1.00 US, which was paid with a 1,000.00 Sucre bill. I could see what it must have been like for the people in Germany, in the 1920s, to go to the store with a wheelbarrow of money to buy a loaf of bread.

Main Plaza, La Paz

Lago Titicaca from Copabaña, Bolivia

A student approached me and said, "My name is Carlos, and I'm to be your guide." This was not unusual as guides had shown up almost like magic in a number of cities, always showing me towns or places I would never have otherwise seen. These guides seemed Spirit-sent, unlike the clamoring swarms of parasites that latched on to me at nearly every city. With these special guides I ended up seeing places and objects I had never heard of anyone else seeing.

Market, La Paz

This was especially true of the Andes. It was an entirely new ambiance, like stepping into the ancient past. I told Carlos I was seeking pre-Inca ruins. He said I should go to Copacabaña. I had never heard of this place so asked him what transportation I would need to take to get there.

"Don't worry," he said. "I'll meet you in the morning and we can take a 'colectivo'. They leave between 6:00 and 8:00 in the morning from the top of the ravine at an Indian Village.

Colectivo loading the ferry to cross the narrows

I was required to report to the police station upon arrival, but I could not find the station. Carlos could not locate it either. When I finally found it, they told me, "Come back on Monday."

The hotel clerk asked me, "Are you Protestant or Catholic?"

"Neither," I said.

"Well, watch out for thieves. I'm a Baptist. We don't steal but you have to watch out for the Catholics."

I started early for a walk to the top of the hill to the awaiting "colectivos". I was in excellent physical shape so I did not strain myself carrying 100 pounds of luggage on a 1,000-foot climb up a cobblestone road. I reached a small park about halfway up where three young men were sitting. They ran over to me to grab my bags. I grabbed one of them back and then one of the others ran behind me to grab the other one. We wrestled until they finally gave up and walked off. I then finished my race to the top, exhausted from the brawl and the climb, which was now turning into a race against time. When I arrived I could see a sea of trucks lined up. Colorful banners were strung across their tops and down the sides, making them look like circus wagons. Most were loaded with people, traveling to market and home from the capitol. I spotted Carlos and another student traveling with him. He beckoned me to one of the trucks and we climbed on. The trucks would not leave until they were filled. This was the only way to travel overland in Bolivia at that time. Each truck was individually owned and charged whatever the traffic would bear.

Approaching Copabaña, Bolivia from mountains

Bay at Copacabaña, Bolivia on Lake Titicaca

I was used to traveling this way but I could see Carlos was uncomfortable. We traveled along dirt roads to lake Titicaca. There wasn't a cloud in the sky, a bright blue, mirroring the blue hue of Lake Titicaca. At one point we waited on shore to cross an isthmus by wooden ferry sailboats. There was little dialogue with the other passengers, who sat quietly, talking in hushed tones among themselves as we bounced across the dirt roads. At one point they all reached into their bags and pulled out bottles of liquor, handing them to me. I looked back, surprised. One of the women said, "Put these in your bag so the police won't find them at the next check point."

Copacabaña, Bolivia. Shrine

I balked at the thought and quickly answered, "I can't do that. They will confiscate all my possessions if I do that."

"But they won't look in your bag. You're a foreigner. They won't look at a foreigner's bag," insisted one woman. I was filled with compassion as I looked into her eyes and said, "I have expensive camera equipment. I can't afford to lose it. I really can't take that chance."

I felt empathy for these people but just couldn't take the chance. I had never seen a checkpoint that did not check my bags, if they checked anyone else. They were unhappy with my answer but quietly placed them back in their bags. We soon arrived at the checkpoint. Each of their bags was emptied and the bottles of liquor confiscated. I carried the pangs of guilt for the rest of the trip. They were right, the customs officials did not inspect my bags; however, had they inspected mine

Llamas in Altiplano, Bolivia

everything I owned would have been confiscated and ruined the rest of my trip.

Colectivos, waiting for ferry at narrows, Titicaca

Lake Titicaca, at 11,000 feet, is the highest navigable lake in the world. A Booth liner traveled regularly from Guaquí, the Bolivian end of the lake, to Puno, Perú, and an overnight trip each way. With the increase in tourism, this interesting voyage has been replaced by hydrofoil boats, which now speed the numerous tourist groups to locations from Puno, Perú.

As we rounded a corner we could see the wonderful views of Copacabaña and the lake about 500 ft. down the mountainside. I became aware of a headache that was beginning to throb. As I arrived at the hotel I found I had Soroche, popularly known as mountain sickness. The best thing for that was rest, which I was forced to do.

Copacabaña, in another setting, would be considered a beach resort. However, the water was 3°C (38°F). At the request of my persistent inner voice, which I had relied on since an early age, I was

Farming in Altiplano, Bolivia, 13,000 ft. altitude

prompted to put on a swimming suit and swim in Lake Titicaca to join with its energy. Believe me, it was a short swim.

We started a trip in a reed boat for the Island of the Sun, site of a pre-Inca ruins, the Temple of the Sun. Unfortunately, it began to rain, making the trip treacherous because of the high winds on the lake, so we were forced to return. Instead, I climbed a phallic rock, about 150 feet high, which sported a shrine to the Virgin Mary. I could feel ancient energy coming off the rock, far prior to Biblical times. Later travel films I have seen of this rock showed many icons to pre-Inca Spirits.

Reed boats, Lake Titicaca

On the return trip the truck stopped alongside the road. I was bored with the endless wait. The passengers carried a small bunch of coca leaves, which they constantly chewed and shared. One woman offered me a leaf. I thanked her and took the leaf. My first bite was obnoxiously bitter. I spit it out and started to discard the remainder of the leaf. "Oh no, cried the woman. Don't throw it away. Give it back." That was my first and

Guaqui, Bolivia. On Lake Titicaca

only bout with the coca leaf. We were still waiting by the truck when one of the children cried out, "Papá, Papá. Onde 'sta?" No one paid any attention. "Onde 'sta, Papá?" (Daddy where are you?) "Oh, la 'sta, está orinando." (Oh, there he is. He's peeing). With that, the women all laughed out loud. I think that was the only time I ever saw a Bolivian laugh.

I was consistently drawn to the ruins of Tiahuanaco, situated on the opposite side of the lake. A voice in my head kept telling me my connection was with the Pre-Incas, who were the original builders of the exceptional stone buildings copied by the Incas. It told me my language was not Quechua; spoken by the Incas, but Aymara, which preceded that civilization. Numerous Indigenous still speak this language in an area, which includes Northern Chile, Eastern Bolivia, and Southern Peru centering in the villages near Guagui and the ruins of Tiahuanaco. On my map I saw there was a road, which went south, forking into a road between La Paz and Guaqui. The ruins were near there. There was no way to shortcut across, even though there was a road connection on the eastern end of Lake Titicaca, so we had to return to La Paz and take another "colectivo" to Tiahuanaco and Guaqui (from which I would catch the Booth Liner to Puno, Perú on the western reaches of the lake). Carlos said he would go with me as far as Guaqui as he had never seen the ruins.

Tiahuanaco ruins, near Guaqui, Bolivia

seen the ruins.

Everyone told us there was no transportation out that day but we found a truck at 6:00 in the morning. This was a lesson I was fast learning in the hinter reaches of Latin America—don't ask, just go and discover. By the time we finished running all over town looking for enough passengers we didn't leave until 10:00. We got to Tiahuanaco at about noon and ran around getting pictures, despite the large sign directing everyone to not take any pictures. It was all I could do to keep Carlos from running around and getting into every picture.

Farming in the Altiplano, Bolivia

Long after my return I read David Childress' book on South America. It was like a magnetic core in my intuition, which validated what I was feeling but could not relate to anything I had read at the time. Tiahuanaco was originally built on a bay in the Pacific. There was a cataclysmic event that caused the land to rise

11,000 feet, blocking the outlet of that sea. This is the present Lake Titicaca. The ruins were lifted with the rising land, keeping its location close to the water. Numerous tunnels honeycombed beneath the ground, connecting the various cities. Ships coming from Atlantis could enter the inland sea (probably near the present mouth of the Amazon) by means of an outlet to the Atlantic. Crossing the vast waters of the inland sea, they could proceed through a canal, which was at sea level at that time (before the uplift of the Andes mountains) that would carry them into the Pacific Ocean. Parts of the canal can still be found in the Andes. I had visions of the cities and having been at Tiahuanaco but did not know the context in which to interpret what I was seeing. Childress' book put all the pieces together for me.

Amara woman walking cow and spinning yarn, at Guaqui on the shores of Lake Titicaca

We found there was no hotel in town so we caught another truck on to Guaqui. As we got off the truck we were gruffly hustled away to the captain of the port.

"Your passport is invalid so you'll have to return to La Paz to get a police exit stamp on it," he barked in an unyielding voice.

He then turned to Carlos and barked, "You don't have enough identification so you'll have to go to jail."

I argued determinedly with the drunken captain and finally he said, "I'll give you the stamp but I'll need some money."

Mountains and Lake Titicaca, Bolivia

Carlos was held for an hour in a dark room being briskly questioned by the inebriated captain on the grounds he was going to rob me.

Booth Liner, which crossed Lake Titicaca, making this the highest navigable lake in the world. It was an overnight trip from Guagui, Bolivia to Puno Perú

After awhile the captain told me, "The boy confessed he was planning to rob you."

I knew this was a lie but went up to get Carlos' stuff ready for inevitable immediate return to La Paz. He suddenly showed up, saying, "The captain set me free but is going to send me home with a soldier tomorrow morning." Despite my repeated efforts, I could get no more information from him. Whatever happened during his detainment will remain a mystery.

We found the captain in the morning. By then he had sobered up and told Carlos, "You can leave by yourself," then turned to me and said, "I'll fix you up when I get back at noon." We, therefore, spent the day taking photographs. A horde of Flamingos formed a large pink mat against the green fields across the isthmus by the boat.

Flamingos on Lake Titicaca at Guaqui

I looked up and saw a woman walking, draped in a dark covering typical of the natives of the village. She was spinning a ball of rough wool into thread. As usual I asked permission to take her picture. She did not speak Spanish so Carlos translated into Aymara for me. When he finished I asked, "Did she say it was all right?" This was usually the expected response.

He looked at me disgusted and said, "Go ahead, and take the picture."

Llamas at small train station on way to Cuzco

"But what did she say?" I asked.

"She said you could not. You just want to take her beauty back with you. Stupid superstition. Go ahead and take her picture." She had passed us by then so I did, with some guilt, take her picture when she wasn't looking. I have since found this a typical belief in many Indian villages in Central and South America. I have also found this to be accepted by a certain segment of the scientific world. I found the Aymara speaking people to be somewhat unapproachable, an awareness that tugged at my heart because I knew I had an ancient connection with these people and must have spoken their language and shared their spirituality in another lifetime.

Walls on Calle Loreto. Colonial buildings were built on top of stones from Inca times because they could not destroy them.

By noon the captain hadn't returned. I checked again at 2:00 and he still wasn't there. I said goodbye to Carlos as he left on a truck. I then went back to work to either get permission to leave the country, permission to enter Perú, or at least buy my ticket on the boat. I succeeded in not one of these things.

By 4:30 the Captain still hadn't returned and I was informed he was drunk again. By 5:30 I was informed he had returned but was completely soused. I decided to try to sneak out of the country if I could get permission to enter Perú.

A Bolivian immigration authority stopped me as I was buying my ticket.

Walls on Calle de Loreto, Cuzco. Our guide is against wall on far left.

"Your passport is out of order," he barked.

"The Captain promised to fix things for me but I understand he's drunk," I answered in my defense.

He then remedied my exit for a price. It was worth that just to get out of Bolivia.

I think this experience, more than any other, convinced me of the dangerous move we are making to take away our individual rights in

Custódia de la Mercéd. Contains 412 diamonds, 1650 pearls, a pearl in the shape of a mermaid. It weighs 45 pounds And dates from 1517. Cuzco

the name of protecting us from "terrorists". The government eventually becomes the one to be feared. There is too much opportunity for abuse of power. It ends up being against the public, doing little to protect the people it is supposed to protect. Bolivia, of all countries, had the tightest security. Even to travel between cities required registering with the police at both ends of the journey, yet I felt the most harassed and least protected by this network. It seemed like every time I turned around an angry police officer who claimed I did not have the proper papers met me. When the authorities were drunk it was even worse.

This is some of the efforts on the part of the Conquistadors to destroy these huge foundations. Failing that, they built on top of them

I got my boat ticket, ran back to the hotel, and dragged my bags on board. I bought second class. Eight young men who were about my age greeted me. I was promptly the center of conversation. They were students from all over Perú who were studying in Buenos Aires. They had come all the way on train. This was a quick change for me. I had used English frequently in Chile as I found it difficult to understand their Spanish. They spoke extremely rapid, cutting and chopping their letters, combining many colloquialisms until they were completely unrecognizable. It was also the first place I ever heard bad Spanish grammar (and that includes the Colombian Amazon). Here, in 85% Indian Bolivia, people spoke a clear, slow Spanish so I could forget English as I understood every word and had no trouble expressing myself. Meeting these students who spoke absolutely the fastest Spanish I had ever heard, but clearly enunciating, I never missed a word. Within an hour I was speaking as fast as they were and keeping three conversations going at once. I was really on the spot as they began asking me questions as fast as I could answer them concerning Nixon's trip, our racial problem, the elections, and the women of the U.S. We talked well into the night so I didn't have a moment's rest.

Musical wall on side of Templo del Sol. These were purported to be the same sounds made by drums in all parts of the world and used in ceremonies outside the Temple.

The students rose at the bright hour of 5:00 a.m.

INTO THE ANDES

At 5:30 breakfast was brought (a small bun and a cup of coffee). We arrived at Puno at about 7:30. I always dreaded an immigration authority asking me to show them my return ticket to the United States, which I was told, frequently happened. My itinerary changed daily as I had no idea whether there was transportation between most remote towns. Finally, that dreaded question was asked by an official.

"How are you getting back to the United States?"

Cuzco. These were purported to be early Inca walls. Some writers claim the Incas built on top of the walls of a previous civilization, which would make these buildings from a culture, which existed prior to the uprising of the Andean mountains. So this wall would then be from the Pre-Inca Empire.

This was the same question that supposedly should be asked in all the countries I had been: Venezuela, Cuba, Colombia, Brazil, Argentina, Uruguay Chile, and Perú. In all these countries no one, fortunately, had asked me this question. I feared this mostly as I did not have enough money to get out of the country.

"It's impossible to buy tickets past Cuzco," I pleaded, hoping that would satisfy that question.

He took my passport, gave me a salvaconducto, and told me, "You can pick your passport up in Lima."

The train left at 9:00 a.m. for Cuzco. The students all gave me their telephone numbers and one of them told me to look him up in Lima. They smiled and assured me, "That train should be as good as your Santa Fe." The train was more like what I would have expected Maverick to ride during his hay-day at the turn of the century. One of the students insisted on loaning me 80 soles and letting me pay him back in Lima because I couldn't change my dollars in Puno. The students went on with their train to Arequipa and I got off and changed to the Cuzco train. It was quite a letdown to get off second class that was better than first in Brazil (the Tavares Bastos) and get on second class that was worse than a cattle car. There were little windows every few feet to let you know you weren't completely boxed in. The interior consisted of a bench along each side and a bench through the middle so they could fit their passengers in back-to-back. It was one of the most fascinating train trips I had had through a mountain valley surrounded by snow-capped peaks. At noon the train stopped by an array of tables with canvases thrown over them where they served us plates of rice, soup and chicken. First serving consisted of a bowl of soup with a bony piece of meat in the middle. Second serving consisted of rice and chicken. Little beggar children stood alongside looking hungrily at the clients, hoping to get a handout. As I finished my soup one of them jerked the bone out so fast that everything splattered all over. I saw a European-looking young man across the car and finally bumped into him. His name was Kristian. He was a Danish lad who had been in Argentina for two years as a tutor. He was taking a vacation before returning to Denmark. I had a rough time communicating with him as his comprehension of Spanish was so bad and I had gotten to a point where I spoke so fast that I lost anyone who didn't understand the language. I bumped into an American taking pictures. He was in first

Cuzco, huge stones carved to fit exactly with the other stones. They are so tight one cannot stick a knife blade between then and one had 14 angles. These could not have been created by a society that did not even have a wheel or steel tool.

Typical balconied street built on the ruins of the Inca

class but came slumming for a while. He didn't speak Spanish and started talking to the Danish boy very fast in English and the Danish boy understood every word. I then spoke my first English since Santiago, Chile and got across to him. We got to Cuzco at 6:00 p.m., and looked around for a room. We walked across town to the Tourist Hotel but were told by the American they had no rooms. The three of us went to the Rosedale Hotel, which was just a little less money but a much worse hotel. We had dinner at the hotel and got exactly what we didn't order about an hour after we ordered it. The American, Art Cohen, thoroughly embarrassed Hans and me as he barked orders at the waiters with his three words of Spanish, sometimes going so far as storming into the kitchen when the waiters didn't understand him.

Clock at Sacsahuaman

Ancient Inca baths at Sacsahuaman.

We had breakfast at the hotel, taking about an hour-and-a-half. We set out with our little guide sheet Hans picked up in Lima and started looking for Inca ruins. Cohen ran off and returned with a twelve-year-old boy, Raul, looking very formal in his blue pants and jacket with a fresh white shirt. As he talked he seemed to have a grasp of Cuzco so we asked him how much he wanted to show us around for the day.

"Whatever you want to pay me," was his casual answer. The first place Raul took us was inside the church of Santo Domingo, which is built on the ruins of the Temple of the Sun and the Temple of the Moon. The Spanish not only melted down golden statues, fountains and plates, but also intended to destroy all great buildings. They found they could destroy them only to the first twenty feet as the stones fit perfectly against each other and weighed megatons. They, therefore, built their new buildings on top of the ruins. Ironically, this left the energy of the Inca temples as the base of new religious structures. At the door of the church, built on the ruins of the Temple of the Sun, I could see the chippings where the Spanish tried unsuccessfully to destroy the lower twenty feet of the temple. Raul's father was killed by a wall that fell in on him while repairing the church walls after the earthquake of 1950. This made him a favorite of the officials of the church. Raul was, therefore, able to talk the priests into opening up a room below the church for us, which housed a lighted custody containing 1600 pearls and 1500 diamonds. Art said they wouldn't even do this for the tour unless requested in advance. I was touched by the energy emitted by this custody and asked if I could take a picture.

Restored houses and farm plots, Machu Micchu

The priest said, "No, no pictures are allowed," then turned and left.

Sacsahuaman. A fine example of stone cutting. Doorway doesn't even have space to fit a knife between any of the stones.

Raul looked at me, smiled, and said quietly, "He left so you can take a picture. He'll be back in a while."

Raul spoke no English so I translated his lecture to Art as we went along. The Peruvians didn't seem to have that shyness of having pictures taken inside their churches so every father

Vendors with delicious items for train passengers

or brother I asked graciously consented to let me take pictures. Our guide took us to parts of the city where walls of old palaces and temples of the Incas still existed and explained them. One street had a wall on the left that was pre-Incan, made with stones and mortar. On the right side of the street was a wall built without the aid of mortar, attributed to the Incas. Like the Pyramid of Giza in Egypt, it is inconceivable how the Incas could have mined, hauled and built these indestructible buildings with such precision, without even the use of the wheel, which they did not possess at the time of the Spanish conquest. I would have loved to have seen what Pizarro and his band of cutthroats saw upon entering Cuzco for the first time: gold fountains, gold trimming and unbelievable wealth stretched out before them. Sadly, most of that gold was melted and shipped back to the Church in Spain.

The Incas built an extensive irrigation system, which carried water to all parts of the Empire. These were also indiscriminately destroyed by the Conquistadors, and little remained of them as their

Remains of Inca bridge, crossing the Río Urubamba between Machu Picchu & Cuzco.

ruins were seen every now and then on the parched wasteland. The Incas constructed way stations for couriers who could run a letter across Perú faster than the present mail system.

On the Temple of the Sun one of the large stonewalls was solid except for three holes, which had been carved into it, perfectly aligned. I stuck my hand inside at Raul's suggestion and thumped the sides, which emitted three hollow tones. He explained these were the same tones you would find in China, Africa, and North America. These were supposedly used for ceremonial dances. I have talked with numerous people returning from excursions to the Andes, and none have seen either the custody of Santo Domingo or the three holes in the stone.

Huaynu Picchu from Machu Picchu

We went up on one of the hills surrounding the city and saw a large Inca fort, Sacsahuaman. The stones were all cut to fit without mortar. One stone had 12 different angles perfectly fit into the surrounding stones weighing an estimated 20 tons. So exact were they in each fitted angle, even a knife could not be inserted between the edges. Most of the other stones weighed equally as much. There were many other remains of the fortress, such as a large sun clock and baths. An Indian student was studying there, sitting in one of the baths. I asked him, "Can I take your picture? I understand these once were baths of the Incas. I would like to have a picture of a descendant of the Incas taking a sunbath in the Baths of the Incas." He laughed and seemed pleased to pose. I sat on a seat purported to be the throne of the Supreme Inca from which he reviewed his troops below. Below I could see Art, grabbing some children in bright native garb and lining them up for a picture. Suddenly there was great commotion below. A young farmer boy was leading his llamas across the field, which was apparently the property of a local farmer. The owner finally overpowered the boy and confiscated one of his llamas; dolefully the boy led his remaining animals back to the farm, sobbing loudly. There were sacrificial tables for the llamas. We found a tunnel that led to the fort, which we squeezed ourselves through.

INTO THE ANDES

On the way back down to Cuzco we were shown a wall of the palace of Manco Copac, the first Inca (around 1145 A.D.). He was the legendary founder of the royal dynasty that ultimately ruled the Inca Empire. According to tradition, he originally came from south of Cuzco, eventually establishing the capitol there. This provided evidence to affirm what I was intuiting, that the real technology of Cuzco was not from the Incas, but their predecessors at Tiahuanaco, who because they left no written record, disappeared into the annals of mysterious history leaving only the remains of their temple grounds and a highly complex language.

Doorways in housing. Machu Picchu

I had a strong intuition the Incas did not build Cuzco. They built on top of a civilization before them that had technology far in advance of our own, which had been all but forgotten.

After about 6:00 p.m. we took Raul to dinner and he then invited us to his apartment to meet his mother. We paid him 305 pesos apiece, which is about $3.60, a good day's wages for Cuzco. We went to the tourist agency to buy passage to Machu-Picchu. The tickets were very expensive but Art bought one as he was short of time. The agent pulled Hans and me apart and offered to let us go to and from Machu-Picchu with the tour for 90 soles. We accepted his offer, as it would otherwise have meant spending two more days waiting in Cuzco.

Ancient stairway going up Huaynu Picchu

The tour cab took us to the station at 6:30 a.m. and we rode the auto car up, slowly climbing the mountains by a series of switchbacks. This was much more efficient than hiring a taxi to go round and round a mountain to get to the top. Part of the old

Inca highway could be seen crossing the Río Urubamba below. The newly discovered ruins of Ollanta came into view and the foundation of an old Inca bridge crossed the river below. The Urubamba, the headwaters of the Amazon, ran along the tracks. At Machu-Picchu we were transferred to old buses and switched back and forth over seventeen loops to reach the ruins on the top of the big hill. The companion mountain of Huaynu Picchu could be seen sticking its head up just beyond, reached by an ancient stone pathway. Some claim this is where they kept the young people as they had only found the bones of youths there. Some ruins remain on top of Huaynu Picchu, some a thousand feet above Macho-Picchu. Machu-Picchu was in pristine condition because it was not found or destroyed by the Spaniards. The stonework of the walls of Sacsahuaman seemed much more impressive because of their size and unsurpassed engineering. Four of us climbed Huaynu Picchu. I was used to the height by this time as I hadn't been lower than 11,000 feet for over a week, but the others struggled out of breath slowly reaching the top. The stone steps and recently installed cables aided the climb to the plateau at the top. There everything was left as it was before. To reach the top I had to go through a cave or across some reeds reached by steps carved into the stones. Some walls were still standing

The road down to the train from Machu Picchu

Abancáy, Perú

and the original steps were still there. At the very top was a carved-out niche for the lookout scout to stand. From there I could see for miles on all sides, Macchu Micchu, a thousand feet below and the Urubamba, another 2,000 feet below that.

Abancáy, Perú

All farming was done on steep terraces. A couple of the farmhouses were restored to show what they looked like. All that had to be added were a couple of pieces of wood and a straw roof to return them to their original condition, so sturdy were the walls. This style of building is still used by the Indians in the mountains. On the return trip we ran into an American and Peruvian who were hunting uranium. One American explorer I met on the train told me he thought they had found the Lost City, the last stronghold of the Inca. They also had found other lost Inca ruins. The Peruvian sounded off with sentiments I had heard all over the back sections of Perú, a condemnation of the Spanish, a lamenting of the fact a great civilization now lives in shacks and huts, more like animals than people. They praised the Inca civilization, which existed before. I ran into a couple that had been in Paraguáy for two years and found out more of how life would be for an American with an American company in Paraguáy. We went out to eat that night and I was again thoroughly embarrassed as Art, with his forthright New York personality, ran out to the kitchen, cussed the waiters out, and stopped people on the streets. Fortunately I managed to smooth things over every time in Spanish after he was finished.

Manco Copac's (First emperor of Inca) Palace, Cuzco

I ran all over the place trying to find a truck going to Abancáy and finally found a bus leaving in half-an-hour. I ran back, threw everything in my bag, and got a taxi out. It finally left after another hour. All the seats were taken so I sat next to the driver (the best seat in the bus). We climbed for five straight hours to the tops of the mountains then dipped down into a hot valley and climbed to the tops of more mountains. At one point I could look straight down, deep into the valley and see the miniaturized view of the town of Abancáy, growing larger during the hour-and-a-half of zigzagging road to reach it. Abancáy was a gem of Colombian architecture.

I got out and soon had met a few towns' people. The price quoted for the Hotel Turista sounded too high so I found a room for 50¢ a night and stayed there.

My dream had been to travel across the tops of the mountains of Peru by bus all the way to Huancayo, where I would find a train down the mountain to Lima. This was the original train I had planned to take on the road to the Amazon River before I discovered the shortcut through Colombia. I found the bus hadn't enough passengers to return so there was no bus or truck out of Abancay that day. My only choice was to wait for a truck from Cuzco to pass through that afternoon. I was taking pictures when I bumped into another American, which at that time would have been considered an amazing experience in Abancáy. His name was John and he had been traveling for two-and-a-half years all over the world. He had gone to Colombia University and MIT. We sat and compared notes for a couple of hours while a couple of Indian students sidled up trying to see how much of our English they could understand. He told me he was going to take a bus straight to Lima, as he didn't care much about the four days it would take to go across the mountains.

Crossing the Altiplano, 14,625' elevation on road from Abancáy to Nazco

I tried to find a truck coming through but finally gave up. I then heard it could be as much as three or four days wait before there were enough people to send a bus from Andahuaylas to Ayacucho. I figured this was too much of a chance so I bought a

INTO THE ANDES

ticket on the bus that went directly to Lima with the other American. That was number One of three foolish decisions I made. My crystal ball failed me on that one.

The bus left at about 6:30 that night and we began to climb into the mountains again. At about 10:00 the unheated bus became miserably cold. Both my jacket and blanket were packed in my bag below, but fortunately I had my sweater with me. The road only allowed one vehicle at a time in either direction so we had to look for a wide spot in the road every time we met a truck, backing up to maneuver around.

Plaza de Armas at night, Lima, Perú

At 2:00 a.m. I was awakened by both the cold and the fact we were trying to maneuver around a truck left in the middle of the road while hanging on the side of a thousand foot drop on our one-lane road. Everyone ran for the door of the bus and left the empty bus for the driver to get around lest it went crashing down the side with everyone on board. We spent a full hour pushing the truck over to the edge so we could maneuver around on the inside. I had a strong urge to urinate but my bashful upbringing came in again to haunt me. I just could not relieve myself in front of all those passengers, many of who were women. Other men apparently had no such disinclination, regularly relieving themselves at the side of the dark road.

Typical Balconied building, Lima, Perú

Finally, at 3:00 a.m. we were off again. I asked if there was any heater on the bus and was told this was the only bus without one. The motor had a terrible sound and I was hoping we would reach civilization before it stopped completely. My bladder was fast moving from urge to emergency. The sun was rising so my inhibitions became even stronger. Finally, we descended into a valley and I spotted a hut. When the bus stopped in front I thought it was possibly a place for coffee and food and possibly had a privy or bathroom. Everyone poured out of the bus and lined up on the side. The women squatted and the men unzipped. Horror swept up inside me. I cursed my conservative upbringing and headed for one of two trees in the distance. I felt reprieved when I looked over and saw a Peruvian heading for the other. "Thank God," I thought, "I'm, not the only shy one in the bunch. There's a native, seeking privacy."

In some places the mountain road was covered with big rocks that we had to remove or where the road was washed out. We had to go less than twelve miles-per-hour almost all the way in addition to the time we spent trying to get around trucks on the narrow precipices. I wished I had taken the other way to Lima. It was a little undependable and took two days longer, but it would have been much more fascinating as it was broken up into five twelve-hour runs with the last big run by train down the steep mountains. Numerous crosses lined the road to mark where cars had gone over the many cliffs. The crosses were so thick on some cliffs; it looked to me like in another year they would have to make double rows.

Argentine Embassy, Lima, Perú

Fortunately, John brought some ham sandwiches along, as I was half-starved. We had stopped at a hut the night before where all I had eaten were three pieces of bread. That morning we stopped at another hut for coffee but found they didn't even have bread. I bought a couple more ham sandwiches from John. The sun was coming up so it began to warm up. We found we had been traveling along a plateau at 4,600 meters (about 15,000 feet), so we understood why it had been so cold. This was the bleakest plateau I had ever seen. There was nothing to look at, either human or otherwise. As we descended a little we passed herds of llama and vicuña, but still no huts. The sputtering motor really had me worried. We were about to approach a town for lunch at noon when the clutch broke down. This was the last straw. As the

INTO THE ANDES

road was only one lane we soon had two busses in back and a bus in front very anxious to help. Our bus had no tools but the others furnished theirs so they soon had removed the electrical system. Fortunately, the problem was in the wiring so the motor was again gasping to a start after only an hour delay. We had an excellent lunch and started for Nazco. According to my map Nazco was only a short way from where we ate but that was deceiving. We were at about 10,000 ft. elevation and had to cross a plateau and descend to sea level. We started at 2:45 p.m. We wound to the top and finally saw the heavy clouds over the ocean at about 5:00 that evening. We wound and wound and wound and at 7:00 p.m. still weren't down the mountain. Finally, at about 7:45 we saw the lights of the city. I was starving again. At 8:00 the motor again died. We pushed the bus back and forth trying to get it started to no avail. John loaned them his flashlight and they pulled the carburetor and distributor apart. We then pushed the truck up and down the hill with no results. Finally, about one-and-one-half hours later we got it going (just barely). The bus puttered and sputtered into the city coming to a dead stop in front of a Japanese restaurant. We were glad to reach Nazco. We were now on a paved road to Lima. The bus amazingly started up again and we were off. It didn't take long to go to sleep with an asphalt road underneath.

I awoke as we were entering another town. The motorist was fighting, as usual, to keep the motor from going dead. He finally lost his battle in the middle of the city at 2:00 a.m. I found this was only ICA (the company that owned the bus). We then spent from 2:00 a.m. until 4:30 a.m. pushing the bus all over town trying to get it started, but no dice. "Why don't you get a mechanic out of bed to fix this?" was a constant refrain from the passengers.

Gingerbread house, San Isidro, suburb of Lima

"We don't need one. We just need one more push," was his persistent answer.

He finally called a mechanic but no mechanic arrived.

Then we changed tactics. "Why don't you put us in taxis

or another bus and let us go on?" we pleaded.

"I have to wait until 8:00 a.m. to call the head office to do this," was his excuse.

At 5:00 a.m. a bus came through. It was a beauty, a Swiss bus with reclining seats, and a hostess to attend us.

"I'll loan you the money. Let's take this," John said to me.

The situation looked hopeless with the Morales bus so we got on. It was wonderful sitting back on a nice smooth bus. I would get to Lima in time to get the money out of the bank, which my bank in Phoenix was supposed to have wired. This was all wonderful until we heard a "ping" and the motor on our luxurious bus stopped. We were way out in the desert and the motor was completely dead. The tools were soon out and the driver and assistant began industriously taking everything apart. After about a half-hour we heard a "ping-pang-cough-put" and looked out to see the Morales bus had started just after we left and passed us on its way to Lima. The mechanics finally got our motor going. We were informed the part would have to be sent out from Lima. This would take three hours. However, they had the motor fixed within two hours and the bus again roared to a start. We were barely out of town when "ping", the part came loose again. We hobbled back to town and the driver and mechanic began again to take the motor apart.

Colonial style house, Lima, Perú

After about two more hours I looked at my watch, sighed, and told John, "I'll bet the Morales bus must be just now arriving in Lima." At that moment our sick motor started again. The desert here was as desolate as what I had observed in Northern Chile. I spotted a few irrigated places but not even the occasional clumps of grass I was used to in the deserts of Arizona, New Mexico, and California. As far as I could see were sand dunes all the way back to the mountains to the East. When I thought about this and the fact nothing grew in the mountains I began to see why Perú had all its progress in Lima. I remembered reading about the extensive irrigation system the Incas had built throughout the mountains and valleys, all irretrievably destroyed by the Spanish Conquistadors.

13. THE PILOT ROAD

We arrived in Lima at about 1:30 p.m. and caught a taxi to a hotel. It was terrible. The shower wasn't working. As I had been almost a week without a bath I used a pitcher and threw water on myself. I went out and tried to find the National City Bank of New York. I kept getting all sorts of addresses so by the time I found it, it had closed. I went on up to their offices and one of the managers took me down and helped me out as he was aware the bank was about to embark on a three-day holiday. All three days I had planned to stay in Lima were holidays. As he was an American I asked, "A friend of mine in graduate school told me to look up David in Lima. Is it possible you know him?"

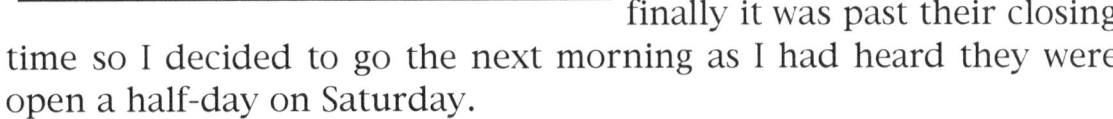
Drive north through the dunes from Lima to Trujillo

"That's me," he answered. He retrieved my $300 and converted some to traveler's checks and said, "Why don't we meet at 1:00 tomorrow?" I happily agreed and thanked him for his help.

Next, I ran around trying to find the authorities to get my passport back. I kept getting the run-around and finally it was past their closing time so I decided to go the next morning as I had heard they were open a half-day on Saturday.

That night John and I decided to try all the restaurants in town as the one we stepped into was too expensive for me to even order an orange juice. We, therefore, had juice at the first place, pizza at another, steak at another, and pastry and tea at another. Each of these places specialized in just these things so we got the best out of each. As John was leaving for Iquítos the next morning I helped him plan his Amazon trip and gave him some people to look up.

Saturday morning the immigration authority asked me to show my transportation ticket out of the country. I laughed and explained the most I could buy was a ticket to Trujillo. I convinced him of my honesty and he gave me my passport.

I ran all over the place trying to locate the student from the Booth Liner, Juan, who had loaned me the 80 soles during the trip across Lake Titicaca. I found the student, at the bank waiting for me. He had gotten back just after I left his father's factory and grabbed a cab over. I invited him to have lunch with us and found that Dave had invited two other Americans from the bank to lunch with us. It took almost two hours to get served, so we had plenty of time to converse. Dave had to return to write some letters so I took off with Juan. I tried to get away as I had so much to do but couldn't get away for five minutes. He had appointed himself in charge of my stay in Lima. I went through his uncle's factory where metal goods are made. Two other students came over and we were off to see the nightlife of the city. The central part of the nightlife they showed me was a house of prostitution in Miraflores. I could tell this was a first for the guys because they had to stop to ask directions. Once again my core values were on a collision course, finding myself in a whorehouse with three other young men. The commercialism of lovemaking was still a culture shock to me, even though the many approaches to the world's oldest profession had fascinated me in each city and town throughout my trip. There was only one girl there I found attractive. As I looked at her on the dance floor she kept disappearing and reappearing with a new partner. Numerous doors surrounded the dance floor. She must have been the top wage earner of the house, so I lost interest. We got back at 4:30 a.m. This nightlife made me bored, so I'm afraid I can't say I enjoyed myself.

One of the many mansions along the shore, Callao

I decided sleep was very important in order to recuperate from the Abancay journey so I slept till noon. I dropped by a travel agency and saw a sign that said "Interamericana de Viajes y Hoteles, S.A. Unusual trips are our specialty". I thought I might pump some information out of them on Southern Ecuadór. Everything was closed all over town but their gate was almost fully open so I smiled at the person who greeted me and asked if the place was open.

The agent spotted me and hailed me in, "Hi I'm Cesar Pardo. Can I help you?"

I asked, "I hear the road to Quito just opened and I don't know whether to go on it or take a boat from Tumbes."

He ran around getting all sorts of information on that area and convinced me, "Why don't you stay over Tuesday morning so you can get some more information from the Peruvian Times before you leave?" We conversed about his business and I was impressed with him. Every travel agency I dealt with throughout Latin America knew nothing beyond air travel. This would help me only if I was interested in flying to the better-known cities and left me with no information sources when I asked about traveling to any of the more interesting remote places.

Perú is probably the most interesting country in Latin American to visit, with its vast desert and enormous jungle. It has one of the two principle towns on the Amazon, the highest mountains in the Andes, the highest road in Latin America, the highest standard gauge railway in the world and the only extensive Indian ruins in South America. Its colonial architecture is unsurpassed in Latin America. These are amazing qualities for any country. Pardo's agency arranged tours to the ruins scattered all around the country, had Amazon tours, bus tours, etc., all extremely interesting.

I took a bus out to the ocean and walked the five miles back. The architecture of Lima was fascinating. Located in a desert backed up by dry mountains had preserved many of the early and 19th Century colonial buildings, beautifully blended with the modern.

I was pleased to find I had kept pretty close to my original budget of $4 a day plus transportation. Elevated prices in taxis, hotels, and other unexpected events squeezed my living into $3.00 a day. However, I was surprised at how few times I had wished I could stay in a better hotel. I found I used my room so little it didn't make any difference where I slept. After six-and-one-half months of living out of a barracks bag I still hadn't grown tired of this life. I had spent less on this trip (about $400.00 less) than a comparable amount of time at college and about $700 less than at graduate school. Yet I figured I had gotten about ten times as much out of this trip as school. I talked with beggars, workers, merchants, factory owners, landowners, bankers, and Indians in the rainforest about the economic, political, and cultural aspects of their country, even including religion. I could never have gotten as much out of this trip had it not been for the good background in Latin America from The School of Advanced International Studies of Johns Hopkins University and American Graduate School of International Management. However about nine-tenths of the information I learned from this trip I could never have gotten from any textbooks or school on Latin America.

"Don't compete with the satellites, slow down and live longer", a traffic sign in Miraflores, a suburb of Lima

In the suburb of Miraflores I saw many traffic warning signs but one in particular gave me a chuckle. It had a picture of a satellite with a car flying around a world that warned drivers, "NO COMPITA CON LOS SATÉLITES, REDUZCA LA VELOCIDAD Y VIVA MAS" (Don't compete with the satellites, slow down and live longer).

I went to the Peruvian Times to get some information on Southern Ecuadór. The common way of traveling overland from Perú to Ecuadór was to leave Perú and take a bus to Sullana, then a short trip to the coast to the port of Tumbes and take a boat to Ecuadór via the port of Guayaquíl. Once there I could easily proceed by train to Quito and then on to Colombia. I found few people who knew anything about the less traveled, but much more interesting, part of Ecuadór between Macará and Cuenca. This trip offered a wealth of splendid scenery and interesting people. I heard there was a newly constructed road connecting the interior of Perú with Ecuador, which sounded like a much more interesting way to go. However, I couldn't find anyone who knew anything about any road to Ecuador. I noticed the travel agencies had no further information either. The Peruvian Times secretary found out I was planning on traveling overland from Perú to Ecuadór, so thought I should talk to the editor, Mr. C. N. Griffis.

Griffis, after talking with me, asked me to write three articles of good length. He gave me an article by a man who had had an easier travel experience than I did over part of that route. He asked me to be a little more kind to the countries than he was. After reading the article I could see what he meant. The writer didn't seem to enjoy any part of his trip. He complained about the hotels, food, transportation, people, and his many cases of dysentery. I was grateful for the editor's warning and glad he gave me the article to go by because the reality of my experiences would have probably provoked me to be equally as unkind in the article I submitted.

The road north circled through mountains of sand dunes, which extended clear out to the ocean. It was an awe-inspiring vista through a far-reaching desert. In places there were small patches of green for short distances where irrigation had made a small amount of farming possible. The bleakness of the desert changed only in degrees, never showing more signs of fertility than the few man-made irrigated locations. When we arrived in Trujillo, I grabbed my bags and was going to stay in the Tourist Hotel because I heard it was so cheap. About a half block from the bus agency I saw a big door and a palatial court inside. I asked someone at the door, "Is this a hotel?"

Nasca Pottery in a museum in Trujillo, Perú

"Yes it is," he answered.

"How much is a room with a bath?"

He said, "12.75 pesos."

I almost knocked him down as I ran inside. The room was a big letdown, except I had a shower and toilet. That's all I cared for at that price. I found out later the Tourist Hotel was about six times that price so was glad I didn't go there.

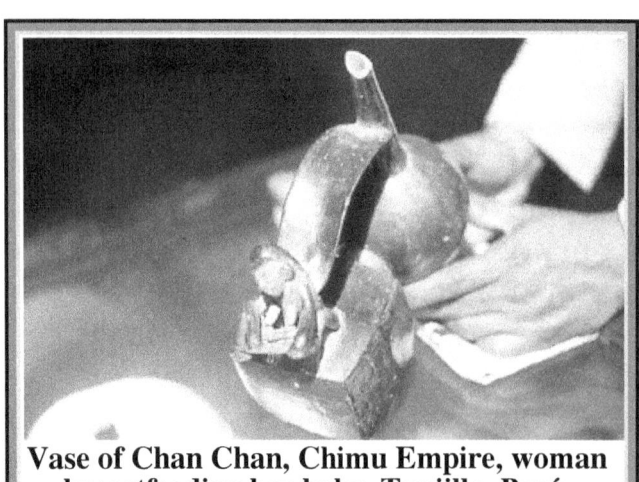
Vase of Chan Chan, Chimu Empire, woman breastfeeding her baby, Trujillo, Perú.

I found Trujillo interesting for her colonial architecture and the ruins of Chan Chan, the only capital of the Chimu Empire. It was a pleasant city with extremely courteous and friendly inhabitants, but life was slow. Even the taxi drivers couldn't be motivated. They placidly sat in their cars or on a park bench awaiting the few customers that patronized them. I tried to barter with a taxi driver but he preferred to continue his siesta rather than lower his price. I found the price of a cab too high to go to the museum, located at an estate fifteen miles from town, but found a bus that passed right by the museum. At the museum I asked if I could just walk around. The attendant answered gruffly, "The museum is closed."

"When will it open?" I inquired

He blurted out, "The entire museum collection is being sent to Lima. We won't be open again."

"I came all the way from Lima just to see the museum," I begged.

"Haven't you been listening to Radio Lima? Haven't you been reading the papers that this museum is closed?" he argued.

It never occurred to me he might mistake my accent for that of a Limeño. I pleaded further but saw my appeal was getting nowhere. I turned gruffly around and started to walk out. That was too much for him. He called me back and told me to go ahead. I was sure thankful he did, because this was a priceless collection of Indian pottery, all privately owned.

The museum keeper warmed to me and began relating the history of the museum. "The gentleman who started this sugar plantation gathered pottery from all the Indian remnants in Perú. He started this museum on the hacienda and opened it to the public. A majority of this pottery was from Nazco."

Most of the pottery looked like it was on the shelf to sell, so perfect was its condition. The realism in the figures was at variance with almost all other South American Indian pottery I had seen. After I was through I asked, "Do you mind if I take a picture?"

He quickly replied, "Yes, go ahead." Then he thought a minute and I could sense he thought maybe he shouldn't have spoken so quickly, so he added, "Just two, no more."

As I was taking pictures he came in and started talking to me about cameras. He then became totally involved in my quest, posing the pottery and letting me know which were the best examples. I thanked him, shook his hand, and started to leave.

"I'm also going to town. Let's take the bus together. Tell me about your trip," he said as we grabbed our seats in the old bus. He began asking me about my trip and when he found out I wanted to go to the ruins of Chan Chan, told me how to get out by bus instead of taxi. I went on into town and he even insisted on paying my bus fare.

I caught the bus to Chan Chan, which took me right to the ruins. I could easily see why there were so few people to explain them. There was nothing to explain. The ruins of the Chimú Empire covered all of Northern Perú from the Gulf of Guayaquil to Southern Perú prior to the Inca civilization (about 800 A.D.). The Incas conquered it in 1400 A.D. The city was made of mud but was in an area of Perú where it never rains. When first discovered the city was in almost a perfect state of preservation. There were frescoes, friezes, large temples, streets, many temples, a canal and houses and gardens. The Spaniards had destroyed a part of it and sacked all the gold and treasure but everything was left standing. Then, in 1932 came a freak rain. It rained so much the hillsides were made into knee-deep rivers. There was nothing to hold back the water as it fell in the mountains close-by because there was no ground cover, so nearly everything was washed away. Only mountains and some rather water-eroded walls remained. After I walked around the once-very-large city I began to get the feeling of its former greatness. Some of the remaining mud brick walls were twenty or more feet high giving me a good idea of what it was like. The

Chan Chan. Alley showing closer view of construction of walls.

taller ones were tapered about four-feet thick at the base to two feet at the top. During construction the walls were covered with a mud coating and probably painted and engraved. The doorways were all long worn away.

I had to get up at 2:00 a.m. to catch the bus north. I found there were cargo trucks that went from Sullana to the Ecuadorian border. From there I was assured I would find buses through Ecuadór. We got to Piura at eleven with a two-hour wait-over.

I spent the time relaxing in the park. The town had a relaxing atmosphere with a nice park and friendly people. They all reminded me of a very friendly chap I met in Abancáy who told me he was from Piura.

I rode a bus the short distance to Sullana. I was warned this was the focal point for immigration to and from Ecuadór. As there was a flare-up between the two nations almost every day there was increased policing the rest of the way to the Ecuadorian border. I was immediately rushed into the immigration office. After I found a truck I had to report its license number and time of departure to the immigration officials. The truck driver, in turn, was given eight forms, all of which had to be signed by each passenger. These were distributed to the police officer at each checkpoint. I went to the bus agency and found the attendant willing to help. All trucks, called Gondolas, left between 4:00 and 8:00 at night. The trucks' frames and motors were American but local companies built wooden extensions on either side to accommodate more passengers.

The truck left at 8:00 p.m. and I reported the name of truck, etc., to the police. We started out and got about three blocks before we hit the first checkpoint. I had to sign 12 sheets of paper. We went on a few more miles and were stopped by another checkpoint. We got out and went through the operation of transferring info from passports, etc. We joked around with the guards awhile and left. We went a few more miles and hit another checkpoint before we could even shift into third gear. We went through the same process again. Another one after that halted us. This was not as exasperating as it might ap-

Closer view of tapered construction of walls of Chan Chan.

pear. The police were generally extremely courteous and each stop was usually followed by a half-hour conversation with the officers. At 1:00 a.m. we encountered a truck with a bad axle. This was a friend of the driver so he got out to help.

At 1:30 they were still working on the other truck so I got my blanket, crawled up on some boxes in back and went to sleep. Soon another truck came along and wanted to get by so we had to move.

The clerk at the bus agency took me to the Ecuadorian Consul and helped me get a tourist card. He told me, "There are a lot of police between here and Ecuadór, but in Ecuadór the police don't bother you." When I told this to a Peruvian, he smiled and retorted with, "Wait and see."

When I returned to the Immigration office, they told me I would also have to go through the police. I went to the police and found them closed. I went back to the immigration and they told me to go back at 1:30 p.m. I had dinner at the Municipal Market, as money was getting a little scarce and returned at 6:30. They took one of my tourist cards and sent me back to the police. The police told me to come back just before I left. I was fast learning how a ping-pong ball feels.

The buses traveling from Suyo, Perú usually averaged about 12 mph. That meant to go 100 miles it took about eight-and-a-half hours. To go the little distance from Macará to Loja, Ecuadór took another fourteen hours, a distance of only 110 miles.

The driver, one of his assistants, an Ecuadorian and I sat in front. The Ecuadorian was going as far as Loja. We got to Suyo at about 3:00 a.m. We had to spend the night there as their immigration office was closed at night. The Ecuadorian and I looked around for a dormitory to sleep. We walked the dirt streets of the town looking for a window in one of the buildings with lighted candles in the windows. A lighted candle signified the room was vacant. I went into a room, extinguished the candle, and the proprietor came by early the next morning to collect.

Leaving town was slow in the morning because all the trucks that bedded down the night before were required to get processed. We got up at 6:00 a.m. I was feeling restless because the bus for Loja, Ecuadór left from Macará, Ecuadór at 8:00 a.m. and I wanted to be on it. My Ecuadorian friend told me not to put much hope in it, as there was still a lot more immigration. We went to the police and they took so long to return with our passports I thought they must

THE PILOT ROAD

have been copying every word. We then reported at the police checkpoint and that was amazingly quick. We were getting ready to go when a dull-witted older man came up and demanded to know, "Are you the owner of this truck?"

I told him politely, "No, but I'll go get him." I went up to the owner and told him, "There is a thickheaded old man who wants to see you." The owner laughed and said, "He can wait."

When I relayed this, the old goat became even more belligerent.

I ran back to the owner and urged, "You'd better see him. He seems rather anxious." He reluctantly put down his tools and started over.

"No, no, not you, him!" the old man said, pointing at me.

"What is it you want?" I asked him.

"I'm the customs inspector here and I'm going to guard your bag."

I said, "You're not going to guard this bag!" The driver backed me up.

The old man turned to the guard and yelled, "Police, police! This guy won't let me look at his bag." No one paid any attention to him.

I said, "If all you want to do is look at it I'll let you do that." We went to his office and I opened up the bag, keeping a very close eye on his hands.

I said, "It's just a camera and equipment, with some film."

"Film?" he demanded, "Where is the camera?"

"In front of your nose," I said.

"Your permit, where is it? Show me your permit," he continued.

"What permit?

"Your permit for the camera."

"You don't need a permit for it in this country," I responded.

"Oh? Well, where's your permit to take pictures?"

"I'm not a professional photographer."

"What do you do?"

"I am a student and am traveling through Latin America, taking pictures for my own private use."

"Student, eh. Well where's your student permit?"

"We don't have such a thing in North America and besides this has nothing to do with my being here as I am in the country on a

Tourist Card." During all this the driver kept urging him to get on the ball and get through, while helping me keep an eye on the officer. Finally, the official saw he could sneak nothing out so closed the bag and asked for my Tourist Card. I showed it to him and he let me go. I thanked him but he just snorted.

The rolling desert hills became more fertile as we moved closer to the border. I could now see tall mountains in the background. A short distance later we approached yet another police check point. I was relieved when someone smiled at me and informed me this was the last police station.

Although it was only thirty miles from Sullana to the border the trip took about fifteen hours, because the border checks slowed passenger movement almost to a standstill. We had nearly reached the border before we encountered another policeman. This was so soon I remarked, "Maybe I'll make the 8:00 p.m. bus yet." Making this bus was important as it meant an extra day of waiting around for another if I missed it. We hit La Tina, the Peruvian border station and I went into the police station. The policeman told me, "I don't have the right book for you."

I picked up the books on his desk and found: FOREIGNERS LEAVING COUNTRY, CITIZENS LEAVING COUNTRY, CITIZENS TRAVELING WITHIN THE COUNTRY. I asked him what was wrong with FOREIGNERS LEAVING COUNTRY. He said that was RESIDENT FOREIGNERS LEAVING THE COUNTRY. I started joking around with one of the men there about the police restrictions. I waited around for quite some time and finally they found a book that pertained to me. They then informed me I would have to go through immigration, which I did in little time. I heard the bus didn't leave until 9:00 a.m. so I grabbed my bags and started to walk across the border. I got about ten feet when I heard shouting. I turned around and a guard called me back, "You forgot to go through the exit customs inspections." Fortunately, the man with whom I was joking in the station was the customs inspector. He asked me what I had in the bag. I said, "Old dirty clothes that no one would ever want to buy, but I have to wear something." He laughed and told me to go ahead. A truck picked me up and we started for the border. We hit a checkpoint and then sailed on through.

Around the corner a little contraband was quickly unloaded to some waiting men and then ferried across the little river, which divides the two countries. This was a good example of the lack of efficiency generated by the numerous police checkpoints within each country to stamp out contraband. To me its only effect was to increase corruption, deprive well-meaning citizens of their rights, and give unrelenting power to those attracted to positions of authority. It's similar to Prohibition in the U.S., which stimulated the growth of the Mafia. Contraband still made it across the border, it just required greasing a few palms along the way. Are we creating the same possible scenario by over reacting to what we call the Patriot Act as a tool against what we refer to as the War on Terrorism?

I swear one third of the nation worked for the aduana, immigration, or police. I had just passed through 12 immigration points to get just a few miles out of Perú. To get across Ecuadór I would go through no less than 44 immigration points. This was worse than Russia. I found little sympathy when I complained among the Ecuadorians who smiled and said, "Well, we have to have control of some sort." I hear many Americans saying the same thing about the Patriot Acts. I could see that none of these hoards of police, multitude of inspection stations and travel restrictions were helping, not here nor in Colombia or any other country in which I had traveled.

We climbed a small hill and then descended into a small cluster of buildings. This was Peru's border station, La Tina. The trucks were required to stop before the group of buildings to unload the cargo that was to remain in Perú. On a small hill stood the small town of Macará, Ecuadór, backed by a high wall of mountains. Although a tiny bridge could unite these two countries, relations had never been good enough to even plan its construction. I took a little boat all 25 feet across the river and it cost me a small fortune. An assemblage of pickups and trucks were backed up to the water's edge on both sides. All cargo was loaded on balsas and poled the short distance to the trucks waiting on the other side. I asked when one was leaving for Macará. One boy said he was going and would take me. I thought he was making the trip anyway so didn't bother to work out a price with him beforehand. After we got started I found he was evidently making this trip just to get plenty of side money. We stopped at the police in town and he offered to wait and take me to a hotel. I argued him out of that as I could see the price going up by the minute. I asked him how much it would be and he calmly said 15 pesos. When he saw me wince he shyly said, "Is that too much?" Seeing my reaction he quickly added, "Is 12 pesos?" This was still high but I figured it was half my fault for not checking fully beforehand.

Macará was a dirty little town but its residents loved conversation. The openly friendly residents made my short stay pleasant. Everyone I saw was usually in a group holding conversation, either in the doorways of stores, seated out in front of the stores, or in the few cafés. Arriving at the border at 9:00 in the morning to meet a bus that goes north at 8:00 a.m. made little sense. The bus had just left so I was in no hurry. The police officer kept me for over an hour in conversation. He then told me to see the aduana. He said, "I'll get you a pick-up to take you there."

"Oh, no" I said, "I'll go broke using those things." He then gave me directions and I climbed up the big hill to the aduana. I went inside and got into a conversation with someone there, who invited me into his office where we talked for a couple more hours. I finally had to admit I was going to expire from hunger. I left my bags with him. After lunch I ran around trying to get some dollar bills. The hotel looked so terrible I felt I would wait until the last minute before checking in. I was told they charged by the bed rather than room, dormitory style. That didn't appeal to me with my $400.00 camera.

I found the rumor about the Pan-American Highway gap being finished was wrong. The only road through was a pilot road pushed through the mountains from Macará and Catamayo several years before, as an experiment to see the rate of deterioration before building the road. During the rainy season, beginning at the end of December, the road just didn't exist. During the dry season the 50 miles of this pilot road was barely passable. The rainy season was just beginning so it was just about the last trip for this wooden bus on a truck chassis. It extended its run from Loja to Catamayo, to Macará during the dry season. My Ecuadorian friend claimed, "This is called 'pilot' road because only an aviator could drive a truck through there."

I found a truck going to Loja but it looked like he was going to take a couple of days so I felt it was better to take the bus the next day. I was finally directed to a store that everyone said changed dollars, the only place in town. The store attendant invited me in, pulled out a couple of chairs and we sat down. This was their way of getting close to the customers. He told me he didn't change dollars as some Chinese immigrants had come through and passed some counterfeit dollars off on the merchants of the town. I finally con-

THE PILOT ROAD

vinced him to change one dollar. He told me he was doing this because he had a daughter and son in the United States and the son had done quite a bit of traveling.

This was enough for my hotel and bus fare, plus a little bit to eat at the open market. This left out anything to drink as soft drinks cost almost as much as a plate of rice and chicken in the street market. He then said he had a hotel. He took me there and gave me the best room in the house for 36¢. Considering the price and outside appearance of this hotel this was a very nice room. It was clean, had a nice view out over the few other buildings of the town and the mountains in the background.

I went to the customs to get my bags and was detained for another couple of hours in conversation with some other workers. They asked me if I had been through immigration yet. I told them I thought this was immigration. They said, "No." They went with me to immigration and got the official out of his house. After this I was officially entered into Ecuadór. I paid someone for a ticket on the next morning's bus and went to the market. I found a nice stall and ordered "the dinner". The food was terrible everywhere I went; the only difference was the price and place. My host and hostess (Indians) were very nice but this was the fiftieth person that insisted on addressing every sentence to me with "Mister". This was something I ran into in the more remote areas of Latin American and it had the same effect on me as someone scraping a blackboard with their fingernails or a black person being called the "N" word. Out of 21 countries the place where I ran into this the most was in Ecuadór.

I went back and was talking with the hotel boy when he suddenly said, "I want you to sign my book."

When he came back in I gave him my card and asked, "Will that do?"

He said, "It would be better if you sign this. He pulled out a book and I looked at the extensive list of names and felt he must have quite a few friends. Everything was outlined—name, nationality, date arrived. Then I noticed passport number and looked closer. This was the hotel register. I looked it over afterward and found I was the second American to stay at the hotel in its three-year existence.

I looked at the bus and wondered how a bus could ever get in such terrible shape in such a short time. It was only a couple of years old but looked like it had been put through a meat grinder—

torn and ripped almost beyond recognition. As we bumped around from stone to stone I could plainly see why. We finally got started at 8:30 a.m. but by the time we got through playing "Ring Around the Bureaucracy' with police, customs, immigration and the control it was well past 9:00. We took a steep ascent from a few hundred feet to about 9,000 feet in a matter of a couple of hours. I began eating little cheap things from vendors who approached the buses to make my money last. I wondered whether the slow ascent had been worth it until we reached the top. I looked back and could see the valley of Macará and Northern Perú, with the river that divides the two countries rambling through the valleys like a small silver ribbon in the distance far below.

I was struck by the incredible isolation of this part of Ecuadór. The towns were few and far between and where they existed they had only a few unpainted mud-brick huts. Outside of these towns I saw few signs of life.

Mangos were cheap and plentiful and quenched both hunger and thirst. We were hours behind schedule because we had quite a bit of freight, short journey passengers, and customs houses, which stopped us at every small village. Each time the officials looked through all the baggage and cargo and checked over the passenger list. We had lunch at 4:00 pm. One passenger attached himself to me like glue. I was embarrassed because I didn't want him to know I didn't have much money, as I was afraid he would offer to buy me something, which so many passengers did. I finally crept up to a waitress in one restaurant and whispered, "How much is your plate for the day?" Two sucres was her answer. I ordered that and a cup of tea. After I was through I asked her how much that would be and she said, "Three sucres." I told her I thought it was only two sucres for the plate. "The tea is one sucre," she said. The proprietor came out and I showed her all my money and asked what I could do. I saw one centavo in pesos Colombian (worth about .3¢) and jokingly asked her how much that was worth in sucres. She laughed and said if I gave her that as a souvenir she would count it as 25¢.

The road was taking a toll on my endurance. We bounced around like jellybeans in a can as the bus climbed rocks, averted holes and clung to the edge of the precipices, where most of the pilot road had washed out. Fortunately the hotel official got me the best seat on the bus, next to the driver, so I had legroom. The seats were hard and it seemed like they got harder the longer we rode. I kept running into people calling me, "Meester, Meester", until I could stand it no longer. After being called "Señor" for six months it was hard to be singled out as a "Meester". I mentioned this annoyance to one of the truck drivers in Perú. He answered, "Some of these people are really ignorant. One time I asked an Ecuadorian if he was a foreigner. He said, 'No, I'm not.' You're not Peruvian are you?" added the driver. "He answered, 'No, I'm from Ecuadór.' Well, then you are a foreigner. 'Oh,' retorted the Ecuadorian, 'I thought that was just for the 'Meesters' and the 'Gringos.'"

The next time I was approached with "Meester" I asked "Why, in that you are speaking Spanish and I am in your country, don't you call me 'Señor?"

"Oh, that's a form of title. They call you 'Meester' in the States, don't they?"

I saw my hint was not going over so told him in more blunt language, "'Señor' in English is 'Sir' and 'Meester' is 'Don' and therefore never used without the surname of the individual." This didn't hit home either so I told him, "The word 'Meester' strikes me about the way the word 'cabrito' would strike you." It was obviously easier for him to break off the conversation than not call me "Meester" at the head of each sentence so he left—much to my delight. I found it impossible to hold interesting conversations with most of the people accompanying me in this part of the country as I had become accustomed in all my other bus trips.

As we passed into a small village I saw they were holding a "Circo Americano," with wrestling, fire-eaters, etc., or so it said on the billboard. Children were squeezing under every part of the tent to get a free look. The whole town of 1,000 was out to see it. Most of the people in the town were Afro-Americans. The bus finally arrived in Loja at 11:00 p.m. morphing itself into a taxi service, taking everyone to his or her various hotels. It stopped first in front of the most expensive hotel in town. The driver said, "Anyone staying at the Hotel Americano?" There were a few chuckles and the bus quickly moved on. I found a clean hotel with no electricity so everyone carried his or her own candle. I managed to get the last gallon of hot water in the shower.

I got out early the next morning. I had to change some money and was told I had to see the police control before I could move on. I finally found a police officer and asked where the control was. He directed me to the main plaza. I asked another police officer at the plaza and he directed me back to the first police officer but kept talking about the control being where the buses left. I then figured I could wait to check out until the bus left. I got my ticket and found the bus companies are also called controls. I guess that was a good name for them, as there was so much control with them. The woman there told me I didn't have to report to the police so I boarded the bus. Before the bus could get started a rather ill mannered policeman came running over to me. My experience here was about the same as with the customs inspector in Perú—asking a lot of dull-witted questions and failing to understand my answers. The clerk's Spanish was terrible and I had to decipher everything he said. On entering the bus I found an Indian woman was sitting in my reserved seat, along with her two rather shabbily dressed children. I smiled and asked, "Could you please move over a little so I can get to my seat?

"No," she said.

"Madame, I have seat number two. What number do you have?"

"I don't understand this number system!"

"But, Madam, I bought this ticket for this number. Didn't you get a number on your ticket?"

"I'm not going to move. We got here before you did and here we stay!"

The woman in front tried to convince her, as did a man on the other side, but to no avail. She then said the station chief said she could take any seat.

"Where's the station chief?" I said. "I'd like to meet him."

"I don't know, but he told me we could sit here so here I stay." The whole thing was so funny I could hardly keep from laughing. I started to get the station chief but the collector came forward and asked, "What is the matter?"

"This lady has my seat and won't let me have it," I said.

"Lady, you'll have to move," he said.

She blurted back "The station master said I could sit here so I'm not going to move." A hot argument followed after which the woman and children were practically bodily removed to the rear of the bus, ranting and raving all the while.

I felt sorry for her but I was finally learning to hold my ground on these buses.

THE PILOT ROAD

Parts of this road were superior to the Pan-American Highway I had experienced in other parts of Latin America. However, the work being done on it looked sloppy and sporadic. The pavement was chopped in every which direction, providing no idea as to what the road would eventually look like. In portions it would be asphalt for a few feet, and then revert back to a one-lane rutted mud road again, then gravel, then split into a bunch of roads leading off in multiple directions. Only the bus driver knew which was the right one. I could see few workers. Most of the machinery lay idle at the side of the road. I felt the government (meaning the dictator in Ecuador) was not too anxious to get the road completed. It seemed to me if they could finish this road and connect it with a good one in Sullana, Perú (which they now have completed) there wouldn't be wars that break out in this area about twenty times a year. The citizens were very tired of the military forays, but the army and police ran the country and they were the ones that usually started these wars. It was never a deliberate attempt on the part of either government but usually a result of a wild party at one of the army camps, when three or four drunken soldiers felt brave enough to conquer the other country. This was usually the Peruvians, as even a drunken Ecuadorian had no illusions about Ecuadór conquering Perú.

The pilot road went as far as Catamayo, about fifty miles. From here to Loja the road was all weather, wide and smooth. We got into Cuenca at about five that afternoon. As Huancayo is to Perú so Cuenca is to Ecuadór. It was beautifully preserved, not only in buildings but also in the way people dressed and acted. I had seen a painting of it in Loja, which inspired me with great expectations. All of them were fulfilled because Cuenca was one of the best-preserved colonial towns in Ecuadór.

I finally had to give in and get a taxi to a hotel near where the bus to Guayaquíl would be leaving. Fortunately, taxis cost little more than a streetcar in the U.S. so I used them often. One thing I discovered about staying at a hotel near the bus terminal in Latin America, I never had to worry about a coat and tie. They never located next to the Ritz-Carlton. I immediately ran over to the station and bought the seat next to the driver, a trick I had learned to do since arriving in Bolivia. The buses were built for the average five-foot passenger. In the regular seats I had to sit with my knees against my chin. Bouncing around all day on the rough roads had given me some painful bruises. I also learned to take my blanket in hand, because the seats were very hard and plastic. It protected me from the heat, which built up under the chassis, as well as adding cushioning. I could also use it as a poncho at night.

That night I went for a walk. Cuenca reminded me of Sâo Luís, Brazil because it was a voyage into the past, little changed since Colonial days. The girls were all in by 6:00 p.m. The women were mostly of Indian and Spanish descent, very beautiful with dark flashing eyes. At night they all came out on their balconies and made eyes at the men below. The parents were safely positioned between the first and second floors so there was little concern on their part. The men were all out for walks at night along the narrow cobblestone streets, sometimes just sitting in the park and thinking. The younger men and boys gathered into larger groups, scattered throughout the park, the volume of their voices increasing the younger the group. On almost every corner near the center of town could be found groups of older youths in light conversation. As with all Latin American cities the radios of the cafes, cheaper hotels and homes raucously competed with each other. At 8:30 or 9:00 p.m. the city rolled up its rug almost as though by signal and noise was limited to a few footsteps echoing in the distance.

There were several companies running buses to Guayaquíl. Everyone had a favorite bus line. I found placing my money on a bus ticket was about the same as placing a bet on a horse. There were always the "most favored", yet the unexpected brought a different winner every time. I purchased my ticket that night to make sure I had the only legroom on the bus, the seat next to the driver.

I got up in the morning at about 5:45. The bus was the same as all buses I had seen in Ecuadór, wide bodies on a GM, Ford, or International truck chassis, which seated three on one side and two on the other. This made the ride a little hair-raising because it gave even less room to pass on the precarious single lane roads. Sometimes we had plenty of room to maneuver around a truck or bus coming our way, but the driver would suddenly slam on the brakes at the last minute and spend five minutes trying to maneuver around as the road narrowed.

This was a very interesting ride on a highway far improved over the previous ones. I was fascinated with the variable colorful clothes of the many Indian tribes. Most of them wore their hair long. Some wore their hair bobbed, others braided, and still others just bobbed it at the back of the head and let it hang. The wool blankets they carried were of bright colors, predominantly red. The women wore a great deal of silver ornaments around their necks. The men wore bloused pants and colorful ponchos (called ruanas in Ecuadór as well as Colombia). They usually wore a scarf around their necks. The Indians were brilliantly dressed. They were what I had expected to encounter in the rainforest. They were very soft spoken and polite. Sometimes it was difficult for me to tell women from men, as their hair was sometimes quite similar. It was Sunday so everyone was out in his or her full dress. The Indians were very cheerful looking (the men much more so than the women) in sharp contrast to the serious Bolivian Indian and the Indians of interior Brazil, especially the Mato Grosso.

We climbed up and down the mountaintops until we finally dropped down from the 8,460 feet at Cuenca into a mass of clouds, which shrouded an endless jungle near sea level. As we broke through the clouds we found ourselves in a deep fog. The architecture of unpainted, mud houses changed to reed houses built on stilts as we descended into the jungle. Whereas most of the people were Indigenous, the population in the jungle was predominantly Afro-American. It was an abrupt, rather than gradual change. An Afro American would probably feel as much out of place in Cuenca as would an Indian in the lower jungle regions. As we passed by the reed buildings, vendors called out their goods and prices from their shabby wooden stands while their children sold them from better vantage points on the bus or through the windows. We finally came to a stop on the other side of the river from Guayaquíl. Some WWII vintage LST Boats ferried us across.

14. THE EQUATOR AND THE MAGDALENA

As I was conversing with two women in the bus, one of them warned me, "Watch out for the people of Guayaquíl. They are very nice but just speak to them and leave. Guayaquíl is the only place where they can steal your shoes off your feet without you knowing it."

"And they usually get your socks, too," added the other.

They told me a good hotel to go to and gave me some information on their country. As usual one of them was working outside the country. It seemed as though every one I met was working in another country. There just seemed to be no available work in Ecuador at that time. They told me how nice and modern Guayaquíl was. When we got to the other side we passed one old stilted building after another all the way to the bus agency. I kidded them, asking if the rather shabby looking building across the street was the hotel they recommended.

Reed building on stilts. Guayaquíl

I found the bus terminal was far from the hotel I wanted. As buses usually leave early in the morning I felt it best to locate myself near it. Then came the usual fight with the porters to rescue my bags. I had to fight with these people at every station so I was grateful I was bigger and stronger than most of them. As soon as they found out which bag was mine they would grab it and wouldn't let go. I would then have to pry the bags loose and push them away. The 65 lb. weight of the bag was in my favor as they would grab it and crumble under its weight. That gave me the opportunity to pluck it off their back and put it on my shoulder as they stared at me, wide-eyed in disbelief. I asked a taxi driver if there was a decent hotel near the bus station. He said there was a more or less regular one there. His idea of more or less differed substantially from mine. I was shocked as I walked through the door. It was absolutely the worst hotel I had seen since the Amazon. The bed was a wooden slat with a thin covering, no windows, dirty and small. I had spent my allotted amount with the taxi so I had no choice but to take the room. I stayed there just long enough to put my bags down and go outside. I went to the bus station and got the seat next to the driver for the next Tuesday. I then went to the park and sat.

An Indian with long hair sat next to me with a pile of weaved goods to sell. I didn't want to buy anything but was so interested in seeing the materials he was able to pique my interest. It wasn't long before he had his entire merchandise displayed around us. I didn't know how I was going to graciously get out of this. I tried to barter him down but to no avail. Finally, after about a half-hour of haggling I got him down 30¢ on a rebolsa.

Another Indian, who had been looking on to make sure I got the right change, sat next to me. I found he was from Quito, and his name was Marco.

He said, "I moved here looking for a job three months ago but there just isn't any work available. I'm a tractor mechanic and driver."

"Why, with all the money the United States is just beginning to put into road building in the country can't you get a job with them?" I suggested.

He said, "The jobs are all filled for the road building and the United States oil companies aren't hiring, either. I hate Guayaquíl but it's the only place there is even a chance to get a job. In all the time I have been here I have not made one friend. I just don't trust anyone. The people stab you right out on the street. Winning an argument is almost sure suicide, as the people don't hesitate to kill you."

"Is this a certain group of people that do these things?" I asked.

"Almost all of the people that do these things are Afro American. You'll find it much better in the Sierra where you're going."

I kept getting hungrier for we had been in conversation since 5:00 p.m. Finally at 8:00 my stomach could stand it no longer so I strongly suggested it was about dinnertime. He was, fortunately, equally as hungry so he went home and I started looking for a restaurant.

After dinner I walked around trying to kill time until the room cooled off so I could sleep. I walked all over the downtown. I went along the port and in one part of the park saw the benches filled with girls, obviously not out for the fresh air. Of all the call girls I had noticed all over Latin America these were absolutely the most repulsive I had ever seen. This was strange because I had found the women of Guayaquíl quite beautiful. The prostitutes painted their lips from ear-to-ear and painted their eyebrows almost clear across so they couldn't have looked more revolting to me. They vocally showed their desperation by loudly hissing and yelling, "Hey you. Come 'ere!" or other such phrases. They would continue this until I was several blocks away, so it was hard to keep my laughter back. The sweet smile and sparkling eyes that typified the prostitutes I saw in other cities was missing. It was just "Pssst! Hey you, come here." (Not very romantic.) Also the male prostitutes, who pass unnoticed in Brazil if one is not looking for them, were all too noticeable here with their painted nails and long hair. It got so I couldn't stop to take a picture without having one slink up to me.

I bumped into someone in one park and talked until I felt my room was well cooled, taking my departure for the hotel. The room had cooled down to a nice 80° F but the bed was so hard I thought I was going to wear the impressions of the splinters.

I got up from my stiff hard bed as soon as I could bend my muscles again. I had slept on a number of hard beds over the past months but never one this hard.

I did not like Guayaquíl. I had been warned in many other places to look out for thieves, that I would not be safe or that they were dangerous. But this was the first city in six months of travel where I actually did not feel safe. I kept my wallet locked in my room and kept just enough change to get me back to the hotel. I finished my sightseeing at 3:00 p.m. and thought I would sit down and write a letter. However, the weather was stifling hot. Even Manaus and Iquítos didn't seem this insufferably hot. The hotel room was oppressive. I got my stationary and fled to the park. It was somewhat tolerable there in the shade. However, the same shoeshine boy came along and I got another good 3¢ shine. His little friends were crowded around so I kept all three hands on my pockets. No sooner had he left than Marco passed by.

I hailed him over to sit down. "Have you found a job?" I asked.

"No, but the army has a mechanical school I might work into. This could raise my chances of getting a job," he answered.

We discussed Guayaquíl, Iquítos, and Ecuadór.

He said, "Don't trust well-dressed men. They are the worst pickpockets. Seems these people get enough money to buy good clothes. Then they bump into people and no one would ever think of suspecting a well-dressed man if they suddenly discovered their wallet missing."

As we were talking two boys walked by and stopped and looked at me. They then came over and sat on the other end of the bench from us, right behind me. Thinking them to be male prostitutes I just ignored them. Suddenly Marco reached into his pocket and pretended to be pulling a pen out, looking first at them and then at me.

When I didn't seem to be responding he turned to me and said, "Let's go for a walk." When we got out of hearing distance from them, he said, "I was trying to tell you those were pickpockets but I guess you didn't get the hint."

I said, "I had my hand in my pocket all the time but they evidently didn't get the hint." Ever since this I practically stood on everything I owned as I could almost feel hands slipping around on the sides. I don't think I met an American traveling through Ecuadór who had not been robbed.

We started talking at about the same time as the day before and after awhile I began to wonder if our growling stomachs or the conversations were louder. I excused myself in vain about fifteen times and finally the sixteenth time managed to find him equally as anxious to get home to his dinner. I asked him. "What does your family do if they eat at 7:30 and you arrive home after eight every night?"

Quito, Ecuador. Cathedral Park.

He calmly said, "They just put the food away and I take it out and eat it when I arrive home."

"Have a happy cold dinner and good luck finding a job. Here's my card. Look me up if you ever get to the United States," I said smiling. He laughed and said, "I can't even get the fare to Quito."

I went on to my outdoor restaurant, walked around until it was cool enough to go back to my room, and then returned to my hard bed.

I was in deep conversation one evening when a middle-aged gentleman approached us and said, "Hello. How are you? Are you an Ecuadorian? You speak wonderful Spanish. Well, goodbye and good luck." He then turned and left. I turned to Marco with a rather puzzled expression and asked, "Who was that?"

"Oh, he's running for political office," he said. Nevertheless, many of my encounters were as spontaneous as this.

I had originally planned to go to Quito on the auto-train but opted for the bus instead. My experience with trains had shown me they usually went through the worst parts of every town and I felt I wouldn't get to see any of the towns. I found the road went through the hot jungle and didn't hit any of the main towns except Latacunga, and it only skirted that town. The morning was hot and muggy. It was like traveling through a sea of warm water. A heavy humid mist and smoggy overhead kept us hostage to the oppressive humidity. The heat from the motor intensified this; the floor so hot I could feel it through my shoes. I took all my film out of the bag and wrapped it in a sweater to protect it from the heat. I was relieved when we hit our first hill, which took us above the hot and sticky fogbank. By the time we stopped for lunch the weather was more comfortable. Above, it was still cloudy but not so hot. Near Latacunga we passed a large finca. The driver told me it belonged to the former President of Ecuadór. We rode for about fifteen minutes and I noticed a post. I asked if that marked the other end of his ranch. He said, "No, that's just the entrance. The end is way up in the mountains." We rode for about another half-hour before we reached the other end of the ex-president's ranch.

Typical shopping street in Quito.

What I enjoyed while traveling in Ecuadór were the steep climbs and descents from the tops of mountains to the jungle, followed by another climb to the next mountaintop. Interspersed were small colonial towns, which carried me back into another era. The views were dazzling.

We arrived at Quito that night. It was a beautiful view, reminiscent of Cuzco, descending from mountains onto the outstretched lights below. I decided to take potluck on hotels so I just turned around on arrival to see which hotel looked best. I had the usual wrestling match with the porters, trying to hold my temper. I found it more difficult here because I not only had to balance a blanket on my shoulders while carrying my handbag in one hand and wrestling for the 65-lb. sack with the other hand—all while watching my pockets. As I made my way through the crowd one chap began pushing vigorously from behind. I quickly slipped my hand over my billfold pocket and tried to move on. He did practically everything he could to pry my hand loose to get at my billfold.

For potluck I did fairly well on my choice of hotels. I was covered with dust, as I had been at the end of every bus trip, including my new powdered-white hair. I got ready for a shower and turned on the hot water. No hot water was forthcoming within the next five minutes so I got dressed and went down to investigate. I found there was only hot water from 8-11 a.m. It was cold in the building and Quito is at 9,200 feet altitude. I was darned glad I had my blanket, as the blankets on the bed didn't even come to my shoulders.

Quito was a complete contrast to Guayaquíl. It was a quiet city with little seeming economic activity. The people were principally Indian or Mestizo and extremely pleasant looking. There were 57 churches in Quito, several museums and many picturesque statues and parks. From the top of Cerro Panecillo there was a beautiful panoramic view of the red-tile roofs of the city below.

I rose early to get a start while the weather was still nice. I was so cold the night before I didn't wash out my frayed clothes or dirty wash-and-wear shirt. The room had an American-type plug so I was able to iron another shirt the next day. I showered with the last gallon of hot water, but when I plugged in the iron nothing happened. There was no electricity. I buzzed the porter to take my shirt out to be ironed but no one came. I went out and asked a man if the bellhop was around. The man just stared at me so I went downstairs. The porter sent my shirt right out and promised me it would be back in fifteen minutes. I got some other things ready and about ten minutes later there was a rap at the door. I opened it and found the porter with my wrinkled shirt in hand. He said, "There's no place that can iron your clothes because there's no electricity."

Frustrated but less vain, I put it on anyway, with my wrinkled tie and my less-wrinkled jacket to cover my more-wrinkled shirt. I found a tourist agency that had a couple of useful maps. I had quit playing this tit-tat-toe game of reporting to the police by the time I got to Loja and had not gotten caught so far. However, one man told me I had better get a signature from the police in Quito or I wouldn't get out of the country. I went to the Colombian Embassy but found I couldn't get a permit to enter because I didn't have transportation out of the country. I begged the official to give me a visa, as I couldn't get to the border before the Consul office closed and would lose a day. She told me the buses would get me there on time. I went around town checking on the various bus companies and finally, at 3:00 p.m., I found one that could accommodate me. I figured the three-hour leeway would give me enough time for flats, breakdowns, delays, etc., so I bought a ticket in the seat next to the driver. I went to the Foreign Office but found I didn't have to report there after all. I finally managed to find the American Embassy to get my mail and to get some more blank pages stapled into my passport book. By 5:00 I had all the pictures I needed and had everything under way.

I went to a movie. Movies helped my comprehension of Spanish. When I was in conversation I never missed a word. But in movies or radio I didn't get the clarity I did in direct conversation. Also, slang and fast talk were thrown in when people talked to each other or in the media. I noticed people were usually careful about using slang when conversing with me so it was easier to understand them.

Hula-hoops were the rage all over South America at this time. No seven-year-old girl would be seen outside without her plastic hoop, and they had become experts. The boys chased them down the street (the hula hoops, that is).

I started my race for the frontier at 8:00 a.m. It was a cloudy misty morning. The road led us up into the cold of the mountains, then down into the rainforest several times. I asked the driver to stop at the Equator Monument, as I wanted to get a picture of it. The road was of the type I had read about in Guatemala. The labor, being so cheap, was used to pave stones in individual mosaics. This made the surface almost as smooth as asphalt. I saw two workmen (man and woman) working on the road. The man used a pick to smooth out the bed. The woman brought baskets of rocks of about the same size, while the man laid them in rows. There were miles and miles of such roads all through northern Ecuadór.

We finally got to the monument and the driver stopped as I had requested. The passengers insisted I take the picture from the bus but I finally convinced them the windows were too dirty and it was too dark, so everyone got out for a breath of fresh air while the collector looked at the motor.

We had breakfast at Cayambe. It was still misty and there were beautiful snow-capped volcanoes that I was told were around there. I had yet to see a snow-capped volcano in Ecuadór, Bolivia or Perú. All over Ecuadór there were volcanoes but I always seemed to arrive just as they went under the clouds.

We went past a couple of interesting lakes, one of which was located by the town of Otavalo. Just above Ibarra was one of the most interesting contrasts I had seen. Colonial and Indian architecture surrounded us. The people were either Mestizo or Indian. Suddenly we dropped down from a mountain onto a cluster of grass huts, none built with bricks. As we approached them I noticed everyone was of pure African descent, with the exception of a few Mestizo, something very unusual for the highlands. It was an African village completely isolated in Indian country.

The residents sold many rare fruits, which I had never seen before. One was a big green pod. When I opened it I felt I should take the cotton off the bean and eat the bean. Instead, I was instructed by the other passengers to eat the cotton (a sweet substance somewhat like chewing on sugar cane) and threw away the black seed. There was another sort of plum. I noticed they would bite a hole in it, suck out the juice, then tear off the skin and eat all the insides except the big seed in the center. This was my first taste of mango. This was delicious and had no similarity whatsoever to any fruit I had ever eaten.

As we got to San Gabriél I noticed we were quite late. The driver was hurrying as fast as he could because there were several of us that were trying to make it to the Consulate that day. We stopped at one of the many checkpoints to hand over the list of passengers. At one checkpoint the collector got out, as usual, to hand it to the police officer. The policeman threw it back in his face and said the list was no good because he didn't like the way he handed it to him. The police officer said he would have to go back to the head office to pay a fine. The driver pleaded he was very late and had to get through. The policeman only became more irate and soon all the passengers were yelling and pleading with him to let us get through because we had to make it to Tulcán. After about twenty minutes we went back to San Gabriél. The collector was put in jail for three days for disrespect of an officer. Then they turned to the passengers and ordered, "You'll have to take the bus back to Quito," while they held out their palms. The driver paid them all off and left the collector to his ill fate. It is the memories of this and a hundred other checkpoints that made me appreciative of the foresight of our American forefathers who enacted the Constitution and Bill of Rights we have so hurriedly dispensed with in our growing fear of terrorism.

We finally arrived in Tulcán at 5:15 p.m. I checked out with the police and ran over to the Consulate. They told me the consul had gone to Ipiales and would be back at 7:00. I waited around until 7:00 and found she wanted $4.00 to serve me at that time. I had to conserve every penny to make it back to the U.S. so I decided to wait until the Consul opened at 9:00 a.m. I ran around trying to find a place to settle down for the night. I wanted only to get as far away from Ecuadór as possible.

By 7:30 p.m. I had everything done I could do and it was too dark to write a letter. A local schoolteacher saved me from the ill fate of boredom by talking to me in the hallway of a restaurant until I was sufficiently tired to go to my room and sleep on the wooden slats. He had two brothers in the States, one teaching at Yale, and the other a doctor in Mississippi. He was among the more interesting Ecuadorians I had conversed with. I found the bus driver's wife very interesting to talk to as well.

"Before I married the driver I worked for an Evangelist Mission," she said. "There I got to know many people from all countries. I spoke seven different languages in the Mission."

She gave me the history of some of the people there and their opinions of Ecuadór. "I long for the United States where there isn't this police-control and corruption like down here. The police live off the people." I wish every American could experience living in a dictatorship. I don't think most people realize how precious our Constitutional guarantees are to our freedom. The only thing worse than fighting for nothing is having nothing left to fight for.

I had a nice talk with her and her husband on the way. They were a very nice couple. There was also a woman with her daughter who made sure I got every type of Ecuadorian fruit to taste before I left. It was when I had left Ecuadór for some time I was able to look at things from a wider-viewpoint; it was these nicer contacts that I remembered. I don't think I've met a more refined boy than Marcos with whom I chatted for six hours in Guayaquíl. The wife of the bus driver and the teacher were the only ones I met in Ecuadór that weren't Catholics. I had taken it for granted everyone was Catholic in Ecuadór. I exclaimed, "I thought this was the most Catholic of all countries."

The driver replied, "The most Catholic but the most tolerant of other beliefs. This is nothing like in Colombia where there is no freedom of religion. The Evangelists are strong in Ecuadór, but the Baptists and Adventists just don't seem to reach the people."

At many points along the road were little shrines with a statue of Mary and a cash box underneath. A sign usually said, "Give a Little Token to My Shrine." The bus stopped at every one of these (I don't know whether that was required by law or not) and the collector took donations from the passengers. In some of the towns a bar or rope was placed across the road to stop the bus. A woman then would come alongside each window to collect donations.

I got up early the next morning, not because I had a lot to do but because I couldn't stand the hard slats any more. I had breakfast and started the long wait for the Consulate to open at 9:00 a.m. When I finally got in I found the Consul to be a woman. She was a little in doubt as to what she should do with a United States passport. I gave her all the details—my medical certificate, vaccination card, police certificate, etc., and she finally got a card and typed it out for me. Had the police not taken my card the last time I was in Colombia I could have gone straight through the night before without even touching the Consulate. I went back to try and find a bus going in and bumped into the bus driver's wife. She said she and her husband were taking the bus onto Ipiales and invited me to come along with them.

The countless encounters I had with border guards, police check stations, police reporting, the constant use of a passport to even register at hotels have made me passionate about the freedoms we have lost ever since the beginning of the '90s in the United States, especially those hurriedly placed into Homeland Security. It has made me not only apprehensive about abuses from the government as much as the power placed in the hands of individual policemen. We are fortunate to have been founded by visionary

Founding Fathers who understood the excesses of abuse by those in power. Do we want to become a police state, like these countries or can we find another way to live with terrorism in a less intrusive, but equally effective manner? Air travel has already become almost unbearable with long lines, inspections and searches in the United States. I spoke with Colombians who were involved in the smuggling of arms from the United States. Despite the great resources, which were placed on road searches, they breezed through customs undetected with their smuggled arms.

The frontier hadn't changed since 1900, except there was a plaque from 1950 commemorating a meeting of Rojas Pinilla with the dictator of Ecuadór. There was a single lane entrance so only one line of cars could go through at once. Processing was quick and efficient. I checked in with the Ecuadorian police and the police and immigration of Colombia. They told me I would have to see the officials in town so I got off there. The driver would take no payment for taking me. He and his wife wished me well and took off for the center of town. I went to the custom office and they told me to go upstairs. When I got there they sent me down the hall where that office sent me back upstairs. I finally got to my destination. After filling out forms the clerk told me I was to go to the Foreign Office. I grabbed my bags and hiked down there. The chief said, "You speak Spanish very well." I thought he was asking if I spoke Spanish so I said, "Yes, I do."

He looked a little puzzled at my answer and stammered, "Well—what I mean is—you speak Spanish perfectly, absolutely faultless." I then caught on and excused myself.

I went to the park and flagged down a station wagon going to Pasto. The fare was less than listed and the time much less. The journey was supposed to take six hours but we made it in four. The prices stunned me. I thought I remembered Colombia as being a cheap country but everyone told me it was expensive in comparison to the other Latin-American countries. However, I still found Colombia nearly as inexpensive as Argentina, which was usually listed as being the cheapest country. I got three cheese sandwiches and two rolls for 10¢. You couldn't do that anywhere else in the world at that time. The people became much nicer and expressed quite a bit more interest in the world around them. The clothes in Colombia were cheap and of good quality compared to the clothes I bought in Brazil, which were falling apart after just a couple of months' wear.

THE EQUATOR AND THE MAGDALENA

The sky was cloudy with a light mist. I felt the weather would be sunnier north of the Equator as this was their dry season, but I guess the clouds were hanging over a little longer into the season. I got a hotel right across the street that looked attractive. I was told it had hot and cold running water. I asked for a room with a bath. A smile came over the clerk's face as he told me there were none. I finally found the hot and cold water all flowed through one sink. I found my bed to be even worse than the others as the slats had spaces between them. The town was a harmonious blend of neon lights and Colonial architecture. Almost all the people were Indian.

That night I settled down to get a couple of letters off when a big commotion started outside. It seemed the local radio was giving a musical program out in front of the hotel. In order to save my eardrums I went inside the room and shut the door. The audience was going wild, with hoots, hollers, and screams. I finally went to bed at 11:00 p.m. Fortunately I was sleepy enough so the noise from the bars below didn't bother me. At 3:00 a.m. the hotel clerk awakened me. The noise from the bars was still going strong. I packed and stumbled over to my bus. I loved Colombia but the country seemed to have one big problem—drunkenness. I found the people very nice when sober but drunkenness was conspicuously prevalent. On Saturday nights the streets were full of men, barely able to stand up or unable to move. When they discovered I did not drink many would say, "I don't like to drink either, but I am socially forced into it."

It was sixteen hours to Popayán and a day from Popayán to Cali. The bus made it in fourteen hours for less money. The ride to Popayán was probably the most dangerous of my entire experience. It was the only part of my trip I was a little wary of. The bus skidded around blind corners for half the day. We had at least three narrow misses. We ran into accidents all the time. One was a head-on collision between two trucks, but luckily no one was hurt. Another was where the embankment gave way under the weight of a truck. Fortunately it was only a slight drop so no one was hurt. In another, a truck had rolled over, etc. To add to the excitement I had some rather nervous women behind me. Their screams and sighs at every narrow miss made the trip much more thrilling. The bus driver smiled after every miss as the conductor running a roller coaster in an amusement park smiles when he hears the passengers scream.

The rain followed us through the journey. There were reputed to be volcanoes surrounding us but I was lucky to see the road in front of us it was so soupy. We made good time, though, and arrived at Popayán at 1:30 for lunch. I could hardly believe I was making this part of the trip in one day. I thought I would make it to Popayán to Ipiales in a good hard day and night drive, but to make it from Pasto to Cali in just fourteen hours was amazing. Perhaps it was due to the driver, who was about the most reckless I had experienced in 18,000 miles. Usually South American drivers, especially Colombian drivers, were very careful but this trip seemed to have the worst drivers. I never ran into anyone who had made the run who hadn't had a hair-raising experience. We dashed around obfuscated corners, passed on blind corners, many times passing when cars coming from the other direction were almost directly in front of us, forcing them to either stop or get off the road. One driver who had to stop ranted and raved, shaking his fist at the driver, who simply smiled and waved back at him. One bicycle turned right in front of us and we swerved just in time to be two inches from adding a few spokes to our wheels.

The weather was so terrible I never really looked around Popayán. It was supposed to be one of the most colonial towns in Colombia. However, all I remembered of it was looking at a bunch of tiled roofs below through the clouds as we descended to it. There was a long row of plain-looking buildings along the main street. I was not motivated to look around.

On the ride to Cali, the scenery flattened out a little. The weather cleared a bit. I met several students. One was a mechanics student. I had heard there was a lack of scientific or mechanical schools in Colombia. He verified this and said he hoped to go to the United States in a couple of years to finish up his schooling.

We encountered our first customs inspection since the border. It had a couple of dumb yokels who evidently had nothing to do so they made everybody get off the bus. Everyone was very disgusted. The Colombians were not used to playing tag with the police as the Ecuadorians were and considered it as much an indignity as an American having to stop for inspection before entering California, or the long inspections at airport security in the States or our more recent cumbersome border crossing stipulations.

I expected Cali to be a beautiful city and was far from disappointed. A small river ran through the middle of town, which was made even more beautiful with parks, quaint bridges, and decorations in similar fashion as the San Antonio River in Texas. It was lined with modern tall buildings in the center, and on one side with sidewalk cafes, shops and a beautiful residential section a little farther on. Cali had probably the most attractive architecture I had seen yet. Brazilian modern was flamboyant but this was solid. As Cali was in a temperate climate the houses were almost all windows with beautiful patios. In nearly every other large city the traditional buildings were copies of Victorian French palatial or chateau or other such reproductions. Here the traditional was Moorish. These were beautifully styled buildings built for a temperate climate.

As I approached I could see the American influence. There were many Americans in Cali, Medellín, Cartagena, and Barranquilla and their influence was significant in these cities. The road was lined with clubs, steak houses, drive-in eating stands, etc. I decided I had had my fill of cheap hotels so I chose the third best hotel on my list. This was the first time I had stayed in a decent hotel with room and bath since San Carlos de Bariloche, Argentina over a month prior. It was really a good feeling. I ironed a shirt and suit (it was the first time I had seen a plug in months) and started out. I had arrived with a three-day beard, dirty shirt, and dirty and torn pants. When I walked into the hotel with a barracks bag over my shoulder and blanket underneath and asked for a room with a bath, the clerks had looked stunned. I spent the evening washing out clothes so I figured the hotel manager must have been pleasantly surprised at my new look. Oh for a Bendix!! I spent two hours doing laundry and still only finished a little more than half of it after expending nearly all my soap.

It was Christmas Day and I was wondering what my family was doing on this holiday. My diary and reference sheets were time-consuming. It had taken 12 hours writing just to fill in the diary from Lima to here, averaging about an hour each night. Laundry was always a problem because I never had the time in one place to send it out and time in the evenings and places to wash were not always forthcoming.

I got up and did some more ironing in the morning. The day didn't look too promising, as the humidity was high. I was sad to find my Kansas City schoolmate had not been transferred here from Bogotá yet. I started looking around for an AVIANCA office to mail some film and letters. I finally stumbled on an office. They told me they wouldn't take packages and sent me to another agency, and the merchant there then guided me to the head office. After waiting in a long line I was told they didn't take packages at that window, and sent me to the package window. That window informed me they didn't take packages until the stamps were bought at the stamp window. I got in that line and the woman there guided me to the next line. This clerk had to go out and powder her nose when I got there but finally came back. I asked her where I could register the packet. She said at the package window but they had just closed for lunch. I sure lost my faith in the efficiency of AVIANCA in a hurry. Later, I went back to AVIANCA and managed to get the registering done in less than five minutes.

I took a good look at my list of hotels to plan my next destination and this time I thought I had picked one that looked like it would be a good one. I started to walk to the railway station but it was 6:30 and I felt I might not make it if I walked. It was a good thing I took a taxi because seats weren't reserved. I got a good one next to the window. The cars were beautiful—chrome, pushback chairs, and food service at a counter right in the car. The weather was so terrible I couldn't see much. The car was smooth and there was no one to talk to so I got quite a bit of writing and reading done. We arrived at a place called Pintada at 12:30. The auto Ferro came to an abrupt stop and ended the journey so I had to look for other transportation. About fifty taxi drivers advanced on me at once. I was persistent in looking for a bus but found both the bus and the station wagon to be full to capacity. I gave up and started looking for a taxi but they were all gone by then. There was a whistle and shout from one bus as one student and his sister called me over. They said it was going to Medellín and they had saved me a place. They have a railway over the mountain pass to Medellín but don't use it. I couldn't get an explanation from anyone as to why they didn't use the tracks. They told me this used to be a train that went over the mountain but it was abandoned. I thought the reason was because the tracks going over the mountain were a narrower gauge than the others and probably faster to transfer everyone to cars and buses for the trip over the mountains than to another slower train.

It was beautiful traveling through the rugged mountains spread out above and below. As we got to the top I could see Medellín in the distance far below. We traveled along a river, the early stages of the Medellín River. This increased in size until it widened into a major river in Medellín. If I was favorably impressed with Cali I was even more so with this city. At the bottom of the hill we turned onto a dual-lane speedway and beautiful industrial section. It was even more beautiful than that of Lima. The factories were modern, fronted by extensive lawns surrounded by exquisite gardens. The river followed us along the other side, beautifully laid out by cement, and carved bridges.

Spanish Jews founded Medellín in the 17th Century. It was the second largest city in Colombia and the capital of Antioquia. It had a history of commerce, with beautiful parks and modern buildings. The bus driver let me off near the downtown section. I couldn't bargain with the taxi drivers so I got directions from someone and hiked on my own. I found the Bristol Hotel and was sadly disillusioned. There was a noisy cabaret downstairs I had to pass through to even get to the registration desk. I pulled out my list and looked for another hotel. A boy stopped to sell me a cow's horn made into a container for whiskey. I told him I didn't drink and started a conversation. In this way I got a run-down on where a good but not too expensive hotel might be located. I must have been an odd sight as I walked through the downtown with the bag and blanket on my shoulder, but I attracted less attention than walking across downtown Cali where I even stopped cars. I ran into a couple of rather ill-mannered cops but got good directions on how to reach the third best hotel in the town. This hotel turned out to be very nice. They must have had the best chef in Colombia because the meat was like bricks but cooked as well as grade D meat could be cooked. I am afraid I was completely spoiled by all the service. Every time I took a sip of water a waiter rushed over and filled my glass. Every time I had any question at the desk the clerks were immediately on the phone getting an answer for me. The minute I stepped out in the morning the maid stepped in and the room

Medellín, Colombia at night on Christmas Eve.

was spotless when I returned. When I came back at night the bed lamp was on and the covers turned down for me.

After I got settled I went out for a walk before dark. I could have found no better place to spend Christmas. The decorations in all the other cities were limited to a few store windows. However, Medellín was beautifully decorated. One walkway displayed numerous lighted trees for about a mile. A park was filled with decorations and lighted trees. The stores were lighted, the windows all dazzlingly decorated. I finally felt Christmas was here. The hotel dining room even had a lighted tree. The people were all scurrying around doing last minute shopping and the stores were still open in the evening. After dinner I went out for what was supposed to be a short walk. I noticed a movie house with a Mexican movie and was drawn inside. Bad movie! The audience added up to no more than 15 people so I judged the picture wasn't the rage of the town. I got back too late and too tired to face another evening of laundry so I just dropped into my wonderfully soft bed and forgot the world.

I had checked into passage on a boat down the Magdalena River. When I asked at a travel agency the agent was very nice but told me passage was booked until the end of January. I told him I had come all the way from Quito to make this voyage and asked if there was any third class or other boat. Unfortunately he was working with a not-so-nice German who blurted out in English, "There isn't a chance in the world. Give up and go home!" The agent was very embarrassed by this and handed me the name of the navigation company so I could talk with them personally. The lady at the office verified there was no room but offered to sell me passage without a bed. I told her I had a hammock. She clasped her hands and said, "Wonderful, then you have no problem. You can put the hammock anywhere you want." The charge was $13.98 for the four-day jaunt with use of everything and food, etc., with the exception of a bed. I think the regular charge was about $24.

I ran around trying to find the AVIANCA office to mail a letter. I found an agency but they told me to go down the block. They only sold stamps there. I went to another agency and they finally directed me to the head office. The girl there told me the registration window had just closed until December 26.

I ate an early dinner and then started out a little before 8:00 p.m. I knew I would run into festivities that would keep me out until at least 11:00 and would make my Christmas that much more enjoyable. At first I was sadly disillusioned because the streets around the hotel were barren. I figured everyone was probably home. I reached the most popular park and found people quietly walking around like myself, enjoying the decorations. I took the street called "La Playa" along which were many decorations up to the poorer part of town. Here there was a sudden change from the quiet main part of town to the sound of many radios, bands, firecrackers, the singing of drunks, etc. Every two feet someone would set off a firecracker. Inside every other home was a fiesta with everyone dancing the Cha-Cha-Cha. It would have been hard to feel alone in this place. I climbed up and down the hills until I got to the end of the street. Below was a beautiful panoramic view of the entire city with its fireworks like thousands of shooting stars. There was a new type of firecracker. It was an asbestos paper sack with a lighted candle inside. This made it rise to great heights. These were floating all over above the city, giving a red glow. Fortunately I didn't see any land on any of the straw roofs in the hills.

In the poorer barrios were many little 7-12-year-old girls smoking cigarettes. I walked to the cabaret section of town. I had never noticed a town with more cabarets. They were going especially wild that night, all of them packed. I stopped at one and was watching everyone dance the Cha-Cha-Cha. It was almost as good as a show. I stood for about a half-hour outside. The bar looked a little rough so I didn't enter, fearing I might get caught in a raid. There seemed to be no age limit. There were some boys there that couldn't have been over 12 years old, so drunk they couldn't see across the table. I was about to leave when someone came dashing up to me and invited me in for a drink. I thanked him but said I would stay outside and watch. He insisted I come in and assured me the owner was a friend of his and would protect my watch. He told me he was manager of the International Division of AVIANCA. After about fifteen minutes of refusing I went as far as the bar. He introduced me to the manager and all his friends. I found just about everyone had spent some time in the United States. I had made the mistake in one city of telling people where I was staying so I told them I was Russian and was going to the States in another month to go to a special school and find work. They finally coaxed me to a table on the other side of the dance floor. I managed to dodge through all the Cha-Cha-Chaers and got to the other side.

I was pleasantly surprised at the interesting people I met. One drunken man came over, and when they told him I was Russian his face lit up. He shouted, "I like Russia. I like Communism." I said I didn't and was going to the United States to look for work. He said he didn't like Americans. I said I didn't know too many Americans but liked all of them I had met. One of the guys asked me if I knew English. I said I knew a little and then proceeded to speak a few broken words for him. He said I had almost an American accent. I pretended to blush and thanked him. He then proceeded to teach me the way the New Yorkers talk. Meanwhile, the Communism lover was still hanging on, lauding me, praising me, etc.

I told him, "If you like Communism you aught to go live in Russia for a while."

"Oh no!" he said. "I don't like Communism as it exists in Russia but I like Communism. Russia has taxes, the United States has taxes, and Colombia has taxes. That's Communism."

"Do you mean you feel the U.S. is Communist?" I asked.

"Yes."

"Well, if that's Communism, Communism is good," I said, hoping this would end that conversation.

"I was in Korea and was taken prisoner so I hate Americans," he added.

I failed to see the significance of that.

He then added, "In the U.S. there's the black here and the white there. In Russia and Colombia they don't separate them. What hotel are you at?"

Thoughtlessly I said the name.

I cringed when he said, "I'm not working so I'll come by and we can talk."

I quickly said, "I'll be leaving town," hoping that would discourage him from coming by the hotel. But I knew I was safe, as the hotel would quickly have told him his party, Carl Endrevich (the Russian name I had used with these people), was not staying at the hotel.

After we finally got rid of our Communist cell-member I proceeded to ask three of the people who had just gotten back from New York how the U.S. was. They told me I should practice my English more and began teaching me some slang. I told them a little about Russia and taught them some Russian phrases. They said there were lots of Russians there in Medellín. I froze on the spot, as my Russian would surely have not passed muster.

Later I met another person who had just gotten back from the States. I was surprised to meet as nice a group of people in such a dump. I was amazed to meet one of the nicest mannered Latinos I had met so far. His name was Orlando. He invited me to come have dinner with the family the next evening along with another friend of his. He said he liked Russia, not the present government, but the country. I was so interested in the conversation. I didn't realize how rough the party was getting. All of a sudden I heard, "Raid!" I looked up and saw the police closing in. There was a mad scramble for the rear. All I could think of was, "Now you've done it, Hinkley." I moved slowly toward the door, conscious I was a head taller than nine-tenths of the rest of the patrons. Soon everything quieted down, a couple of girls and several people were hustled out by the heavy arm of the law, and that was it. My heart was stuck in my throat. We settled back to our conversation. It wasn't more than a minute before there was another fight. The owner jumped in the middle trying to break it up. Fortunately, he was bigger than all three participants put together so it soon ended. Then another fight started, this time with tables being thrown at each other. No sooner had this one died down than bottles started flying. When the fight settled down a couple of us decided the party was getting a little rough. I excused myself, claiming 2:30 a.m. was my bedtime. The whole table got up and walked me back to my hotel. What an inappropriate way to celebrate the birth of Christ. The town was still going wild. The streets were even fuller than they were earlier in the evening. As I walked up the quiet steps to my room I could hear my hosts singing and hollering as they ambled down the street.

I didn't get to bed until 3:00 a.m., as I had to wash my shirt for the next day. However, to my dismay I found I couldn't sleep past 6:00 a.m. I got up and ironed my shirt, deciding I would get everything done and take a nap that afternoon. I found the cabarets still going full blast, drunks lying all over the tables, sidewalks and streets, and recognized some of the same people staggering around. I felt a little uncomfortable with my camera hanging around my shoulder.

I had told Orlando the night before I would tell him something when I met him for dinner. I didn't even want my nationality known at the bar. My experience with the wrong person getting my name in

Guayaquíl had made me wary of giving any correct information to anyone I didn't completely trust. After Orlando left with the group I began to be a little sorry I didn't tell him the correct information. He had probably told his family he was bringing a Russian home for dinner. I couldn't get hold of him, as all he gave me was his post office box number. At 6:00 p.m. I went over to the AVIANCA office to meet him. He and Jorge were there waiting for me. I learned one thing about Medellín. Whereas nine-tenths of my appointments had either failed to show up or were pitifully late, this just didn't seem to be the case in Medellín. The day before Orlando was just a few minutes late in meeting his mother for a noon appointment and found a note from her saying she could wait no longer. Such promptness would never be expected in other parts of Latin America. They told me Orlando's sister had been ill so the dinner at his house was off. We then went to my hotel restaurant. I told them the meal was expensive there but they insisted on accompanying me. After we got there they ordered drinks and no food. They claimed they weren't hungry, although I could hear their stomachs growling from where I was sitting. We walked around until the last movies were about to start and went to see "Cielito Lindo". This was a good show, considering it was Mexican with excellent filming in good color, but the speakers weren't too good so Orlando had to clue me in every so often. After the movie Orlando and I walked around for a last look at the Christmas decorations. I got my camera and we got a couple of pictures of the neon lights at night. We sat in the park and talked about Colombia until about 2:00 a.m. and then I remembered I had to get up at 5:00 so it was best to get some sleep and if he was going to see me off as he had insisted he had better get home too.

It was an awful feeling when the phone rang at 5:20 a.m.; an equally sleepy clerk told me to get up. Six hour's sleep in two nights was not quite what I was used to. As this would make equally as few hours sleep for Orlando I doubted he would show up at the train station. I got ready in good time considering the condition I was in and started for the station. It took a good half-hour to walk to the train station but this was great exercise with my 65 pounds of luggage. I took one look at the block-long line for second-class tickets and decided I would go first-class so I could get some writing done. I ran down and threw a blanket on a good seat and then waited for Orlando to show up. I was about to give up and return to the train before it left when Orlando came dashing into the station, huffing and puffing. He handed me a Colombian record he had bought for me as a souvenir. I was really deeply touched by this. Here he was slaving away helping to support his family on a salary that was barely sufficient and he had insisted on paying for every soda we drank, ice cream, we ate, etc., and had bought a record for me to remember his country. It was a mystery that in a country, which had a reputation of being the most dangerous of any South American country, I found such extreme generosity and selfless thinking on the part of many of the people I met. Every time I encountered another person in this country I got to like Colombia more. Only in Paraguáy had I found such graciousness and hospitality.

Orlando warned me I was going into the most dangerous part of Colombia and expressed fear I might lose my life as there was so much killing going on there. I assured him I would stick to the more crowded areas of Puerto Berrío, but he cautioned me, "Don't take the bus under any circumstances. You'll be exposed to too much danger. Take the train. It is safer and you will be more protected." He continued, "I was there for several days with some friends. We were in a bar when one of the meanest of them was sitting with some of his gang on the other side of the room. Suddenly he sent someone over who demanded one of us go to bed with him. We had to think carefully as offending him could mean death so we agreed. Then when he was not looking we sneaked out of the bar and headed for home. One time he got into a disagreement with someone. The next day he proudly walked down the street displaying the head of that man. No one dared touch him or go against him in any way. Another time a schoolteacher was dragged into their place and thirty of the men raped her before they let her go. She did not dare report it."

When I boarded the train to Puerto Berrío I found two young boys occupying my seat. As a hint I picked up the blanket they had moved and put it next to the window explaining that was my seat. They quickly squeezed together on the other side of the seat. It was so unusual to meet a well-mannered boy outside Brazil that I was pleased to meet these three boys. One of them, who couldn't have been over twelve, began asking me very intelligent questions about my odyssey. He began explaining the transportation system of Colombia. I swear if I hadn't seen him I would have said he was at least eighteen. He explained the reason they don't run the train all the way from Cali is that there is a division of States and another company has rights past the State line for Antioquia. Formerly you got off the Auto Ferro and got on the train for Medellín but they shut down the other half. I felt with this new government things were going to improve. The Colombians, for the first time in their history, actually admitted they had a good President. The boy explained to me they were moving the Capitol of Brazil the same way they moved the capitol after a war in the States. He then named the capitols of the provinces of Colombia. I was really held spellbound by the intelligence of this little mulatto boy from Puerto Barrio. When I first saw him I wondered if he could read. At about 8:00 a.m. I was getting very hungry and expressed this fact. He hailed down the coffee man and brought me a cup of café con leche. I started to pay but he said, "No, my brother has already paid for it." This was only 1-1/2¢ but I was touched with this show of generosity shown me by these people whom I might have considered poverty-stricken.

At noon we entered a long tunnel, which took six-and-one-half minutes to pass through. I would judge it was about three or four miles long. Some people left doors and windows open so the ventilator did little good. The smoke from the engine wafted in. I thought we'd never reach fresh air again. The scenery was spectacular on the ten-hour run. We passed from a valley into a ravine, following the Medellín River. Then we went up into the mountains, passed through a tunnel, and came out on the other side of the mountain range. We passed down into a valley and then followed another river. We began to drop into a dense rainforest, the day became progressively hotter; the train stopped more often to pick up passengers.

David Arrango, our boat to descend the Río Magdalena

I went to the diner to get something to eat and finally, after 36 days of travel all over Colombia, I ran into what everyone told me would be the typical mean surly Colombian. Upon seeing no vacant tables I politely asked if a seat was free at one table. The seats were filled with second and third class passengers. No one was eating. I went up to a woman who was standing and asked if there were any seats. She just stared at me as though I just landed from Mars and looked in the other direction. I finally got a rise out of a helper when I finally loudly bellowed, "What the hell am I supposed to do—stand up and eat?" Having finally gotten his attention the waiter took me to a table where four rough-looking men were seated. He asked them to move and they stared at me with looks that could kill. I could feel the negative energy they hurled at me with their expressions as they got up to give me their seats. Then came the problem of getting something to eat. When I saw the waiter was attending people who came in after me I yelled at him that I would like a meal. I was very happy I didn't buy third class. The third class passengers looked the most serious and mean spirited I had seen in all my travels.

We got into Puerto Berrío at 3:30 p.m. I was pleasantly surprised to find it rather lovely. The weather was oppressively hot and muggy. I started to disembark and found the boat was already docked only a block or so away from the station so I walked directly to it. The "gerencia" of this boat was not as nice as the clerk at the head office. I told the captain I was ticketed without a bed and he told me that was impossible. They never sold tickets that way. He finally weakened from his obstinate posture and we finally got a closet to put my things in. He told me this was one of the worst ports so I had better watch everything closely. I took a quick walk around the town but swiftly returned.

Riverboat on Río Magdalena, Colombia

At 8:00 p.m. dinner was served. I sat at a table with another man and we were soon graced with the pleasure of two charming women. We discussed Colombia and Colombian women. I think my opinions were music to their ears as I could truthfully say little against Colombia. After dinner the girls excused themselves and the other gentleman and I talked for a couple of hours on the political situation. I was perpetually impressed with the intelligence of the Colombians I met having just been freed from a ruthless dictatorship and how freely they discussed politics. He said, "The U.S. should think more about Latin America."

I explained, "I feel the growth in Latin America has been so fast the people of the United States haven't kept up with it, but they are beginning to change."

He chuckled and said, "Nixon's thinking more of Latin America than he did before his trip."

I told him, "We aught to be glad that wasn't Ike or Dulles they threw pebbles at, because there would have been war for sure."

He expressed, "I have the same concern as you, that the government of the United States couldn't raise its head above military thinking."

Our conversation moved from a majority of Americans supporting neutrality until 1941, to involvement with the darker side of international relations put into affect by the creation of the CIA by Allen Dulles and a war mentality with our Foreign Service under the direction of his brother, John Foster Dulles. Americans don't see this from inside our country, but my travel in other countries, especially at the worker/Indigenous level, gave me an entirely altered view of our foreign policy. When America wakens to its mission of bringing peace to the world, the weapons of terrorism will lose their ammunition. New approaches to drug abuse will diminish its tentacles into our society and drastically reduce our prison population.

At about 10:30 p.m. I thought I'd better put my hammock up and asked the Captain where I could put it.

He gruffly told me, "You can't put your hammock anywhere on this boat."

I asked him, "Where am I going to sleep?"

"I don't know," he barked and started to walk away.

Moonlight on the Río Magdalena

I told him, "They told me at the head office I could put my hammock anywhere I pleased on the boat."

It was apparent I was getting nowhere with him, so curled up on one of the deck chairs and went to sleep. After six hours sleep in two nights I wasn't too anxious to do this but I had to sleep somewhere.

I thought of four more nights in a deck chair and shuddered at the thought. At 11:30 p.m. I was awakened by one of the waiters who told me they had set up a bed in the salón for me. I slept very comfortably.

Having finally had a good night's sleep I found I had all the facilities I needed. I discovered a shower I could use in back and went back to my battery razor after three luxurious days with my electric razor. I bumped into my friend of the night before and we ran into the girls and had breakfast with them. I was adjusting to beefsteak and egg breakfasts after my two pieces of toast and a cup of coffee, the Continental breakfast I had become accustomed to being served.

After breakfast we got into an interesting group conversation. I found Colombians talked freely about their country and spoke with great knowledge about it. The people seemed to love to travel so I was always bumping into Colombian tourists wherever I went. This boat was a tourist boat but I was the only non-Colombian on it. This appeared to be the best-advertised and most popular tour in Colombia. I mentioned to one passenger the lack of any foreigners and she said, "Oh, Americans all take the plane. This trip is for idlers like you and me."

I found this boat trip especially interesting. Although nearly a half-mile wide, the river was very shallow so we wove in and out of the channels. This boat was an old paddle wheeler. It had been reconditioned and much of it was air-conditioned. The river was full of paddle wheelers so gave me the feeling I was riding the Mississippi in 1850. The Magdalena River has its source above San Agustín, where I had been the prior June on my trip to the Amazon. I crossed it at a point called the "Estrechas del Magdalena" (Magdalena narrows) where it was only nine feet wide. It flowed almost from one end of the country to the other. Until recently it was the only way of getting to Bogotá from Barranquilla, the principal port on the Gulf. There was now a road from Cartagena to Medellín and from there to Bogotá by train. The government,

Traveling down the Río Magdalena

at that time, was planning to build a bridge across the river at Puerto Berrío, which they eventually did, which now provides an even closer connection. Many American oil companies had built a large oil pipeline running from Puerto Berrío to Barranquilla.

Some of the passengers explained to me the view of the mountains was supposed to be very good on a clear day but all I could see was jungle. The day before I was sitting in an open café at one of the ports, sipping a cola when an older drunk came up to me and offered to give me some money and a bill that looked like it was more than the money. He claimed he had paid the bill. I finally wormed out of that one. He then offered to sell my watch for me. I finally convinced him I loved my watch. He threw his arms around me and wished me well. I wished him well, too, as I quickly checked all my pockets to make sure everything was still there. This drew another older gentleman over who explained there was no work in the area. He expressed to me an American oil company came in but more people flocked there than there was work. He was missing so many teeth I could get little of what he said (Spanish is spoken off the teeth) so I ended up nodding in agreement or disagreement (depending on the expression on his face).

Paddle wheeler on the Río Magdalena. Some of these were purchased from the U.S., so traveled the Mississippi River at one time.

My dinner companion explained to me the present situation in Colombia was something new (combining the liberal and conservative into one government) in Colombia's history. "This all resulted from Rojas Pinilla. He cultivated the criminals to keep himself in power. He also divided the country into two camps. With a combination of these two there was a lot of political killing and then open robbery and killing. The government is now successfully combating it and it is becoming less and less of a problem. This new government setup is helping to bring the two sides together."

He said, "The real popular American down here is Adlai Stevenson. He carries a lot of respect as being a very honest, straightforward man with good ideas and the force to carry them out. Colombia felt deep sorrow after Stevenson lost the election."

My writing was about the best way to attract attention, especially the children. I couldn't get back to my writing once they found me. They hung all over my shoulders, knees, etc., grabbing the sheets of paper and re-arranging them. One would yell at me while the other one would keep kicking me. There seemed to be absolutely no discipline or respect for their elders. I finally just gave up writing after awhile. It would have been very smart to pretend I didn't know Spanish on this trip, except for the fascinating conversations I had with other passengers.

There were two men traveling together who the children loved. This relieved me of that burden as they were much more patient with them than I. Suddenly the father of one of the children came at the two men in a tirade. "Stay away from my children!" he yelled. "Don't get near them!" He pulled the children away.

"What's going on?" I asked.

"They're homosexuals and they will abuse my children," he fired back.

"Not necessarily so," I said in their defense.

"Yes, they will. That's what they do," he fired back.

I had no evidence one way or the other, so decided to bow out of that conflict.

This trip was hotter than the trip down the Amazon. Every time we stopped it became oppressively hot. Even while moving the air remained quite hot. There was air-conditioning in the bar but not very efficient in this humidity. We stopped in the middle of the afternoon at Barrancabermeja where there was a big oil refinery. Elia, Telesa, Oliva (my three dinner friends) and I set out to see the town. The girls were wearing slacks but the ones that Oliva was wearing looked like they had

Carriers unloading sugar and cement at Magangue

been sprayed on. Several men couldn't stop staring, others fell over pebbles in the road and the rest just stood and watched as we passed. The city was in good shape for a river town. It was so miserably hot we headed right back to the boat. We found little relief there. The day was filled with conversations from the nonsensical to the more serious. One thing about being on a boat in Colombia, there was never a dull moment. Some of the crew were planning to present a play and a beauty contest to be held that night for the women, and a most-beautiful leg contest for the men. The play was directed by a rather masculine woman and her milk-toast husband (both wonderful people). I tried to evade the leg contest but the director insisted I be on the program. I was the first one called so I had to march down between two rows of packed chairs of women with my legs bared. They measured the muscle and ankle. I won but somehow couldn't seem to feel very proud over being known as having the best male pair of legs on board. The party went on and on with singing, comedy and much, much drinking on the part of a few. I thought the salón would never clear so I could get some sleep. Finally, at 1:30 a.m., the salón was clear and the bar still full. I made up the cot on the other side of a pony wall and went to sleep.

At 6:00 a.m. I felt I had better get up and get dressed before the crowd arrived. The night before had been miserable. We pulled alongside another boat at a small town at about 6:00 p.m. and stayed for the night. It was stuffy and the mosquitoes were unusually hungry. Like the Amazon they were used to an early breakfast furnished by the passengers. By 10:00 a.m. I either ran out of blood or the mosquitoes finished their breakfast because they no longer bothered me. We were coming to the mouth of a river ahead that made the channel unusually shallow so we had to stay for the entire night. It was miserably hot until midnight (95°F) and then became bearable. I guess I was the luckiest one on board. The salón was big and had a lot of windows. The camarotes where the other passengers were sleeping must have been

Boats in Barrancaberameja on Río Magdalena

miserable. I spent most of the day trying to keep away from the brats. They somehow attached themselves to me as chief friend and nothing could change their minds. We didn't stop at any towns of interest. At night we pulled up at the town of El Panco. It was unusually nice shape and had one of the most beautiful hotels I had seen in Colombia. The girls were dressed in snazzy strapless eveningwear so all eyes were again popping among the townspeople. Entertainment that night was guitar-playing, singing, and comedy. I was heavily requested to sing "cowboy" or Rrrock 'N Rrrol. I told them my voice was like a horse but they kept insisting. After I gave them a short demonstration the requests were withdrawn. At 12:30 a.m. the party was still going strong. The steward offered me the use of an office so I pulled my cot in there and went to sleep. The party continued until 2:30 in the morning.

Shouting native vendors passed by my open window, which awakened me abruptly. I looked out and saw we were in a small shantytown. The natives of the town were running all over the boat trying to find someone awake to sell some mangos, chickens, etc. A woman stuck her head in the window and yelled "Mangos!!" I told her, "Not today," and she left. I suddenly felt a sharp awakening. I had forgotten to put my billfold under my pillow. I was relieved when I checked and found it safely in my pants. We hit the port of Magangué in the morning. I got off and took a short walk through the town. It was very dirty. We stayed there for several hot hours and then moved on.

The rest of the day was quite hot. We were supposed to arrive at Barrenquilla at 1:00 a.m., which would give me an extra day. The big fiesta held that night was an evening of fun. I wasn't expecting a fiesta so I quickly washed a shirt out, found an electrical outlet in the girls' camarotes, and ironed it dry. The captain was brought in for trial on crimes he supposedly committed at the various ports we hit on the way down. The hairiest beast, husband of the director, dressed up as a ballerina with mustache still intact, and flirted with various members

Church in Barrenquilla, Colombia

of the court (which brought down the house). Most of the show was written in poetry. It still amazes me the way Spanish-speaking people can speak and write so freely in poetry. I finally got tired of being the only one dancing so I went out on deck just to sit and watch the beautiful moonlight shining on the water.

I got up at 5:00 a.m. and found the shower and everything all shut down, so I decided to disembark and find a hotel. It wasn't hard to find a taxi, as I had to fight to keep from getting one bag put in one car and another bag in another by the large number of anxious cabbies. I saw a taximeter in one cab and chose it so I could monitor any overcharge. The cabbie talked me into going to another hotel, which he said was closer to the center than the one I chose. I looked at the meter after we had been gone about a minute and saw it wasn't working. I asked how much it would be. He calmly quoted me ten pesos. After coming out of shock I told him that was a lot. He answered, "Oh, you're spending in dollars so that's nothing." I told him I was a student and was spending practically no dollars. He knew he had me over a barrel as we were in the middle of a field and I could never get another taxi from there. We got to the hotel and I was still fuming. I mentioned to the hotel clerk the driver was charging ten pesos and the driver quietly whispered to him, "He's a foreigner you know." I gave him a bill for twenty and he ran out the door. I ran and grabbed him, asking for ten back. He finally gave me ten. My first thought was, "I feel like I'm back in Cuba."

Old wall, Cartagena, Colombia

After all this, the hotel had no room. I started to grab my bags and the clerk grabbed my bag from me and said another hotel paid him a tip for carrying pas-

Cartagena from top of fort

sengers to it. I got to the other hotel and found it had no single rooms, only dormitory. My two señoritas, who had traveled with me on the boat, were sitting there waiting for their room to be cleaned. I finally said I would take a dormitory room. I was given a room with a man from Medellín. The hotel was very expensive in comparison to Medellín and Cali and very poor in quality. I was again back in the madhouse tourist Caribbean.

I went down to check on transportation. I found a thick-skulled clerk behind the desk of the tourist agency in the hotel lobby. Every time I asked for information he would give me information on something completely different. He insisted I was going to go to Cartagena in express taxi and I insisted I was going on the bus. Every question I asked would lead back to the taxi. He finally said, "Well, if you don't want to cooperate with me you can go to another agency." I continued asking questions and he finally divulged the information I wanted and he told me to come back at noon. I went to the banks and found they were all closed on the 30th, too. I then went to KLM and found the camera I bought in the Dominican Republic had still not arrived. It had now followed me through every South American Country and was still in flight, somewhere in the world. I could now understand frequent fliers who say, "I would love to travel to all the places my luggage has been."

Typical side street in older section of Cartagena, Colombia

A business specialist at the Consulate gave me a rather gloomy picture of business in Colombia. He said, "The dollar situation has scared American businesses so they are afraid to invest capital. They usually enter in partnership with a similar Colombian business, buy a business out, or license to a Colombian firm. This eliminates a lot of the risk and allows for a steady flow of capital in return. The peso, in a little over a year, had jumped from $2.50 to the dollar to $8.14. This could eat up profits real fast when one considered they would have to receive around three million pesos from a million dollar investment to just break even. Also, there was the same problem as in México. The Colombians had developed to the extent American enterprises found it more profitable to hire a Colombian for $1,000 pesos a month than send an American down for $10,000 pesos."

I went to the Panamanian Consulate. It was located in the back of a shop. The clerk asked me for my ticket out of the country. I laughed and told him I couldn't purchase transportation outside the country. I argued with him and finally pulled the official-looking letter I had from my bank reserved for just such emergencies. It had never even been opened. I told him the Panamanian Consul in the United States told me this would be sufficient. The Consul finally told me he would give me a visa for ten pesos (under the table). That hurt but there wasn't much I could do about it because to buy a ticket and get a refund after leaving would cost me just as much in mailing and tax charges. He told me to come back in the afternoon.

When I finally got started at 2:00 p.m. I found it took up the entire afternoon. I had to get my visa, go get money exchanged (with the banks closed that was something), process the ticket, and go to the head office. I found a very nice person at the head office. We soon forgot all about the ticket and had a map of Central America on the table, working out my future trip together. He had been overland in Panama as far as David within the last six months so he had a lot of current information. He told me he had heard there was overland travel within Costa Rica on four-wheel-drive vehicles that might carry me over the unfinished Pan-American Highway and they might carry some passengers.

That evening I went out and found the town completely dead in comparison to Medellín. I had dinner with my two girlfriends from Medellín and talked to them for a while afterwards. The women of Medellín are the most talkative and charming of any women I met during my journey and the men were also most friendly and cultured.

I couldn't see getting up at 4:00 a.m. to catch the 5:00 bus to Cartagena so I got up at 6:00. My roommate was journeying to Medellín, his home, so he got up at the same time. I asked the hotel to put me on the European plan (which does not include meals), as I wasn't eating there that day. They said they only had an American plan so I decided to find another hotel. It was 7:00 a.m. and I bought a ticket on the 7:30 bus over the protest of the hotel manager (who was agent for the station wagons) and the station wagon men who were surrounding the bus company. I ran to the best hotel in town (a real beauty) and found it was cheaper than remaining in my other lousy room I was sharing. I ran back and the hotel charged me a higher price because I was going to another hotel. After he was through robbing me the hotel manager smiled and said, "At your service."

I muttered back, "Yeh, for a price." He got a big kick out of this and I could hear his roar as I walked out. It was 7:20 and I threw my bags on the counter and signed the register of the other hotel, told them to find me a good room and ran to catch the bus.

Cartagena is absolutely the best city in the world for fortifications. There is a wall all around the old city, an enormous big fort, and many other fortifications. The downtown was a perfect replica of a colonial fifteenth century town. At 3:00 p.m. I found the station wagon full and decided the extra money I saved made it worthwhile to take the bus, which would arrive only one-half hour after the next station wagon.

I went out that night to enjoy New Years' Eve but found the town dead, except for children with firecrackers. I was so exhausted anyway that I came back and went to bed at 10:00 p.m.

I got up and went to the snazzy hotel restaurant. My room was the best so far. I was on the top floor, with a beautiful view above the city. The entire front of the room was windows. It was also brand new. It cost only $3.13. I went around looking for a taxi that might take me to the airport for little money. I found a woman leaning out a door of an airline office. I asked her if there was a limousine to take me to the airport. She led me to a man who led me to another individual who worked for AVIANCA. He told me to drop by at 10:00 a.m. and he would get me a cheap taxi. I ran around and got a few more pictures of the town. I carried my bags down and there was my man with a taxi that would take me for only 62¢, even though it was about three times the distance of my $1.30 ride into town.

The plane was an hour late out of Cartagena, affording me some time to do some reading. The plane ride was short but interesting. I was surprised at the speed with which we crossed the Isthmus. I never realized Panama was so narrow. I became apprehensive as we landed, as I could see we were far from the city and the cab would probably be prohibitive. It was like "little America" flying with Pan-American. I don't think I heard a word of Spanish from anyone until I hit Panama City where some people still stubbornly hung onto their native tongue. I found a limousine for $1.50. It was a Cadillac and I really felt like a king in the back seat. I ran into a Spaniard who was working for the United Nations. He spoke beautiful English so I spoke my first English since Lima. It was strange to hear English again after so long. The driver was very nice. I explained my financial position to him and he got me a hotel that wasn't quite as expensive as the others. It was a terrible hotel and worse room. There were no windows, just a curtain over the door, two beds squeezed into the room. However, it was $4.50 a day with meals (what there was of them). I really felt terrible. My beautiful hotel with room, bath and meals for $3.75 in Medellín had spoiled me.

    I figured up my finances that evening and found with everything I had to buy I had less then $2.50 a day for room, board, taxi and extra fare for the remainder of the trip. I was worried for a while but figured I had gotten down as little as $1.50 a day by conserving on my room and meals. I was sure I could do this until I reached the United States border in another month. I looked at my thinning body and said to myself, "Here goes another ten pounds." I went out that night to see the nightlife and was disappointed. There were a few cantinas, a few drunks but nothing near what I thought there would be for the New Year.

15. UNFINISHED ROAD

Panama was way above my expectations. I had heard it was just one big house of prostitution. My memory of Cuba with little boys and grown men tugging at my arm at every corner to drag me to the house of their choice made me feel I wouldn't like Panama. However, in my two days in Panama I was never hassled in any way (this is more than I could say for any five-minute period of my stay in Cuba). The architecture was fascinating. It was like a population polyglot. I saw beautiful homes, modern buildings, ruins, world buildings, and squalid slums.

Balconied streets, Panama City

I got up early in the morning. I was hoping to get my money out of the bank, get my visa, pick up any mail, get some shopping done, get to Colón, go to Panama Viejo, see the city and get my bus travel arranged plus the trip up through Costa Rica. I accomplished none of these things. I first ran over to the bank. It was closed for the day. I called the Costa Rican Embassy because they had moved and the Ambassador told me the Consul was open. I finally found the place with the help of a kind American who picked me up in his car but found they were also closed. I called the Consul's home and found the Consul wasn't home. I had to get my visa as I would arrive at David on Sunday and everything would be closed then. I walked back to where I had caught the bus and found it only took 25 minutes to walk the same distance it took forty minutes by bus. The stores were closed so I couldn't do any shopping. I really felt cramped, as this had all started December 23 when everything closed down for Christmas and none still were open for business.

Panama City, Balconies.

I went over to where the buses were and went to the first company. They had a station wagon and said they would take me for $6.00 to David ($2.50 under the listed price in my book). I put my name down for a reservation and started to leave. I thought they had a bus so I went a little way down the street to see it. I asked the attendant to let me see it. He asked if I had bought my ticket. I pointed to the office and said I had my name down for one. He told me this was a different company. I asked him how much this was and he said $5.00. He soon had me in the company, signing my name for a ticket there. I told him I had to save money as I only had $3.00 or less a day for everything and was paying $4.50 a day for my hotel. He said he would get me a bed for 75¢ and I could leave my baggage at his place. I went next door to cancel my name and the woman offered to lower her fare to $5.00. I told her I felt I had better stick with the others because they offered to keep my bags, get me a hotel, etc. She became very angry and said, "They work dirty." I finally got out of there and was called over by a man who took me down the street to see his bus. It was a brand new Mercedes Benz wagon. I got inside and found a chair next to the driver that was plush and had lots of legroom. I asked him how much and he said $6.00. I told him I was broke and would go with the Ferguson bus for $5.00. He then said he would take me for $5.00. That jolted me as the difference between this and Ferguson was like night and day. Ferguson was a bunch of boards tacked on a truck chassis. The seats were hard and there was absolutely no legroom. I was emotionally caught between loyalty and efficiency because Ferguson had offered me so many services. At the time I wished I were my friend, Art Cohen, who I went around with in Cuzco who spared no tact in getting what he wanted. The trouble with me is I

Panama City. Ruins of the convent of Santo Domingo (1678), Destroyed by fire 1761

have a soft and loyal heart that sometimes overpowers my better judgment.

I went back to the hotel. I had struck up quite an acquaintance with all the other guests at the hotel. All of them were from Medellín, Colombia. Touring together were two sisters with two other girls traveling with the mother of the sisters, and two single women (about 35), who had joined them. I got into a conversation with the women about Medellín women and said they would be the most preferable of all the women I had met for marriage because they have nice personalities, a deep sense of love, are intelligent and are nice looking. She asked me if I was a Catholic and I said I wasn't. She said, "Oh, Medellín women are the most firmly Catholic of all Latin American women." We then got on the subject of religion. She asked me about my religion. I ended up with all the guests crowded around asking me about it. They were most interested in the healing aspect of my faith. After my lengthy explanations one of them remarked, "If you were a Catholic you would probably be a Saint." I told her to be a Saint you have to be good and dead and being neither I would stick to my own sense of spirituality. We agreed anyone who is good in his religion and open-minded toward others necessarily radiates good in his or her actions, no matter what religion they are. At the end of the conversation I found it was 4:00 p.m. and I could no longer go to Colón and return. They also had missed Mass and I told them not to worry as they had probably gotten as much out of our conversation as they would have out of Mass. To their compliments I said, "It is one thing to talk about your religion and another to live it. I don't even come near to living my religion but would like to gradually work toward this goal. It is in this desire my spirituality helps me."

Typical balconied buildings around a plaza, Panama City

I was in a store run by one of the many obnoxious German storeowners I met in many cities. A young man was politely waiting on me and I was getting all my information in Spanish. I needed a part for my camera but did not know a Spanish word for the part I needed. He was patiently helping me as I was describing what the part looked like and where it went. The owner butted into the conversation in English and asked if I spoke English. I said I did. He then yelled at the boy, "Why aren't you speaking English? You shouldn't be speaking Spanish to an American. Get back there in the corner."

The clerk cowered and ducked into the corner. I could tell this happened to him often. The owner then went over to a girl working on some papers and yelled and fumed and roared at her. He turned to a Panamanian and yelled, "These Panamanians are Devils." I have never considered myself prejudiced against any nationality, race, or religion. However, I found many German storeowners in all the countries had been were gruff, impolite, and even cold to their customers. I had gotten so that when I even heard someone speaking with a German accent I cringed. I didn't want to carry this intolerance, and made an effort to block these feelings from my mind, but the next German proprietor I met would be like a nail driven into the coffin of my consciousness.

I went to the bus station and got my ticket with the later bus, rather than Ferguson. I figured comfort was better than loyalty. I went back to cancel my name with Ferguson and you could have cut the air between us. He said the latter worked dirtier than they as the other bus driver was drunk all the time and declared I would never leave town with them. I went back to the hotel and got into another conversation with my two friends. This time we talked about love and marriage. One of the women had to laugh when I told her I felt less like getting married every year. She said it had been the same with her. Every year she got choosier, going from one engagement to another until she finally couldn't find anyone she could see spending the rest of her life with. She told me I would make a good husband. I thanked her but told her I wondered if I would ever be one. She said she was much happier now than she would be if she were married. I told her that was the trouble with me. I was enjoying bachelorhood too much.

I got out early the next morning. It was good to see everything open for a change. I got my money out of the bank, my letters out of hock with the American Embassy, and then went to the Colombian Consulate. I passed my time shopping, waiting for the consul to open. When I got there she told me I couldn't get a visa without buying transportation out of the country. There was no way of buying ground transit out of the country because there was still no road to Costa Rica from Panama. I went over to C O P S A., another bus company, and bought a ticket from San José to Managua on Pan-American. This I would be able to turn in with a 90¢ loss in San José. I got the visa, did some shopping, and checked on the road. Someone told me a bus had come down from San José on the road so I figured they must have some transit over that stretch, the only non-completed stretch of the Pan-American Highway between the United States and Panama. The bus had extraordinary service. All the buses went around and picked up each passenger. We were to leave at 1:00 p.m. but I didn't get to my hotel until 2:30. We went back to the agency and waited and waited. We didn't finally get started until 4:00. It was a smooth ride but we were forced to wait for what seemed like hours in the line for the ferry across the canal. I thought with all the money the United States had sunk into the canal they could have at least put a bridge across it. I wondered how the people of Panama must have felt about the United States presence there. They seemed very nice and were extremely courteous to me as an American but I just couldn't imagine how they must have felt with foreign troops right across the middle of their country. It must have been like a knife in their back. The government couldn't move without United States approval of everything and the people couldn't move against their government. The Panamanian people seemed too good-natured to get into a serious revolution.

I was in the middle of a demonstration in Panama on New Year's Eve; the day Fidél Castro took over Cuba. A large crowd of people were drawn from everywhere by the passionate young orators. The police pushed their way through the crowd and the orators began yelling at them, saying, "You're working against the people. You are a part of a dictatorship. You can't fight the people..." etc., etc. The police calmly observed the demonstration and the crowd seemed peaceful. Three of the leaders were obviously students. The speaker was very serious in his revolutionary fervor. I moved to the front so I could hear. I felt the many eyes, which were focused on me, standing a foot above everyone else in the crowd, but I somehow felt safe.

The speaker continued, "People, that which happened in Cuba is not only important to the Cubans. It is an indication of what is happening all over Latin America. The people are throwing out their dictators and putting themselves in power. In Venezuela they took over, in Argentina they threw Perón out, in Colombia they threw Rojas Pinilla out, in Guatemala they killed Castillo Armas, and now in Cuba Batista is out. Masses! Tomorrow the same thing will happen in Panama. The people will rise up and take over the government." This brought a mixture of laughter, consternation, and shouts of, "Viva Fidél Castro!" A student, standing on the platform behind him whispered to the leader, "Hurry up. I have to go. My sweetheart is waiting for me. She's been waiting for three hours. What am I going to do?" This turned the whole thing into a show. I had the feeling everyone was there for amusement rather than revolution. The student repeated his pleas every ten minutes until finally the police began gathering up all the orators and hauling them off. This was probably because they were tired of waiting for the demonstration to die down of its own accord. I never found out what happened to the leaders, but the calm methods used by the police were less offensive than I have seen in some of the demonstrations in our own country. The crowd dispersed amicably.

I wish I could have taken the trip north during the day. I had no idea Panama was so beautiful. The jungle growth there was so much more varied and beautiful than in the Amazon and the flowers so much more abundant. The mountains loomed up as green hills in the background. The highway was as smooth as glass all the way to Santiago. From there it was a mixture of good gravel road and old torn-out road paved two years before. It now had only bits of pavement left, winding, narrow, with many single-lane bridges. As usual this Mercedes-Benz was beautiful, comfortable, smooth but powerless with a motor that took up half the front seat.

We arrived a half-hour late so I missed any chance of catching the train out. I asked around but could get no information as to when there was a train going north. I decided if I could get to the border I could find things out and find rides north easier. I went to L A C S A and found it closed so I couldn't find when there was a plane to San José, Costa Rica from Davíd, Panama. I finally found there wasn't one until the next Wednesday. I called the train depot and found there wasn't a train on the banana line until the next Tuesday, which would take me to Delfito where I could catch a boat up the coast to Costa Rica. I noticed a line that went to Palomar Norte, which was further up the Pan-American Highway but could get no information on when there was a train on it. I finally got hold of a station wagon going to La Concepción. I got off at the train depot there and tried to find a truck going to the border. It was useless as it was Sunday and no trucks were traveling. I finally got the 3:00 p.m. train and bought a ticket to Jacú, which was closer to the border on the future Pan-American Highway that would lead to the Costa Rican border. The train was old and rickety with people hanging on wherever there was room. I was left stranded between two cars, hanging on for dear life. Soon a soldier got on who must have thought his uniform belonged to King George. He immediately started yelling what I would translate to be "Get the hell back!" He started pushing and jamming people into the cars. He got to me and said, "Where are you going?"

I said, "Jacú."

He said, "Are you a foreigner?"

I said, "I am."

"What are you doing here?"

I told him I was a student and was just passing through. He started getting rougher with me but was diverted by some other people who he felt more urge to boss around. Soon he yelled at me from the other car, "Get inside that car!" I tried to argue that there wasn't enough room but I finally turned to shove my way in. "Pardon my feet, animals," I yelled jokingly as I pushed my way through. This added a little levity to this experience. They laughed and let me in. I even managed to find a place to sit down.

I had stocked up on food in Concepción with enough bread to carry me through any emergency. A woman came through, selling ugly pieces of meat for ten cents. I bought one and found mostly grease and bone. I figured I had better eat one good meal a day to save money. I hadn't had anything solid in over twenty-four hours and that evening didn't look too promising.

We stopped at a town and I asked what station this was and was told it was Progresso. I remembered Jacú came before Progresso so I asked where Jacú was. "Way back there," one woman said. I quickly grabbed my bags and blanket and got off. I did some hard and fast debating on whether to get back on or go to Puerto Armueles where I could catch a Grace Liner to Dominicál or further north. I finally figured I didn't have enough money so I would have to go the highway even if I had to walk. I figured I could walk most of the gap in two or three days if I had to, and as this was jungle, I could always find some trees to hang my hammock. I stopped a man and asked him how far it would be to the Pan-American Highway. He said he was walking that way and it would take about one-and-one-half hours to reach it. I put a wary eye on my 75 pounds of luggage and asked how far it was to Jacú. He asked around and said it would take about an hour to walk. So I told him I would go with him. We started on a jungle path and left the city behind. After about a half-hour we reached a river. The water was hot and not very refreshing. We continued for about another half-hour and came to a customs shack for Panama. My walking companion was very interesting. His wife's daughter was studying in the United States. We talked over the political situation of Panama.

When we arrived at the customs shack a surprised guard greeted us. He copied the information from my passport and showed me a shortcut to La Cuesta, Costa Rica. He told me, "Follow this path straight through. It should take only twenty minutes." I started down the path and noticed it was full of water. I tried to skirt the water but my bag fell in the mud. I finally skirted the road through a field, almost having a tangle with an inhospitable bull. I walked for more than twenty minutes and didn't encounter anything. I passed a banana field but still saw no one. I finally saw the road turn 90° ahead and felt that would take me back to Panama. I continued for another quarter of a mile but saw nothing so I walked back to the banana field and took the road. I was dead tired. I threw the bag down, pulled the blanket out, and lay down, completely exhausted. I hadn't had a meal in two days, hadn't slept in two and the temperature was just beginning to fall below 90° Fahrenheit. I was tempted to sleep there as it was nearing 7:00 p.m., but remembered I had been told there was a small plane that went from La Cuesta, Costa Rica to San Ysidro where the construction met the highway north and San José every morning at 8:00. I figured if I didn't find La Cuesta that night I might not find it before the plane left that morning. I also felt I had better get started right away as snakes are a danger after dark since you can't see them. I looked at where the sun had been and oriented my road map. None of these passes were on the

Main Street, La Cuesta, Costa Rica

map so I figured out every direction I had been on the first path. I reasoned if it turned left it would take me right to La Cuesta. I got back on the path and after about ten minutes heard a motor, then faint rock and roll music. I thought, "That's strange. I'm here in the middle of the jungle and I hear pop music. I've got to be close to a town." Then I saw some lights and soon was walking between two rows of wooden buildings. As I reached the third building I looked and saw a restaurant. Suddenly the jukebox sang out with a Mexican melody and I knew I was in civilization. I found the customs inspections and entered.

One of the more abominable customs officials was interested in everything I had because he ordered me to empty absolutely everything from my duffle bag and carefully scrutinized every item. I began a friendly conversation with another customs inspector who invited me out to eat. He introduced me to everyone in the restaurant. We went back to get my bags and take them to a hotel. He pointed into a dingy room with the boards all falling off the wall. He said this was a dormitory for the workers and there was an unoccupied cot if I wanted to use it. I gladly took him up on that, as my money was getting shorter. I pulled out my blanket, wrapped myself in it, and did not wake for ten hours.

It was good, in a way, to be away from Panama. It was a pleasure to run into the Costa Rican women. I noticed a heavy Greek influence. Many of the Costa Ricans were blond. I got tired in Panama of being addressed in rough English. It was always, "We'ah you goin', Mack?" "Make room, boy," etc., etc. Also, nearly every sign was in English and everyone expected me to speak English.

I bumped into an American. When I detected a Scottish accent I asked him, "Where are you from?"

"I'm from Texas," he said.

The accent surprised me so I asked,

Death Pass, Costa Rica. From the peaks at 11,000 ft altitude, you can see both oceans on a clear day.

"Your accent isn't Texan."

"I was born of Scottish parents and I got this accent from them," he responded.

"I've been in Latin America for twenty years. I've been digging up Indian graves looking for gold. I'm working on the Pan-American Highway gap with a construction company from Kansas City, Foster Williams. I've been digging for gold in México for some years but I go to sea once in awhile. It's too soon after the rainy season for even a jeep to get through the lower end of the highway. But you can catch a train to Palmer Norte on Tuesday and you'll find company jeeps there that will take you to paved areas. You should, by the way, fly from Oaxaca to Mérida because that train trip is miserable."

"That sounds great," I told him, "but there's no way I could find the money to do that."

I found there was room on the small plane, which I could afford, flying to San Isidro del Generâl where the paving began. I had to pay quite a bit for excess baggage, as the plane was just a three-passenger Cessna. The plane came in at 8:00 that morning but it was full. Half the passengers were going to San José and half to San Ysidro del General. The plane took the three passengers and then returned for the rest of us at 9:00 a.m.

I found the plane trip even more interesting than the road would have been. It seemed strange to zip right up in the air with a small plane, having been accustomed to commercial planes especially at no more than 1,200 ft. altitude. We flew into the mountains just barely skimming the tops until we reached San Ysidro del General, the then terminus of the Pan-American Highway.

I met an interesting older Greek man there, who proceeded to tell me, "I'm seventy-five years old, and I've never been ill. I rely on God for my health. I also never drink or smoke. Church is for the ignorant. I have had a vision others haven't. I believe in reincarnation. The intelligence of a person depends on the number of times they have reincarnated. A per-

Oxcart, San Isidro del Generál, Costa Rica

son can reincarnate as many as twenty times. You must have reincarnated at least ten times."

"Thank you for the compliment but I feel more like a first timer," I said as I was interrupted by the bus to San José. This was supposed to be a fabulous trip, climbing to 11,000 ft. where we would be able to see both oceans on a clear day, but this day was so cloudy I could barely see in front of me. What interested me most were the churches. I had gotten weary of seeing these formless piles of concrete they call churches all over Latin America and longed to see a good old quaint New England church. I found a great deal of Greek influence in Costa Rica. Almost everyone appeared to me to be of Greek descent. Even their accent seemed Greek. It was a joy to see the Greek cupolas on the churches. Most of the buildings were frame and un-Latin. There was much more variation in style then I usually found in Latin American small towns. I arrived in San José at 5:00 p.m. It was amazing to me to have made the trip from Panama City in just fifty-one hours. I asked the bus driver where I could find inexpensive accommodations. He recommended one close to the agency. I went there and found a very nice woman running it. The room was only slightly larger than the bed, but clean. I went out that night and found a nice restaurant above the bar. I had never seen a finer dinner than that for just 80¢. The waiter explained this, "Costa Rica exports meat, so we have plenty for domestic use."

I was sitting at my meal when the owner came and said, "Hay un paisáno aquí (There's a fellow countryman here)." I was never overjoyed when people approached me to tell me there was a fellow countryman they wanted to introduce me to, because it usually turned out to be an American who knew two words in Spanish, one of them being "cervesa" (beer). She soon appeared with a young man and I greeted him in English. He looked at me strangely and asked me in German if I spoke German. We then switched to Spanish, which he spoke perfectly. It seems the proprietor had told him I was one of his compatriots. We both laughed and talked for the next two hours. He was working on a construction crew in San José. I was impressed with his friendliness and openness.

Soon I felt confident enough to ask him a very frank question, "Excuse me, but I have to ask you this question and I hope you will not feel offended. I have met many Germans over the past eight months I have been in Latin America and, if you don't mind my saying so, you are the first one I've liked. Every one of the Germans has been rude, inconsiderate, and just not nice. Why is this so? You are the nicest person I have met in a long time."

He chuckled, "You know, Carlos, we have a saying in Germany and that is, 'God save us from the Russians . . . . and the Germans abroad'. The Germans who emigrate to other countries are different. Many of them are selfish and only concentrate on getting ahead. The Germans who stay in Germany are generally warm and friendly people."

Costa Rica seemed surprisingly reserved, especially after having experienced so many other gregarious Latin American countries. It is the only country in North or South America that spends more on education than the military. It has a government patterned after Switzerland and is the seat of the University of Peace. It is the only Central American country to evade the constant bickering and wars of its neighbors. It seemed to me more like a European country than Central American.

The next day was hectic. I had to get a visa, sell my ticket, check on buses, and do some shopping. All this sounds simple unless you've been in San José. I first tried to sell the ticket but was told I had to buy the bus ticket first. I couldn't buy the bus ticket until I had my visa. I then spent an hour looking for the Nicaraguan Consulate. My budget abolished taxis so I had to walk all over town, as no one seemed to know where the address of any of the places I needed were. The Consul told me my visa photos were no good so I had to go back downtown and get others made. I ran back down and found the photoshop he recommended. It was after 11:00 a.m. before I finally got waited on. I told the photographer I needed the pictures by noon so I could get to the consul before it closed at one o'clock. I went back to the photoshop and waited until 12:30 p.m. for the pictures. I then went to the consulate and got there at 12:45 p.m. The counsel delayed and delayed until 1:00 and then finally waited on

Typical Wooden church, San Isidro del Generál, Costa Rica

me. This gave him a chance to get the overtime charge I had to pay for after-hour service. Getting my visa gave me some relief. I ran back and looked for the transportation company with a bus to Nicaragua. I then went to PAA and they rather begrudgingly returned my money, less tax. I went back at 5:00 p.m. and flopped on the bed, completely exhausted, more mentally than physically.

16. MAYALAND

I had to be at the bus agency at 4:30 in the morning to get my papers in order before the bus left at 5:00 a.m. The bus was a brand new Mercedes-Benz, and as with all Mercedes-Benz's I had taken it was comfortable and beautiful but ran like a washing machine. I was lightly annoyed with the cattle that kept passing us, but especially annoyed when the turtles began passing us. Costa Rica is a beautiful country. The mountains are green and full of trees, in complete contrast to the barren brown mountains of Perú, Bolivia, and Ecuadór. We stopped at every dog that barked in the highway so were soon two hours behind schedule. We arrived at the Costa Rican customs at 3:00 p.m. and I thought we'd never get processed. The Nicaraguan customs was even less efficient. We went into one building and filled out papers one-by-one. Then we went to a second building and filled out papers, again one-by-one. Then came the baggage inspection. By the time we got to the third building it was 4:45. They delayed us until 5:15 so they could charge each of us for services rendered after 5:00 p.m. I was really getting concerned about my money by this time. The two overtime charges, the extra photos, and the big expenses were running me way over my less than $2 a-day. By the time we finally got to Lake Nicaragua, the sun was down and I could see it would have been a beautiful picture had we passed it earlier when the sun was still up. Two magnificent volcanoes rose out of the middle of the lake.

Parque Nacionál, Managua. Nicaragua. Monument to poet Rubén Dario.

We finally arrived at Managua at 9:00 p.m. The bus didn't go into town, having us disembark at its edge. I grabbed my bags and started walking. I followed directions to the center of town but couldn't find a hotel. I walked over and finally a man on a bicycle stopped and asked if I was looking for a hotel. I laughed and asked him if there was such a thing in Managua. He gave me some directions and I finally checked into a dive called the Hotel Central. I went out to find a bite to eat because I hadn't eaten a meal in the last couple of days. I found a stand open and ordered a sandwich. I thought it was a house of prostitution so figured that must be the reason for its high price. I guess I should have asked if they furnished company with the sandwich for that price.

I went to the Honduras Consulate but found they had moved and no one seemed to know where it was. I then looked for the El Salvador Consulate and was told they had moved. The police told me the Nicaraguan Consul was there now. I got the address of the Honduran Consulate, which had also moved. Within one-and-one-half hours after I entered the Honduras Consulate I had Tourist Cards for Honduras, El Salvador, and Guatemala, which left me time to see the city.

On the top of my list was the famous FDR Monument. I had seen this in a textbook in the seventh grade and was impressed Nicaragua had been so grateful to President Franklin Roosevelt for saving their government they built a monument in his honor. I started to take a picture of it. All of a sudden a police officer shouted at me from the top of the hill behind the monument, "Don't take that picture!"

"Why can't I?" I asked with a loud but questioning voice.

"The President's Palace is on the hill behind it. No one is allowed to take any pictures in the area."

He was joined by other police who came at me from every direction, waving their arms and yelling, "No, no, no!!" A squad car stopped and a guard called me over. I was stunned, yet I was laughing inside; the whole thing seemed so ridiculous. It was difficult for me to take any of this seriously. I laughed and said to one officer, "Don't tell me I can't take a picture of the Monument?" They said, "The president's palace is up on the Hill in back of it."

"The President's Palace was not even in the picture I was going to take," I said in my defense. "I didn't even have the palace in the picture." I didn't tell any of them I had already taken the picture.

Like a SWATT team police came from all over, led by an officer who came back from his car, and one asked me, "Did you take the picture?"

"No, I didn't have time to," I answered as affirmatively as I could. "Can I take a picture of the city from here?"

"No, but you can take a picture from the Officers' Club," one of the police finally said, in a slightly more civil tone.

I went in front of the plush Officers' Club and took a picture. I suddenly heard a loud commotion behind me and saw all the personnel of the club running out the front door coming toward me, waving their arms wildly and shouting at the top of their voices, "No, no, no, don't take a picture from there!!" By this time I was riled up myself and was extremely tempted to yell, "Viva, Fidél Castro," but decided I was a little too close to being hauled off to jail to dare do anything like that. I then pulled out my map and decided to go out to the volcanic lake and take some pictures. I found the road blocked by a guard, so asked him, "Is this the only road to the lake?"

He said, "You'll have to get permission from the commander."

I asked, "Is there another road to the lake?" I got the same answer.

I then told them, "It isn't worth the effort," turned around and walked off in disgust. I found another road to the lake but there were too many soldiers with guns leveled in my direction to want to take any pictures. I went to the American Embassy to pick up a letter. It felt good to be in free territory even if for only three minutes.

I found a newspaper tacked on a wall of a news house. The front page was filled with news about Fidél Castro, so I read the entire article to see what this ruthless dictatorship, Nicaragua, had to say about another one being overthrown. It was extremely interesting to read. The paper was free and liberal but exceedingly careful in its wording. It lambasted Batista as being a ruthless tyrant. Then it attacked the U.S. for supporting Batista with arms. It mentioned the "Hon. General Somoza" (The dictator of Nicaragua) was helping the Cuban rebels and had recognized the new government. It also had some more agreeable things to say about Nicaragua's wonderful President. It continued, "This ought to be a lesson for the U.S. they can't support ruthless dictatorships and give them arms to fight the people with and expect to win. This is not only an incident in Cuba but a movement of all the people of Latin America to throw off the shameful dictatorships and also a lesson to dictators they cannot lend their own against the will of the people." By mentioning Somoza as helping the rebels, this made the article acceptable to the censors. By blasting the U.S., they presented something the special interpreter for the American Embassy would relate back to their superiors — stop sending arms to dictators. And by blasting the dictators they got the word to the people of Nicaragua. I thought the paper was exceedingly brave to stick its neck out that far.

The people who gathered in the hotel were very approachable and welcomed conversation, but when I mentioned the incident at the Roosevelt Monument, they scattered out of the lobby, especially when I mentioned the name Somoza. This was obviously not like the Dominican Republic where the people talked openly about their dictator. These people were visibly scared.

I was glad when I got my ticket for a bus leaving at two o'clock the next morning. I went to bed at 9:00 p.m. but the hotel was terrible. The walls had about a 4 ft. gap between the ceiling, so the laughter, etc., sounded like it was inside the room. When that finally died down the house of entertainment next door was still blasting away. A man, who was definitely not born to sing, screeched away, while a piano futilely tried to play louder than his bellowing. I didn't sleep a wink until the alarm went off at 1:30 in the morning.

I got ready to go by 2:00 a.m. The bus company ran house service so it was to come by at that time. I walked the streets back and forth to kill time. The "house" next door was still going strong, the jukebox blasting away. At three we began to get worried. I went to the bus agency and found it closed. At 4:15 I went again. The patrol officer told me to pound on the door. I whammed, banged, kicked, and pounded the door for fifteen minutes. Finally the door opened and a sleepy woman's head peeked out. I asked where my bus was. She told me in a sleepy voice the driver must have overslept, then shut the door and left me standing outside. The patrolman was still there and raved about the lack of responsibility of that company. I packed up my bags and thought I would park myself in front of the agency to assure myself of a good seat. I no sooner had bags in hand than I heard the beeping of a horn. I ran out and a sleepy chauffer came running over with a sheepish "Good Morning," in English. I was his first passenger. He said his clock wasn't working. It took us about another hour or so to pick up the other passengers. We finally got rolling about 6:00 a.m. I was pleased with the little car because it was a Volkswagen. It had a lot of power on the hills, unlike its Mercedes cousins. The trip was quiet. Some of the passengers talked in hushed tones, quite different from the noisy conversations I had experienced on nearly all other buses, and even Managua itself. By 8:00 we arrived at the Honduras frontier. The Nicaraguan customs was inefficient and considerable time was spent processing our exit visas. When we crossed the border it was like a gathering at a convention, with all the passengers suddenly opening up and beginning to talk freely. Everyone was friendly and the driver was even better than hiring a guide. I couldn't have felt better attended had I been on a tour.

We were a little delayed at Honduras and ran over the Saturday noon deadline, but they didn't charge us extra. We looked at our watches and found we had made up all our lost time. I met a couple of American students on the Honduran border. They were headed into Nicaragua, traveling in the same type of Volkswagen bus as us, and economizing with a kitchen they had inside. They were working with geology in Guatemala, and had just taken a swing down to San José, Costa Rica for vacation. They told me to look for them in Guatemala City.

I was fearful to even mention the word "police" in Nicaragua. I did this once with a group in Managua just to see what would happen. The two men I was talking with about dropped their teeth, looked both ways, and quickly changed the subject.

Safely across the border I mentioned my little Managua photo-taking incident to the driver. He laughed and said, "My country is in trouble now. The police nab you off the streets. A group of students held a little rally to celebrate Castro's victory and all the leaders were picked up and shot. Anyone who even mentions anything against the government is picked up and shot."

I mentioned, "I think it will probably be less than a year before Trujillo will have trouble and will probably be fomented by forces outside. A group has already formed in Cuba with the aim of ousting Trujillo. Trujillo is very safe but signed his death warrant when he took on Batista. This was a bit too close a place for that. I was in the middle of a riot in Panama and the leader said, 'The people threw out Jiménez, and now Batista, and tomorrow it will be the government of Panama.'"

He quickly added, "And next Somoza. (Running his finger across his throat)."

I told him, "Now I am talking freely against your government but didn't dare do that inside your country."

He said, "I wouldn't dare say the things I am saying to you while inside my country."

I watched how the soldiers and officers pushed the people around and walked on them, how the Officers' Club looks like a palace, and everyone that worked for the government was looking for a tip for every official document I needed. The Dominican Republic was never like this and I can say that Paraguáy wasn't either. I had traveled extensively in a number of dictatorships and some that had overthrown their dictators. In none of these tightly controlled countries did I feel any safer because of the police control. In fact, it was quite the opposite. I felt threatened in Guatemala, harassed in Colombia, Bolivia, Ecuadór, and Perú. And I felt victimized by imbecilic oafs who exercised insolence by means of their misplaced authority.

When we got to a high mountain pass the driver stopped and showed us where we could see the three countries of El Salvador, Nicaragua, and Honduras.

One of the most uncultured men I had ever met argued the driver into taking him to the Tegucigalpa junction from the border. He pushed me into the center of the bus where my knees touched my chin, dumped all the baggage on me, and put my bag where the driver couldn't use the brake. Whenever the bus passed a truck we always closed our windows so the clouds of volcanic ash wouldn't come in, but this man left his window open. One of the women begged him to close it but he loudly answered, "We are made of the earth here. We live and breathe the earth." When we finally managed to get rid of him the driver turned around and said, "I'm sure he is descended from a savage."

The driver told me, "Any time you want a picture just yell, and I'll stop." He gave me details on the transportation I would need to use ahead to help me out. I was sorry when we got to the junction of the Tegucigalpa highway because I had to leave such a pleasant ride. The driver took me over and got me right on an inexpensive Land Rover going to Tegucigalpa. The road was paved almost all the way for the two-and-a-half hour ride.

I went to the embassy to pick up my mail, and found a room at a dreadful hole-in-the-wall. It was the first time I didn't have a light in my room. I had a terrible meal there for 50¢, but it was my first meal in twenty-four hours so it tasted good. I ran out and got my bus ticket and found the bus would come by my door at 4:30 a.m. I came back and sat on the bed, drifting off immediately into a deep sleep.

I awoke at 2:30 a.m. and asked the porter to wake me at 4:00 a.m. At 5:30 a.m. I was still waiting for the bus, and by 6:00 I got worried and called the agency. They said the bus was still picking up passengers. Finally at 6:30 a.m. the bus came by. We still had to get some more passengers so we didn't get started until 7:40 a.m. Unfortunately, the bus was a Mercedes-Benz so there was no chance to make up for lost time. The passengers lovingly named the bus "La Tortuga" (The turtle) and made little puns about its definite lack of speed. It was fortunate I had gotten all the visas in Managua because all the consulates were closed during my short stay in Tegucigalpa. I would be in San Salvador on a weekend and wouldn't be able to get my visa for Guatemala there.

Every frontier got progressively better as I went north, so this one was a little easier than the one before it. In Costa Rica the road was mostly paved halfway to the Honduras border. In Honduras none of the Pan-American Highway was paved. They were also rebuilding the bridges all at once so all the rivers had to be forded. Fortunately, the Pan-American Highway only went through ninety miles of Honduras. The dirt was all volcanic ash, which filled the bus with a cloud of dust, completely covering our clothes.

Bridge on the Pan-American Highway in El Salvador, only 100 miles border to border

We arrived in El Salvador at 6:00 p.m. The bus boardinghouse was recommended to me as being cheap and good so I decided to stay there. On the bus I had become acquainted with another young man, Andino, who was staying in a hotel about three notches above my budget. Andino was a student of Commerce in Tegucigalpa and worked for the Bank of Honduras. He asked me to come stay there but I explained my budget restraints. He finally said he would stay at the bus boardinghouse with me. I got a good view of the city at night because the bus spent one-and-one-half hours unloading passengers all over the city. Andino and I found a room at the hotel, which was the best I had found since Barranquilla. It ran over my budget but at least it provided three meals a day for a change. I was beginning to feel my strength give out so I figured I had better get some food in my stomach.

We were exhausted when we got the room so Andino retired while I looked around and found a laundry area with a sink. I could make up sleep later but another day of dirty clothes won my attention. I went into the room and dumped my clothes into the tub of water. The proprietor walked into the room and doubled up with laughter. I asked her what I had done but she was laughing so hard she couldn't answer. When she calmed down she said, "I'm sorry, Señor but I've never seen a man doing laundry before."

"I have to do this. I'm never in a place long enough to send it out," I offered, joining her laughter.

"Leave it there and I'll have one of the maids do it for you in the morning," she offered.

"No, thank you very much but I'll just finish it tonight. I need clean clothes in the morning." I protested.

Two-and-a-half hours later I had clean laundry and ironed shirts. It was sure good to have clean clothes again. I had been wearing dirty laundry for weeks.

We got an early start in the morning and walked the streets until 10:00 a.m., catching a bus to Lake Llopango. As we were walking through the streets I was talking to Andino, when I suddenly became aware he was either not listening to me or could not understand what I was saying. Then my mind clicked and I realized I had absent-mindedly been speaking English. This had never happened to me before. I was not even conscious of it. I asked him if he had understood me. He said, "No, I knew you were talking in another language and figured it must be English." I guess I was getting ready for the anticipated return to the U.S. We found it was a six-mile walk over volcanic ash to the lakeshore so we satisfied ourselves with pictures from the hills above. We went back, had lunch, and then went out again. I liked San Salvador and its people.

Volcán San Martín, El Salvador

The next day Andino returned to Tegucigalpa. We exchanged Christmas cards for several years after I returned to the States. His last one saddened me. He told me his father had been killed because of a political run-in. He cursed the crooks running their government. I read later in a book by a friend the crooked workings of the government of Honduras, about the drug connections between the CIA and the Mossad. In cooperation with the drug cartels they financed the Contras who fought against the government of Nicaragua to defeat that government, which had finally freed itself from the iron hand of the U.S. backed dictatorship Somoza. But that is another story. It is with great sadness I read the accounts of the slaughters taking place in El Salvador to defeat the populists fighting their U.S. backed government of the affluent. I remember the friendly and open peasants who were struggling with their very survival.

Post Office arch, Guatemala City

I bumped into a Spanish immigrant from São Paulo, Brazil who had come from Tegucigalpa with us. He lacked a visa to enter so had been forced to return to the Nicaraguan border. He now had his visa and was going to Guatemala. The proprietor got us the last two seats on another bus. This was an old broken-down station wagon with seventeen of us crammed inside. It ran the usual door-to-door service, so we did not get started until nine-thirty. The road through El Salvador was all paved so it was smooth going to the border. The border was modern and efficient and processed us for both countries in less than an hour. Guatemala lacked thirty miles of paving from the border to Guatemala City so we had a dusty ride. We arrived at 6:00 p.m. but had to run bus service at that end as well. I found a cheap hotel recommended to me for only a dollar a day with meals. A Spaniard I met from Brazil tried to argue me into going to a better hotel with him but he finally decided to try the cheap one with me. I am sure all this was quite a shock to him, as he was not used to such meager hotels. For a dollar a day with meals in Guatemala I didn't feel it was that bad. The bath was a pigsty and the room a rattrap but I wasn't expecting Buckingham palace. The dinner was a disaster. Outside of my paddle wheeler trip down the Putumayo River I had never turned away food. However the soup was unpalatable and the fried banana was rotten.

I got an early start to get things done and plans made. I picked up my mail, which contained a letter from my father telling me he was wiring me money for my birthday. This was great news because I did not have the money to fly from Yucatan to the U.S., nor the time to take land transportation. I went to the American Express to get the telegram with the money. They had nothing so I went to American Cable. They said they had no record. I read over my mail and returned a little later, but there was still nothing anyplace. I asked them to recheck it but they wouldn't do it unless I paid an additional fee. This would knock a big hole in my budget so I finally gave that up. I went to Radiogram but they claimed no responsibility. I finally went to the American Embassy and they told me to come back the next day. I went back to American Cable and they reluctantly went through everything and found nothing. I went to the bus agency and got my future trips planned. We went to a tourist agency and found the planned tour was discontinued. That put $14 in my till that I would have had to spend there. I checked a couple more times but no telegram was received. My emergency plans were to take a bus directly to the border through Tapachula, but this would mean aborting my plans to explore the Mayan ruins of Yucatan and Southern México. Although I could travel by bus directly to Nogales, I still opted to include Yucatán. I could still make this trip but would have to travel under the

Aqueduct, Guatemala City

Iglésia, Capuchinas, Antigua, Guatemala

lowest class fares and worst hotels. I had no idea how much my birthday money awaiting me in the deep hole of bureaucratic maze was but any amount would raise the level of the final leg of my travels to 'tolerable'. I had so far traveled 27,000 miles on $1,700 — not bad.

The night before I got the addresses of the buses that went to Antigua. When I finally found the bus it had just left. I bought a ticket for the next bus and went to check on a few things. The agency was closed and there was still no telegram so I returned to the bus. All the seats were taken so I sat in a folding seat in the aisle. The ride only took an hour.

Antigua was the regional capital of Guatemala for over two hundred years. It was destroyed by earthquake in 1773 and the capital was then moved to its present location in Managua. Many of the courtyards and parks were landscaped and furnished just as they must have been before the earthquake. Of special interest were the frescoes in the churches, which were painted by Indian slaves and initiates. They painted the scenes as instructed by the padres, but with their revered Indigenous spirits rather than the Western renditions. This way, when they worshipped they prayed to their own venerated souls and masters. The change in worship was only surface. There was a blend of spirituality between the Christian beliefs and the ancient spiritual values of the Mayans that transcended time.

Antigua was probably one of the most thriving cities of Latin America so the ruins were magnificent.

Lake Atitlán, Guatemala

On leaving the bus I was hit by what seemed like at least 2,332 guides and 5,412 taxi drivers. I pretended I didn't know any English, told them I was going to use a guidebook as it was cheaper, and that made it easier to get detached from them. The ruins were extremely interesting as they were so old, dating back to the fifteen hundreds. I went to the market and had some rice, beans, and tortillas. When I got back the agents told me I would not be able to take the next bus, as it was full, but when I flashed my ticket they found a place for me.

Kids at San Rafaél, Guatemala

Back in Managua I went into the American Express and still found no telegram. I was about to give up when I thought, "I'm not going to let American Cable get off that easily." I went in and the agent shrugged his shoulders when he saw me. I made him go back and look through the telegrams. He finally found one hidden under everything that said to change the words American Express to American Embassy. I ran over to the Embassy and finally found a note that something was waiting for me at the Agriculture Bank. I ran over there and they had just closed. I told them I had to have the money that I was sure was in their bank because my bus would be leaving early the next morning and there was no other bus out of there that day. He gave me a definite "No," to that and slammed the door.

I knew there was a very important message for me from my father, which contained money for my birthday. I could not leave before tracking it down because without that I would have to skip Yucatán.

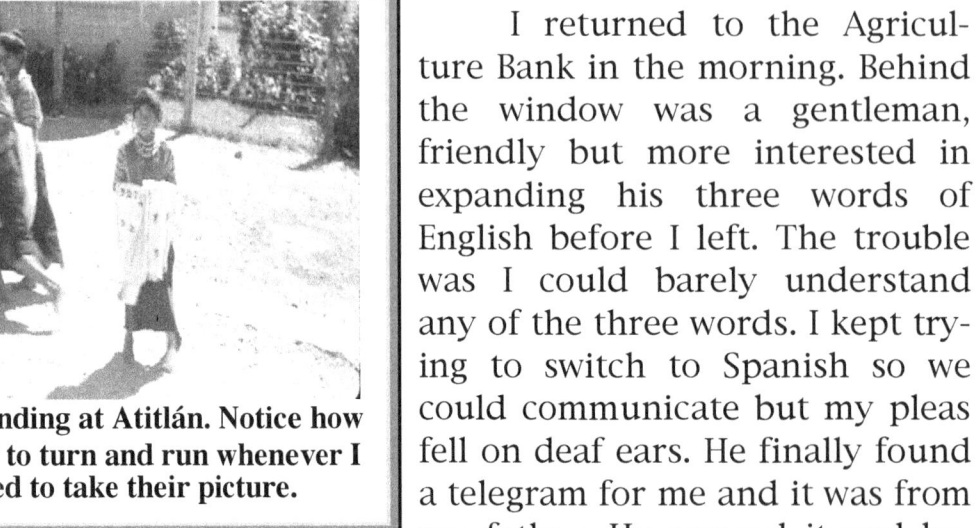
Girls vending at Atitlán. Notice how they try to turn and run whenever I tried to take their picture.

I returned to the Agriculture Bank in the morning. Behind the window was a gentleman, friendly but more interested in expanding his three words of English before I left. The trouble was I could barely understand any of the three words. I kept trying to switch to Spanish so we could communicate but my pleas fell on deaf ears. He finally found a telegram for me and it was from my father. He opened it and began reading it to me, "Happy Birthday, Chuck. I thought you could use this $100 I am sending you as a present." Hooray! I could now cancel my plans for a direct trip through Tapachula. I had just heard of the blowing up of the bridge at Tapachula by a group of Guatemalans. For that reason I had decided to cross the border through the newly completed Pan-American Highway through Ciudad Cuatémoc. This entered through the center of México, giving me the opportunity to go east to Yucatán and the ruins around Oaxaca, rather than West for the direct route to Nogales I thought I would have to take. AGSIM had just written me I had three additional days before I had to be back in Phoenix. I now had both time and money to complete the portion of the trip I had planned eight months before.

Zaculéu from the hills, Guatemala. This center of the Mayas formed a culture different from the Mams called Chima Bahul, was constructed by the Quidres in the 12th Century under Chin Chicab & received the name Zaculéu (Tierra blanca). It was discovered in July 1525 by Gonzalo de Alvarado and offered him terrific resistance.

The Mayan ruins were the most important places to me now. It was a short jaunt out to see the beginnings of the uncovering of the ruins just outside Guatemala City of Kaminaljuyú. This ruin, which belonged to the Preclassic Period between 800 B.C. and 300 A.D., originally had 350 buildings. Only the beginnings of excavation were visible at that time because it had been so recently discovered. I found Managua to be a combina-

Zaculeú, Left side temple from top of temple with ball court in background.

tion of ancient civilization, living much as it had before the Spanish conquest. Spanish Colonial represented most of the government buildings dating back to the earthquakes, which destroyed the former capital at Antigua. A strangely homogenized modern architecture was present in some of the more exclusive homes in residential districts. Of special interest was the aqueduct, dating back to Spanish Colonial days, which still ran through the center of the city.

Ball Court, Záculéu

Lake Atitán lay like a crown jewel, deep within the surrounding volcanoes. It reflected a bright blue against the sky above. As we descended the dirt road leading down to it we left behind the bustle of traffic, limited only to ox carts loaded with goods destined for the market. I not only saw the lake, I felt it and a quiet energy resonated peacefully around us.

I caught an early bus to Huehuetenango on my way to the Mexican border. I planned to transfer to another bus, which would take me the rest of the way. We arrived late at night so I settled down to sleep in the bus until the other bus arrived. I was awakened in the morning, dreaming in Russian. This was strange because I had never dreamed or thought in Russian and had been away from speaking it for so long I was no longer fluent. I looked out at the day, which was just breaking, and worried that the 7:30 bus for the border might have left already. Just then a conductor boarded the bus. I called to him and asked, "Could you tell me whether the bus for the border of México has left yet?"

Zaculéu. Templo del Agua.

"There's no bus to the border from here."

"I was told a bus would leave from Huehuetenango at 7:30."

"I don't know, but there is no bus that leaves from Chichicastenango for the border."

"This is Chichicastenango?" I said in shock. "How do I get to Huehuetenango?"

"You'll have to return to Guatemala City to catch the bus to Huehuetenango."

Colonial front on church, Oaxaca, México

I was also aware I might not have the proper papers for crossing the border so this would give me an opportunity to get properly documented, just in case they wouldn't accept what I had at the Mexican border.

It was another day's ride going to Guatemala City, obtaining proper papers, and taking a bus north to Huehuetenango.

Mexico, Monte Albán, near Oaxaca. Temple of the Dancers

Mexico, Mitlá. Temple & court.

Huehuetenango gave me the opportunity to visit the ruins of Zaculéu. Zaculéu was the capital of the Mam kingdom of the Mayan Civilization. Many of the natives still spoke the Mam language and many of the original inhabitants still lived around Huehuetenango and Quetzaltenango. It was reached by a dirt road, but there was no transportation leading out to it. I walked endlessly up and down this road but could see no ruins. I passed a young man traveling in the opposite direction and asked, "Do you know where Zaculéu is?"

He smiled and gave me directions. His clear and lilting accent was typical of the many other Indians I had met where Spanish was their second language.

Stone engraving at the Temple of the Dancers, Monte Albán, Mexico

Mexico, Mitlá. Front of temple. Original paint still showing.

"It's just over that hill and down in the valley. Are you going to be going to the dance tonight?"

"No, I would like to go but I have to leave tonight for México."

"Oh, that's too bad," he said with a somewhat sad tone. "Well, go you well."

I followed his directions and was completely surprised by what unfolded in the valley below. An ancient city spread out, every building a brilliant white color. It was almost the way it must have looked when the Mayans abandoned it. The temples and outer buildings, as well as the plazas, and ceremonial grounds were little changed from the Pre-Hispanic era. I strolled around in awe, examining the buildings. I was completely alone.

Back in town I could feel the tensions among the residents of Huehuetenango and México. The people still felt disenfranchised. Half their territory, which was now the state of Chiapas in México, contained a large section of what were their ancestral lands. The people of Chiapas still felt a kinship to Guatemala and those in Northern Guatemala felt the same. Constant battles had flared up

Head sculptured in basalt, Villa Hermosa, Mexico. Represents a god or young warrior smiling. Work of art of la Venta, found in time of La Venta, town of Huimanguillo, Tabasco. Found in 1940. Weighs 4 tons. Contributed to the classical Maya I, II, and III, Teotihuacán culture of the Gulf Coast. Appears to have had a long duration.

in that section of México because of the cultural differences between the Mayans and Mexican government. Many felt they belonged to México. Revolutionaries had just blown up the international bridge at Tapachula in México. In the central park was a sign, which read: "No Óigan Musica Mexican, no Lean los Periódicos de México, No Excuchan el Radio Mexicano. (Do not listen to Mexican Music, Do not read Mexican newspapers, Do not listen to Mexican radio stations)."

The trip to the Mexican border on the newly completed, well graded, dirt Pan-American Highway was pristine and beautiful, passing between a series of low lying mountains. A converted school bus took me from the border to San Cristóbol de Las Casas, a short trip of four hours. At San Cristóbol I found another bus for the ten-hour trip to Oaxaca. Other than the police who met us at every checkpoint, the peasants were nearly identical to their Guatemalan counterparts. As the bus passed through Tuxtla Gutierra I was fascinated with the natives. I had read men tend the children while the women work. Unfortunately, without disembarking and visiting there was no way I could see evidence of this

State Capitol for State of Tabasco, Villa Hermosa, Mexico

looking out the window of a bus.

It was a long-time fascination for me to visit Oaxaca. I was attending the University of México six years prior when an election spawned a revolution in Oaxaca. There were several Zapatéc ruins around that city and a famous church. Later, during the Harmonic Convergence of 1987, a tree attributed to legend, called the Quetzalcuátl tree, was said would live until the second appearance of Quetzalcuátl, at which time it would die. Several seers witnessed it dying at that time.

I was privileged to see the ruins of Mitlá, 25 miles south of Oaxaca, which had just shortly been restored. At that time the original red paint on most of the walls was still intact. Pictures I have seen since do not show the red paint as I saw it. Mitlá was the residence of the Zapotéc high priest at the time of the Spanish conquest. The site was first occupied in the 6th century B.C., but the oldest surviving palaces belonged to the period A.D. 200-900, the time when the Zapotéc still ruled the Valley of México, Tenochtitlán, from their capital at Monte Albán.

With the northern part of the Valley under Mixtec control, Mitlá became one of the main centers of southern Zapotéc culture. New palaces were constructed after 1200 A.D., decorated with elaborate raised mosaic patterns made of small, individually carved pieces of stone arranged in geometric designs. The numerous mosaics showed Mixtec influence, as did frescoes at the site, executed in the same style as the famous Mixtec painted manuscripts. This use of Mitlá made it unique compared to any of the other ruins, including Teotihuacán, outside México City. Whereas Mitlá is the remains of palaces and gracious living, Monte Albán, just west of Oaxaca, showed Olmec influence.

Temples — de la Cruz del Sol, Palenque

By 200 B.C. Monte Albán had become the most prominent center in Zapotéc territory, and by A.D. 200 it dominated the area surrounding the central valley of Oaxaca. The civic center atop the ridge included temple-pyramids, palaces, richly furnished tombs, and an astronomical observatory. The lower slopes were terraced for dwellings, which housed a population of 30,000 or more. Relief carvings and hieroglyphic texts, though not yet fully deciphered, appeared to emphasize themes of military expansion and conquest.

Palácio de Las Princesas, Palenque, Mexico

Although there were indications of ties with Teotihacán in the period 200-600 A.D., Monte Albán maintained its independence. Monte Albán declined after 800 A.D.

I went by bus to Coatzacálcos (pr. Co-at-sa-cualcos) (it took me a week to learn to pronounce this). This city also goes by another name, Puerto México. I changed buses there for Villa Hermosa.

Villa Hermosa offered a strange mix of isolated village, being the terminus of the railroad and the beginning of road travel to the major ruins of Yucatán. It housed a small museum, among which was the famous stone carving of the Olmecs, a civilization which preceded most of the ruins left by the Maya civilization as far back as 1200 B.C. They were known for creating huge basalt heads, one of which was displayed at the museum. This drew my interest, as did the Pre-Colombian ruins of Tiahuanaco at Lake Titicaca. I felt a relationship to the people who created these carvings.

Gate to Campeche, Mexico

From Villa Hermosa I caught another bus to Teápa. From there the only way to get to Yucatán was by train or plane as there were not yet any roads from the mainland into Yucatán. I took a train to the village of Palenque, located a half-hour ride from the ruins which I reached by pickup.

When I arrived by train at Palenque the ruins were steeped in fog, making them mysterious, almost exotic. I was positive I had been here before and it had been a university or place of learning. I climbed the main pyramid and looked down on the excavated buildings below. I could close my eyes and visualize the ancient people I had known. I walked among the buildings, stood spellbound in the small niches with their carvings and monoliths. I could sense I was alone, yet knew on one level I was not. I could feel the ghosts of the past gathering around me. The mist accentuated the mystique. The astronomical observatory appeared to have been placed there by a subsequent civilization, so disparate was its design. I knew I had been a teacher there. I felt the presence of some of my students.

I befriended several passengers on the train as we traveled slowly through the night. "How can your government be so stupid?" shouted one Mexican when Fidél Castro's name was mentioned. He has you duped by his rhetoric. He is a Communist and he is going to be trouble for the rest of the governments of Latin America. The United States is playing soft on him and Castro is using you."

I was somewhat surprised. I was secretly cheering the win of Castro in Cuba, because I felt the government of Batista was so repressive. This was the first time I had heard anything against Castro in all my conversations.

Temple at Uxmál, Mexico. Author slept at its base in full moon.

To say the train was slow from Palenque to Campeche was a gross understatement. It was a 22-hour ride to make the short distance of 250 miles. I could swear I saw cattle passing the train at times. It was interesting as we passed by numerous huts scattered along the railroad tracks, each with its culinary delight of the numerous delicious offerings the vendors approached the train to sell at each of the countless stops.

The Spanish founded Campeche in 1540 at a Mayan site. It was significant because it was one of the three ports in the area permitted to trade with Spain. The entire city was declared an architectural monument because of the many buildings dating from the colonial period. I felt like I was walking through a remote village in ancient Spain.

A bus took me to the ruins of Uxmál. It was déja vu when I saw the pyramids of Uxmál. Uxmál was a major capital of the Mayan Empire. These buildings were abandoned in the tenth century, but still seemed almost untouched by weather and the purposeful destruction of the Spanish in colonial days. I learned the only hotel in the area was four times my daily allowance so I asked at the local village if I could put my hammock up inside the housing area. They refused but said I could do that outside the fence.

Entrance to Labná, Mexico

The Uxmál compound was closed so I decided to walk to the ruins of Sayíl and Labná. I left my bags in the care of the village people and took a bus on the three-hour trip to Km 22 where I began walking the six miles on the dirt road to those ruins. After a few miles I became weak from the heat and humidity. Finally, I was exhausted, not knowing whether this was even the correct road. As I weaved down the road several men came by on horseback. I asked them, "Is this the right road to Labná?"

"Yes, it is the right road, but you don't look like you can walk much further. Why don't you spend the night in the village? There is a person there who will take you in," said the voice of one of those angels on horseback. They were right; I wouldn't have been able to make it back out before dark. They walked me to a few huts in the jungle. A young man came out of one of the huts. When they explained the situation to him, he said,

Road to Sayíl & Labná, Mexico

"Come with me. My father is away for the night. You can sleep on his hammock. Follow me."

I went inside the one room hut. I had no food or drink because nothing was available at the Uxmál ruins. I saw a hammock and stumbled over onto it and lay down. In the morning the boy cooked an egg breakfast and I was on my way.

Labná was still nearly in the condition it was when the Spanish found it. An archeologist was very slowly and meticulously reconstructing it. The masonry and design was unique, with an arched doorway to the entrance, about twenty feet high.

Sayíl, three-story building, Mexico

A few miles further on the return loop of the dirt road, was Sayíl. Although mostly in ruins at that time, it was impressive because of the palace, which contained 98 rooms in its three stories. Sayíl and Labná were built during the height of the Mayan civilization of that era, the ninth and tenth centuries. It is estimated that at Sayíl's height there were as many as 10,000 living in this vicinity. Their ruins were hidden from the Western world until 1871.

The hot noonday sun amplified my exhaustion from the heat and lack of food, and I was soon overcome with exhaustion and heat prostration. I became delirious, spending little time at Sayíl. I began

Sculpture above doorways, Sayíl, Mexico

to whirl my camera around on its strap, crashing it to the ground in an erratic convulsion. My photography was over and done with until I could return to Phoenix and repair the damaged camera there. I finally strung my hammock between two poles outside the village next to Uxmál and crawled in to sleep.

The night was dark, the pyramids beckoning me in the moonlight. There was a strong feminine energy emanating from the Nunnery and main pyramid, looming 120 feet overhead. As the winter skies darkened early in the evening, the moon began to rise behind the Great Pyramid. Everything present was blocked out as I slipped into a past lifetime when 25,000 people inhabited this complex. Uxmál flourished during the Classical period of the Mayan Empire between 600 and 900 A.D. It was now reduced to a few acres of fenced-in area, housing a small number of grass huts. The tourist hotel was hidden in the surrounding low-lying forest. I lay for hours watching the moonrise behind the pyramid and illuminate my sleeping area. It was a date with destiny sleeping beneath this pyramid, glowing in the warmth of the moon at that site.

Chichen Itzá, Observatory, Mexico

The next morning I caught the first bus passing on its way to Mérida, destination Chichén Itzá. I learned there was an airline strike so I would have to take trains and buses the long distance from here to Nogales through México City. I took a bus the short distance to those ruins. Here, again, were many past life remembrances. I knew I had trod this area in distant times, experiencing the greatness of both that era and its opulent living.

Mercéd de Santana Bridge. Colonial promenade dating from 16th Century, Campeche

I returned shortly to Mérida, so I could catch the first train out to Coatzacuálcos. That night I met an indigenous man in the park and we began a lengthy conversation. His name was Medardo Ix Ukam. At that time the Bracero program was still active which brought Mexican workers to the United States for seasonal work on the farms. This was a controversial program because housing conditions were shoddy on many of the farms, and there was a claim Mexicans were taking jobs away from Americans. Medardo, as well as many other Mexicans with whom I talked, enthusiastically supported the Bracero Program.

He explained, "Our families line up to be on that program. Each guest worker on the program can save around $500 after expenses during a season. No one is allowed to be on the program for two years in a row and families are limited to one member at a time, so each family signs up a different member of the family each year. That person returns with enough money to add a room to the family house or begin building a home. The next year another member signs up and another room can be added. It is impossible to save that amount of money in México, even if they can find a job."

A room inside temple at Mitlá, Mexico

I had to agree with Medardo. The Mexicans that signed up for the program usually had no interest in emigrating to the U.S. They loved their land, their families, and their homes. Granted, the program was in need of some modifications, but when the program was abandoned Mexicans still were obliged by financial necessity to go to the United States to earn enough money to send back to their family. Without government protection they were now forced to use "coyotes", (traffickers), at considerable expense, to lead them across the border, braving extreme heat and possible death in the desert and detection by the immigration. Those that made it to the U.S. found a different set of circumstances which obliged them to remain so they could make up for expenses and the fact any other member of the family would have to hire a "coyote" to help him or her cross the

Palenque, Templo de las Leyes. Mexico

the border. Many were caught by our immigration service and shipped back, and then needed to accumulate money in México to return home. Thousands have died in the desert. Once in the U.S. many become victims of unscrupulous employers who threatened to turn them in if they don't accept substandard conditions and pay. Now, instead of emigrating for a season and returning with a part of their earnings, they have been left with no choice but remain as undocumented workers, bringing others in their family who would ordinarily never have left their homes to join them, including brothers, sisters, children, mother, aunts, etc. Deprived of public services and assistance offered through the Bracero Program, they now have become a burden on the welfare, education, and health programs open to them as they remain in the United States. Following the demise of the Bracero program the focus shifted from seasonal work in the U.S. of various members of the family with an occasional permanent illegal alien to massive undocumented immigration of entire families who would never have considered leaving their land. This has led to some twenty million undocumented workers and their families abandoning their land and country and a border fence,

Palenque, Mexico, Palacio patio

which has raised the ante for those forced to penetrate it due to financial deprivation. We are in need of a comprehensive immigration program between Mexico and the U.S. that has moved beyond platitudes, political expediency, racial profiling and greater walls. The border problem has been over forty years in the making and will only become worse if the two countries cannot come together and resolve the many facets of those on the bottom of the economic ladder in both countries. Neither a new law nor a bigger fence is going to resolve it.

The next morning I caught a train for the 33-hour trip to Campeche and Coatzacuálcos. From there I caught a train for México City, getting a brief glimpse of Puebla as we passed through, which I had not seen for six years, The five-hour wait for a bus in México

City gave me just enough time to ride out and see the now completed Universidad de México, which was still being constructed when I was attending that University six years before.

Mexico, Mitlá. Detail of wall. Notice the original paint can still be seen.

As we approached the United States border I became frightened. I didn't know whether I was going to be able to speak and understand English right away and was concerned about customs, possible duty on the camera and other items I had purchased. I was actually trembling as we approached Nogales.

I was amazed when the border guard greeted me, stamped my passport, and let me through without hesitation or problems. I boarded a bus to Tucson and heard the bus driver and a passenger talking in English. I could understand everything. When I began to speak I was as comfortable with English as I had been before.

When I sat on the bench in Glendale, waiting for a bus to AG-SIM, I felt almost dizzy. I had traveled 29,000 miles through Latin America, stayed within my $1750 limit, seen 21 different countries, and made it back alive, which is more than I can say for the camera I bought in the Dominican Republic which did not arrive to my home for another three months, along with import taxes and shipping costs. I was possibly the first person to make it down one side of South America and back. I was a person who went to Latin America 250 days before and another one very much changed when I returned. I grew with each person I met and every experience I had. Today, 48 years later, I still see every tree, person, building, river, and moun-

University of Mexico, Mexico City

tain as clearly as I did each day of my journey.

For me it was a spiritual journey, in a vision quest, which my restless spirit had required me to take. This trip was a journey into my past giving me a fuller understanding why I had chosen to incarnate at this time, what I was to become — both student and guide to lead myself and others into higher dimensions as the world and its inhabitants evolve as the ancients predicted for eons of time. I hope each person who reads this is changed by my experience and will view the world in a more expanded way, and know we are all one, in love and peace.

BORN OF THE SUN
The Story of Akhenaten

Pharaoh Akhenaton was popular with the masses, a heretic to the Amun Priests of his day. His city, Akhetaton, was destroyed —his name intentionally expunged from history. Yet, his struggle continues today as the author makes him alive in this book.

Hinkley shows not only the royal side of Akhenaton, but the human feelings and spiritual struggles of a man deliberately erased from history. His renowned endeavors continue today as the world searches for its common relationship with the Creator.

Akhetaton was magical in both appearance and the energy it created. Light, color and sacred geometry were incorporated in each building, especially that of the Temple of Light, a holy temple which has as its objective, to be an instrument in elevating the thinking and body manifestation to Christhood of fifty men and fifty women. To draw the attention of the Amun priests and military officials away from the real objective of the city, Akhenaton built a magnificent temple at its entryway and a majestic palace to his queen, Nefretiti, who continued to receive dignitaries.

Many indignities were perpetrated on Akhenaton by his half-brother, disgruntled military officers, and the priesthood in an attempt to defame what they regarded as their "heretic king." Only his and Tyi's popularity with the masses saved him from being prematurely dethroned. However, he knew he was in a race with his inevitable demise, that eventually he would lose both his life and his throne. It took five years of concentrated effort to elevate the requested number of people to the purity he desired and when this was accomplished they were sent to the Dead Sea. With Egypt crumbling and unable to either find or pursue them, they wrote and lived among the people of that area. Their writings on scrolls were hidden in caves. They were eventually known as the Essenes. They were there to write and pave the way for the man known as Yeshua ben Joseph, Jesus the Christ.

www.ingramcontent.com/pod-product-compliance
Lightning Source LLC
Chambersburg PA
CBHW081208230426
43666CB00015B/2673